DATE DUE

My Fellow Soldiers

ALSO BY ANDREW CARROLL

Here Is Where

Grace Under Fire

Operation Homecoming

Behind the Lines

War Letters

Letters of a Nation

My Fellow Soldiers

GENERAL JOHN PERSHING

AND THE AMERICANS WHO HELPED

WIN THE GREAT WAR

ANDREW CARROLL

PENGUIN PRESS | *New York* | 2017

PENGUIN PRESS
An imprint of Penguin Random House LLC
375 Hudson Street
New York, New York 10014
penguin.com

ISBN 978-1-59420-648-1 (hardcover)
ISBN 978-0-698-19266-9 (e-book)

Printed in the United States of America
1   3   5   7   9   10   8   6   4   2

Frontmatter maps by Jeffrey L. Ward
Designed by Marysarah Quinn

This book is dedicated to
Erwin Blonder and James Carroll Jordan,
two extraordinary veterans who served their country with honor.

Contents

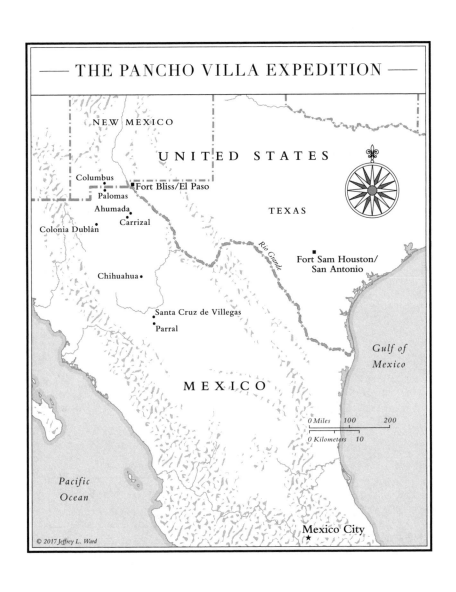

— THE PANCHO VILLA EXPEDITION —

NEW MEXICO

UNITED STATES

Columbus

Palomas

Fort Bliss/El Paso

TEXAS

Ahumada

Carrizal

Colonia Dublán

Rio Grande

Fort Sam Houston/
San Antonio

Chihuahua

Santa Cruz de Villegas

Parral

Gulf of
Mexico

MEXICO

0 Miles   100   200

0 Kilometers   10

Pacific
Ocean

Mexico City
★

© 2017 Jeffrey L. Ward

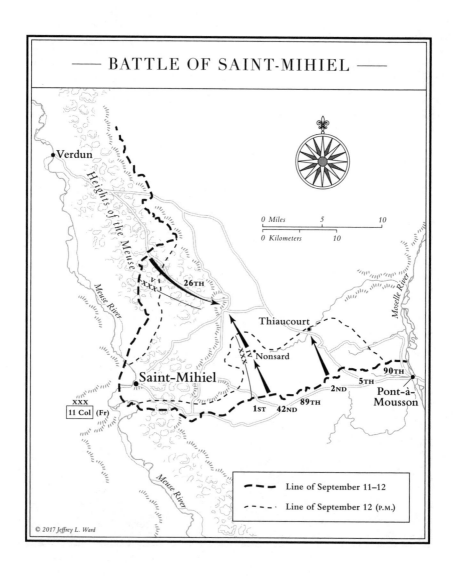

— BATTLE OF SAINT-MIHIEL —

Verdun

Heights of the Meuse

Meuse River

Moselle River

0 Miles   5   10

0 Kilometers   10

XXX V I · 26TH

Thiaucourt

XXX · Nonsard

Saint-Mihiel

90TH

5TH

2ND

Pont-à-Mousson

XXX
11 Col (Fr)

1ST   42ND   89TH

Meuse River

- - - - Line of September 11–12

– – – Line of September 12 (P.M.)

© 2017 Jeffrey L. Ward

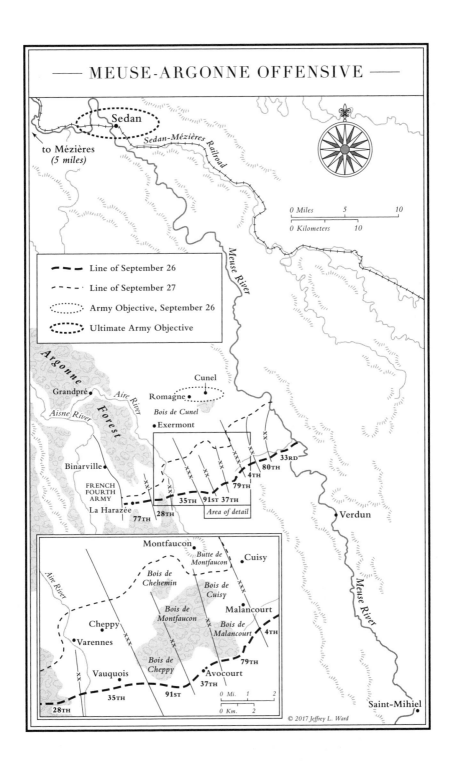

MEUSE-ARGONNE OFFENSIVE

Sedan

to Mézières
(5 miles)

Sedan-Mézières Railroad

Meuse River

0 Miles — 5 — 10
0 Kilometers — 10

— — — Line of September 26
- - - - Line of September 27
⬭ Army Objective, September 26
⬭ Ultimate Army Objective

Argonne Forest

Grandpré

Aire River

Aisne River

Cunel

Romagne

Bois de Cunel

Exermont

Binarville

FRENCH
FOURTH
ARMY

La Harazée

77TH   28TH   35TH   91ST 37TH   79TH   4TH   80TH   33RD

Area of detail

Verdun

Meuse River

Montfaucon

Butte de Montfaucon

Cuisy

Bois de Chehemin

Bois de Cuisy

Cheppy

Varennes

Aire River

Bois de Montfaucon

Malancourt

Bois de Malancourt   4TH

Bois de Cheppy

Avocourt   79TH

Vauquois   37TH

28TH   35TH   91ST

0 Mi.   1   2
0 Km.   2

Saint-Mihiel

© 2017 Jeffrey L. Ward

American Expeditionary Forces
Chain of Command and Organization*

PRESIDENT OF THE UNITED STATES

SECRETARY OF WAR

  (renamed the Secretary of Defense in 1949)

ARMY CHIEF OF STAFF

AEF COMMANDER

GENERAL OR LIEUTENANT GENERAL

  Commander of a field army, each consisting of two to five corps

  (By the end of World War I, the United States had two field

  armies, First Army and Second Army. General Pershing created

  "VI Corps," but it existed mostly on paper and was used to deceive

  the Germans before the battle for Saint-Mihiel in September 1918.)

LIEUTENANT GENERAL

  Commander of a corps, each consisting of two to five divisions

MAJOR GENERAL

  Commander of a division, each consisting of three brigades

---

*The information presented here is specific to World War I and differs, in places, from the military's modern-day structure. In World War I, for example, a division could include forty thousand soldiers while currently the number is closer to fifteen thousand.

BRIGADIER GENERAL OR COLONEL

Commander of a brigade, each consisting of two regiments

COLONEL

Commander of a regiment, each consisting of two or more
battalions

LIEUTENANT COLONEL OR MAJOR

Commander of a battalion, each consisting of three or more
companies

CAPTAIN

Commander of a company, each consisting of three or more
platoons

LIEUTENANT

Leader of a platoon, each consisting of four or more squads

SERGEANT

Leader of a squad, each consisting of four to twelve soldiers or
Marines

Foreword

STASHED AWAY FOR DECADES and found by chance in a garage attic, the small bundle of World War I–era letters sent from France by a U.S. serviceman had never been published or shown to anyone outside of his family. In the letters, the soldier expresses how meaningful it is to receive mail and be reminded that he hasn't been forgotten. "Dear Aunt Eliza," he wrote on November 9, 1917. "It was very delightful to get your letter and to know that you still think of me; also to know that I have your sympathy and good wishes."

And to a friend he had *not* heard from, he added a short, plaintive handwritten note at the end of a typed letter to her, stating: "Dear Anne: I don't know why you do not write to me. I asked you to do so but have I think received but two letters from you in the past two years—It is not easy to understand. Best Love. J.J.P."

"J.J.P." was John Joseph Pershing, the fifty-seven-year-old general who was commanding the entire American Expeditionary Forces in World War I at the time. His leadership and the decisions he was making on a daily basis were affecting the lives of millions of individuals and even the fates of nations. But all of Pershing's prestige and power couldn't mitigate the very human longing he felt to be thought of and remembered while he was thousands of miles from home.

Woven through these newly discovered letters are also references to a catastrophic personal loss that Pershing suffered before the war that caused those close to him to fear he might, emotionally, never recover. In the same November 9, 1917, letter to his Aunt Eliza, Pershing remarked that his focus on the war helped distract him from thinking about the tragedy he had endured, confiding: "Only by being continually at work in positions requiring my whole thought have I been able to live during the past two years."

To the soldiers of the American Expeditionary Forces serving under Pershing, these intimations of emotional vulnerability would have come as a shock. Pershing was notoriously strong-willed, to the point of seeming cold, rigid, and humorless, almost more machine than man. He was especially unforgiving when it came to matters of discipline. From the youngest privates to senior officers, including other generals, Pershing would lash out if he noticed the slightest imperfection, be it an unpolished boot or a missing button. (Ironically, Pershing had one pronounced failing throughout his entire military career: He was constantly late. The reason wasn't laziness though; Pershing often became so absorbed in what he was doing that he lost his sense of time. Nevertheless, it irritated his staff members and, in particular, the obsessively punctual French and British officers with whom he worked.)

Pershing's private letters reveal that the crusty old general was in fact a doting and sweet-natured father, a husband passionately in love with his wife, and an empathetic soul, quick to offer solace to friends and strangers alike coping with their own trauma. And regardless of what many AEF soldiers might have thought of Pershing, his letters frequently conveyed his deep pride in them for their courage, their resilience, and their sense of duty. Whatever sternness he displayed outwardly, he would argue, was because of his concern for his troops. He believed that those who pushed themselves to their physical limits and could function under enormous pressure in the face of extreme hardships were the ones most likely to survive. If his unyielding strictness and lack of warmth caused him to be unpopular, he couldn't care less.

Personal.

AMERICAN EXPEDITIONARY FORCES
OFFICE OF THE COMMANDER-IN-CHIEF

France, November 9, 1917.

Mrs. H. E. Stanton,
Huntington, Massachusetts.

Dear Aunt Eliza:

I have your letter of October first and have
often had in mind to write you, but my time is so
fully occupied that I have not found a moment to
spare.

It was very delightful to get your letter and
to know that you still think of me; also to know
that I have your sympathy and good wishes. Only
by being continually at work in positions requiring
my whole thought, have I been able to live during
the past two years. It is of course quite unlikely that I shall have occasion to see young Lindsey,
although I believe his regiment is here now. I
shall inquire for him the next time I make an inspection of his command.

I am glad you realize, and I hope all Americans
will realize the vastness of our undertaking and the
necessity for very loyal support whatever may happen.
We are fighting for a cause that has made us great as
a nation, and we must all stand together.

Thanking you again for your letter, and hoping
to hear from you when you have time to write, I remain,

Yours with sincere affection,

John J. Pershing.

*Pershing's letter to Aunt Eliza. The censor's mark on the left side of the envelope indicates
that even the commanding general of the American Expeditionary Forces
had his correspondences inspected before they were mailed.*

In the years immediately following World War I, people across the United States heralded Pershing as one of the country's greatest heroes, on par with George Washington and Pershing's own idol, Ulysses S. Grant. Communities bestowed countless awards on him, organized parades to honor his service, and named streets, plazas, squares, schools, and parks after him.

By the time of his death, in 1948, the general's prestige had undoubtedly waned. In part it was simply that he was now overshadowed by a new generation of leaders such as George Patton, Dwight Eisenhower, Douglas MacArthur, and George Marshall. Another reason Pershing's reputation lost some of its shine was that in the wake of World War II, World War I itself increasingly appeared to Americans to have been a hollow victory. The Great War, as it was often referred to before 1939, gave the United States no appreciable gains and, if anything, would come to be perceived as the cause of World War II. Some argued that President Woodrow Wilson should have allowed Pershing to fight the Germans all the way to Berlin in November 1918 to ensure that they'd be so thoroughly annihilated they could never dominate Europe again. (Pershing himself contended that this is what the United States should have done.) In any event, the prevailing opinion remains that the penalties imposed on Germany in 1919, particularly the substantial financial reparations, sent its economy into a downward spiral and enabled Adolf Hitler and his henchmen to prey on their country's wounded pride to elevate the Nazis' in their rise to power.

The full story of World War I, of course, begins well before America's entry, back to the summer of 1914, when a Serbian terrorist group known as the Black Hand sprang their plot to kill Archduke Franz Ferdinand and his wife, Sophie, during their visit to Sarajevo. Ferdinand was the nephew of Franz Joseph I, emperor of Austria-Hungary, and the presumptive heir to the throne. The Black Hand had wanted Serbia to unite with Bosnia-Herzegovina and liberate itself from Austria-Hungary, and its members thought that by assassinating Ferdinand they could ignite a larger war that would lead to independence.

By sheer luck, they had learned of Ferdinand's schedule weeks in advance, giving them ample time to prepare. Nedeljko Čabrinović, one of the conspirators, had bumped into a friend of his father's, and he happened to be an officer in Sarajevo's police department, who told Čabrinović the exact day the archduke would be touring the city.

On the morning of June 28, when Ferdinand's slow-moving procession approached where Čabrinović was standing, he lobbed a grenade directly at the archduke, but missed. The bomb hit the back of the vehicle and dropped into the street, and then exploded under the next car, wounding more than twenty passengers and bystanders.

Realizing that they had come under attack, Ferdinand's driver accelerated out of the scene and sped past three of the other conspirators—Cvjetko Popović, Trifun Grabež, and Gavrilo Princip—so quickly that the men didn't have a chance to use their weapons.

Understandably rattled, the archduke excoriated Sarajevo's mayor, Fehim Čurćić, when he arrived at the town hall for a reception. "I came here on a visit," Ferdinand raged, "and I am greeted with bombs. It is outrageous!" Sophie was able to calm her husband down, and the mayor returned to officiating the prearranged welcoming ceremony.

Afterward, Ferdinand insisted on changing the day's schedule and going to the hospital to visit the people wounded by Čabrinović's grenade. On the way there, Ferdinand's driver took a wrong turn and, upon realizing his mistake, stopped the car and backed up—right in front of a café where the nineteen-year-old Bosnian Serb Gavrilo Princip was sitting. Princip walked over to the car and, nearly at point-blank range, shot Ferdinand in the neck, severing his jugular vein, and then fired a bullet into Sophie's stomach. With blood spurting out of his neck, Ferdinand leaned over to Sophie and implored her to live for their children's sake. She slumped forward and died moments later from internal bleeding. Ferdinand was delirious from shock and repeated, "*Is nischt, is nischt*"—"It is nothing, it is nothing"—but suddenly he could no longer speak and emitted a loud, gurgling death rattle.

Gavrilo Princip swallowed a cyanide pill, but it was too weak to be fatal. As police officers rushed toward him, he aimed his gun at his head and was about to pull the trigger when someone grabbed the pistol, and he was taken into custody.

Emperor Franz Joseph had no love for his nephew (and even less regard for Sophie; the emperor didn't attend either their wedding or their funerals), but, if sanctioned by another government, the assassination of the archduke could be considered an act of war.

Austria-Hungary began an inquiry into whether the Serbian government itself was complicit in the murders. Regardless of the outcome, Germany's Kaiser Wilhelm II, Chancellor Theobald von Bethmann-Hollweg, and Foreign Minister Gottlieb von Jagow wanted to use the crisis to destroy Serbia, which they considered a destabilizing force in the region.

On July 6, senior German officials, with the kaiser's blessing, urged the Austro-Hungarians to go to war against Serbia, promising the German military's full support. Austria-Hungary's hawkish foreign minister, Count Leopold Berchtold, began drafting an ultimatum so draconian that Serbia would have to reject it; Austria-Hungary could then argue that they had at least *attempted* diplomacy. Berchtold, in fact, had no desire for a peaceful resolution.

Nor did the kaiser and his advisers. They understood the reasoning behind the document, but they were impatient and felt that in order to ensure that the attack on Serbia was successful, war should commence as soon as possible. A swift victory, they believed, would also prevent Russia from coming to the aid of their fellow Slavs.

On July 11, the German Foreign Office was consumed with a somewhat awkward situation: July 11 was King Peter of Serbia's birthday, and normally the Germans would send a congratulatory message to his highness on the special occasion. In light of the fact that their government was currently plotting the destruction of Serbia—and, if necessary, its king—they were flummoxed as to what to do. The matter was finally presented to the kaiser, who, not wanting to raise any suspicions whatsoever, ordered that the foreign office send King Peter happy and hearty best wishes for his birthday. So they did.

Gavrilo Princip.

*The Archduke Franz Ferdinand and his wife, Sophie,
minutes before they were shot to death.*

Austria-Hungary presented the ultimatum to Serbian officials on July 23 and told them they had forty-eight hours to accept it. That same day, Kaiser Wilhelm and other prominent German officials went on vacation to maintain the fiction that they had nothing to do with Austria-Hungary's demands to Serbia.

Once the document became public, however, there was a sudden frenzy of diplomatic maneuvering across Europe, especially in France, Russia, and England. The British cabinet was already meeting over another contentious matter, the brewing civil war in Ireland, when they learned the news. "The Cabinet was about to separate," First Lord of the Admiralty Winston Churchill recalled of the moment, "when the quiet grave tones of [Foreign Secretary] Sir Edward Grey's voice were heard reading a document which had just been brought to him from the Foreign Office. It was the Austrian note to Serbia." Upon hearing its contents, Churchill called it "the most insolent document of its kind ever devised" and that "it seemed absolutely impossible that any State in the world could accept it, or that any acceptance, however abject, would satisfy the aggressor. . . . Europe is trembling on the verge of a general war."

England's prime minister, Herbert Henry Asquith, was equally pessimistic. "The situation is about as bad as it can possibly be," he wrote privately to a friend. "Austria has sent a bullying and humiliating ultimatum to Serbia, who cannot possibly comply with it, and demanded an answer within forty-eight hours—failing which she will march. This means, almost inevitably, that Russia will come to the scene in defence of Serbia and in defiance of Austria, and if so, it is difficult for Germany and France to refrain from lending a hand to one side or the other."

But incredibly, the Serbs seemed willing to accept almost all of the terms. England, France, and Russia all pressured Austria-Hungary to negotiate with Serbia. Not knowing that Germany was complicit in the scheme, the various foreign ministers and ambassadors also implored Germany to use its influence over Austria-Hungary.

Country after country began preparatory actions in case the talks failed. The French government informed all of their soldiers that leaves had been canceled. Winston Churchill put the British Navy on "war footing." And Russia, which was in the middle of a massive rebuilding of its armed forces, called the Grand Military Program, debated whether to begin assembling troops as well. Which is precisely what the Germans wanted them to do in order to accuse Russia of inciting a larger war.

At 1:00 a.m. on July 30, the Austro-Hungarians declared that Serbia was delinquent in responding and used its ships to bombard the capital city of Belgrade from the Danube River.

Russia's Tsar Nicholas II, who was Kaiser Wilhelm's first cousin (they had played together as children while staying in England with their grandmother, Queen Victoria, and called each other Nicky and Willy), engaged in one last back-channel attempt to prevent hostilities from expanding throughout the region. At 1:00 a.m. on July 29, the tsar cabled the kaiser after Wilhelm had returned from his "vacation":

> Am glad you are back. In this serious moment, I appeal to you to help me. An ignoble war has been declared [by Austria-Hungary] against a weak country [Serbia]. The indignation in Russia shared fully by me is enormous. I foresee that very soon I shall be overwhelmed by the pressure forced upon me and be forced to take extreme measures which will lead to war. To try and avoid such a calamity as a European war I beg you in the name of our old friendship to do what you can to stop your allies from going too far.

Thus began a series of communiqués between the two cousins that culminated in a final exchange beginning on July 31. The tsar wrote to the kaiser:

> I thank you heartily for your mediation which begins to give one hope that all may yet end peacefully. It is *technically* impossible to stop our military preparations which were obligatory owing to Austria's mobilisation. We are far from

wishing war. As long as the negotiations with Austria on Serbia's account are taking place my troops shall not make any provocative action. I give you my solemn word for this. I put all my trust in God's mercy and hope in your successful mediation in Vienna for the welfare of our countries and for the peace of Europe.

Your affectionate Nicky

The next day, the tsar made one final plea:

Understand you are obliged to mobilise but wish to have the same guarantee from you as I gave you, that these measures do not mean war and that we shall continue negotiating for the benefit of our countries and universal peace dear to all our hearts. Our long proved friendship must succeed, with God's help, in avoiding bloodshed. Anxiously, full of confidence await your answer.

Nicky

The kaiser replied hours later, barely able to hide his disdain:

Thanks for your telegram. I yesterday pointed out to your government the way by which alone war may be avoided.

Although I requested an answer for noon today, no telegram from my ambassador conveying an answer from your Government has reached me as yet. I therefore have been obliged to mobilise my army.

Immediate affirmative clear and unmistakable answer from your government is the only way to avoid endless misery. Until I have received this answer alas, I am unable to discuss the subject of your telegram. As a matter of fact I must request you to immediately order your troops on no account to commit the slightest act of trespassing over our frontiers.

Willy

The cousins had reached an impasse, and on August 1, Germany declared war on Russia. France actively began preparing its troops, and the Germans now faced a two-front war, one to their east and the other to their west. Their greatest hope for victory was that Belgium would let German troops pass through their country, without resistance, so they could strike a decisive blow against France while it was still mobilizing. That decision was in the hands of Belgium's King Albert, who also happened to be a cousin of Kaiser Wilhelm. The two men weren't as close as Willy and Nicky, but they were still relatives.

On August 2, 1914, the German government sent the Belgian minister of foreign affairs a letter that began by insisting that French troops were about to march through Belgium in an attempt to invade Germany. The Germans were afraid that Belgium, "in spite of the utmost goodwill," would not be able to repel the invasion without assistance, so it was therefore necessary for the Germans to go through Belgium first.

Germany would "feel the deepest regret if Belgium" thought the Germans were "in any way acting in a hostile manner" and emphasized again that this was purely a defensive act. And, just so there was no misunderstanding, the Germans promised they would not occupy Belgium and would make sure that, at the end of the war, Belgium would maintain both its "possessions and independence." They also assured the Belgians that if they went about all of this with "a friendly attitude" and let German soldiers pass through Belgium, the Germans would reimburse Belgium "for any damage that may [be] caused by German troops."

At this point in the letter the tone abruptly shifts into a stern warning. If Belgium should resist or impede the German advance, including by destroying railways, tunnels, and roads, Germany would "to her regret, be compelled to consider Belgium as an enemy" and treat her and her citizens as such.

Having gotten that uncomfortable little matter out of the way, the letter returns to its more cordial tone. "The German Government entertains the distinct hope that this eventuality will not occur, and . . .

the friendly ties which bind the two neighbouring States will grow stronger and more enduring."

Belgian officials didn't quite see it that way.

In their August 3 reply, they let the Germans know that the letter had "made a deep and painful impression" on them. After rejecting the preposterous claim that France was planning to invade their country, the Belgians cautioned the Germans that an "attack upon [their] independence . . . constitutes a flagrant violation of international law" and that they were "firmly resolved to repel, by all means in their power, every attack on their rights."

German troops stormed into Belgium the next day. This caused Great Britain to honor its 1839 treaty with Belgium and, on August 4, declare war on Germany. Chancellor Theobold von Bethmann-Hollweg was incredulous that England would go to war with Germany, as he famously remarked, "over a scrap of paper!"

GENERAL JOHN PERSHING didn't arrive in Europe with the first contingent of AEF officers and soldiers until June 1917, almost three years after Gavrilo Princip murdered Archduke Franz Ferdinand. But Pershing was hardly idle in the time between. He closely followed the battles from day one as they were being reported in the American press, and he requested early on to be sent over as a military adviser. (The appeal was denied.) In 1916 he was deployed to Mexico with twelve thousand U.S. soldiers to hunt down the Mexican outlaw Pancho Villa without sparking a war south of the border, a mission that had earned him the admiration of President Woodrow Wilson. Now, tasked with commanding the AEF in Europe, Pershing was responsible for building, supplying, and training an army twenty times its current size, and in just over a year.

This book tells the story of the American experience in World War I, with General Pershing as the unquestionable protagonist. It does so primarily through the letters, journals, and other personal writings that

Pershing and his countrymen composed throughout the conflict. The focus of this book is not to detail the movement of every platoon in every operation of the war. An example for this reasoning can be found in Pershing's own memoirs, *My Experiences in the World War*, in which he lays out the order of battle for the Meuse-Argonne Offensive:

> From east to west, the II Corps (Bullard) was on the right, with the 33d Division (Bell) nearest the Meuse to cover the river and protect the flank of the army, the 80th Division (Cronkhite) in the center, and the 4th Division (Hines) on the left, with the 3d Division (Buck) in reserve. The V Corps (Cameron) consisted of the 79th Division (Kuhn) facing Montfaucon, the 37th (Farnsworth), and the 91st (Johnston), in that order, while the 32d Division (Haan) was in reserve. The I Corps (Liggett) was on the left of the army with the 35th Division (Traub) on its right, the 28th Division (Muir) next, west of the Aire River, and the 77th Division (Alexander) facing the Argonne, with the French 6th Cavalry Division and the American 92nd Division (colored) (Ballou) in reserve, except for one regiment which was attached to the French Fourth Army.

This goes on, roughly, for four more pages until Pershing himself concedes that it's all a bit overwhelming: "The numbers engaged, the diverse character of the fighting and the terrain, the numerous crises, and the brilliant feats of individuals make a detailed description of the battle extremely complicated and necessarily confusing to the reader."

Pershing also emphasizes in his 857-page memoirs that his purpose is not to write a complete history of the war or expound on every country's involvement. Italy, for example, proved to be a valuable ally; its soldiers thrashed Austrian forces so thoroughly that they hastened the collapse of the entire Austro-Hungarian empire. But Pershing barely mentions Italy in his writings. Instead, he mostly concentrates on Great Britain and France. And the latter, in particular, represented to Pershing the epicenter of the war. It was there that the Americans, serving with the Foreign Legion, first encountered German troops only months after hostilities broke out in 1914. It was there that he set up his headquarters. And Pershing knew that it would be there, in France, where the most decisive battles of the war would be fought and where the majority of the Americans under his command who saw combat would fight and bleed and die.

The aim of this book is to portray an overall sense of what these men and women, especially those who volunteered, lived through and felt and expressed during the war and, if they survived, in the years and decades that followed. Battles are indeed related here in detail, but through the lens of individual soldiers, pilots, ambulance drivers, nurses, doctors, and journalists. Endless tallies of body counts and casualties can be potentially numbing, making war almost too large and abstract to comprehend. Some of the most powerful accounts don't necessarily record the enormity of war, but demonstrate, in fact, how small—and personal—it can be.

Serendipity is often an author's greatest ally, and finding previously unpublished letters by Pershing was one of several fortuitous discoveries and unforeseen events that inspired this book. The first, actually, came years earlier during a visit to a small museum in Columbus, New Mexico, to research a historic raid on the tiny town almost a century ago. In this case, it wasn't a letter that sparked my interest in Pershing, but a photograph. The moment it caught my eye, I knew it was significant. But it wasn't until I delved into Pershing's life and the epic story of World War I that I realized just how remarkable it truly was.

My Fellow Soldiers

Left to right: Mexican general Álvaro Obregón, General Francisco "Pancho" Villa, and General John Pershing.

I.

August 26

I bought Warren a corduroy suit in regulation Norfolk
jacket pattern. He was so delighted that he told the
conductor on the car all about it. You should see your
children. They all look so blooming. Mary Margaret is a
perfect little fascinator with cheeks like a red apple. Anne
wrote you a darling letter. She dictated her thoughts, and
Helen was her secretary. Both did a pretty good job, I
thought.

—Helen "Frankie" Warren Pershing, writing from
San Francisco to her husband, General John Pershing,
about their four young children: Warren,
Mary Margaret, Anne, and Helen

IN A BLACK-AND-WHITE PHOTOGRAPH taken at Fort Bliss in El
Paso, Texas, a grinning General John Pershing is standing next to
General Francisco "Pancho" Villa and the future president of Mexico,
General Álvaro Obregón. (On the far right is a young lieutenant named
George S. Patton Jr.) Villa, the provisional governor of Chihuahua, had
maintained cordial relations with the U.S. government. Within Mexico, he was seen as a Robin Hood–like figure, raiding the haciendas of
wealthy businessmen and redistributing the money and land to destitute farmers, laborers, and widows.

The picture was snapped in 1914, on the twenty-sixth of August. On that very day, 5,360 miles away, German soldiers were systematically setting fire to the Belgian town of Louvain, a city famous for its architectural splendor, including the Katholieke Universiteit Leuven, the oldest Catholic university in existence. The school's world-renowned library held almost a quarter of a million priceless medieval, Gothic, and Renaissance manuscripts. When evening came, the sky was a swelling, rippling mix of smoke and fire. Everywhere, tiny bits of paper drifted down like black snowflakes, their edges aglow with bright red embers. To the horror of the townspeople, it was clear that countless rare books and manuscripts from the library were going up in flames. By morning, the building was a heap of smoldering ruins.

For weeks, British and French newspapers had been reporting on German atrocities in Belgium. The German government had asked the Belgians to let German troops march peacefully through their country to invade France, but Belgium's King Albert, citing national honor, refused. In retribution, the Germans implemented a policy of *Schreck-lichkeit* ("frightfulness" or "terror") during their invasion, under which any perceived act of violence against even a single German soldier would result in brutal and widespread punishments. The point was to spread so much fear that the entire population would be deterred from offering any resistance whatsoever.

British and French newspapers reported that German troops were executing innocent civilians en masse; setting homes on fire and then shooting the residents as they ran out to escape the flames; and turning tens of thousands of Belgians, many of whom were frail and elderly, into refugees who had to trek for miles to seek out a safe haven in another town or village. The articles became increasingly lurid. There were accounts of German soldiers raping nuns, chopping off the hands and feet of small children, and impaling infants on doorways with their bayonets. Many of these stories came from secondhand sources, and even those sympathetic to Belgium and its people questioned their veracity. But the demolition of an ancient library struck a particular chord around the world because the proof was evident for all to see; it seemed like an attack on civilization itself. "Remember Louvain!" was the first of many rallying cries for those who wanted the United States to enter the war.

Richard Harding Davis, a correspondent from the *New York Tribune*, was in Louvain during the invasion, and days later he wired back a detailed account of what he saw:

> The Germans sentenced Louvain on Wednesday [August 26] to become a wilderness, and with the German system and love of thoroughness they left Louvain an empty, blackened shell. Great architects and artists, dead these six hundred years, made [the city] beautiful, and their handiwork belonged to the world. With torch and dynamite the Germans have turned these masterpieces into ashes. . . .
>
> In each building, so German soldiers told me, they began at the first floor, and when that was burning steadily passed to the one next. There were no exceptions—whether it was a store, chapel or private residence it was destroyed. The occupants had been warned to go, and in each deserted shop or house the furniture was piled, the torch was stuck under it, and into the air went the savings of years, souvenirs of children, or parents, heirlooms that had passed from generation to generation. . . .
>
> Outside the station in the public square the people of Louvain passed in an unending procession, women bareheaded, weeping, men carrying the children asleep on their shoulders, all hemmed in by the shadowy army of gray wolves. Once they were halted, and among them were marched a line of men. They well knew their fellow townsmen. These were on their way to be shot.

President Woodrow Wilson, as a former college president, was especially furious about what the Germans had done, but he refused to make a public statement about Louvain. When asked to comment about it, Wilson referred journalists back to his speech from barely a week earlier on his decision for the United States to remain neutral in the war. "America," he had said, is "a nation that neither sits in judgment upon others nor is disturbed in her own counsels and which keeps herself fit and free to do what is honest and disinterested and truly serviceable for the peace of the world."

Wilson's stance was a matter of principle to some extent, but he also well knew that the vast majority of Americans were opposed to interceding in the war, and Wilson had a reelection campaign to win. The largest community of immigrants in the country were German Americans, who believed that their native land was being unfairly maligned, and the second largest were Irish Americans, many of whom were happy to see their longtime foes the British entangled in a major war. Combined, these two groups could ensure Wilson's defeat. But Wilson had another consideration in mind: when the fighting was done, he—as a neutral player—could mediate the armistice and come out shining as an international peacemaker. And the prospect that the war would, in fact, be over soon looked increasingly likely.

HAVING PUSHED THROUGH Belgium over the previous four weeks, 1.5 million German soldiers under General Helmuth von Moltke swept into France from the north through Belgium and by early September 1914 were thirty miles from Paris, putting the city well within range of Germany's massive siege guns. The French government fled to Bordeaux, and an invasion of the capital seemed imminent. General Moltke was confident that a resounding victory was all but guaranteed, fulfilling Kaiser Wilhelm II's promise to his troops that they would triumphantly return home in autumn, before "the leaves fall from trees."

Although the French forces were outnumbered, Marshal Joseph Joffre, their commander, was able to reassemble one million French and British troops and strike the enemy from three different directions, blunting the German juggernaut at the Marne River. Short of transpor-

Louvain after the Germans had leveled most of the city's homes and buildings.
The Maison Americaine, an American cultural center (far right),
was spared because the United States, at the time, was a neutral nation.

tation and manpower, the French Army recruited taxi drivers to help bring men and supplies to the front. (The taxi drivers actually kept their meters running throughout the offensive and were later reimbursed, collectively, more than seventy thousand francs.)

When General Moltke realized that his troops would have to retreat, after having come so close to success, he suffered a nervous breakdown and was relieved of his command. Joffre, by contrast, remained the epitome of calm. Every afternoon he enjoyed a leisurely lunch and took a nap.

Paris was saved for the time being, but the Germans still occupied all of Belgium and hundreds of square miles of French territory. Both sides dug in, creating an elaborate network of trenches along a front that soon zigzagged for roughly 440 miles from the Swiss border to the North Sea. Any celebration by the Allied forces was tempered by the fact that an estimated eighty-one thousand French and British soldiers had been killed in what would be called the Battle of the Marne. German losses were approximately the same.

Americans had nothing with which to even compare such a staggering loss of life. At Gettysburg, a total of seven thousand Union and Confederate soldiers were killed, and that was the deadliest battle of the Civil War. In Fort Bliss, Texas, the *El Paso Morning Times* was one of the main sources of international news, and General John Pershing was devouring everything he could read about the German invasion of Belgium and France. At first, censorship prevented many of the details from being reported. On August 27, 1914, the very morning that Pershing's picture appeared on the front page of the paper, the two largest headlines were: WARM WELCOME FOR VILLA AND OBREGON IN EL PASO and CLOSED VEIL DRAWN OVER PROGRESS OF WAR.

That "closed veil" started to lift the next day. On August 28, the entire upper quarter of the *El Paso Morning Times* featured a graphic picture, stretching from margin to margin, that showed Belgian casualties being treated by doctors and nurses. Underneath was the headline: CONFLICT OF MILLIONS APPEARS TO AT LAST BE IN PROGRESS IN EUROPE. Pershing had wanted to be there from day one. Between August and October 1909, Pershing had traveled with his family as a tourist throughout Russia and Europe, and he was fascinated by the region. Pershing recalled of his trip to Berlin:

> As I particularly wished to see something of the German army, I at once got in touch with Colonel John Wisser, our military attaché. He took me the following day to call at the [German] War Office, where I found, as expected, every sign of smartness and efficiency. Through this visit I arranged to see an artillery regiment and barracks at Potsdam. The Colonel showed me the preparation they had made for quick transformation of the regiment's civilian reserves into fully-equipped soldiers ready to take their places in the ranks. I had never seen such perfect preparation. . . .

The discipline of the German people was evident at every turn. All things seemed to be done in military fashion. The army, so to speak, was the nation. This was especially noticeable to one who had just come from Russia. There the army seemed a thing apart from the people; here it was a model which they were proud to emulate.

Pershing also had a memorable stay in France:

While there I went to Metz and with a guide and maps went over the battlefield where the Germans captured Marshal Bazaine and his army in 1871. The visit was especially interesting to me not only as a soldier but because I remembered how as a ten-year-old boy I had eagerly read the dispatches about the Franco-Prussian War as they appeared in the *St. Louis Globe-Democrat*. It was the first great war that I was old enough to read about at the time it was being waged. The sight of the battlefield brought back to mind how the wiseacres of Laclede, my old hometown, used to gather in front of father's store and Dick Mitchell's drugstore next door and, whittling in Missouri fashion, hold forth on the strategy of the campaign—comparing the French and German generals to Grant and Lee.

In August 1914, senior U.S. commanders floated the idea of sending generals to Europe *solely* to evaluate and report on the situation. Pershing appealed directly to Major General William Wotherspoon, the Army's chief of staff, to be picked. "I am among the younger general officers and the special personal benefits that I should derive should make my services that much more valuable to the government," the fifty-four-year-old Pershing pointed out. He reminded Wotherspoon that he had been a military observer during Japan's war with Russia ten years earlier, but he had not, as of yet, "had any opportunity to visit European maneuvers or see anything of their armies." Wotherspoon replied that, with the possible exception of Great Britain, none of the warring nations wanted observers from other countries, and he assured Pershing that if the governments changed their policy, Pershing's name would be considered.

Pershing soon found himself restless and lonely in Texas. His wife, Helen Frances "Frankie" Warren, and their four children—nine-year-old Helen, seven-year-old Anne, six-year-old Warren, and three-year-old Mary Margaret—were all still living at the Presidio, the military base in San Francisco. They had never been separated for so long.

Frankie was the daughter of the powerful Wyoming senator Francis Warren, chairman of the Committee on Military Affairs. Warren was seventy-one years of age, and the oldest living veteran of the Civil War in the U.S. Senate. As a nineteen-year-old Union soldier, he had charged into a volley of shot and shell to disable a Confederate cannon during the siege of Port Hudson, Louisiana, and sustained a head wound so severe that he was left for dead in a ditch. Surrounded by corpses, Warren was almost buried alive until an observant doctor noticed that he was breathing faintly and got him to a hospital. For his actions at Port Hudson, Warren was awarded the Medal of Honor.

General Pershing had originally been stationed at the Presidio in January 1913 to command the Army's 8th Brigade, but he and his men were moved to Fort Bliss, Texas, in April to help protect the border from Mexican bandits, who were crossing over and stealing horses, cows, and other livestock. As much as he missed his family, Pershing wanted them to stay in San Francisco for the time being, where they would be safe: Mexico was in the throes of a violent revolution. Pershing would later blame himself for not bringing them to Fort Bliss earlier.

On the morning of August 27, 1915, a reporter named Norman Walker from the Associated Press called General Pershing's headquarters to confirm a story coming over the wires about a house fire at the Presidio that had broken out on August 26, just before midnight.

Certain that the voice at the other end was Lieutenant James Collins, General Pershing's military aide, the reporter asked somewhat matter-of-factly if he could get a quote from Pershing's office about the incident.

*General Pershing in the Philippines in 1911 with his wife,
"Frankie," and their children: Anne, left; Helen, middle; and Warren, right.
Mary Margaret was not yet born.*

There was a pause, and then the voice demanded, "What fire? What has happened!?"

Suddenly Walker realized that it wasn't Pershing's aide he was speaking to, but General Pershing himself.

Caught off guard, Walker stumbled through the report as the general listened: Mrs. Pershing, thirty-five, and their three daughters were all killed when a fire swept through their house at the Presidio a few hours past midnight. Only six-year-old Warren survived.

"Oh, God! My God!" Pershing cried. "Read that again!"

Walker repeated the story.

"My God! My God!" Pershing kept saying, traumatized by the news.

After Walker expressed his sympathies, Pershing was silent for a moment, and then asked, "Who is this? Who am I speaking to?"

Walker told him, and Pershing said, before hanging up, "Thank you, Walker. It was very considerate of you to phone."

As word of the tragedy spread, sympathetic messages came in from around the world. One was by former president Teddy Roosevelt, who wrote: "Am inexpressibly shocked and grieved pray accept my deepe [sic] and heart felt sympathy."

Another telegram read: "With enormous sorrow I heard that your estimable family had the misfortune to perish in a house fire and for this unfortunate accident permit me to send my sincerest condolences. Yours faithfully." The sender was Pancho Villa.

One thought consumed Pershing as he began the agonizing two-day journey by train to California: Had his wife and daughters slowly burned to death, or did they die instantly?

Pershing's first visit was to the funeral home, where he saw the four coffins—three tiny ones next to a longer one—and collapsed in grief. After composing himself, he went to the Presidio and immediately began asking eyewitnesses what had happened. By then it was determined that a spark from a burning piece of coal had leaped out of the fireplace and onto the newly lacquered, and highly flammable, floor, which set off the blaze.

Guests of the Pershings had made it out safely, and when soldiers on base rushed to the frantic scene and saw a small family huddled outside the home, they assumed it was Mrs. Pershing and her children. Once they realized it was not, they charged into the burning house and were able to drag out Warren, who was barely conscious. By the time they found the three girls and their mother, all four had died from smoke inhalation.

"Not even their hair was singed," an officer told Pershing. "They went quietly in their sleep." His friends would later say that this fact, along with Warren's survival, was all that kept Pershing from going mad with grief.

Frankie and the three girls would be buried in the Warren family plot in Cheyenne, Wyoming, where Frankie was born and raised, the place that Senator Warren considered his true home. The senator had gone to the Presidio as well, and although also devastated, he realized his son-in-law was barely functional and unable to handle all the heartbreaking little details that had to be arranged. The local undertaker had to be notified to begin preparing for the funeral. Hearses were needed. And pallbearers had to be found. Senator Warren decided on using twelve; just two each for the three girls, since their coffins were so much lighter, and the rest for Frankie.

Six-year-old Warren had no idea what was going on, and Pershing and the rest of the family believed it was best, at least for the time being, not to tell him the truth. It would simply be too overwhelming. Pershing told him that his sisters and mothers were off vacationing for the next several months. Warren would go to Texas with his father.

When Pershing returned to Fort Bliss there was a short letter waiting for him. "The world is so clean this morning," it began. "There is the sound of meadow larks everywhere. And God be thanked for the sunshine and blue sky! Do you think there can be many people in the world as happy as we are? I would like to live to be a thousand years old if I could spend all of that time with you." Frankie Pershing had written it to her husband just before her death.

2.

The First to Go

THERE HAS BEEN VERY little action here since we arrived, and practically no ground lost or gained," twenty-seven-year-old Private Edward Stone wrote to family members on January 20, 1915. A machine gunner in the French Foreign Legion, Stone was near the Craonne region of France, ninety miles northeast of Paris. "If there is a battle of any importance, we probably shall not take part in it," he lamented. "We shall in all probability go ingloriously to the rear, giving place to fresh troops."

Unlike most of his comrades, Stone was not French. Born in Chicago on January 5, 1887, he was an American citizen who had joined the Foreign Legion after the war erupted in early August 1914. And despite his efforts to downplay the risks he faced, Stone was very much in danger. On February 15, 1915, German forces unleashed an artillery barrage on Stone's battalion. Instead of running for shelter, Stone remained by his machine gun. Seconds later, a small but razor-sharp shell fragment punctured his right lung. Stone was rushed to a military hospital, and after an excruciating twelve days—every breath a labored effort, every jostle a stab of pain—he succumbed to his injuries. On February 27, 1915, Edward Stone earned the sad honor of becoming the first American combatant killed in the Great War. Other than a tribute from his alma mater, Harvard, his death received scant attention back in the United States.

The day before Stone died, another Harvard graduate in the

Foreign Legion described to his father a close call he had near the front lines. Twenty-six-year-old Alan Seeger wrote:

> I was shot a few days ago coming in from sentinel duty. I exposed myself for about two seconds at a point where the communication ditch is not deep enough. One of the snipers who keep cracking away with their Mausers at anyone who shows his head came within an ace of getting me. The ball just grazed my arm, tore the sleeve of my capote and raised a lump on the biceps which is still sore, but the skin was not broken and the wound was not serious enough to make me leave the ranks.

Close call notwithstanding, Seeger deemed the soldier's life to be a rather boring one overall. "We are just watchmen at present," he wrote at the end of his February 26 letter to his father, "which does not please me, but which ought to comfort Mother."

Mother was not pleased at all. She had castigated him in a letter for making a rash and foolhardy decision. He defended himself vociferously in response: "You are quite wrong about my not realizing what I was going into when I enlisted. I had not been living for two years in Europe without coming to understand the situation very well, and I was under no illusion that the conflict which was to decide the fate of empires and remake the map of Europe would be a matter of months." In this Seeger was more prescient than many senior French, German, and British commanders, who assumed when the war began in August 1914 that it would be over by fall. "I knew that it would be a fight to the finish, just as our Civil War was. The conflagration, far from diminishing, seems to be spreading. The lull during the winter has allowed each side on this front to fortify itself so strongly that, in my opinion, the deadlock here is permanent."

Alan Seeger, Edward Stone, and other Americans had volunteered to serve in the Foreign Legion because, as U.S. citizens, they were legally prohibited from enlisting in the French Army, so long as the United States remained a neutral nation. Soldiers in the Foreign Legion technically swore an oath of allegiance to the Legion and not to France, a distinction that the Germans, not unfairly, contended was ludicrous.

Seeger was an unlikely candidate to be part of one of the world's toughest and most fearsome paramilitary forces. Tall but skinny, he was a romantic at heart. After graduating from Harvard in 1910, he moved to Paris in 1912 to live a bohemian life—reading, writing poetry, drinking wine, and falling in and out of love. Even his friends considered him moody, free-spirited, and something of a loner, not exactly the ideal traits for a soldier, whose existence revolved around discipline, obedience, and camaraderie.

But Seeger had become enamored with France, and when the country was threatened, he enlisted. He was also drawn to what he thought would be the exhilaration of warfare. "Every day from the distance of the north has come the booming of the cannon around Reims and the lines along the Meuse," he wrote to his mother. It was the day before he hoped he was finally going to experience combat.

> We have had splendid sham battles [in training], firing dozens of rounds of blank cartridges. . . .
>
> But imagine how thrilling it will be tomorrow and the following days, marching toward the front with the noise of battle growing continually louder before us. I could tell you where we are going but I do not want to run any risk of having this letter stopped by the censor. The whole regiment is going, four battalions, about 4,000 men. You have no idea how beautiful it is to see the troops undulating . . . as far as the eye can see. . . .
>
> The hard work and moments of frightful fatigue have not broken but hardened me and I am in excellent health and spirits. Do not worry, for the chances are small of [my] not returning.

Much to his disappointment, Seeger and his regiment remained in an area relatively far from the front. His greatest concern would be the safety of the only manuscript of his poetry. "Unfortunately I left my MS with a printer in Bruges," he wrote to his mother, "which is now in the hands of the Germans and the center of the fiercest fighting." Trying to soothe her worries, he added, "After the war I shall return there and look it up. . . . So wait and count on my being with you next summer."

SOME AMERICANS, like Seeger, were already in France when Germany invaded, but others heard the news while still in the United States and did everything they could to join the fight. On August 3, 1914, a twenty-one-year-old Tennessee native named Kiffin Rockwell, living in Atlanta with his older brother Paul, contacted the French consul in New Orleans, Louisiana, declaring that he and his brother greatly admired France and were willing to sail to Europe immediately and enlist. Rockwell emphasized that he had been trained and educated at the Virginia Military Institute, but this was an exaggeration: he had indeed attended VMI, but only for a year before dropping out.

Rockwell didn't wait for a reply. After calling steamship companies in New York to see if any of their liners were going to Europe, he learned that only one ship—the *St. Paul*—was willing to brave the voyage in the face of warnings from the German Navy that even passenger liners might be targeted by their fearsome fleet of submarines, the *Unterseeboote,* or U-boats.

On August 5, 1914, Kiffin and Paul received word that they could purchase two steamship tickets, but they had to be in New York by the morning of August 7. Almost giddy, they hastily packed their belongings and boarded an express train, first to Washington to get their passports, and then to Manhattan. They were in such a rush that they discarded the idea of making a side trip to North Carolina to say good-bye to their mother, Loula, and sister, Agnes. Their father was no longer alive. He had died when the boys were young, and the three children were raised by their mother and her father, a proud Confederate veteran of the Civil War.

The Rockwell boys had grown up listening to their grandfather's war stories, and Kiffin, in particular, held rather romantic notions of combat. On the eve of his departure, he wrote to his "Dear Mamma" from the Hotel Imperial:

> Well, Paul and I Are Sailing on the American Liner, *St. Paul*, Tomorrow Morning at 10 O'clock.
>
> We would have gone home to see you and explain things if there had been time. But we had to do some hurrying to catch this boat and it was practically our only safe chance. It is the only boat leaving here in two weeks time flying the U.S. flag and we did not want to wait two weeks.
>
> I don't want you to worry or feel bad. You have always told me that you wanted me to live my life without interference and this opportunity is one that only comes once in a lifetime.

Worry, of course, she did, and in her first letter to Kiffin, she begged her boys to reconsider and come home. Kiffin tried to convince her that there was no reason for her to be concerned. He admitted that his motivations had as much to do with his own self-respect as his sense of patriotism. "I realize how you feel," he wrote, "but I don't think you should worry or feel bad. I am of such a temperament that if I didn't do things that seem strange to you, I could never be satisfied, myself, or make a success of my own life. . . . If I should be killed in this war I will at least die as a man should and would not consider myself a complete failure."

By the end of August 1914, Paul and Kiffin Rockwell were training with the Foreign Legion. By the fall they were in the line. Paul was knocked out of the war early by a shell that broke his collarbone. He survived but did mostly administrative work for the French government. Though Kiffin would carry on without his brother, he didn't lack for companionship. Kiffin was impressed by the "diversity" of the Americans in the Legion. "Yale, Harvard, Michigan, Columbia, Cornell and several other schools are represented [here]," he told his mother; the men were all "fine fellows."

Kiffin Rockwell.

On January 31, 1915, Kiffin began another letter to his mother by saying, "I suppose you are a little worried about me, owing to recent happenings, but have spent eight days in a position where we couldn't send any mail. . . . Don't worry about my welfare, for the more I see the more convinced that I am coming through safe and whole."

Those "recent happenings" he alluded to were a bit more intense than Kiffin let on to his mother. In a letter to Agnes, he gave the real story of how close he'd come to dying. "I have had practically no sleep for the last eighty hours, but I can't sleep now so will write you and try to keep my mind occupied," he wrote on January 7, 1915. After spending Christmas in the trenches, Rockwell and his regiment were marched through swamplands in the dead of night until they reached a French village demolished by the Germans. Not a single house or building was intact. Still standing, however, was a stone wall that surrounded what had been a park, and Rockwell and three other men, including Alan Seeger, were positioned at various points along the wall as sentries. German troops were entrenched on the other side.

At 7:00 a.m., Rockwell and the others started back to a rear section to get breakfast. But once they were exposed, the German troops opened fire. The men sprinted to small dugouts and were pinned down for the entire day. As Rockwell wrote to Agnes:

Alan Seeger.

At 10:30 p.m., the communication sentinel came up to me. Just as he started to speak something fell at my feet and sputtered a little and then went out. We each said, "What's that?" I reached down and picked it up, when the other sentinel said, "Good god! It's a hand-grenade!" I threw it away and we both jumped to attention, asked each other what to do, and finally decided for Seeger (the other sentry), to go to the *petite poste* for the corporal, while I watched.

Seeger did so, and he and their corporal, a full-blooded German named Weideman (his first name is unknown) who had spurned his native country to become a French citizen, were on their way back to find Rockwell just as another grenade landed nearby. Unlike the previous one, this wasn't a dud, and after it exploded, a squad of Germans came leaping through the smoke. Corporal Weideman screamed out, *"Aux armes!"*

Rockwell continued in his letter:

> The corporal and I both were in an open position at their
> mercy, so we turned and jumped for cover. I went about ten
> feet when a rifle flashed and I dropped to the ground. When
> I dropped the corporal fell beside me and I knew by his fall
> that he was dead. I crouched and ran, the bullets whizzing by
> me, but I made it into the woods. . . . I lay in the woods and
> watched, not daring to move lest I be seen.
>
> While [the Germans] had us in this position, part kept
> firing while others ran down to the corporal, dragged his
> body, . . . cut off his equipment and coat and took them and
> his gun, broke his body up with butts of their rifles and then
> got away without a shot being fired on our side.
>
> The Germans had no military point to gain by doing
> what they did. It was done as an act of individualism with a
> desire to kill. The top of poor Weideman's head was knocked
> off, after he was killed, by the butt of a rifle.

To ROCKWELL's even greater fury, the Germans, having already mutilated Weideman's body, sought to humiliate him further. "About two hours after all this happened," Rockwell wrote, "there came from the German trenches the most diabolical yell of derision I ever heard. It was mocking Weideman's last words, his 'Aux armes,' and it practically froze the blood to hear it. Up until that minute I had never felt a real desire to kill a German. Since then I have had nothing but murder in my heart, and now no matter what happens I am going through this war as long as I can."

Rockwell wasn't the only one who had heard the Germans ridiculing Weideman's last words. Alan Seeger had been sending dispatches to the *New York Sun* about his wartime experiences, and after giving an account of the German attack that he and Rockwell barely survived, Seeger ended his story by writing:

About midnight, from far up on the hillside, a diabolical cry came down, more like an animal's than a man's, a blood-curdling yell of mockery and exultation. In that cry all the evolution of centuries was levelled. I seemed to hear the yell of the warrior of the stone age over his fallen enemy. It was one of those antidotes to civilization of which this war can offer so many to the searcher after extraordinary sensations.

In Seeger's reports to the *New York Sun*, as well as in his letters and journal entries, one topic dominated almost everything else—the trenches. Life in the trenches was an immediate and overwhelming assault on the senses. Men went days and even weeks without bathing, and everyone reeked. Latrines flooded when it rained, and the men had to wade through a thick, rancid stew of mud, excrement, vomit, and urine. Even in the driest conditions, men were often afflicted with dysentery, and it was not uncommon for them to lose control of their bowels and relieve themselves wherever they happened to be standing.

After a few days, troops would start itching, and it would only get worse. The culprit was lice, or "cooties." The tough little parasites thrived in the environment and spread quickly from man to man, causing extreme discomfort and spreading diseases like malaria, typhoid, and trench fever. There was no relief. Troops were constantly scratching themselves, their hair, their necks, in between their toes, and behind their ears, but to no avail. They would eventually stop complaining about it because there was little to be done.

The trenches were also infested with rats. Men stabbed at them with their bayonets and tried to crush them under their boots, but over time the rats became unafraid of the soldiers and scurried over their bodies while they were trying to sleep or went after their food as they ate. Most disturbing to the men, however, was that the rats were becoming larger, some said bigger than cats, from feasting on the bodies of their fallen comrades in no-man's-land, the battlefield in front of the trenches. (In some instances Allied and German troops would stop fighting and agree on a quick truce to let each side collect its dead, but this was rare. Particularly during the warmer months, the unburied corpses became bloated and attracted hordes of flies. The stench of decaying remains permeated the entire area.)

Each season was wretched in its own way. During late spring and summer, the men broiled in their woolen uniforms, and they were often thirsty because getting freshwater to the front was difficult. In the fall, the nights got colder, and the men shivered under their thin, worn-out blankets. Early winter was the worst, when it rained. Ice-cold water would fill the trenches up to the men's waists, even flooding into the cubbyholes they had dug in the side of the trenches to sleep.

Regardless of the weather, the taller soldiers developed back spasms from constantly walking hunched over. If they stood up straight, they became perfect targets for patient German snipers. Alan Seeger made a point of depicting how trenches were often constructed, describing them to the *New York Sun* as "catacombs more than anything else. Its dimensions are about those of the cages which Louis XI devised for those of his prisoners whom he wished especially to torture, that is, the height is not great enough to permit a man to stand up and the breadth does not allow him to stretch out."

Trenches had to be as narrow as possible, usually no wider than the space for two men to pass each other, to limit the damage from incoming artillery. If a shell dropped right into the pathway, the blast could wipe out an entire platoon.

Both sides were shelled at all hours; mentally, troops had to adjust to the reality that at any time, a well-directed bomb could land on top of or next to them, and that would be it. Seeger wrote to the *New York Sun*:

> [The shelling] is the most distressing thing about the kind of warfare we are up against here. Never a sight of the enemy, and then some fine day when a man is almost tempted to forget that he is on the front—when reading or playing cards or writing home that he is in the best of health—bang! and he is carried off or mangled by a cannon fired five kilometers away. It is not glorious. The gunner has not the satisfaction of knowing that he has hit [his mark], nor the wounded of at least hitting back.

An American soldier in a flooded trench.

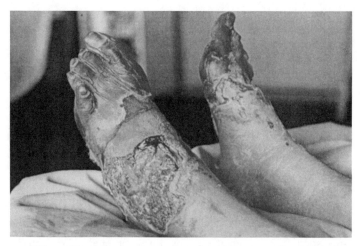

When soldiers' feet were constantly immersed in water and mud, some troops developed trench foot. In winter, their feet sometimes froze solid and had to be amputated.

Troops developed a kind of fatalism in the face of this relentless danger. Seeger captured it memorably in his poem "I Have a Rendezvous with Death," which would become the most famous poem of the war by an American. Seeger wrote in his final lines:

> *At midnight in some flaming town,*
> *When Spring trips north again this year,*
> *And I to my pledged word am true,*
> *I shall not fail that rendezvous.*

"IT MAY INTEREST you to know that this letter is written in the trenches, 30 yards away from the enemy's lines, with the continual ★ ★ ★ crashing of artillery all around and shells ★ whizzing directly over our heads," another American, nicknamed Champy, wrote to a friend back in the States. Champy explained that every time he added a star (★) in his letter, it indicated that a shell had just passed above him. "The cannonading goes in wave motions. For an hour, like from 11 to 12 this morning, it may be very violent, then, calm down, and then begin again."

Champy was the first American to serve in the French Army, as opposed to the Foreign Legion. His situation, however, was unique. His real name was André Chéronnet-Champollion, and he was born in France. His great-grandfather, the linguist Jean-François Champollion, was revered for having helped decipher the Rosetta stone, and his American mother, Mary Corbin, had inherited millions of dollars from her father, the railroad magnate Austin Corbin.

Champy left for the United States as a teenager, after his mother died, to attend the elite New Hampshire preparatory school St. Paul's, and then Harvard. He fell in love with his adopted country and eventually earned his U.S. citizenship. But when Germany invaded France, he felt it was his duty to join the French Army and, as a native Frenchman, he was allowed to do so. Thirty-four years old, married with a young son, and accustomed to a luxurious lifestyle, Champy nevertheless signed up as a private. Early on he told friends that he had no desire to be an officer, because he merely wanted to "shoot at France's enemies" and not be responsible for organizing or leading other troops. He also expected the war to end quickly. But by the spring of 1915, he realized that it would continue for at least another year, and that once the weather warmed up, the fighting would only intensify. "There will be," he predicted to a friend, "a tremendous pile of cracked skulls this summer."

As the realities of a soldier's life sank in, Champy's letters became more and more laced with ambivalence and regret. He launched into tirades about every aspect of his existence: he had to eat from a tin bucket, he washed himself using water from an outdoor faucet even when temperatures had dipped below freezing, and before being moved into the trenches, he was sleeping on a straw-covered concrete floor inside a factory converted into temporary housing. On one particular night, when a group of haggard French soldiers returning from battle had the audacity to take off their boots inside the barracks, Champy was infuriated. "It was quite the most formidable odor I have ever endured for more than a few seconds," he griped. "But in this case I was obliged to stand for it all night!"

Depending on his mood, Champy was either desperate to see the front to break the mind-numbing boredom of training or appalled by the notion that he might end up losing his life because of how inept and callous the French Army was toward its own soldiers. He was especially embittered that he wasn't allowed to perform liaison work between the British and the French as a translator. In light of his education and social status, he couldn't believe his superiors didn't see the value of employing him in that capacity. (As his disgust for the military grew, Champy concluded that any idea that was too sensible would, by definition, be rejected by the French Army.)

He also confessed that he'd been partly motivated to enlist out of the fear that others would have labeled him a coward if he had not. He was stricken to find that the French troops with whom he was serving, as well as his friends back in America, had expressed "puzzled curiosity as to how any one with as good excuses as mine for staying away could voluntarily have plunged himself into such an ocean of trouble."

By March 7, 1915, Champy had survived his baptism of fire in the frontline trenches and told a friend he referred to only as "Old Top" that the experience was so intense and unreal that it was "like walking in a dream," starting with the train ride that took them to the depot nearest to their final destination. Crammed together for twenty-four hours, the "men with me indulged in the rather gruesome amusement of yelling, 'A l'abbatoir—moa—maa,' imitating the cries of cattle going to the slaughter-house."

ONCE THE SOLDIERS were in the trenches, Champy also noted in his letters, death could come from any direction. Artillerymen could aim poorly, the arcing rounds falling short, hitting their own men. Sniper and machine-gun fire came straight on, killing soldiers who had peeked above their trench for only a split second. Both sides were also frequently throwing grenades at one another. The bravest scrambled to pick them up before they exploded and tossed them back, but in many cases, they were too late, and they lost a hand or an arm or were injured even worse in the attempt. Among the most unnerving realizations was that death could also come from below. "Another danger," Champy wrote to Old Top, "[is] that your trench may be mined, and that you are standing over several pounds of high explosives." Whereas the whistling of an incoming shell gave a soldier at least some warning, underground mines could explode at any instant, day or night. Sentinels were instructed to listen for the sounds of digging, but the din of gunfire and artillery barrages often made it difficult to hear the muffled scrapes of a shovel under mounds of earth. The miners themselves were often killed when their tunnels caved in or the notoriously temperamental explosives detonated prematurely.

On March 14, 1915, Champy and his unit were returning from a rest period in a local village and were approaching their secondary position when, about six hundred feet away, a massive rumbling came from beneath the frontline trench. The ground erupted with volcanic fury, sending into the air a jumbled mass of earth and trees and men so gigantic that, according to Champy, it seemed to obscure "half the sky" before taking the shape of a mushroom cloud that dissolved into a shower of rocks, shattered branches, and body parts. Champy and his men were far enough away that they weren't injured by the explosion, but they dove for cover into their shelters, and "almost immediately there came the sound of thousands of heavy rain-drops on a stiff canvas," Champy wrote.

Once the deluge subsided, German soldiers attacked what remained of the frontline trench, but Champy and his men were ordered to stay where they were. With their ears ringing from the blast and some almost knocked unconscious, the French soldiers who had survived managed to push the Germans back. According to Champy, the French lost sixty men in the assault, and two hundred more were injured. Champy was deeply affected by the casualties. "I saw many dead and wounded men carried out of the trenches on stretchers," he wrote on March 20, 1915, to his friend Old Top. "Some of the wounded seemed more mauled than some of the dead. Behind a hedge at the end of the communication trench, which is erected to conceal our movements, I counted 25 dead men lined up for burial. Their faces were usually concealed by part of their uniforms, but their arms assumed every imaginable attitude, gestures of prayers, [and] attitudes of men pleading." Champy ended his letter demoralized by the notion that there was not even "the ghost of a chance" that he would ever be made an interpreter. He was a combat soldier, and now a veteran one at that. "All I can do is to stick it out to the end, and have faith and confidence in the future. . . . Write often, Old Top. You are a brick to communicate so regularly. Your faithful friend, 'Champy.'"

Seventy-two hours later, Champy was piling sacks of dirt to create a barricade at the front of his trench when a German bullet went through his forehead. André Chéronnet-Champollion's name was added to the rolls of French casualties, which by March 1915 totaled approximately half a million.

NOT EVERY AMERICAN contributing to the war effort joined the French Army or the Foreign Legion. Some weren't fit enough or had a physical defect (even stuttering could make one ineligible to fight), were too old, or opposed killing on moral or religious grounds but still wanted to serve. There was another much-needed role for such individuals—ambulance driver. The work might not have seemed as glorious as donning a soldier's uniform and shooting Germans, but it was vitally important, and at times just as dangerous.

Abram Piatt Andrew was forty-one when he left for Europe in December 1914 to drive ambulances for the American Military Hospital in the Parisian suburb of Neuilly. He had graduated from Princeton in 1893 and then lived in Germany and France for fifteen years before the war, studying their central banking systems. He had taught economics at Harvard, served as the director of the U.S. Mint, and was the assistant secretary of the U.S. Treasury. Now, upon his arrival in Paris again, he expected to find the capital either deserted or in a state of panic, and he was stunned by how normal it appeared.

Over the course of the next two days, he began to notice the signs of war. "If you go down to the Louvre," he wrote to his parents on December 31, 1914, "you will find that its doors have been closed to the public for five months. If you pass some of the larger hotels, you will find that many of them bear Red Cross signs and are evidently used to-day as hospitals. . . . [And] above all, if you regard the women you pass on the street you will note that about one in three wears mourning."

Andrew was eager to begin his training, but he first had to acquire a permit, and he discovered one slight hindrance: he could barely drive.

On January 6, 1915, he set out with a "fussy and pompous old" French official who administered licenses. By Andrew's own admission the outing was nearly a disaster. Unused to the refitted Ford Model Ts, he barely missed colliding with a tram car and came close to picking off several pedestrians. By the end of the examination, the shaken administrator compared Andrew's performance to that of an "assassin" but nevertheless granted him a license.

Andrew's first assignment was to pick up injured soldiers at a railroad station in Dunkirk, two hundred miles north of Paris. "So long as I shall live, whether it be weeks or months or years, I can never forget this night," Andrew wrote to his parents at 3:00 a.m. on January 29. Andrew had been at the train station since 9:00 p.m. waiting for the wounded to come in, when German shells came shrieking into the city. "When the bombardment was over, we started out with our ambulances to see what havoc had been wrought," Andrew wrote. "On the third floor of a house near the station, a bomb had pierced the roof and a poor old woman lay torn in pieces. She was evidently getting ready for bed. . . . On two streets I saw whole fronts of houses torn to pieces; and in several places hideous streaks of blood dripped down the sidewalks to the gutter."

Andrew ended his letter by expressing outrage at the German attack. "No military advantage," he fumed, "can be gained by dropping bombs indiscriminately over a sleeping city, and currently the world at large and the judgment of the future will not endorse the wanton slaughter of civilians and women."

Supervising the American Military Hospital in Neuilly was a longtime friend of Andrew's, Robert Bacon, president of the American Hospital Board. Bacon was a former ambassador to France, and was secretary of state under President Theodore Roosevelt. Bacon quickly came to the conclusion that Andrew was better suited to working in a managerial role, assisting Bacon in expanding the ambulance corps. Bacon put Andrew in charge of the newly formed American Ambulance Field Service, later shortened to the American Field Service, or just AFS.

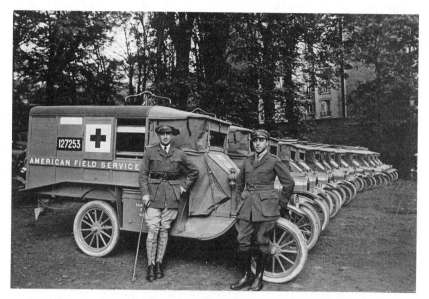

American Field Service founder Abram Piatt Andrew (left) and ambulance driver Stephen Galatti standing next to a fresh line of automobiles.

While Andrew based his operations out of Paris, the wealthy forty-two-year-old American archaeologist Richard Norton was building up his own organization in London, the American Volunteer Motor Ambulance Corps. Norton began with funding from the French millionaire Henry Herman Harjes. Norton preferred large vehicles such as Packards, Cadillacs, Daimlers, Peugeots, and Mercedeses. They were sturdier and could carry more wounded. Andrew's car of choice was Henry Ford's Model T, also known as the Tin Lizzie. It was faster, nimbler, and cheaper. And, indeed, Andrew's AFS became the larger of the two fleets.

WITH A MONOCLE OVER ONE EYE and an affected speaking manner, Richard Norton came off to many as a snob, and in a sense he was. He preferred that his drivers come from distinguished families and had been educated in America's finest universities. An ambulance driver, Norton articulated in a recruiting letter, "has, for quite a period of time, very little to do; the result is that time hangs heavy on the men's heads and there is a great chance for a troublemaker to make trouble, and accordingly . . . a volunteer must be a man of good disposition, possessed of self-control—in short a gentleman."

Working under the auspices of the British Red Cross, Norton's corps had to be neutral, helping both Allied and German troops. Andrew's corps was part of the French Army, and even though his drivers occasionally picked up injured Germans, Andrew was proudly pro-French and had adopted the motto *Tous et tout pour France*—"Everyone and all for France."

There were no German equivalents of Andrew's and Norton's units, so most of the reports coming from Europe about ambulance drivers focused on the Americans risking their lives to aid troops and civilians alike in France. Since their work was purely humanitarian in nature, as well as extremely perilous, their actions—and words—were subtly influencing public opinion.

Leslie Buswell, a professional actor in the United States before the war, sent letters to loved ones chronicling his time in Andrew's AFS, and the letters were passed around to a growing circle of admirers in the States. Leslie did not sugarcoat his feelings or experiences. He openly expressed his initial fear of getting killed: "It is difficult to accustom one's self immediately to the possibility of receiving a bullet in one's head or a shell in one's stomach." He emphasized how survival often depended on pure chance: "My friend the médecin chef had been blown to pieces by a shell which landed exactly where my car had stood the night before." Somewhat ashamed, he admitted that he'd taken a "souvenir" off the body of a German soldier who had died on the way to the hospital: "I picked up his overcoat, and I noticed that the top button was pierced by a bullet, so I cut it off and kept it as a remembrance." While on duty one Friday night, a fresh regiment of troops came through the town where Buswell was working and, appreciative of his service, hailed *"Bon camarade!"* to him as they marched off to the front. When they asked him what he knew of their destination, he found himself unable to speak. He later wrote:

I could not tell them that they were going to a place where
between their trench and the German trench were hundreds of
mangled forms, once their fellow citizens,—arms, legs, heads,
scattered disjointedly everywhere; and where all night and all
day every fiendish implement of murder falls by the hundred—
into their trenches or on to those ghastly forms,—some rotted,
some newly dead, some still warm, some semi-alive, stranded
between foe and friend,—and hurls them yards into the air to
fall again with a splash of dust, as a rock falls into a lake.

Twenty-four hours later, the men returned. "Saturday night they
came back, some of those poor fellows I spoke a cheery word to on
Friday—no arms—no hands—no feet—one leg—no face—no eye,"
Buswell recalled. "One glorious fellow I took [in the ambulance] had
his hand off, and although it was a long trying drive to Dieulouard he
never uttered a word. I touched his forehead when I arrived and whispered, 'Bon courage, mon brave!' He looked at me a moment and answered, 'Would God had taken my life, my friend.'"

Richard Norton's drivers were writing letters equally as graphic,
and they, too, were being shared among friends and family members
and then gaining a wider readership by being reprinted in local newspapers and literary magazines. The purpose wasn't merely to arouse
sympathy for war-torn France, but to dissuade potential volunteers
who romanticized life as an ambulance driver. "It is not surprising that
we receive letters from quantities of persons who are firmly convinced
that their mere desire to help in our work is all that is needed to make
them of use to us," Norton wrote to his treasurer, H. D. Morrison.
"The fact is, however, that what nowadays are considered battles occur
only at long intervals, and most of the time the ambulances are performing an essential, but by no means thrilling, service."

This applied to female drivers, too. "We must be very particular
about the type of women we bring back [to France]," the socialite Ethel
Drake was quoted as saying in the *New York Times*. Drake saw no reason why women couldn't serve as drivers as well, and she began an

aggressive recruitment campaign to enlist women in the ambulance corps. "They must be of the right physique and with a well-balanced mental equipment," she added, and "must be financially able to pay all their expenses. . . . [They] must be in the pink of condition, and must have poise and that essential capacity for individual action at the right moment. We want no neurotic women to whom the romance of the cause is the first appeal."

Amy Owen Bradley, from Boston, was one of the few female drivers whose letters appeared in American newspapers. Bradley would zip around Paris and its surrounding villages in her Model T ambulance to bring the wounded from one hospital to the next, depending on the soldier's condition, and to deliver medical supplies and "comfort bags," which were extremely popular. Packed by generous Americans and shipped to France, the bags contained whatever tiny gifts the sender hoped might bring a few moments of happiness to the bedridden patients: harmonicas, finger puzzles that could be played with on one hand, decks of cards, packets of cocoa, and various other treats. The doctors and nurses told Bradley that these bags greatly improved the men's mental health, which accelerated their physical recovery.

Some items caused the occasional problem due to cultural differences. Many of the French soldiers had never seen or heard of Wrigley gum, a popular item, and they ate it like candy, swallowing it, which caused rampant indigestion throughout the hospital wards. Efforts to educate them on chewing the gum and then spitting it out were not entirely successful, so Bradley and other volunteers picked through the bags and removed all the gum.

Bradley's letters focused on these lighter, poignant moments more than the blood-and-guts descriptions that others related. But she did reflect deeply on a theme that many of the other drivers had touched on as well: the surreal juxtaposition of splendor and horror in wartime. The most striking moment for Bradley came while driving through the French countryside and watching the transformation of the land, and how it silently told the story of the war. "I have seldom seen anything as beautiful as the spring in France," Bradley began her short story about this one particular trip.

> We went for miles on straight roads between rows of feathery trees, with fields of brilliant green on either side. . . . The sky was the most heavenly blue, and the fields and woods were filled with hyacinths and violets and primroses and lilies of the valley and with the songs of birds. Sometimes, instead of going through green trees we went through valleys of pink apple blossoms that almost overpowered with their sweet smell of spring. Everything seemed jubilantly full of life.
>
> Then, all of a sudden, perhaps an hour from Paris, we came on a grave by the roadside, a rustic cross, with a little red white and blue cockade on it, and "Patrie" ["Home"] on the little fence that surrounded it. After that, we came upon another and another, then on a little group, and finally to mounds with large crosses on them, all the same. Some had the number of the regiment on them and a very few had the names of the soldiers. And all the time we were driving along the perfect quiet roads under the blue shadows of the trees, with great splotches of sunlight filtering through them.

Mary Dexter, another female ambulance driver, started out working at the Medico-Psychological Clinic in London studying and helping patients with a newly diagnosed affliction called "shell shock," a term coined during the war. Men whose bodies were uninjured nevertheless manifested physical ailments such as tremors, tinnitus, blistering headaches, irregular heartbeats, and soaring blood pressure, and some also suffered from depression, severe insomnia, amnesia, and suicidal thoughts. One searing image could trigger an acute emotional reaction that would disturb a soldier for days, weeks, or months. "One man [in our clinic] saw the back of another man's head blown off, right up into the air, leaving him standing there for a second with only a face," Dexter wrote to her mother. "No wonder that sometimes they have nightmares, and that some of them can't sleep."

Once Dexter was assigned to her ambulance duties, she would have her own firsthand experiences to remember.

> I was dreadfully upset a day or two ago, over two injured civilians. They arrived on a train, and were carried out and put in one of our cars—the man's chest blown to pieces—dying— and the woman legless, hit by an obus [shell], also dying, from shock and lack of care. Twenty minutes later I saw the car return and . . . to my horror I found that they had been refused at the hospital, because of being civilians. . . . They were [eventually] taken in, but it was just about too late—their faces haunted me all that day.

Dexter herself had to have her spine treated as a result of the constant strain she'd been putting on her back lifting patients, cranking up her car to get it started, replacing popped wheels, and driving for hours on clapboard seating over rocky, uneven roads. Doctors found one of her vertebrae sticking up almost an inch under her skin. She would return to the psychiatric clinic in London to continue her work with troops suffering from shell shock.

Of all the individuals who supported the ambulance corps, no one did more to ensure its success than the American philanthropist Mrs. W. K. Anne Harriman Vanderbilt. In 1910, Vanderbilt had contributed the funds that helped build the American Military Hospital in Neuilly, and when the war came four years later, she bought dozens of Ford Model Ts for the ambulance units and encouraged her wealthy friends to support the corps in whatever manner they could. (Henry Ford was of no help whatsoever; personally opposed to the war, he refused to donate any of his cars, and he charged the full price for each vehicle.)

"The person to whom we are most indebted is Mrs. W. K.

Vanderbilt," Andrew wrote in a letter to his parents after meeting her in France. "Mrs. Vanderbilt is a wonderful personality," he gushed. "She has a man's intelligence and force and a woman's grace and charm, very frank, utterly genuine, distinguished in appearance, [and] interested in everything."

Andrew was in good spirits; he had recently convinced two affluent Parisians to loan out their grand estate for him to use as the AFS's new base of operations. Ideally situated in the heart of Paris and close to local hospitals, it also had enough space to provide sleeping quarters for the drivers and officers. Andrew was enchanted by the mansion's history and the exalted list of previous visitors, including Ben Franklin, Honoré de Balzac, and Jean-Jacques Rousseau. The house was situated on a beautifully landscaped five-acre estate with lush gardens and fountains.

Mrs. Vanderbilt had helped Andrew secure the property, and in appreciation, he arranged for her something that she had particularly coveted: a tour of the front lines.

This was no small request. Civilian women weren't allowed at the front, certainly not for sightseeing. But Vanderbilt was insistent, and Andrew eventually plotted out a route that would take her close to the German lines but not *too* close. He was torn between wanting to please his main benefactor and not getting one of the world's most famous philanthropists killed. Andrew disguised Vanderbilt in white to make her look like a war nurse, and they set out for the village of Pont-à-Mousson. Andrew recounted in his letter to his parents that her exact words were: "It will be my luck never to hear a gun. But I shall never admit when I get back that I haven't." Later that night, Andrew recalled:

> I was suddenly awakened by a series of heavy crashes like claps of thunder, and then I heard the familiar whistle of shells overhead and more crashes, and more crashes, and gradually it dawned upon my drowsy consciousness that the city was being bombarded. Whir-r-r bang! Whir-r-r bang! Bang! Crash!

> Bang! Whir-r-r, bang! They were coming in fast and falling very near. . . . The boys downstairs were calling, "Doc, Doc, come down to the cellar." I called, "Mrs. Vanderbilt," got a quick reply, "Yes, yes." "Let's get down in the cellar." We reached a dimly lighted shelter where already twenty or thirty half dressed Americans and Frenchmen were gathered. . . . Some were in pajamas, some had their shirts outside their trouser—no one was really dressed.

The next day they went up to Campigny, where they saw the destroyed summer home of the French president Raymond Poincaré. "The Germans," Andrew wrote his parents, "have shelled it day after day for no particular reason except childish 'Schadenfreude.' The house is on the slope of a sunny hill, and we picked an armful of roses from the President's deserted garden. In the neighboring village not a single soul remains—everything silent, serene and like a dream."

Vanderbilt jotted down her own impressions of the journey, noting that the "quaint old town" of Pont-à-Mousson had been bombed two hundred times since the beginning of the war. "On the right of the road to the *poste de secours* [aid station]," Vanderbilt wrote, "we passed by the famous *Bois le Pretre*, once a wood, now a wilderness. Here is the grave of André Champollion, an American, killed in the early months of the war." Vanderbilt wanted to get out of the car and put flowers on Champy's grave, but she was told that this was too dangerous. They were in range of not only artillery but also sharp-eyed German snipers and machine gunners.

Moments later, "a battery of '75s, concealed in a wood at the edge of the road, opened fire with ear-splitting detonations," Vanderbilt continued, "and, almost simultaneously, a German shell whistled over our heads and, landing in a near-by field, splashed dirt and smoke over us." Vanderbilt was done. "It was enough for me," she wrote. "I have never felt any further desire to be under fire."

Her final stop was to see the Cathedral of Reims, which the Germans had also bombed but not entirely destroyed. Vanderbilt believed

Mrs. Anne Harriman Vanderbilt, disguised as a war nurse, standing in front of the Reims Cathedral and under a statue of Joan of Arc.

it should be left almost exactly as it was, as an eternal testament to France and her resilience. "It still stands in all the grandeur of its magnificent outlines," she wrote. "Its burned roof, its pierced walls, its broken statues envelope it with a new nobility, because these scars tell and will tell forever for the great tragedy through which France is passing. . . . History has always been written on its walls, and the courage and faith in the heart of France to-day are worthy of this recording."

Vanderbilt had been a Francophile long before the war had begun, but the conflict became all the more personal to her when her nephew, Alfred Gwynne Vanderbilt, was killed by the Germans. Alfred, however, died not on the blood-soaked fields of France but in the cold waters of the Atlantic.

NICKNAMED THE LUCY, the RMS *Lusitania* was the largest and most opulent ship in the world. To the delight of the ship's passengers, a lingering mist began to dissipate in the early afternoon of May 7, 1915, revealing Ireland's sparkling green coast less than twenty miles away. Children skipped rope on the main deck. Couples held each other's hands as they leaned up against the ship's railings and soaked in the salt air and beautiful scenery around them. Others, having enjoyed an elegant lunch, settled comfortably into sundeck chairs and read or took a nap.

The ship's crew greeted the disappearing fog with ambivalence, however. Across the clear, sunlit water, they could better watch for German U-boats, but this went both ways; their ship was now a hard target to miss. The *Lusitania* was nearly eight hundred feet long and had four towering funnels, three of which were belching out huge clouds of black smoke.

From the moment the ship had left New York City en route to Liverpool, England, on May 1, passengers and crew had been fully warned that they were putting their lives in danger. Printed directly below the *Lusitania*'s schedule in local newspapers, especially in New York, the German embassy had run the following advertisement:

NOTICE!

TRAVELLERS intending to embark on the Atlantic voyage are reminded that a state of war exists between Germany and her allies and Great Britain and her allies; that the zone of war includes the waters adjacent to the British Isles; that, in accordance with formal notice given by the Imperial German Government, vessels flying the flag of Great Britain, or of any of her allies, are liable to destruction in those waters and that travellers sailing in the war zone on ships of Great Britain or her allies do so at their own risk.

IMPERIAL GERMAN EMBASSY
WASHINGTON, D. C., APRIL 22, 1915.

Passengers took some comfort in knowing that, despite its immense size, the *Lusitania* could outrun any U-boat, and in dangerous waters, the ship would move in a zigzag pattern that made it harder for the vessel to be hit.

At about ten minutes after 2:00 p.m., Seaman Leslie Morton was on the *Lusitania*'s starboard side, scanning the waters for periscopes and any other signs of submarines, when suddenly he noticed a huge burst of air bubbles less than half a mile away and realized that a torpedo had just been launched.

So clear was the water that Morton, and numerous passengers, saw the twenty-foot-long torpedo shooting forward at more than forty miles per hour about ten feet below the surface. As the torpedo swam forward, a tiny propeller at the tip caused the nose to unscrew, exposing a trigger, which, upon impact, would detonate more than 350 pounds of explosives. Morton cried out to his crewmates that a torpedo was coming, but it was too late to change course. Moments before impact, the torpedo seemed to disappear, and those who had seen it approaching hoped, during those few seconds, that it had passed underneath the ship.

The torpedo, in fact, could hardly have struck at a more sensitive point—directly under the bridge, where there was both a boiler room and a coal bin. The explosion tore a forty-by-fifteen-foot hole in the side of the ship. Other boiler rooms, filling with seawater, began to explode as well, causing some passengers to believe that the ship was being hit by multiple torpedoes.

Due to the warm spring weather, many passengers had opened their portholes to let in the fresh air, and as the ship dipped below the waterline, hundreds of tons of water flooded in, causing the *Lusitania* to descend even faster.

The electricity cut out, and those walking through indoor corridors found themselves in total darkness, unable to find an exit or a way back to their rooms, where their life preservers were stored.

Only a third of the ship's twenty-two lifeboats successfully made it into the water. Because the *Lusitania* was tilting to the side and its aft was so high in the air, the boats on the starboard side were hanging eight feet away from the ship. Some of the older children were able to take a running start and leap into the boats, but for most of the passengers this simply wasn't possible. And those who tried and missed fell more than sixty feet into the water, high enough to kill. Several lifeboats that were close enough to step into became overwhelmed with passengers; one flipped over, sending everyone into the ocean. Another plunged when the pulleys gave out and crashed directly onto the passengers below them. A crew member grabbed the rope and tried to slow it down but burned his palm raw in the attempt. And boats on the port side were so firmly pressed against the ship that they couldn't be budged.

The ship went down in eighteen minutes (by comparison, the *Titanic* sank in two hours and forty minutes), and with so many lifeboats destroyed or rendered useless, most of the *Lusitania*'s passengers ended up in the sea. Wealthier passengers were among the first to drown, weighed down by heavy mink coats, corsets, evening jackets, and extravagant jewels. Entire families perished, including the Cromptons, eight in all. Mr. and Mrs. Crompton were originally from England, but they had lived in Philadelphia for several years, and three of their youngest children were American.

The *Lusitania* had been able to send out an SOS signal, and initially the British Navy dispatched the cruiser HMS *Juno* to rescue the survivors. But minutes later it was called back. A decision was made that the U-boat was still prowling the waters and might torpedo the *Juno*, too.

"The ship was sinking with unbelievable rapidity," an eyewitness named Walther Schwieger recalled. "There was a terrific panic on her deck. Overcrowded lifeboats, fairly torn from their positions, dropped into the water. Desperate people ran helplessly up and down the decks. Men and women jumped into the water and tried to swim to empty, overturned lifeboats. It was the most terrible sight I have ever seen." Schwieger was the captain of the German U-boat that had fired on the *Lusitania*; he had watched the ship go down and its passengers drown through the periscope of his submarine.

Of the 1,962 individuals on board, including three German

stowaways held in the ship's brig who suffocated to death, 1,198 died in all. Among the 123 American fatalities was Alfred Vanderbilt. The Vanderbilts offered a $5,000 reward for Alfred's body, but it was never recovered. Adding to the family's grief was the fact that they had been through this before three years earlier; when the *Titanic* sank on April 15, 1912, Alfred Vanderbilt's name was printed in the next day's paper as "deceased." In fact, although Vanderbilt had indeed bought a ticket to sail on the *Titanic*, he changed his plans at the last minute and returned home to America on another ship, very much alive.

Germany was technically in the right when they argued that the *Lusitania* was carrying war-related matériel and that passengers had been warned that the ship was, in their eyes, a legitimate target. But throughout the world Germany was condemned for the wanton murder of women and children. From the one place Americans expected righteous anger, however, there was silence. On May 7, 8, and 9, President Woodrow Wilson made no public statements about the *Lusitania*. On the Saturday after the sinking, he went golfing.

On May 10, while officiating at a naturalization ceremony in Philadelphia, Wilson used the opportunity to articulate what America should stand for—and what it should not:

> You have taken an oath of allegiance to a great ideal, to a great body of principles, to a great hope of the human race. You have said, "We are going to America," not only to earn a living, not only to seek the things which it was more difficult to obtain where you were born, but to help forward the great enterprises of the human spirit—to let man know that everywhere in the world there are men who will cross strange oceans and go where a speech is spoken which is alien to them, knowing that, whatever the speech, there is but one longing and utterance of the human heart, and that is for liberty and justice.

Wilson didn't mention any countries specifically, but he went on to emphasize that those who had arrived from nations currently at war against one another must cut those ties and pledge their complete loyalty to America. "You cannot become thorough Americans if you think of yourselves in groups," Wilson stated. "America does not consist of groups. A man who thinks of himself as belonging to a particular national group in America, has not yet become an American, and the man who goes among you to trade upon your nationality is no worthy son to live under the Stars and Stripes."

Wilson then made comments that thoroughly disheartened those who expected a fervent condemnation of the German attack on the *Lusitania*: "The example of America must be the example not merely of peace because it will not fight, but of peace because peace is the healing and elevating influence of the world and strife is not. There is such a thing as a man being too proud to fight. There is such a thing as a nation being so right that it does not need to convince others by force that it is right."

Those last two lines in particular were, to Wilson's detractors, abject cowardice sugarcoated in the syrup of idealism. On the home front, few were more scathing than Theodore Roosevelt. In a pamphlet he quickly had published titled "Murder on the High Seas," Roosevelt began by reminding his readers that the *Lusitania* was not the first ship to be attacked in such a manner. "A number of American ships had already been torpedoed in similar fashion. In one case the lives lost included those not only of the American captain, but of his wife and little daughter. . . . Centuries have passed since any war vessel of a civilized power has shown such ruthless brutality toward non-combatants." Roosevelt hammered the point. "The day after the tragedy," he wrote, "the newspapers reported in one column that in Queenstown there lay by the score the bodies of women and children, some of the dead women still clasping the bodies of the little children they held in their arms when death overwhelmed them."

Without saying his name, Roosevelt excoriated President Wilson for being, essentially, a fainthearted sheep:

In the teeth of these things, we earn as a nation measureless
scorn and contempt if we follow the lead of those who exalt
peace above righteousness, if we heed the voices of those feeble
folk who bleat to high heaven that there is peace when there is
no peace. . . .

Unless we act with immediate decision and vigor we shall
have failed in the duty demanded by humanity at large, and
demanded even more clearly by the self-respect of the American Republic.

Abram Piatt Andrew, who watched every day as hundreds of dead
and wounded men were brought from the front on his ambulances, felt
compelled to add to the chorus of voices criticizing the government's
neutrality. Andrew unleashed a verbal barrage that was published in his
hometown paper, the *Boston Herald*:

We Americans of to-day are onlookers upon one of the greatest
struggles in the world's history. We have sat silently by while
clause after clause of treaties, of which we, too, were signato-
ries, were treated as scrap-paper. We have sat silently by while
an utterly unoffending nation was devastated, its towns and cities and peaceful farms pillaged and burned, its universities and
libraries and churches destroyed. We have sat silently by while
7,000,000 people of this innocent nation were driven from their
homes. We have sat silently by while officers of this medieval
monarchy allowed their cohorts, drunk with stolen wine, to
rape and murder and commit crimes of cannibals and beasts.

Andrew repeated the "We have sat silently by . . ." refrain with
growing fury, like a preacher hitting his stride, and then culminated in
a fiery challenge to America's essence, even questioning the manhood
of its leadership (the words in quotation marks are from President Wilson's speeches):

> We have behaved as if our souls were dead and the ideals of the founders of our government were extinct. We have behaved like a soft-bodied man, who, seeing a ruffian beating and kicking and spitting in the face of a woman on the street looks on for hours with indifference, says that it is not his business, shows no resentment until a misdirected blow accidentally strikes him in a tender spot, and then explains his previous inaction on the ground that he had not hitherto observed that the ruffian was not "humane," "enlightened," and "engaged on the side of justice."

Coming from a man who had run the U.S. Mint and the Treasury Department, his concluding statement was especially potent: "Is America no longer a country of ideals beyond success in business and the accumulation of material wealth and comfort? Is America no longer capable of making sacrifice except to mammon? Is the generous spirit which animated the founders of our government, and which a century and more ago inspired the admiration of the world, extinct? . . . As a nation, do we represent nothing which makes us worthy of an enduring future? Are we headed on the road to Carthage and Rome? A. Piatt Andrew. March 19, 1915."

Two days later, Andrew drove up to Dunkirk, the first town in which he had served as a driver, to check in on the AFS ambulance unit stationed there. Since the time of his last visit, the German shells were getting larger, their range even longer. "Think of it," Andrew wrote to his parents, "a projectile six feet high, and weighing at least a ton and a half, thrown twenty-two miles!" Their accuracy was poor, but the blast radius was so wide that precision hardly mattered. "One shell struck in the cemetery as an internment was taking place," Andrew wrote, "and the coffin and nine or ten mourners, mostly women and children, were transformed into debris in the twinkling of an eye." Another shell dropped on the street in front of the convent where Andrew had slept during a previous stay. Along with destroying the building, "it killed a group of children at play; nobody knew exactly how many, the fragments were so scattered."

Andrew crossed the border into Belgium, found a farmhouse being used as a temporary dressing station, and offered to take the two wounded men inside to a better-equipped tent hospital in the Belgian town of Woesten. These drives were hellish for the patients because of the rocky, uneven roads, but they were also exhausting for the men behind the steering wheel. They traveled in the dark and without lights, so as not to attract the attention of German artillery, and the drivers had to be as alert as possible for any obstacles, and they often had to stop to fix a busted tire or push the car out of a muddy rut. The experience was emotionally taxing as well. "We took our men into the tent, and as one of them had been shot in the breast he was immediately put on the table," Andrew wrote to his parents. "It is the same story that has happened hundreds of thousands of times in the last ten months and I won't harrow you with the details. The poor boy had already lost much blood, and before morning he had doubtless given his life for his country, dying without a friend or acquaintance near, lying on the ground in a dimly lighted tent in Belgium."

ALTHOUGH IT MAY have seemed fitting retaliation for the sinking of the *Lusitania*, the French attack along the German lines in northeastern France on May 7, 1915, had been planned weeks beforehand. Having fought defensively since August 1914, France was now launching its first major offensive of the war.

"A big battle is going to commence soon," Kiffin Rockwell wrote to his brother, Paul, on May 5, "and we have already received instructions as to what our position will be in it and what we have got to do. It is no rumor this time." Rockwell could not reveal where he was headed, but the destination was the Artois Ridge, where four divisions of German troops were protecting a critical railroad junction.

After forty-eight hours of constant bombing, employing more than 1,000 artillery guns to launch 250,000 shells on the Germans, the French followed up on May 9 with an infantry attack nearly twenty miles wide. Rockwell was hit in the thigh within minutes of going over the top, and he dragged himself into a shell hole to bandage his wound. Inside the small crater he found a friend from another regiment who had been shot through both hips and hit with shrapnel in the stomach. Rockwell tried to staunch the bleeding, but the wounds were too severe and his friend died in Rockwell's arms. Shells continued to drop everywhere, and whenever Rockwell heard one screeching above, he would shut his eyes, say to himself, "Well, it is over," and wait for the impact. Three shells landed just feet away but did nothing more than cover him with a shower of dirt. Realizing he couldn't stay there indefinitely, Rockwell crawled out of the hole and, using his elbows to inch forward, slowly snaked his way back to the French lines.

Rockwell was hiding behind a haystack when he was found by a Red Cross worker, who told him that it was doubtful that any ambulances would come for at least a day. Rockwell picked up a sturdy stick and hobbled several miles to a railroad depot, and from there he went by train to a hospital. So many patients were crammed in the wards and hallways that Rockwell had to wait another four days before his leg wound, which by then was black and festering, could be treated.

On May 13, Kiffin Rockwell wrote from his hospital bed to his brother Paul with almost breathless excitement about the battle:

> At ten o'clock [a.m.], I saw the finest sight I have ever seen. It
> was men from the Premier Étranger crawling out of our
> trenches, with their bayonets glittering against the sun, and
> advancing on the Boches. There was not a sign of hesitation.
> They were falling fast, but as fast as men fell, it seemed as if
> new men sprang up out of the ground to take their places.
> One second it looked as if an entire section had fallen by one
> sweep of a machine-gun. . . .
>
> To think of fear or the horror of the thing was impossible.
> All I could think of was what a wonderful advance it was,
> and how everyone was going against that stream of lead as if
> he loved it.

With not much else to do in the hospital, Rockwell corresponded frequently with family members and friends. He remained upbeat in the letters to his mother, assuring her that he was fine, but that even if he was killed, she shouldn't worry. "When you write of the chances of my being killed I can see that you have a great horror of it. But I don't see anything so terrible in death," he wrote. "If I should be killed I think you ought to be proud in knowing that your son tried to be a man and was not afraid to die, and that he gave his life for a greater cause than most people do—the cause of all humanity."

Rockwell did concede to his mother that he understood her perspective. "Of course, anyone with any feeling at all hates to see a loved one or a friend die. I didn't watch a friend of mine continue on after I was wounded because I did not wish to see him if he fell."

That friend was Paul "Skipper" Pavelka, another American. Rockwell and Pavelka had forged a strong bond since their days of training together in the Foreign Legion. Pavelka was stabbed through the leg by a German bayonet after Rockwell had been shot at Artois, but he was able to find out Rockwell's whereabouts and let him know that he was alive and okay.

Rockwell promptly mailed Pavelka some francs "for tobacco" and instructed Paul to send him money as well. "He is a good lad and brave," Rockwell wrote to his brother. "He has no way of getting money from home and no friends in France. Now I want you to find someone in Paris who appreciates that a chap like this is fighting for France, and who will take him when he gets his convalescence, so that he can enjoy it before returning to the front."

Pavelka was proof that not all American volunteers came from privileged backgrounds. Born to Hungarian immigrant parents in New York City, Pavelka set out to explore the world in 1906 when he was only sixteen. He bounced around New England first, doing odd work on farms in New Hampshire and Vermont. He crossed into Canada to work as a lumberjack, then went back to New York to become a handyman at a mental hospital. He gave that up and rode boxcars across the

Midwest until he arrived in Montana, where he herded cattle and sheared sheep. Then he took a train up to Washington State, eventually finding a cozy shack by the Washington River, where he fished and hunted throughout the summer of 1909. When fall came, Pavelka followed the sun south and ended up as a migrant laborer in California. In 1912, after having steamed across the Pacific to Japan and Australia, Pavelka joined the U.S. Navy. He was honorably discharged in 1914, and when war came to Europe, he joined a Belgian unit before switching over to the Foreign Legion.

Three months after getting bayoneted at Artois, Pavelka was sent back into action as a message runner at the battle for Champagne in September 1915. Another sweeping offensive against entrenched German forces, Champagne cost the French twice as many casualties as the Germans—145,000 to 72,500. Pavelka had badly mangled his hands setting up barbed wire and was granted a leave to Paris to recuperate. Kiffin Rockwell was no longer there, having been assigned to a new unit, but Pavelka tracked down Paul and stayed with him for a week. Pavelka hadn't had the chance to bathe or clean his uniform for two months, and while washing his clothes, he and Paul picked out the bullet slugs and pieces of shrapnel that were embedded in the jacket's heavy lining. When piled all together, the metal weighed nearly a pound.

WHATEVER MILITARY SUCCESS Germany was having, its ruthless tactics were causing it to lose the war of public opinion. In April 1915, less than three weeks before the sinking of the *Lusitania*, reports came that the Germans were using a weapon outlawed by the Hague Convention of 1907. At approximately 5:30 p.m. on April 22, French North African colonial soldiers at the Ypres Salient watched as a strangely colored fog started to drift toward them. Initially they presumed the smoke was meant to conceal a German infantry raid, and the troops braced themselves for an attack. But as they strained to look through the mist, there were no signs of approaching soldiers. Within minutes the gray-green clouds were upon them, and they clutched their throats in agony as chlorine gas entered their lungs. Thousands of panicked troops fled to the rear. Those who stayed put and dropped back into the trenches, thinking the gas would drift above them, fared the worst; chlorine was heavier than air and floated down over their bodies, covering them from head to foot. The Germans had unleashed almost 170 tons of the poisonous gas from more than 5,700 containers across four miles, and even they were so surprised by how effective the gas was that they failed to take advantage of the massive break in the line. On April 24, the Germans struck again, this time targeting Canadian and English troops. "I saw one man near me turn a sickly greenish-yellow," said a Scottish officer with the British Army named Scott Parker. "His eyes began to bulge from his head; froth filled his mouth and hung from his lips. He began tearing at his throat. The air wouldn't go into his lungs. He fell and rolled over and over, gasping and crying out while with his nails he tore open his throat, even wrenched out his windpipe. Then his chest heaved a time or two, and he lay still. Death had brought its blessed relief."

One of Germany's most controversial actions involved only a single person but reinforced the growing perception that the country was a nation of barbarians. On August 3, 1915, German agents arrested a forty-nine-year-old British nurse named Edith Cavell in occupied Belgium. Cavell had been treating the wounded, including German troops, but she was also helping British and French soldiers evade capture and return to England and France. The Germans considered this an act of treason, punishable by death. Hugh Gibson, a member of the U.S. Department of State's legation in Brussels, tried to convince Germany's civil governor of Belgium, Baron von der Lancken, to commute her sentence. But von der Lancken could not be persuaded.

"We reminded him of the burning of Louvain and the sinking of the *Lusitania*, and told him that this murder would rank with those two affairs and would stir all civilised countries with horror and disgust," Gibson recalled. Gibson also noted that another German officer, Count

Franz von Harrach, "broke in at this point with the rather irrelevant remark that he would rather see Miss Cavell shot than have harm come to the humblest German soldier, and his only regret was that they had not 'three or four old English women to shoot.'" (Austrian by birth, Harrach had been Archduke Franz Ferdinand's personal bodyguard and was in the car when Ferdinand was assassinated.) On October 12, 1915, a firing squad executed Cavell, sparking worldwide condemnation.

Soon, however, the public's attention would shift elsewhere, to the French town of Verdun.

Propaganda postcard widely disseminated among the Allies.

PLANNED BY CHIEF of the German General Staff Erich von Falkenhayn and code-named *Unternehmen Gericht* ("Operation Judgment"), the assault on Verdun was not only about gaining new ground or advancing toward a strategic position. The intent was also to attack a sacred French region in order to draw in as many defenders as possible and bleed their army dry. It was, primarily, a battle of attrition, killing for killing's sake.

Von Falkenhayn knew the land had special meaning to France. The Germans had been victorious there in 1792 and in 1870, and the French could not lose it again. By mid-February 1916, von Falkenhayn had amassed close to 1.25 million troops—the largest number of soldiers ever organized for an offensive—around the region and had also brought in, under camouflage, approximately 1,600 pieces of artillery, ranging from the light but devastatingly accurate 77mms to the Big Berthas, whose shells weighed 1,800 pounds each.

On February 21, the Germans began a bombardment that lasted for nine hours, followed by waves of infantry attacks. "I thought I had seen fighting in other battles, but no one has ever seen anything like Verdun," Eugene Bullard recorded in his diary. Bullard was the son of a slave and had run away from his native Georgia at a young age to make his way to France, where he had heard blacks were treated the same as whites. Bullard stowed away on a ship headed for Europe—where exactly he didn't know—and, starting out in Scotland and then England, made a name for himself as a professional boxer before the war. After Germany invaded France, he joined the Foreign Legion and was a veteran of both the Artois and Champagne campaigns before his regiment was rushed to Verdun in late February.

Bullard wrote of the battle:

> To describe the slaughter at Verdun would be absolutely impossible. We were ordered to go forward and die rather than to retreat, and dying is what thousands upon thousands did.
>
> On the morning of February 22nd, the German artillery bombardment was resumed with the same violence [as the morning before]. The French forces were obliged to withdraw from the position we were holding. The whole front seemed to be moving like a saw backwards and forwards. . . .
>
> During the nights that followed, droves of German soldiers surrendered or wandered into the French lines. Were they lost? Were they disgusted or crazy from the slaughter? No one can say. The earth was plowed under. Men and beasts were hanging from the branches of trees where they had been blown to pieces.

Eugene Bullard.

On March 2, Bullard and several other members of his unit were inside an abandoned farmhouse when it was hit by artillery fire. Bullard sought cover under an old bed, but a shell fragment ripped through the mattress and smashed into his mouth, shattering his front teeth. When one of Bullard's commanding officers ordered him to the rear, Bullard replied, with blood dripping down his chin, that he wanted to stay with his comrades. "The real truth was that I didn't know where to go," he wrote in his diary. "There was no such place as a safe place at Verdun." He was surrounded, he recalled, by what seemed to be "millions of shell holes, dead men, dead horses, and dead mules."

Three days later Bullard sustained another shrapnel wound, this time in the leg. Fortunately, he was able to spot an ambulance and was taken to an evacuation point in the town of Bar-le-Duc. From there he traveled by train, over the course of a week, to a hospital in southern France where his injuries were treated. While reflecting on the carnage he had witnessed at Verdun, Bullard noted in his diary an observation made by other survivors of the battle. What surprised them the most wasn't how many men were killed in the savage, relentless fighting, but that anyone, on either side, came out of it alive at all.

A small mountain of skeletons of French and German troops killed at Verdun. The anonymous remains were later placed in a massive ossuary.

3.

Hunting Pancho

VERDUN WAS COVERED EXTENSIVELY in American newspapers, and on March 6, 1916, the *El Paso Morning Times*, which General John Pershing read on a regular basis, ran two front-page accounts of the battle. The longer one, sent in by the Associated Press, declared: GERMANS MOWN DOWN BY DEADLY FRENCH FIRE—GRUESOME PRICE PAID FOR SIX MILES OF GROUND. The article estimated that the Germans had brought up 250,000 reinforcements but that they were being wiped out at an astonishing rate by machine-gun fire. "It must be demoralizing to the Germans," the AP reporter noted, "to see some 40,000 to 50,000 corpses of their comrades lying before the French lines." There was no tally of French casualties (and no reference whatsoever to the presence of American soldiers like Eugene Bullard), but the last two paragraphs did describe another weapon relatively new to warfare that was killing the French in a horrific manner.

"The Germans, in their assaults, are using several sorts of burning liquid projectors. One of these is in the form of a small tank, which is carried on the back, filled with a composition liquid which seems to be mostly kerosene." The reporter was referring to a *Flammenwerfer* (flamethrower). "Some French soldiers have been burned to a crisp by the flaming liquid." It was a particularly ghastly way to die because death wasn't instantaneous. The streams of burning fuel often covered the entire body, and the victims flailed about madly for up to a minute as they were roasted alive. So despised were German troops who used flamethrowers that if they tried to surrender, Allied soldiers executed them on the spot instead of taking them prisoner.

But of greater interest to General Pershing was another front-page story in the El Paso newspaper: VILLA TROOPERS ARE REPORTED MARCH-ING ON EL TIGRE. Whatever goodwill had existed between Pancho Villa and Pershing when they were photographed together with General Ál-varo Obregón in late August 1914 had evaporated by January 1916. Villa was furious at President Woodrow Wilson for supporting his po-litical rival, Venustiano Carranza, to be president of Mexico. Wilson had continued to send Carranza military arms and supplies from the United States, while halting similar shipments to Villa.

Feeling betrayed by Wilson, Villa and his band of Villistas began harassing and killing U.S. citizens in Mexico. El Tigre was a mining town seventy-five miles southwest of the border, where about two dozen Americans lived. They had every reason to be afraid. Less than three months earlier, on January 10, approximately fifteen Villistas stopped a train outside Santa Isabel, Mexico, and commanded the American passengers to get out. Most of them were workers on their way to the silver mines of Cucihuriacic, an area that President Carranza had assured the United States was safe. Pablo Lopez, one of Villa's most trusted and vicious officers, told the eighteen Americans to strip to their underwear and group together. (Villa himself wasn't there.) Lopez then selected two of his men to shoot every one of them. Within sec-onds the firing began. "The Americans lay on the ground, gasping and writhing in the sand and cinders," an eyewitness named José Maria Sanchez recalled. "The suffering of the Americans seemed to drive the bandits into a frenzy. 'Viva Villa!' they cried, and 'Death to the grin-gos!' Colonel Lopez ordered the 'mercy shot' to be given to those who were still alive, and the soldiers placed the ends of their rifles at their victims' heads and fired, putting the wounded out of their misery." The Villistas stole everything of value off the victims and left their bodies to rot on the side of the tracks.

Villa denied having anything to do with the killings, and President Carranza told President Wilson that because the incident had taken place inside Mexico, his federal troops would bring the perpetrators to justice. Wilson, not wanting to spark a larger conflict, initially did nothing.

For Pershing, the weeks and months between August 26, 1915, when his wife and daughters were killed, and March 9, 1916, were essentially a blur. "I have been trying to write you a word for some time but find it quite impossible to do so," he wrote in an October 1915 letter from Fort Bliss, apologizing to a friend named Anne Boswell.

> I shall never be relieved of the poignancy of grief at the terrible loss of Darling Frankie and the babies. It is too overwhelming! I really do not understand *how* I have lived through it all thus far. I cannot think they are gone. It is too cruel to believe. Frankie was so much to those whom she loved and you were her best friend. . . .
>
> I am trying to work and keep from thinking, but oh! the desolation of Life! The emptiness of it all, after such fullness as I have had. There can be no consolation.
>
> *Affectionately yours,*
> *John J. Pershing*

In December 1915, three months after the fire, Pershing confessed to another friend that he still could not bring himself to tell his son the truth. "Warren doesn't know his loss, but includes Mama and Helen and Anne and Mary Margaret in his prayers every night. I just cannot tell him [they are gone]. He thinks they are in Cheyenne [with Frankie's parents]." As he had told his aunt Eliza before, Pershing was burying himself in his work, and the turmoil in Mexico was, almost mercifully, requiring much of his attention.

Pershing was getting reports from the War Department about Pancho Villa's whereabouts, but most were false leads. The March 6, 1916, story in the *El Paso Morning Times* about Villa possibly attacking El Tigre turned out to be incorrect as well. Villa and four hundred of his

An excerpt from Pershing's letter to Anne Boswell.

men had in fact set their sights on the town of Columbus, New Mexico. Their plan was to charge into Columbus in the dead of night and steal horses, weapons, food, money, and anything else they could get their hands on. The raid started on March 9 just after 4:00 a.m. (The railroad depot clock was hit by a stray bullet, stopping the hands at exactly 4:11.) Villa expected the residents to offer little to no resistance. He had sent spies into Columbus the day before, and they informed him that there were only about fifty U.S. soldiers at Camp Furlong, which was right next to the town. There were actually five hundred members of the 13th Cavalry garrisoned there.

The soldiers were initially caught off guard and groggy from sleep, and it took them time to scramble around and find their rifles, including a Hotchkiss machine gun, in order to save Columbus. The fighting went on for almost two hours, but once the sun began to rise, Villa called for his men to retreat, and they galloped back into Mexico. Eight U.S. soldiers and ten civilians lay dead, among them a Mrs. Milton James, who was pregnant. Several bullets had passed through the coat of a young girl named Edna Ritchie, but she escaped unharmed. Moments earlier, however, she was forced to watch her father beg the Villistas to spare his life if he gave them everything in his pockets, a total of $50. They accepted the money and then shot him anyway.

Even with the element of surprise, Villa and his men sustained massive casualties. Estimates ranged from 160 to 200 killed, and many more injured, including the man who had massacred the 18 American miners in January, Pablo Lopez. Lopez had been shot badly in both legs. Months later, still crippled, he surrendered to President Carranza's troops, who treated his legs enough so that he could stand up in front of a firing squad. Brash to the end, he refused a blindfold, and his last words were an order to his executioners to take careful aim: "In the breast, brothers! In the breast!"

Villa's brazen assault on U.S. soil and the deaths of eighteen soldiers and civilians ignited widespread condemnation throughout the United States. (There was one exception: the *Santa Fe New Mexican* newspaper actually scolded Columbus in a front-page editorial for "being [too] close to the border," thus all but inviting an attack.) President Wilson knew he had to respond militarily, but he was still concerned about an action escalating into full-blown war. And President Carranza was an unreliable ally. Carranza recognized that Villa had crossed a line, but he was also aware of how popular Villa was in Mexico, and striking the United States had only made him more of a folk hero.

March 9, 1916, when the Columbus raid occurred, also happened to be the very day that a man named Newton Baker became America's new secretary of war. Within minutes of starting his job, Baker found himself embroiled in one of the most sensitive diplomatic situations the country had faced since the *Lusitania* was torpedoed in May 1915. Baker hadn't wanted the position and had even tried to talk Wilson out of appointing him. He insisted he knew virtually nothing about the military and described himself as a "pacifist," claiming that he had "never even played with tin soldiers" growing up. The two men had been friends for almost fifteen years, starting in 1891 when Wilson was a visiting professor at Johns Hopkins University and Baker was one of his students. Baker went on to become a successful lawyer and politician in Ohio, and he was elected the mayor of Cleveland in 1911. When Wilson ran for president in 1912, Baker helped him win over critically needed delegates from the Buckeye state, enabling Wilson to secure the Democratic Party's nomination. Wilson asked him to join his cabinet, but Baker refused because it would have meant quitting as mayor. When his term was over, he finally relented and accepted Wilson's offer. Completely lacking in expertise in military affairs, Baker nevertheless had other attributes Wilson admired. He was decisive and willing to take risks, and he excelled at finding and delegating authority to the brightest and most competent people.

After a cabinet meeting on March 10, the White House announced that an "adequate force will be sent at once in pursuit of Villa with the object of capturing him and putting a stop to his forays." The statement emphasized that "this can and will be done in entirely friendly aid of the constituted authorities in Mexico and with scrupulous respect for the sovereignty of that republic."

Now President Wilson and Secretary Baker had to select who would lead this unprecedented operation, the largest manhunt in U.S. military history. Major General "Fighting Fred" Funston and the general who served under him, John Pershing, were the top two contenders.

Funston was not only in charge of Fort Sam Houston, he was responsible for the entire Southern Department of the Army. Those who saw him for the first time could be forgiven for thinking his nickname was intended as a joke; Funston stood barely five-foot-four and weighed just over a hundred pounds. But despite his diminutive stature, he was a whirlwind of energy and had extensive combat experience.

His path to leadership was an unusual one. After being rejected by

West Point, Funston worked a series of jobs—train porter, botanist, journalist—before, almost on a whim, he decided to go to Cuba at the age of thirty-one to join the Cuban revolutionaries rebelling against their Spanish rulers. Malaria forced him to return to the States, but for his actions in Cuba, Funston was made a full colonel with the 20th Kansas Infantry and shipped to the Philippines in 1898, where he fought Filipino nationalists. Funston was daring in combat: during one especially heated battle, he swam across two rivers, under fire, to single-handedly overwhelm an enemy position. He was also responsible for capturing the leader of the Filipino insurgents, Edward Aguinaldo, receiving the Medal of Honor for his actions.

Unlike General Funston, John Pershing seemed destined to become a soldier since childhood. Born in January 1860 in Laclede, Missouri, he had vivid memories of Confederate troops storming into his hometown and almost killing his father during the Civil War. As a boy, Pershing delighted in dressing up in a little Army uniform and marching around Laclede saluting veterans and joining in Fourth of July and Memorial Day parades. He applied to the U.S. Military Academy at West Point, and by correctly answering a grammar question that stumped his one remaining rival, he went on to gain admission to the school in 1882. To get in, Pershing even claimed his birthday was September 13, 1860; if he hadn't fibbed, he would have been rejected for being too old.

But in truth, Pershing never intended to make a career as a soldier. What he most aspired to be was a lawyer, and the sole reason he applied to West Point was for the free education. Although he did eventually attend law school, Pershing found himself increasingly drawn into a military life. His first assignment was with the 6th Cavalry, fighting against Lakota Sioux tribes throughout the West. Pershing became an officer at the age of thirty-two, taking command of troops in the 10th Cavalry Regiment, comprised of African American soldiers serving under white officers. After the Spanish-American War broke out, Pershing distinguished himself in Cuba, where he and Teddy Roosevelt's Rough Riders confronted Spanish forces on the San Juan heights in July 1898. When Roosevelt became president in 1901, he so admired

Pershing that he made the unprecedented move of promoting the young major three full ranks, to brigadier general, a decision that generated considerable bitterness among the large group of officers he had leapfrogged. There was much speculation that Pershing's father-in-law, Senator Francis Warren, played a role, forcing Roosevelt to publicly deny any favoritism in vehement terms.

Pershing had also served in the Philippines as the governor of the Moro province. The Moros were indigenous Muslims who had been notoriously hostile to Americans, but Pershing made an effort to learn about their culture and treat them with respect, which led to better relations. (He had also made it *very* clear that he would fight if attacked.)

Wilson and Baker ultimately chose Pershing because the Punitive Expedition was to be as much of a diplomatic mission as a military one, and Funston, for all his experience, was also hotheaded and rash, while Pershing was known for his political sense and cool demeanor.

Pershing's aide was an eager lieutenant from a prestigious military family named George Patton who was hell-bent on participating in the hunt for Villa. Patton had camped out in front of Pershing's office every morning to insist, respectfully, that he go along. Partly annoyed by Patton's persistence but also impressed by his zeal, Pershing relented and gave him the assignment.

Though Pershing was given close to twelve thousand soldiers to hunt down one man, the odds were in Villa's favor. There was no contingency plan for such an expedition, and Pershing had to improvise on a daily basis. Villa knew the terrain intimately, while Pershing and his men were given maps from the War Department that were so useless a soldier went out and bought a more accurate one published by Rand McNally for fifteen cents. Villa had runners and scouts who could get messages to him quickly. Pershing had "wireless sets," but their range was less than thirty miles and his cavalrymen were covering upward of a hundred miles in a day. Telegraph machines required an actual wire to run between the devices, and the government-issued wire was fragile and uninsulated. A single misplaced horse step or a few drops of rain and all communication would be cut off until the wires were patched up again.

President Carranza hindered Pershing at every turn. He refused to let him use Mexican railroads to move troops and supplies, forcing Pershing to rely on horse- and mule-drawn carts as well as new Dodge trucks and Ford cars that had never been used in a military operation of this size. They also added an extra $450,000 to the expedition's cost, and, by law, only Congress could approve such a purchase. But when the request came to the desk of the Army's assistant chief of staff Tasker Bliss, Bliss knew there wasn't time for a lot of bureaucratic back-and-forth, so he just put in the order with the quartermaster and the vehicles were shipped off to Pershing. Bliss told Secretary of War Newton Baker what he had done, and Baker applauded his actions and offered to take responsibility for any backlash, saying: "If anybody goes to jail, I'll be the one." Congress let the matter slide, and neither man was punished.

President Carranza may have loathed Pancho Villa, but he was deeply suspicious of Pershing as well, and he questioned why President Wilson was sending into Mexico a force the size of a division—with artillery, infantry, and cavalry—for one individual. To Carranza, it reeked more of an invasion than a manhunt.

Pershing was ordered not to occupy any town, and so he set up his first headquarters outside Colonia Dublán, a Mormon community 116 miles south of Texas. (Members of the Church of Latter-day Saints had been settling in Mexico since the mid-1880s, after the United States outlawed polygamy in 1882.) Pershing's men were astonished by how erratic the weather could be. One day the desert was a furnace, broiling hot even in the shade. Sandstorms came whipping through with such violence that the men had to scurry into their tents and lie down flat on their stomachs, with goggles covering their eyes and handkerchiefs over their mouths. A day later, it would snow.

To cover as much ground as possible, Pershing sent columns of troops to spread out across Mexico. On March 28, Colonel George Dodd was traveling with the 7th Cavalry, George Custer's old unit, through the town of Bachiniva, more than 250 miles south of Texas, when he learned that Villa had been shot in the leg by Carranza's troops and was hiding in

Guerrero, only 20 miles away. Unbeknownst to Dodd, his Mexican guide was sympathetic to Villa, and he took the 7th Cavalry on an intentionally meandering route, allowing Villa time to escape. The delay was critical to Villa because his wound was causing him to move slowly.

"The leg of his pants and drawers were cut away nearly to the hip, leaving his leg bare, and after some days it turned very black for about twelve inches above and below the wound," recalled Villa's driver, a Mexican farmer named Modesto Nevares. Nevares recalled that Villa "would cry like a child when the wagon jolted and curse me every time I hit a rock. After we . . . started south through the mountains, he got so bad that he could not stand the wagon any longer." Villa instructed his men to attach poles to his bed and carry him on foot. Sixteen men were required to take Villa 110 miles east to the town of Parral.

Conflicting rumors about where Villa was hiding sent Pershing's men chasing numerous dead ends, and they suspected that many of the Mexicans provided them with erroneous information on purpose. There was also speculation that Villa was already dead. President Carranza jumped on that idea, calling for Pershing to abandon the entire expedition and return to the United States.

Pershing doubted Villa was dead, but he understood how delicate the diplomatic situation was, and, on April 3, he issued the following statement to the press: "After having progressed 350 miles into the interior of Mexico it is very gratifying to be able to state that our relations with the Mexican people, both military and civil, have been exceptionally cordial and friendly. From the military forces of the de facto [Carranza] government we have received hearty co-operation." In fact, relations with Carranza were worsening by the day.

On April 1, Pershing traveled to Bachiniva to confer with one of his senior officers, Major Frank Tompkins, who proposed heading to Parral. When Pershing asked why, Tompkins said, "The history of Villa's bandit days shows that when he's hard pressed he invariably holes up in the mountains in the vicinity of Parral. He has friends in that region." The hunch was no better or worse than any other that Pershing had heard, and he put 175 soldiers from the 13th Cavalry under Tompkins's command and equipped them with five hundred silver pesos, a dozen mules, and about a week's worth of rations.

Tompkins and his men arrived outside Parral on the morning of April 12. They had been told the night before, by a messenger from the town, that the local Mexican commander, General Ismael Lozano, would be there to greet them, allow them to stock up on provisions, and then take them to a habitable spot just outside Parral where they could set up camp.

When neither General Lozano nor any of his aides were present to meet him, Tompkins rode into Parral, found Lozano at his headquarters, and discovered that the general had no intention whatsoever of helping him. Lozano said that if Tompkins came into town with all of his men, it would be perceived as a hostile act by the townspeople and they would respond accordingly. A crowd was already assembling in the main plaza, and it began chanting, "Viva Villa! Viva Mexico!" One of the more vocal agitators looked to Tompkins like a German spy. Hundreds of Germans had allegedly infiltrated Mexican villages to stir up anti-American sentiment and, ideally, provoke another war with the United States.

Tompkins also cried out "Viva Villa!" to break the tension, but whatever laughter it elicited vanished the moment that gunshots rang out. Tompkins realized that Mexican soldiers were emerging from the crowd and forming into lines around the Americans. And these were Carranza's troops, not Villa's. General Lozano told Tompkins that he had no control over the mob or the soldiers and that he and his men should retreat immediately. Whether it was meant as a warning volley or actually to hurt someone, a shot was fired by a Mexican soldier in Tompkins's direction and ended up killing a young sergeant named Jay Richley. Tompkins and his men rode out of Parral, with Carranza's troops close behind. As Tompkins crested a ridge that swerved to the right, he quickly set up an ambush, placing twenty of his soldiers behind the hill. When the unsuspecting Mexicans came around the corner, dozens were struck down by a hail of bullets.

Tompkins and his men reached Santa Cruz before the Mexicans

could catch up with them. From half a mile away, they watched as the Mexicans rode cautiously toward the town. A captain named Aubrey Lippincott, known as a crack shot, lay down on the roof of a house, aimed his rifle at the first Mexican in the group, and fired. The man slumped over, dead. All of the Mexican soldiers behind him pulled up on their reins, turned around, and hightailed it back to Parral.

Tompkins never found out if Villa had even been there.

Pershing, upon hearing that Carranza's troops had fired on and killed some of Tompkins's men, was apoplectic. The *New York Tribune*'s Robert Dunn, who had been following the Punitive Expedition, started to write about what had happened at Parral, calling it an "ambuscade." When Pershing saw the draft, he crossed out "ambuscade" and replaced it with "treachery."

Dunn pushed his luck and typed out a fake headline he thought would amuse the general: PERSHING DECLARES ALLEGHENY MOUNTAINS AT ANY COST MUST BE DEFENDED, referring to the mountain range safely located four thousand miles away in the eastern part of Appalachia.

Pershing didn't crack a smile. Another reporter, from the *Kansas City Journal*, published a story that did go to press, and it was explicitly mocking the whole expedition and the myriad rumors surrounding Villa. "Since General Pershing was sent out to capture him, Villa has been mortally wounded in the leg and died in a lonely cave," the article began.

> He was assassinated by one of his own band and his grave was identified by a Carranza follower who hoped for a suitable reward from President Wilson. Villa was likewise killed in a brawl at a ranch house where he was engaged in the gentle diversion of burning men and women at the stake. He was also shot on a wild ride and his body cremated. Yet through all these experiences which, it must be confessed, would have impaired the health of any ordinary man, Villa has not only retained the vital spark of life but has renewed his youth and strength. He seems all the better for his vacation, strenuous though it must have been.

Pershing was beginning to hate the whole country. "[Mexico] is given over to banditry," he wrote to a friend, "the main purpose of the bandits being to live without work and have first call on all the young girls as they arrive at the age of puberty or even before." After telling another friend, General Enoch Crowder, who was back in Washington, that he felt like a man "looking for a needle in a hay stack with an armed guard standing over the stack," he remarked, "I do not believe these people can ever establish a government among themselves that will stand. Carranza has no more control over local commanders or states or municipalities than if he lived in London."

This line of reasoning, coupled with his anger over Parral, prompted him to send a telegram to General Funston with a bold idea on how to solve the Villa problem once and for all. "The tremendous advantage we now have in penetration into Mexico for 500 miles parallel to the main line of railway should not be lost," he cabled Funston on April 18. "With this advantage a swift stroke now would paralyze Mexican opposition throughout the northern tier of states and make complete occupation of entire Republic [a] comparatively easy problem."

Unable to catch one man, Pershing was now suggesting taking over all of Mexico.

The recommendation went to President Wilson, and he dismissed it out of hand. As he told the journalist and historian Ray Stannard Baker, he believed that the first "Mexican-American War was a blot on our nation's honor," and, regardless of the country, the citizens of a nation had the right "to do what they damned [well] pleased with their own affairs."

Pershing vented his frustrations privately and kept his cool in public and with the press, just as President Wilson had hoped. Wilson, nevertheless, was worried about how events were unfolding, and he sent the Army chief of staff General Hugh Scott to the border to meet with General Funston and high-ranking representatives from Carranza's government, including General Álvaro Obregón. Talks went on and off for weeks. Obregón insisted that Villa was dead and Pershing's troops should be pulled out immediately. Scott and Funston countered that there was no proof Villa had been killed, and that attacks on border towns in the United States had to end before American forces withdrew. (In early May, even as the negotiations were taking place, Mexican bandits crossed into Texas twice and murdered four people and kidnapped two others.)

Funston ordered Pershing to move the bulk of his troops to the district of Namiquipa, northwest of Chihuahua City. Funston was hearing reports that President Carranza had deployed twenty thousand soldiers to Chihuahua City and was bringing up thousands more to the west. Carranza claimed it was to go after the Mexican bandits Funston had expressed such concern about, but Funston suspected Carranza was, in fact, preparing a massive strike against Pershing and his men.

FRUSTRATED AT HOW LITTLE his Punitive Expedition had accomplished during the two months it had been in Mexico, Pershing finally received some good news. On May 14, Pershing told Lieutenant George Patton to take three cars and fourteen other men to find food for the

General John Pershing during the hunt for Pancho Villa.

troops. After securing a whopping six-hundred-plus acres' worth of corn, Patton realized that they had ventured close to the ranch where Pancho Villa's bodyguard and second in command, Julio Cárdenas, was suspected of hiding out. In this case the rumor was true. Cárdenas and two other Villistas were inside a hacienda, and when they saw the American cars driving up, they all jumped onto their horses with guns in hand. Patton yelled at them to halt, and three shots came back in response, one kicking up dust right in front of him. Patton unloaded his pistol on the first man, about twenty yards away, hitting his arm. Patton then remembered the advice of a friend who had said that when confronted by cavalry, aim for the horse; he brought a second bandit down by shooting his horse in the hip. The animal fell on top of the man, and Patton—"impelled by misplaced notions of chivalry," he later said—let the man stand up before riddling his body with bullets.

By the end of the firefight, Cárdenas and the two other Villistas were dead. Patton and his men tied the bodies to the front of one of their cars like hunted deer and drove back to headquarters to show off their "trophies." Upon his return, Patton dashed off a short letter to his wife, Bea, about his first experience shooting a man. "As you have probably seen by the papers, I have at last succeeded in getting into a fight," he wrote. "I have always expected to be scared but was not nor was I excited. I was afraid they would get away. I never heard a bullet but some say that you do not at such close range. I wondered a little at first that I was not hit, they were so close."

Several days later, the incident still very much on his mind, Patton sent Bea another letter. "Gen [Pershing] has been very complimentary telling some officers that I did more in half a day than the 13 Cav. did in a week. He calls me the 'Bandit,'" Patton wrote on May 17. "You are probably wondering if my conscience hurts me for killing a man. It does not. I feel about it just as I did when I got my sword fish, surprised at my luck. From the latest news we may stay here some time. I hope not as it is very stupid unless we have war."

Another month passed, with the War Department frequently reminding Pershing to act "conservatively" so as not to trigger a larger clash. Pershing was also being warned by General J. B. Treviño, commander of Mexican troops in Chihuahua City, that he had orders from his government "to prevent American forces that are in this state [of Chihuahua] from moving to the south, east or west of the places they now occupy."

Outnumbered two to one, Pershing refused to be intimidated. "I shall," he replied to Treviño's June 16 message, "use my own judgment as to when and in what direction I shall move my forces in pursuit of bandits or in seeking information regarding bandits. If under these circumstances the Mexican forces attack any of my columns the responsibility for the consequences will lie with the Mexican government." In the diplomatic equivalent of "Go to hell," Pershing ended his cable to Treviño by stating unequivocally, "I do not take orders except from my own government."

Hunkered down near his original headquarters at the Mormon missionary in Colonia Dublán, Pershing learned on June 18 that a large force of Carranza's troops were advancing on Ahumada, just to his east. Pershing tasked Captain Charles Boyd with gathering a small scouting party to head toward Ahumada. "This is a reconnaissance only," Pershing sternly instructed Boyd, "[and] I want you to avoid a fight." Pershing didn't want Boyd to go directly into Ahumada itself, but stay as far away as possible while still being able to determine the size of the Mexican forces. Pershing's orders could not have been clearer.

En route to Ahumada, Boyd and his men rode past the Santo Domingo Ranch, and an American foreman there who knew the area told him that there were more troops in Carrizal, five miles south, and they were tough fighters. Lieutenant Henry Adair, in Boyd's company, mocked the very idea of "Mexican courage" and assured Boyd that if they encountered Carranza's soldiers, the Mexicans would drop their guns and flee at the first sign of real trouble.

Boyd's scout, a bilingual Mormon named Lem Spilsbury from Colonia Dublán, disputed this. "You're just mistaken," Spilsbury said. "I know Mexicans that are just as brave as any Americans I have ever heard about."

After heading out of the Santo Domingo Ranch at 4:00 a.m. on June 21, Boyd was within a mile of Carrizal by 7:30 a.m. Using Lem Spilsbury as his translator, Boyd told Major Genevo Rivas, a Mexican officer who had ridden out to meet them, that Boyd and his men were going to enter the town.

"There are no Villistas in this part of the country," Major Rivas said to Boyd with a sneer, "and if there are any enemies of yours over here, we're them!"

At this point, another one of Major Rivas's commanders, General Félix Gómez, appeared on the scene. His tone was more cordial, but he nevertheless informed the Americans that they could not continue any farther. Gómez said that he would, however, be more than happy to go back to Ahumada and send a cable to the senior general in the region, J. B. Treviño, for a final decision.

But before Gómez left Carrizal, Carranza's troops began stealthily taking positions behind walls and barricades around the Americans. Perhaps hoping for his own Patton-like moment of fame, Boyd marched up to Lem Spilsbury and demanded that he translate the following to Gómez word for word: "Tell the son of a bitch that I'm going through," Boyd exclaimed, spittle flying out of his mouth. "God damn you! I've never disobeyed an order yet, and I'm not going to now."

Boyd's words didn't have to be translated.

"You might pass through the town," Gómez replied calmly, "but you'll have to walk over my dead body."

Boyd was convinced by Lieutenant Adair's assessment of Mexican troops that once the Americans made a move, the Mexicans would run away. Seconds later, Boyd and his soldiers raced directly into the Mexican positions, and were shot down like penned hogs. Boyd's low regard for the fighting spirit of the Mexican soldier cost him his life. General Gómez was also killed in the shoot-out. With several of their officers dead, the remaining Americans realized they were outgunned and without leadership, and they retreated as rapidly as possible. In the end, nine Americans were killed, a dozen injured, and twenty-four more taken prisoner.

President Wilson, Army Chief of Staff Scott, and General Funston had all thought that tensions were deescalating in Mexico, but the catastrophe at Carrizal reminded them that they were still one needless firefight away from a full-scale war. President Wilson called up 110,000 National Guard troops to protect the American side of the border and assured Carranza, as best he could, that this was not the buildup to an invasion. It was also insurance that Mexican troops would not suddenly surround and massacre Pershing and his relatively smaller force of 12,000. Pershing remained close to Colonia Dublán. Carranza by this time had more pressing matters to deal with: south of Mexico City, 20,000 heavily armed rebels under the leadership of Emiliano Zapata were conducting hit-and-run strikes against Mexican troops.

Pershing's Punitive Expedition had for all intents and purposes run its course. While they never captured Villa, the operation wasn't a total failure. By June 30, 1916, of the estimated 485 Villistas who had raided Columbus, New Mexico, four months earlier, approximately 270 had been tracked down and killed, more than 100 were seriously injured in firefights, and 60 had been brought in by the Carranza government, which left only about 25 of the original attackers at large. Still, Pershing was a proud man, and he believed that if Carranza had actually helped him, they could have caught Villa.

One of Pershing's greatest disappointments was the ineffectiveness of the airplanes assigned to the operation. The impressively named 1st Aero Squadron consisted of a mere eight planes. The first one broke apart on its way to Colonia Dublán, and the other seven didn't have enough power to fly above the mountainous terrain, rendering them useless. Days and weeks of agonizing marches could have been spared by even one plane able to dart miles in advance to find Villa's men.

Pershing doubted that planes would ever be of much use in warfare. He wasn't alone in underestimating their influence; General Ferdinand Foch, the Allied commander in chief, had considered airplanes "very well for sport" but not "for the army." By June 1916, aviators on all sides of the war were proving the generals wrong.

4.

Lafayette's Boys

M
Y WOUND HAS CLOSED up very nicely," Kiffin Rockwell wrote his mother on June 8, 1915, a month after receiving "a nice clean bullet through the thigh" during battle in the Artois region of France.

After six weeks recuperating in a French military hospital, Rockwell stayed for several days in the Paris apartment of Alice Weeks, whose son, Kenneth, a graduate of the Massachusetts Institute of Technology, had joined the Foreign Legion in August 1914 along with Alan Seeger, the Rockwell brothers, and about forty other young men from the United States. Mrs. Weeks had the means to move to Paris in January 1915 from her home in Boston to be closer to her son, and she became a "mother hen" to many of the young American men in the Legion, sending them care packages on the front lines or providing them with a comfortable place to stay if they traveled through Paris. Kiffin Rockwell often addressed Mrs. Weeks as "my dear second mother" when he wrote to her.

Rockwell's wound prevented him from returning to the infantry, but a chance encounter with William Thaw, a native of Pittsburgh, Pennsylvania, raised the prospect of an exciting new opportunity for him to fight for France—in the air. William Thaw's affluent parents had bought him his own airplane in 1913, when he was only nineteen, and he proved to be a skilled pilot. A year later he was in Paris to compete in a flying contest that offered a whopping $100,000 prize. When hostilities broke out between France and Germany in August 1914, the competition was canceled and Thaw signed up for the Foreign Legion. Months later he was reassigned to the Service Aéronautique, becoming the first American to fly for France. His dream was to create an entire squadron of American pilots.

The French government was less than keen on the idea. Officials were concerned that German agents, posing as Americans, could infiltrate the unit. And indeed, one spy was caught and executed for joining the Service Aéronautique after having forged a U.S. passport to get in.

Nor were the French convinced that a new squadron was needed. Aviation was in its halcyon days, and there was no shortage of daring young men wanting to participate in this thrilling new enterprise. Pilots were surpassing race-car drivers in popularity, constantly setting world records and risking their lives in air shows and races, to the admiration of gasping crowds below. Even under the best conditions, flying was extremely dangerous, as the planes themselves were often death traps. Constructed mostly of wood and canvas and held together in places by a highly flammable glue, they burst into flames quite easily. A single engine spark could set the whole contraption on fire. They were also structurally unstable; hit with a sharp crosscurrent of wind, propellers and wings broke apart in mid-flight, sending pilots hurtling to the ground.

Military planes were at first used primarily for reconnaissance. The pilots went scouting over enemy lines, made a mental note of where opposing troops were assembling, and then reported the information back to their superiors when they landed. As technology progressed, pilots physically held a camera over the side of the plane and took as many pictures as possible before they risked losing control of their aircraft. Since they weren't engaged in trying to kill one another, there was almost a friendly bonhomie between Allied and

German aviators, who would give each other a jaunty wave as they passed.

Some pilots started bringing pistols with them, not only to fire at their enemies, but in case they caught on fire and opted for a quicker way out. The first machine guns were fixed on the wings of the planes, and pilots had to reach over and pull the trigger with one hand while keeping their other hand on the throttle. To change the cartridge, they had to stand up in the cockpit, lean over the old drum and pry it out, and then replace it with a new one. Two-seater planes eventually came along, allowing pilots to focus on flying; the rear seat was for manning a machine gun or dropping bombs. A Dutch inventor named Anthony Fokker perfected the idea of placing a fixed machine gun directly in front of the pilot and using a "synchronized interrupter," enabling him to shoot through the propeller blades without blasting them to pieces. Other inventors attempted something similar, but Fokker's design was the most copied. (The French wouldn't be able to figure out how to replicate Fokker's synchronized system until March 1916, when they finally captured a German plane and dismantled it.)

Throughout the summer of 1915, William Thaw continued to press his case for an all-American squadron, and with powerful new backers like Dr. Edmund Gros, one of the main funders of the American Military Hospital in Neuilly, the French government gradually opened up to the idea, reasoning that it might help rouse public support in the United States for France and its allies. By August 1915, Thaw and another American pilot, Norman Prince, were recruiting men, and Kiffin Rockwell signed up right away. On September 8, he sent home his first letter from training camp. "Dear Mamma," he wrote, "I am transferred to the aviation as a student-pilot. That is a jump from the lowest branch of the military to the highest. It is the most interesting thing I have ever done, and is the life of a gentleman, and I am surrounded by gentlemen."

Rockwell reserved the more gruesome updates for his brother, Paul, working at the Ministry of Information and for the *Chicago Tribune*. "The last flying we had at all was Friday morning and it was an unlucky morning, as we had three men killed and one badly injured," Kiffin wrote on September 27, 1915.

> A puff of wind caught their aeroplane and almost upset it, then something went wrong and it shot straight up in the air, then fell. The instructor and the mechanic were imprisoned in the wreckage and there was an explosion and the whole mass went up in flames, and they were burned alive with all the men watching but unable to do a thing.

At the end of the letter, Kiffin mentioned in passing that an "American named Chapman, from the 3eme de Marche [of the Foreign Legion], arrived here this morning and seems to be a very fine fellow indeed."

Victor Chapman felt the same, writing to his father on September 27 that he had found "a compatriot I am proud to own here. A tall lanky Kentuckian, called Rockwell."

Grandson of Henry Grafton Chapman, former president of the New York Stock Exchange, Chapman was another wealthy and idealistic Harvard graduate who had been studying in Paris when the war broke out and joined the Foreign Legion. Chapman quickly distinguished himself for being one of the hardest-working Americans in his regiment, no matter how menial or mindless the assignment. If ordered to peel potatoes, he went about it as if it were the most essential task of the war. The same was true when it came to the backbreaking job of digging trenches. One officer observed him shoveling away with such intensity that he asked Chapman if he was a ditchdigger by trade.

"You're off there, Captain," said another soldier familiar with Chapman's background. "He's a millionaire."

(The only recorded instance of Chapman even hinting at his family fortune occurred when he was desperate to help a gravely injured comrade. "Save him, sir, and I'll give you a hundred thousand francs," Chapman begged the attending surgeon. But the wound was too severe, and Chapman's friend bled to death in his arms.)

Chapman had been transferred into aviation only a few weeks before Kiffin Rockwell had, and he was trained in a different region of France. He conducted his first mission over Germany on August 24, 1915, as a bombardier, with a more experienced officer flying the plane. Chapman wrote to his brother Conrad the next day:

> This is by far the most difficult operation, for the 155 shell with its tin tail looking like a torpedo four feet long, is hung under the body and without seeing its nose even one has to reach down in front of the pilot, put the *detonateur* in, then the *percuteur* [firing pin] and screw it fast. After which I pulled off the safety device. You may imagine how I scrambled round in a fur coat and two pair of leather trousers and squeezed myself to get my arm down the hole.

Flying was so rudimentary at the time that Chapman, sitting behind the pilot, communicated with him by passing back and forth hastily scribbled messages. (The roar of the engine also drowned out their voices, even if they screamed at each other.) After hitting their target, Chapman, to celebrate, "drew out some chocolates and fed some to the Lieutenant," hand to mouth.

Chapman was especially struck by the beauty of the multicolored landscapes below. "From a good altitude the country looks like nothing so much as a rich old Persian carpet," he observed to his brother.

> Where the fields are cultivated one sees the soil now a rich pinky red fading into a light yellow, or running into dark browns. The green fields, oblong patches and the brick-roofed villages like figures on the carpets connected by threads of roads and rivers; superimposed upon it here and there in big and little patches always with straight edges are the woods, a dull, darkish green, for they are pine woods. In the direction of the sun the bits of water shine silver.

Victor Chapman.

ONE BY ONE, more Americans were taking to the air.

Raoul Lufbery worked as a mechanic for the popular French exhibition pilot Marc Pourpe, who enlisted in France's Air Service in August 1914. When Pourpe died attempting a night landing in December 1914, Lufbery vowed to avenge his death and (even though it was accidental and not due to combat) spent the summer of 1915 earning his wings.

A graduate of San Antonio's West Texas Military Academy, Clyde Balsley volunteered to drive ambulances in May 1915, and then quit in late September 1915 to become a pilot.

Paul Pavelka recovered from the bayonet wounds he received while fighting in Champagne and joined his friend Kiffin Rockwell in December 1915.

Edwin Parsons had fallen in love with flying after dropping out of the University of Pennsylvania in 1912 and befriending Glenn Curtiss, inventor of the plane that bears his name and an aviation pioneer on par with the Wright Brothers. Parsons gained such a reputation as a gifted pilot that by 1913 he was receiving requests from other countries to train their soldiers to fly. One of those appeals came from a representative of Pancho Villa. Parsons spent almost a year in Mexico trying to train the Villistas in a Curtiss biplane, but most were too scared to venture much higher than a few feet off the ground. When relations between Villa and the United States soured in early 1915, Parsons reenrolled in the University of Pennsylvania. Upon learning of the American squadron forming in France, he followed the route of many of the other men and served as an ambulance driver first, in January 1916, before finally becoming a pilot.

While he breezed through the actual training, Parsons almost failed the eye exam because, ironically, the accomplished pilot was actually nearsighted. By this time France desperately wanted more Americans, and they were allowing—and even helping—individuals with what would normally be considered disqualifying defects to pass their physicals. Standing ten feet from an eye chart, Parsons was essentially told by the French doctor what was in front of him.

"In the second line," the doctor would say, "the third letter. I see there a *B*. What do you see?"

Parsons stated that he, too, saw a *B*.

"*Bon!*" the doctor exclaimed, and the charade continued.

All of the men, including Victor Chapman, William Thaw, and Norman Prince, were the founding members of what became known in April 1916 as the Escadrille Américaine. German officials protested that the squadron's very title suggested that it wasn't neutral, and France's minister of war agreed. So he simply had it renamed the Lafayette Escadrille, in honor of the Frenchman who had aided the Colonies during its War of Independence. Nothing else about the squadron was changed, but there really wasn't much more the Germans could do but complain.

By May 1916, the escadrille was making history. "Well, at last I have a little news for you," Kiffin Rockwell wrote to his brother on May 18. Rockwell had just returned from a harrowing mission that began with his engine sputtering off and on. But before returning to base, Rockwell caught sight of a German two-seater Boche plane below him with a pilot and a machine gunner. Outmanned and flying with a motor that might conk out at any second, Rockwell nevertheless went after them. "[The gunner] immediately opened fire on me and my machine was hit, but I didn't pay attention to that and kept going straight for him, until I got within twenty-five or thirty meters of him," he wrote to Paul.

> Then, just as I was afraid of running into him, I fired four or five shots, then swerved my machine to the right to keep from running into him. As I did that, I saw the mitrailleur [machine gunner] fall back dead on the pilot, the mitrailleuse fall from its position and point straight up in the air, the pilot fall to one side of the machine as if he was done for also. The machine itself fell to one side, then dived vertically towards the ground with a lot of smoke coming out of the rear. I circled around, and three or four minutes later saw a lot of smoke coming up from the ground just beyond the German trenches.

Rockwell had just become the first member of the Lafayette Escadrille to make a confirmed kill. Less than a week later, he almost became the first member to be killed as well. Rockwell, Victor Chapman, and several other pilots flew to Verdun, where the battle that had started three months earlier, on February 21, was still raging, and French troops needed air support. A German gunner fired a bullet that shattered Rockwell's windscreen and sent shards of glass and metal fragments flying into his face, nearly blinding him. Rockwell made it back to base but refused to be hospitalized.

He was granted a leave to Paris, and he ended up knocking on the door of Alice Weeks, who was shocked by what she saw. "His face was pretty badly disfigured," Mrs. Weeks wrote to a family friend. "At the ambulance they took out the pieces of shell, and the Captain wished him to go at once to a Hospital for fifteen days, but he told them he wanted an eight-day leave, to come home to us." Along with the physical wounds, the attack had clearly taken an emotional toll, too. "He looks terrible with those dreadful eyes men always have after going through heavy firing," Mrs. Weeks wrote. "I cannot describe them. They are sunken and yet have a sharp look."

Edwin Parsons, who had more experience flying before the war than most of his comrades, was the least romantic about it. It was, in fact, "pure agony of mind and body." What especially made it miserable, Parsons later recalled, was the open, unheated cockpit. Even during the spring and summer months, the air could be freezing cold thousands of feet above the ground. Parsons wrote:

> The sub-zero temperature penetrated the very marrow of your bones. Despite three or four pairs of gloves, fingers coiled around the [control] stick would be paralyzed in five minutes. Then they would have to be forced open and pushed away from the stick with the other hand and the paralyzed hand beaten against the side of the fuselage to restore circulation. A few minutes later the process would have to be reversed. . . .
>
> Feet were twin lumps of ice, rigid and unfeeling; shooting pains throughout the entire body, eyeballs and teeth smarting and burning, icy scalp contracting till it felt as if the skull must burst through and explode in a shower of bones, heart pumping half-congealed ice water instead of warm blood—thus it can be easily understood why liquor was a necessity.

Drinking wasn't a topic the men addressed much in their letters, but it was a pervasive problem. If a pilot wasn't an alcoholic before he joined the escadrille, odds were he soon became one. The men drank before heading out on a mission to bolster their courage. They drank while flying to keep warm. They drank after they landed to calm their nerves. At dinnertime, they drank together and were notorious in French bars and restaurants for brawling with other patrons or one another, just for the hell of it. And then when they went back to their barracks, they drank before bed to help them sleep.

Edwin Parsons described the escadrille men, ultimately, as a "devil's brood of grousing, reckless, undisciplined, irresponsible wildcats, all a trifle screwy (for to be war aviators we had to be just a little nuts), but a loyal crew, ready to fly, drink or fight at the drop of a hat. Motives were as varied as the men themselves. Some sought adventure, others revenge, while a pitiful few actually sacrificed themselves in the spirit of purest idealism."

The man who particularly stood out in this motley crew, Parsons observed, was Victor Chapman, "the best-beloved pilot of the Escadrille." What Parsons found so admirable about Chapman was that, while "he fought like a fiend" in the air, he was gentle and gracious at heart. Parsons wrote that Chapman's "artistic soul was able to see the beauty in anything: in shell-torn earth, in ruined villages, in a sea of clouds, in the dark skeletons of fire-blackened forests."

That artistic spirit was reflected in Chapman's letters, even as the war dragged on and the other men were becoming increasingly discouraged and shaken by the experience. "This flying is much too romantic to be real modern war with all its horrors. There is something so unreal and fairy like about it," Chapman began a letter to his father on June 1, 1916, having spent almost nine months as a pilot. He wrote with untempered enthusiasm how he recently coasted above "a purple sea of mist" almost ten thousand feet in the air, and was playfully "popping in and out" of "rolly-poly cotton wool clouds."

Four days later, after telling his stepmother not to believe any newspaper accounts of his death ("I am reported killed twice already"), he went on for pages about all the different types of clouds he'd seen and how they kept him endlessly fascinated. "Everyone says they get tired of flying, 'It's monotonous,'" Chapman wrote. "I don't see it, but on the contrary, an infinite variety is this, when there is a slight sprinkling of clouds."

What Chapman did not mention, in either letter, is that he had been awarded the Croix de Guerre only days before for taking on three German Fokkers and downing one of them. Chapman kept upping the stakes. On June 17, he went after a formation of five German planes, knocking one out almost immediately. The other four seemed as if they were about to scatter until they realized they were being attacked by a single pilot and swooped back around to descend on him. Chapman's machine gun had run out of ammunition, and he tried to change the magazine drum while evading four attackers. Bullets shot up the side of his plane, and one gashed his scalp. Blood started to pour into his eyes, and Chapman, barely able to see, feigned death, slumping over in his seat and letting the plane spin toward the ground. Apparently this convinced the Germans that they had been successful, and they peeled away. Once they dispersed, Chapman wiped away the blood streaming down his face and wrestled with the control stick until he leveled off, with seconds to spare, and landed in one piece.

On June 18, Chapman's friend Clyde Balsley went off on his first combat mission, a predawn patrol over Verdun. Balsley spotted a German Aviatik biplane and headed straight for him. Balsley was only about fifty yards away when he began firing his machine gun, which spat off a single round before jamming.

Three other German planes came out of nowhere and opened up on him. A bullet pierced his right pelvis and then sliced into his intestines. Balsley looked down and saw that he was still over enemy lines, so with what little energy he had, he aimed toward the French side and crashed behind a frontline trench, the wheels of his plane getting tangled in barbed wire and causing him to be thrown out of the cockpit. As German artillerymen adjusted their guns to target where the American pilot had fallen, four French soldiers crawled out of their trench and dragged Balsley to safety.

Balsley was taken to a field hospital ten miles away, but the small medical staff was overwhelmed by the constant stream of injured soldiers coming in from Verdun, and Balsley received little attention. The facility itself was something out of a nightmare; grotesquely mutilated men, many with bloody stumps for arms and legs, were wheeled in one after another, the living replacing the dead within hours or even minutes on uncleaned cots. There was no ventilation, and the June heat only exacerbated the stench of decaying limbs and bodies. Along with the excruciating pain, Balsley was going mad with thirst. The doctors said that, due to his internal wounds, he couldn't drink water but only suck on a wet cloth. Balsley became dehydrated and developed a high fever worsened by a growing infection and malnutrition.

His first visitor was Victor Chapman.

Despondent over his friend's condition and pleas for water, Chapman asked the doctors if Balsley might benefit from eating fresh oranges. In theory, the doctors said, yes, but oranges would never be found anywhere near the war-torn village where the hospital was located.

Chapman had the answer he needed. He promptly flew off to Paris and returned with fresh oranges for his friend. The next day, he got into his plane and did it again.

On June 23, Chapman was back on base when he saw three of his squadron mates—Raoul Lufbery, Norman Prince, and their commander, Captain Georges Thenault—fly off to the front lines. Chapman impulsively decided to follow along, just in case they needed backup. When the patrol went after two slow-moving German observation planes, they suddenly realized that it was a trap; flying overhead were three Fokkers, hoping to catch the escadrille pilots by surprise.

Once Lufbery, Prince, and Thenault realized what was happening, they quickly turned around and went back to the French lines, not knowing that Chapman was behind them. Chapman didn't see them change course, and he was now facing five German airplanes all alone. This time, they knew they had him surrounded and there was no escape. With machine-gun fire raking him from all sides, Chapman was shot through most of his body, and the plane broke into pieces before slamming into the ground. Inside was another bag of oranges Chapman had planned to take to Clyde Balsley.

Victor Chapman was the first American pilot to die in the war, and his death hit the escadrille hard, and no one harder than Kiffin Rockwell. He wrote to Alice Weeks the day after Chapman was killed:

> Victor had about the strongest character of any boy I have
> ever known. We used to kid him a lot and tell him that a lot
> of his ideals were very foolish and all, yet it didn't affect him
> and he still believed these old ideals and died a glorious death.
> As we all have to die sometime, it isn't so bad, yet by living
> he could have accomplished a great deal in his life. Last night
> I went to bed, but I couldn't sleep thinking about him,
> especially as his bed was right beside mine.

It took Rockwell a week before he could muster the strength to write to Chapman's parents. In a long, emotional letter he emphasized how impressive their son's character was and gave them a detailed account as to how Victor was killed.

Rockwell added that, as much as he missed Victor, "he is not dead; he lives forever in every place he has been, and in everyone who knew him, and in the future generations little points of his character will be passed along. He is alive every day in this *Escadrille* and has tremendous influence on all our actions. . . . You must not feel sorry, but must feel proud and happy."

Three days before he died, Victor Chapman wrote to another relative, his Uncle William, and made a comment that was not in any of his letters to his immediate family members: "Of course," Chapman wrote, "I shall never come out of this alive."

On June 28, 1916, five days after Chapman died, Alan Seeger was about to head into the Battle of the Somme, the British-led offensive intended to break the German lines in northern France and take pressure off the French at Verdun, where they had been fighting for five months. "We go up to the attack tomorrow," Seeger wrote to a friend on June 28. "This will probably be the biggest thing yet. . . . I am glad to be going in the first wave. If you are in this thing at all it is best to be in to the limit. And this is the supreme experience."

The attack began on July 1, and Seeger and the other legionnaires were kept in reserve for the next few days. Their first mission was to liberate a French village occupied by the Germans called Belloy-en-Santerre.

Back in Paris, a memorial service for Victor Chapman was being organized. His body hadn't been recovered, but French officials decided to hold the public ceremony anyway in hopes that his death would help galvanize U.S. support for France. Hours later, Alan Seeger was darting across an open field toward the little town of Belloy-en-Santerre when he was cut to pieces by German machine-gun fire.

Newspapers throughout France and the United States reported extensively on the loss of the two notable young men, the first American pilot to die in the war and the prominent poet, one honored and the other killed on the same day—the Fourth of July. The coincidence, to many, seemed almost providential.

Week by week, little by little, it increasingly appeared that the question was no longer *if* the United States would officially join the Allies in their cause but *when*. A single piece of paper, filled from top to bottom with what looked like random numbers, would push the moment to its crisis.

5.

Countdown

O N T H E N I G H T of the 1916 presidential election—Tuesday, November 7—the *New York Times* and other major newspapers announced that President Woodrow Wilson had been defeated by his Republican opponent, former justice of the Supreme Court Charles Hughes. Wilson even lost New Jersey, the state he had governed only three years before.

"I am doubly thankful as an American for the election of Mr. Hughes," Wilson's longtime foe Theodore Roosevelt said to the media. "It is a vindication of our national honor."

On Wednesday, November 8, however, reports began to trickle in that the election might not be over. A candidate won a state definitively only when all of its ballots had been tallied, and California, with its crucial thirteen electoral votes, hadn't finished the process. Sierra County, in particular, was behind because a snowstorm had made it harder for the mule-drawn wagons to plod from one precinct to the next, gather up ballots, and count them by hand.

On the morning of Friday, November 10, it was official: California had gone for Wilson, and he would remain as president for another term.

Key to Wilson's victory was his slogan: HE KEPT US OUT OF WAR. Charles Hughes had seemed the more likely of the two candidates to declare war on Germany. During the summer and fall of 1916, as Wilson and Hughes campaigned against each other, Americans were shocked by the carnage overseas. The Battle of Verdun, which had started in February 1916, was still being waged, at a cost of over three hundred thousand men killed and hundreds of thousands more wounded.

Verdun had been the worst battle of the war—until the Somme Offensive, launched three months later on July 1, 1916. More than 19,200 British troops died on the first day alone, and by the time the fighting was over in mid-November 1916, there were 1.2 million Allied and German casualties combined. (The Allies claimed victory because they had gained ground, but they had actually lost 200,000 more men than the Germans.) British field marshal Douglas Haig, who had argued for and led the Somme Offensive, was soon being referred to as Butcher Haig, and British politicians were so aghast at the fatality counts that they temporarily withheld additional troops from Haig to prevent him from feeding them into what many viewed as nothing more than a meat grinder.

"The officers and men along the [Mexican] border and in my command followed closely the press reports from abroad and kept themselves informed as far as possible on the progress of the war," General Pershing would recall. "The German attempt to take Verdun excited deep interest, and the determination of the French to defend that fortress at all hazards was highly praised. The battle of the Somme, fought during the summer by the British and French to relieve pressure on Verdun, furnished fresh examples of the so-called warfare of position." Pershing believed in this more aggressive strategy and called it "open" combat or warfare. "Many Allied writers had proclaimed that trench warfare was a development of the World War which had made open combat a thing of the past," Pershing argued. "But trenches were not new to Americans, as both the Union and Confederate armies in the Civil War had used them extensively. While my command in Mexico was taught the technique of trench fighting, it was more particularly trained in the war of movement. Without the application of open

warfare methods, there could have been only a stalemate on the Western Front."

This was all pure theory and speculation at the time because the
United States barely had a military and was far from being a world
power: the regular army numbered just over 127,500 soldiers and the
National Guard had only 66,500. Even combined they wouldn't have
lasted more than a few weeks at Verdun or the Somme. Pershing had
the prudence not to criticize President Wilson publicly, but privately he
felt it was "almost inconceivable that there could have been such an apparent lack of foresight in administration circles regarding the probable
necessity for an increase of our military forces and so little appreciation
of the time and effort which would be required to prepare them for
effective service." Worst of all, Pershing thought, Wilson's "inaction"
played into the hands of Germany, for she knew how long it would take
us to put an army in the field, and governed her action accordingly. . . .

> Thus, through a false notion of neutrality, which had pre-
> vented practically all previous preparation, a favorable oppor-
> tunity to assist the Allies was lost, the war was prolonged . . .
> and the cost in human life tremendously increased.

Throughout November and December 1916, Wilson was crafting a
"peace note" to the foreign ministries of all nations involved in the war.
"Perhaps I am the only person in high authority amongst all the peoples
of the world who is at liberty to speak and hold nothing back," Wilson
recorded in his journal. Deeply religious, Wilson honestly believed that
God had chosen him to do His work on earth, and Wilson's political
opponents bristled at the president's often self-righteous and sanctimo-
nious preening. His goal now was to bring about, in his words, "peace
without victory," so that no side felt that a settlement was being forced
upon it. In the first draft of the peace note Wilson stated that, since
"the causes and objectives of the war are obscure," the parties should
articulate specifically what it is they hoped to achieve, so that represen-

tatives from each nation could meet together and try to forge an overall agreement. Wilson indicated that he, of course, would be happy to preside over the conference.

The president read the first draft of the document to his closest adviser, Colonel Edward House, and asked for his opinion. (Although he had no official title, House was such a trusted and close friend that he could call on Wilson at any time and was even given his own bedroom inside the White House.) More hawkish than Wilson, House couldn't believe what he was hearing. Respectfully, he replied that the letter was "wonderfully well written," but he feared that the Allies would be upset by the notion that the "causes" of the war were somehow "obscure," considering that Germany was clearly the aggressor. "Germany started the war for conquest," House thought, and it "broke all international obligations and laws of humanity in pursuit of it." Wilson disagreed and made only minor changes to the document before having the Department of State send it off to the respective foreign ministries.

On January 22, 1917, Wilson met with the U.S. Senate to brief them on what he had done and how the other countries had responded. "On the eighteenth of December last," Wilson began, "I addressed . . . the governments of the nations now at war requesting them to state . . . the terms upon which they would deem it possible to make peace."

The main thrust of Wilson's argument, which he reiterated to the senators, was that "every people should be left free to determine its own polity, its own way of development—unhindered, unthreatened, unafraid, the little along with the great and powerful." He emphasized that these were "American principles, American policies. . . . And they are also the principles and policies of forward-looking men and women everywhere, of every modern nation, of every enlightened community. They are the principles of mankind and must prevail."

Germany had replied "that they were ready to meet their antagonists in conference to discuss [their] terms," Wilson told the senators, and Great Britain and France were also amenable to negotiations "but with sufficient definiteness to imply details, the arrangements, guarantees, and acts of reparation which they deem[ed] to be indispensable conditions of a satisfactory settlement." Wilson remarked, optimistically, that the world was "much nearer a definite discussion of the peace which shall end the present war."

Reactions within the United States fell mostly along party lines, with Democrats praising Wilson for his eloquence and vision, and Republicans waving it off as quixotic nonsense. General John Pershing's father-in-law, the Republican senator from Wyoming, Francis Warren, ridiculed Wilson and voiced a judgment shared by many that "the president thinks he is the president of the world."

Whatever overtures of peace the Germans had offered to Wilson after his first diplomatic cable on December 18 became absolutely meaningless a month later. Unbeknownst to Wilson, Germany had already decided on a more forceful military policy and was nurturing new alliances to bring the war to America's borders. The British knew this and were debating whether they should tell the Americans what they had learned.

On January 16, less than a week before Wilson met with the Senate, members of the German Foreign Office had gone to the U.S. embassy in Berlin and requested that it wire an urgent message to the German ambassador in Washington, Johann von Bernstorff. It was written in numeric code that the Germans knew the Americans couldn't decipher. Indeed, the Americans assumed it related to Wilson's last-minute peace efforts. It was nothing of the kind.

"We intend to begin on the first of February unrestricted submarine warfare," Foreign Secretary Arthur Zimmermann wrote to Heinrich von Eckardt, Germany's ambassador to Mexico. Germany's plan was to encircle Great Britain with submarines and sink any vessel, including American ones, in order to starve the British of food, oil, munitions, and matériel. Zimmermann went on to write that if the United States entered the war on the Allied side, Germany should create its own alliance with Mexico that would entail "generous financial support" as well as "an understanding" that Germany would help Mexico wage war against the United States directly and reclaim Texas, Arizona, and New Mexico. Zimmermann also encouraged Mexico to form an allegiance with the Japanese, who were providing some aid to Great Britain but not substantially so.

Zimmermann concluded the telegram by instructing Ambassador Eckardt to "call the President [of Mexico, Venustiano Carranza]'s attention to the fact that the ruthless employment of our submarines now offers the prospect of compelling England in a few months to make peace."

On January 17, code breaker Nigel de Grey was working in the British Navy's crypto-analysis department when he began poring over a stack of telegrams transmitted to America the day before. The British had cut Germany's telegraph cables below the Atlantic Ocean at the beginning of the war, preventing them from wiring countries in North America directly, which is why the Germans brazenly used America's own cables to send Zimmermann's telegram. In 1914, the British had surreptitiously acquired several German codebooks and could crack secret communiqués.

De Grey's heart started pounding faster as the significance of the January 16 message became more apparent. Once he had enough of it deciphered to make sense, he rushed in to see Admiral William Reginald Hall, the director of the intelligence division.

"D'you want to bring America into the war?" de Grey asked his boss, somewhat mischievously.

In true British fashion, Hall responded with utter calm. "Yes, my boy. Why?"

Explaining that his transcription was not entirely complete, de Grey went on to summarize the telegram.

"This may be possibly the biggest thing of the war," Hall remarked, after taking it all in.

Hall also realized they couldn't act on the information right away. The U.S. State Department had no idea that England was eavesdropping on its international conversations, and if Hall showed them the

The coded version of the Zimmermann telegram.

cable, he'd be revealing that the British had been snooping on the Americans, even if it was for their own good. Also, the British could not appear as if they were baiting the United States into the war. Hall instructed de Grey to keep working on the full text and ordered him not to tell anyone about it, not even their superiors.

Hall hoped that some other incident or development would make it unnecessary for him to reveal Zimmermann's plot against America. On January 31, that appeared all the more likely when German ambassador Johann von Bernstorff sent U.S. Secretary of State Robert Lansing a positive reply to Wilson's peace note, emphasizing that they were in agreement on most points. But in the penultimate line of the message, after enumerating all of the ways Germany had been treated unfairly by the French and the British, von Bernstorff announced that his government "is now compelled to continue the fight for existence, again forced upon it, with the full employment of all the weapons which are at its disposal."

By "all the weapons which are at its disposal," von Bernstorff meant U-boats, just as Zimmermann had outlined in his telegram to Mexico. Germany now intended to torpedo any vessel, regardless of its cargo. Not even passenger ships would be spared.

German officials recognized that the declaration alone risked bringing America into the war, but they were also aware of how passionately Wilson wanted to remain neutral and how weak his country was militarily. The earliest the United States would be able to get troops to Europe would be the summer of 1917, the Germans estimated, and by then they would have already brought France and England to their knees.

When the news of Germany's decision to resume unrestricted submarine warfare was released, pro-war advocates in the United States assumed that, at long last, President Wilson would *have* to declare war. On February 3, Wilson went before Congress to make what they expected to be a historic announcement.

Wilson began by repeating the news that, two days earlier, the Imperial German Government had publicly vowed to use its submarines "against all shipping seeking to pass through certain designated areas of the high seas." Wilson reminded his audience that, after torpedoing a steamship called the *Sussex* almost a year earlier, on March 24, 1916, "without summons or warning" and killing several U.S. citizens, Germany had assured the world that it would cease such attacks. Wilson quoted from one of Germany's own government memos to its naval force, ordering that merchant vessels "both within and without the area declared a naval war zone, shall not be sunk without warning and without saving human lives." Germany was now reneging on this pledge.

Wilson reached the climax of his speech and laid out the consequences to Germany for enacting a policy that would lead to the deaths of countless innocent crew members and civilian passengers alike: Germany's ambassador in Washington, Johann von Bernstorff, had to give back his passport and return home because Wilson was temporarily suspending diplomatic ties with Germany.

"I cannot bring myself to believe that [the Imperial German Government] will indeed pay no regard to the ancient friendship between their people and our own or to the solemn obligations which have been exchanged between them," Wilson said, ending his speech on a softer note. "We are the sincere friends of the German people, and earnestly desire to remain at peace with the Government which speaks for them."

Theodore Roosevelt and other interventionists were incensed. "He is yellow all through in the presence of danger," Roosevelt wrote to Senator Henry Cabot Lodge, once again calling the president a coward and questioning his patriotism. "Of course it costs him nothing, if the insult or injury is to the country, because I don't think he is capable of understanding what the words 'pride of country' mean."

The new U-boat policy remained a vague threat against U.S. citizens until February 25, when Germany's SM U-50 torpedoed the RMS *Laconia* twelve miles south of the Irish coast. There were nearly three hundred individuals on board, including twenty Americans. One of them was the famed war correspondent Floyd Gibbons, who had covered General Pershing's Punitive Expedition in Mexico.

"I have serious doubts whether this is a real story. I am not entirely certain that it is not all a dream," Gibbons wrote at the beginning of a 4,700-word account describing the incident with literary flourish. "I am writing this within thirty minutes after stepping on the dock here in Queenstown from the British mine sweeper which picked up our open lifeboat after an eventful six hours of drifting and darkness." At the very moment the passengers had been discussing the odds of being sunk by a sub, "the ship gave a sudden lurch sideways and forward." The torpedo had hit the stern on the starboard side, but there were no secondary explosions, so the passengers and crew had time to reach the lifeboats. The ship began to list, however, hindering the release of the boats. Some crashed into the ocean while others dangled above the water at a precarious angle.

"As we pulled away from the side of the ship, its ranking and receding terrace of lights stretched upward," Gibbons continued. "The ship was slowly turning over. 'Get away from her; get away from her,' [one passenger] kept repeating. 'When the water hits her hot boilers, she'll blow up, and there's just tons and tons of shrapnel in the hold!'"

The U-boat fired again, this time striking the engine room.

"We watched silently during the next minute, as the tiers of lights dimmed slowly from white to yellow, then to red, and nothing was left but the murky mourning of the night, which hung over all like a pall."

Gibbons then related an extraordinary encounter that occurred minutes later. "A black hulk, glistening wet and standing about eight feet above the surface of the water, approached slowly and came to a stop opposite the boat." It was the German sub, its captain needed information for his log. Gibbons recorded the conversation:

"Vot ship was dot?"

"The *Laconia,* Cunard line," responded the steward [William Ballyn].

"Vot did she veigh?" . . .

"Eighteen thousand tons."

"Any passengers?"

"Seventy-three," replied Ballyn, "men, women, and children, some of them in this boat. She had over two hundred in the crew."

"Did she carry cargo?"

"Yes."

"Vell, you'll be all right. The patrol will pick you up soon."

And with that, the submarine slipped away.

Six hours later they were rescued by a British sloop, and from another survivor, Able Walley, Gibbons learned the fate of the two Americans who were killed in the attack.

"Our boat—No. 8—was smashed in lowering," [Walley] said. "I was in the bow, Mrs. Hoy and her daughter were sitting toward the stern. The boat filled with water rapidly. It was no use trying to bail it out—there was a big hole in the side and it came in too fast. . . . Every swell rode clear over us and we had to hold our breath until we came to the surface again. The cold water just takes the strength out of you.

"The women got weaker and weaker, then a wave came and washed both of them out of the boat. There were lifebelts on their bodies and they floated away, but I believe they were dead before they were washed overboard."

Gibbons's dramatic retelling of the disaster sparked a fresh wave of outrage across the United States, if not quite the level as the response to the *Lusitania* sinking, given the relatively small loss of American lives.

In England's naval intelligence office, Admiral Reginald Hall determined that the time had come to reveal the Zimmermann telegram. By February 19, Nigel de Grey had completed his word-for-word decryption of the entire message, and Admiral Hall had devised a cover story to explain how they had come across it. Instead of claiming that the message had been intercepted, they would say that it had been found, already deciphered, in Mexico, and given to an undercover British agent by a worker at the Mexican Telegraph Office.

On February 23, England's Foreign Secretary Arthur Balfour invited Walter Page, America's ambassador to Great Britain, to his office and gave him the translated message. Page was thunderstruck and rushed back to the U.S. embassy right away to forward the telegram to the Department of State in Washington. At 8:30 p.m. on Saturday, February 24, the transmission came clattering over the department's own encryption machine. Secretary of State Robert Lansing was gone for the weekend, and the acting secretary, Frank Polk, decided the matter was too urgent to wait for Lansing's return and hurried over to the White House to show Wilson the telegram personally.

Wilson was livid. The British feared he might think they had fabricated the message as part of a ploy to draw America into the war, but the president didn't doubt for a moment that it was genuine. He even considered releasing it to the press that evening, but Polk persuaded him to wait for Secretary Lansing to return.

When Lansing saw the telegram, he, too, was furious. By this time, his staff had also learned how the Germans had cabled it from the U.S. embassy in Berlin to Washington, for Ambassador Johann von Bernstorff to forward it to Mexico. When Lansing told the president of this subterfuge, Wilson was almost more angered by the German government's audacity of using America's own telegraph cables than by the actual content of the message. "Good Lord! Good Lord!" Wilson kept saying after Lansing informed him how they'd been duped.

An Associated Press reporter named E. M. Hood was summoned to Lansing's home on the evening of February 28, and the secretary of state granted Hood an exclusive if he agreed not to disclose how the telegram was obtained or who had leaked it. This was the biggest story of the war since the sinking of the *Lusitania*, and newspapers nationwide featured it on their front page. GERMANY SEEKS AN ALLIANCE AGAINST US;/ASKS JAPAN AND MEXICO TO JOIN HER;/FULL TEXT OF HER PROPOSAL MADE PUBLIC, proclaimed the *New York Times*. Hood kept his word, and the article began by stating that "the Associated Press is enabled to reveal . . ." without mentioning any specific American officials as his source.

Some journalists were not convinced. George Viereck, founder of the pro-German weekly *The Fatherland*, predictably judged the telegram a "preposterous document, obviously faked" and "planted by British agents." Even the influential publisher William Randolph Hearst, who had used his newspapers in February 1898 to incite the nation to fight the Spanish in Cuba, considered it "in all probability a fake and forgery."

With the telegram's authenticity in doubt, the majority of Americans were not clamoring for military action. There was only one man who could put the debate to rest, Arthur Zimmermann, but surely he wouldn't do so; as long as there was skepticism about the telegram, the United States would most likely remain neutral. And then, surprisingly and without provocation, Zimmermann admitted to the press on March 3 that he had indeed authored the document.

Public opinion in the United States changed overnight. Newspapers that had previously defended Germany and promoted neutrality in the conflict now insisted that the U.S. declare war. There were still those against going to war under any circumstances, but they were now decidedly in the minority. One young pacifist walked up to Henry Cabot Lodge, the pro-war senator from Massachusetts, outside a committee room in the Capitol and claimed that Lodge was opposing the will of his constituents. Lodge told the man he was wrong and that "national degeneracy and cowardice" were "worse than war." The man shot back that those who supported military action were the real cowards, prompting Lodge to slug the man in the face so hard that he was knocked to the ground.

During his second inaugural speech, on March 5, Wilson did not articulate any specific plans, but he was clearly preparing the nation for some form of intervention. "The tragic events of the thirty months of vital turmoil through which we have just passed have made us citizens of the world," he said. "There can be no turning back. Our own fortunes as a nation are involved whether we would have it so or not."

Thoughtful and methodical to the core, Wilson was not finished deliberating on exactly what to do. He talked with Colonel House, who advised him to request from Congress the declaration of war. Then, speaking more as a friend, House remarked that Wilson wasn't really "well fitted" to be a wartime president, because he was "too refined, too civilized, too intellectual, too cultivated not to see the incongruity and absurdity of war."

Wilson held the first cabinet meeting of his second term on March 20, and the members unanimously favored war. Secretary of State Lansing was among the most vocal proponents, to the point that he grew so excitable Wilson had to tell him to calm down and lower his voice, lest anyone outside in the hallway hear what they were saying.

Josephus Daniels, despite being the secretary of the Navy, had been the cabinet member least willing to use military force, but now, with tears in his eyes, he told the president that war was inevitable.

Postmaster General Albert Burleson reminded Wilson that the American people were calling for action, to which Wilson replied, "I do not care for popular demand. I want to do right, whether popular or not."

Without stating whether he had reached a conclusion, Wilson thanked the men for their counsel, and the meeting was adjourned. Before Lansing and Burleson left the room, Wilson asked them when would be the earliest he could convene a session of Congress. Monday April 2, they said.

Over the course of the next several days, Wilson kept thinking. By Friday, March 30, he had finally made up his mind and began working on his address to Congress. He wrote it and even typed it up on his own. After finishing the speech, he asked Frank Cobb, editor of the *New York World* and a close friend, to come to the White House. Cobb remarked how exhausted Wilson looked. The president told Cobb he hadn't slept for days. Wilson also said that he had "tried every way he knew to avoid war," but could no longer see an alternative. "I think I know what war means," Wilson added, thinking back on his childhood during the Civil War when he saw horribly wounded young men return home. "Is there anything else I can do?" Wilson asked plaintively. Cobb assured his friend that Germany had given him no other option.

At 8:30 p.m. on April 2, 1917, President Wilson stood before Congress, his cabinet, the Supreme Court, and fifteen hundred special guests, all packed into the House chamber. "I have called the Congress into extraordinary session because there are serious, very serious, choices of policy to be made, and made immediately, which it was neither right nor constitutionally permissible that I should assume the responsibility of making," Wilson said, his hands visibly trembling.

He began by focusing on Germany's submarine attacks. "Vessels of every kind, whatever their flag, their character, their cargo, their destination, their errand," Wilson stated, "have been ruthlessly sent to the bottom: without warning and without thought of help or mercy for those on board . . . even hospital ships and ships carrying relief to the sorely bereaved and stricken people of Belgium. . . . The present German submarine warfare against commerce is a warfare against mankind."

Wilson's strength seemed to be building, his voice more resolute, his manner more confident.

> With a profound sense of the solemn and even tragical character of the step I am taking and of the grave responsibilities which it involves, but in unhesitating obedience to what I deem my constitutional duty, I advise that the Congress declare the recent course of the Imperial German Government to be in fact nothing less than war against the government and people of the United States; that it formally accept the status of belligerent which has thus been thrust upon it, and that it take immediate steps not only to put the country in a more thorough state of defense but also to exert all its power and employ all its resources to bring the government of the German Empire to terms and end the war.

Wilson then made it clear what must happen next. America would have to organize and mobilize all the "resources of the country to supply the materials of war and serve the incidental needs of the nation in the most abundant and yet the most economical and efficient way possible." The Navy would have to be fully equipped "with the best means of dealing with the enemy's submarines." The Army needed to be built up to "at least five hundred thousand men, who should . . . be chosen upon the principle of universal liability to service, and also the authorization of subsequent additional increments of equal force so soon as they may be needed and can be handled in training."

Wilson was also adamant about articulating that our "object now, as then, is to vindicate the principles of peace and justice in the life of the world as against selfish and autocratic power and to set up amongst the really free and self-governed peoples of the world." Wilson accentuated that Americans

> have no quarrel with the German people. We have no feeling towards them but one of sympathy and friendship. It was not upon their impulse that their government acted in entering this war. It was not with their previous knowledge or approval. It was a war determined upon as wars used to be determined upon in the old, unhappy days when peoples were nowhere consulted by their rulers and wars were provoked and waged in the interest of dynasties or of little groups of ambitious men who were accustomed to use their fellow men as pawns and tools.

The Imperial German Government was America's enemy, not Germany's citizens. "We are accepting this challenge of hostile purpose because we know that in such a government, following such methods, we can never have a friend," Wilson exclaimed. "We are glad, now that we see the facts with no veil of false pretense about them to fight thus for the ultimate peace of the world and for the liberation of its peoples." And then Wilson uttered the most consequential lines of the speech: "The world must be made safe for democracy. Its peace must be planted upon the tested foundations of political liberty. We have no selfish ends to serve. We desire no conquest, no dominion. We seek no indemnities for ourselves, no material compensation for the sacrifices we shall freely make. We are but one of the champions of the rights of mankind."

Wilson informed his countrymen that this would be a ferocious contest between mighty powers, warning:

> There are, it may be, many months of fiery trial and sacrifice ahead of us. It is a fearful thing to lead this great peaceful

people into war, into the most terrible and disastrous of all wars, civilization itself seeming to be in the balance. But the right is more precious than peace, and we shall fight for the things which we have always carried nearest our hearts—for democracy, for the right of those who submit to authority to have a voice in their own governments, for the rights and liberties of small nations, for a universal dominion of right by such a concert of free peoples as shall bring peace and safety to all nations and make the world itself at last free. To such a task we can dedicate our lives and our fortunes, everything that we are and everything that we have, with the pride of those who know that the day has come when America is privileged to spend her blood and her might for the principles that gave her birth and happiness and the peace which she has treasured. God helping her, she can do no other.

Wilson received a prolonged standing ovation, with many audience members openly weeping. Congress formally declared war on Germany on April 6, by a vote of 82 to 6 in the Senate and 373 to 50 in the House.

After giving his speech, Wilson drove back to the White House with his wife, Edith, and his personal secretary, Joseph Tumulty. Thousands of people were lined up along Pennsylvania Avenue. A soft rainstorm had come through, and the black streets were glistening. The crowds burst into applause when the motorcade passed. Once Wilson returned to the White House, the shaken president asked Tumulty to join him in the cabinet room, where they sat in silence for a few minutes. There was one thing Wilson couldn't get out of his mind. "My message today was a message of death for our young men," he whispered. "Think of what it was they were applauding."

6.

The Promotion

WITH TENSIONS ON THE border with Mexico at their highest level since Pancho Villa's rampage, General Pershing remained in San Antonio, Texas, and was not in Washington, D.C., when Wilson spoke to Congress. "As an officer of the Army, may I extend to you, as Commander-in-Chief of the armies, my sincere congratulations upon your soul-stirring patriotic address," Pershing wrote in a fawning letter to the president after reading a transcript of Wilson's speech in the newspaper.

> Your strong stand for the right will be an inspiration to humanity everywhere, but especially to the citizens of the Republic. It arouses in the breast of every soldier feelings of the deepest admiration for their leader.
>
> I am exultant that my life has been spent as a soldier, in camp and field, that I may now the more worthily and more intelligently serve my country and you. With great respect,
>
> *Your obedient servant*
> *John J. Pershing*

Pershing sent an equally gushing letter to Secretary of War Newton Baker. "In view of what this nation has undertaken to do, it is a matter of extreme satisfaction to me at this time to feel that my life has been spent as a soldier, much of it in campaign," Pershing added. "I thus formally, to pledge to you, in this my personal manner, my most loyal support in whatever capacity I may be called upon to serve."

Pershing was not being immodest in presuming that there would be a significant role for him to play in the war. His hopes were raised on May 3, when he received a telegram from his father-in-law, Senator Francis Warren, the chairman of the Committee on Military Affairs, instructing Pershing: "Wire me to-day whether and how much you speak, read and write French."

Pershing responded without delay: "Spent several months in France nineteen eight studying language. Spoke fluently; could read and write very well at that time. Can easily reacquire satisfactory working knowledge."

This was, as the French might say, *une petite exagération*. Pershing was taught basic French at West Point, and it was by far his worst subject. Pershing's time in France in 1908 certainly improved his proficiency, but nine years had passed since then, and it was unlikely that he could become fluent anytime in the near future. Pershing was not, however, going to let subpar French skills exclude him from the Great War, so he slightly embellished his abilities.

On the morning of May 10, Pershing arrived in Washington for a series of appointments, the first with the Army chief of staff, Major General Hugh Scott. Pershing was honored to learn that he had been chosen to lead the first U.S. division in France. His enthusiasm was tempered, though, upon learning how short of men and supplies the American military and its General Staff truly were. "In view of the serious possibility of war that had confronted the nation since the sinking of the *Lusitania*, there was no apparent reason why the General Staff should not have developed definite basic plans for the organization and employment of our armies in anticipation of the rapidly approaching emergency," Pershing recalled after his visit with General Scott. "To find such a lack of foresight on the part of the General Staff was not calculated to inspire confidence in its ability to do its part efficiently in the crisis that confronted us."

After calling on Scott, Pershing met with Secretary of War Newton Baker, and Pershing had to mask his surprise at how tiny and young Baker looked in person. Pershing was fifty-seven years old and stood six feet tall. Baker was forty-four and five-foot-six. This was their first face-to-face encounter; all of their previous communications, during and after the Punitive Expedition, had been conducted by telegraph or phone. Once they started talking, however, Pershing came to admire the bespectacled little man in front of him, who looked like a grade school math teacher but spoke with authority and an unshakable sense of resolve. The two men ended up having a pleasant and substantive conversation about Pershing's division, how it should be organized, and what it would need from the War Department. Baker expressed his full faith in Pershing's leadership, and Pershing thanked him for his confidence. He left Baker with, in Pershing's words, "a distinctly favorable impression of the man upon whom, as head of the War Department, would rest the burden of preparing for a great war to which the wholly unready nation was now committed."

Less than forty-eight hours later, Pershing was summoned back to Baker's office. Baker didn't say so, but part of the reason for their first meeting was to enable Baker to size up General Pershing in the flesh before making a final recommendation to the president. Baker was even more impressed than he expected. He had seen photographs of Pershing before, but in person he was magnetic. With his ramrod straight posture, sharp blue eyes, and square jaw, he couldn't have looked the part any more than if he were an actor sent over by a Hollywood casting agency. He emanated strength and had the bearing of a true leader, someone who could inspire millions of troops. Baker also appreciated that Pershing expressed his views frankly but respectfully.

Baker had conferred with President Wilson, who heartily agreed with the choice. Wilson had been ruminating for months about who would command the entire AEF in Europe if the United States did go to war.

His first choice was actually Major General "Fighting Fred" Funston. Pershing had been better suited for the Punitive Expedition because it required a more diplomatic touch to avoid sparking a larger war, and Funston could be a loose cannon. This would be less of an issue in Europe, where an ability to lay out bold strategies while also grasping the nitty-gritty details needed to execute them, which Funston was known for, was more imperative for this assignment than political tact. But it was not to be. On February 19, six weeks before Wilson's speech to Congress, Funston was in the lobby of a San Antonio hotel, leisurely enjoying the music of a local orchestra, when he suddenly clutched his chest, cried out in pain, and dropped to the floor, dead, from a heart attack.

Major General Leonard Wood was another contender. Wood out-ranked Pershing, and he was venerated by many of Washington's most influential politicians, most notably Theodore Roosevelt. Wood hadn't been seriously considered for the Punitive Expedition because of ongoing health problems. Commanding the AEF would certainly be stressful, but it was more of a "desk job," not as physically strenuous as galloping around Mexico's deserts and mountains for weeks at a time. Wood had also been at the forefront of the Preparedness Movement, a campaign started by Wood, Theodore Roosevelt, and other prominent Americans to drastically expand the armed forces and require mandatory military training for boys when they turned eighteen. Wood and Roosevelt had been able to establish officer's training camps, first in Plattsburgh, New York, then in other parts of the country. With the coming of war, Wood's actions seemed farsighted.

Along with his poor health, however, Wood had several glaring drawbacks. He often treated those below him condescendingly and acted with overbearing obsequiousness toward his superiors. During one meeting with Wilson, Wood belittled Theodore Roosevelt to try to win favor with the president, but Wilson saw right through him. Wood was also notorious for being unable to keep a secret, and he thrived on adulation and almost fanatical loyalty from his staff. He was also politically ambitious. There was no question he was going to run for the presidency on the Republican ticket, and a brief stint commanding the AEF would only add luster to his already distinguished career.

Pershing, by contrast, showed no interest in politics. President Wilson and Secretary Baker did not want on their hands another George McClellan, the Union general who ran against his former commander in chief, Abraham Lincoln, during the Civil War. Pershing certainly valued loyalty, but not if it deterred his subordinates from speaking to him candidly. He had no desire to be adored, and he extolled just and equal treatment, regardless of rank. In one oft-told story, a private conducting security outside a restricted area was told to stop all vehicles coming in, order the occupants out of their cars, verify their identity, and then allow them to enter. When Pershing's limousine approached the gate during a heavy storm, the driver told the sentry that he had General Pershing inside and to let them proceed. The private refused and instructed Pershing to stand in the rain like everybody else. Pershing got the soldier's name and rank—but not to demote him. He commended the young man for his strict adherence to the rules and had him promoted to sergeant.

Of the senior generals, Pershing was also the only one to have led more than twelve thousand men in battle, even if they were unsuccessful in capturing Pancho Villa. Secretary Baker, in fact, didn't judge the manhunt a failure. "People used to tease me about not catching Villa, but I never dared tell them the truth: I was in hopes they would *not* catch him," Baker said in a speech.

> As long as he was still at large and running from one hiding place to another, there was an excuse for having Pershing's expedition hang like a pendulum down in Mexico, and as long as his army hung down there, no [major] attacks on the border were to be feared. . . . Every Mexican commander realized it was unhealthy to attack. . . . If we had captured Villa, we would have had to retire and then would have the problem of what to do with him, which nobody was particularly clever in suggesting solutions for.

The operation gave Pershing and numerous other officers, including George Patton, real-world combat experience, and it helped the Army improve everything from footwear (the regulation shoes turned out to be too flimsy) to "rolling kitchens" that fed the troops more effectively. Mostly it revealed how woefully ill prepared the military was, prompting some in the War Department to informally and discreetly draw up contingency plans for a larger conflict.

Not since Ulysses S. Grant took control of all the Union's armies in March 1864 had an American general been saddled with more responsibility. And Grant's situation was significantly more advantageous than Pershing's. The Union soldiers were, for the most part, already assembled and ready to fight, Grant was familiar with the territory he'd be attacking, his supply lines were within the same country, and his forces vastly outnumbered those of his enemy.

Pershing would have to expand the Army almost twentyfold. The barely trained Americans would be going up against battle-hardened German troops spread out across thousands of miles of concrete-fortified trenches on the Western Front. The Germans had three years to prepare countless tunnels and rows of barbed wire, and they were already skilled in the use of flamethrowers, machine guns, and deadly gas, all of which were relatively new to warfare and causing mass fatalities at a rate virtually never seen before.

An army of at least two million troops would have to be mobilized and brought across three thousand miles of oceans teeming with German submarines, along with millions of tons of matériel. Ports and warehouses had to be constructed and hundreds of miles of train tracks laid to bring an estimated forty-five thousand tons of supplies—primarily food, water, and fuel—to soldiers and Marines on the front lines *each day*. Factories were needed to manufacture tanks, warplanes, trucks, rifles, machine guns, and millions of shells, mines, grenades, and bullets. (Approximately six hundred thousand rounds of ammunition were used in a single day of fighting at the Somme.) Hospitals had to be built and thousands of nurses and doctors trained. A mail delivery system also had to be set up, as Pershing knew that letters between loved ones were essential to keeping spirits high. And because there were so many first-generation immigrants being drafted into the AEF, censors would have to read through correspondences written in fifty different languages.

Along with the million and one details pressing down on him after he was named AEF commander, Pershing was flooded with requests from friends and associates who wanted to serve with him or have family members join his staff. His old comrade in arms Theodore Roosevelt wrote:

My Dear General Pershing:

I very heartily congratulate you and especially the people of the United States, upon your selection to lead the expeditionary force to the front. When I was endeavoring to persuade the Secretary of War to permit me to raise a division or two of volunteers I stated that if you or some man like you were to command the expeditionary force I could raise the division without trouble.

I write now to request that my two sons, Theodore Roosevelt, Jr., aged 27, and Archibald B. Roosevelt, aged 23, both of Harvard, be allowed to enlist as privates under you, to go over with the first troops. The former is a Major and the latter a Captain in the Officers' Reserve Corps. . . . But they are keenly desirous to see service; and if they serve under you at the front, and are not killed, they will be far better able to instruct the draft army next fall, or next winter, or whenever they are sent home. . . . The President has announced that only regular officers are to go with you; and if this is to be the invariable rule then I apply on behalf of my two sons that they may serve under you as enlisted men, to go to the front with the first troops sent over.

Trusting to hear that this question has been granted, I am, with great respect,

Very sincerely yours, Theodore Roosevelt

P.S. If I were physically fit, instead of old and heavy and
stiff, I should myself ask to be under you in any capacity
down to and including a sergeant; but at my age, and
condition, I suppose that I could not do work you would
consider worth while in the fighting line (my only line) in
a lower grade than brigade commander.

Pershing was able to secure assignments for Roosevelt's sons, but he
knew that the letter's postscript was slightly disingenuous; Roosevelt,
as he noted in the letter, had already asked Secretary of War Newton
Baker if Roosevelt could raise and lead a division in France, and Baker
had unequivocally said no. Roosevelt had reminded Baker: "I wish to
point out that I am a retired Commander in Chief of the United States
Army, and eligible to any position of command over American troops
to which I may be appointed." Legally, there was no merit to this argument, and Baker had told Roosevelt that his health was a primary concern; he was blind in one eye, had diabetes, and was overweight. But
regardless, Baker knew that Woodrow Wilson would never have consented to Roosevelt's request, considering the snide and insulting comments Roosevelt had been making about the president in public and
private for years. Roosevelt wasn't going anywhere.

Theodore and his sons weren't the only members of their prestigious
family eager to fight; Theodore's thirty-five-year-old cousin, Franklin
Delano Roosevelt, wanted to be deployed as well. Franklin had never
seen battle, but he was physically much more fit than Theodore, and for
the past four years he'd been serving as the assistant secretary of the Navy
under Secretary Josephus Daniels, and was an expert in military affairs.

Like Theodore, Franklin Roosevelt exuded a youthful vigor that
bordered on recklessness. When Franklin traveled to the West Coast to
tour U.S. Navy installations, he was scheduled to take his first dive in
a submarine. Only days before, another American sub had malfunc-
tioned underwater and was unable to resurface. All twenty-one sailors
inside slowly suffocated to death. The incident was a devastating blow
to Navy morale, and the only thing that could have made matters worse

would have been if Roosevelt was killed in another ceremonial dive, so it was scuttled. Roosevelt overruled the decision, and he went aboard a sub off the coast of Los Angeles right as it was being hit with massive swells. Roosevelt ordered the sub to dive, and it went down and came back up without a hitch. Roosevelt spoke with the press afterward, claiming that he felt so safe and comfortable that it was "the first time since we left Washington [I felt] perfectly at home."

From the very first day of the war, Roosevelt had been more prescient about the conflict than his boss, Secretary Daniels. When Germany marched through Luxembourg on Sunday, August 2, 1914, on its way to Belgium and France, Roosevelt was ordered back to Washington from Pennsylvania, where he had been giving a speech. From the train, he hastily wrote to his wife, Eleanor, that the conflict would be "the greatest war in the world's history. Mr. D[aniels] totally fails to grasp the situation and I am to see the President Monday a.m. to go over our own situation." The August 3 meeting didn't take place, because President Wilson was spending all of his time with his first wife, Ellen, who was dying of kidney disease. Wilson wouldn't leave her side until she passed away three days later, on August 6.

Upon returning to Washington, Roosevelt was mortified by how complacent his colleagues and their superiors, including Secretary of State William Jennings Bryan, appeared to be. Roosevelt wrote to Eleanor:

> I went straight to the [Navy] Department, where as I
> expected, I found everything [*sic*] asleep and apparently
> utterly oblivious to the fact that the most terrible drama in
> history was about to be enacted.
>
> To my astonishment nobody seemed the least bit excited
> about the European crisis—Mr. Daniels feeling chiefly very
> sad that his faith in human nature and civilization and similar
> idealistic nonsense was receiving such a huge shock. So I
> started in alone to get things ready and prepare plans for what
> ought to be done by the Navy end of things. . . .

These dear, good people like W.J.B. [William Jennings Bryan] and J.D. [Josephus Daniels] have as much conception of what a general European war means as Elliott has of higher mathematics.

Elliott was the Roosevelts' four-year-old son.

"All this sounds like borrowing trouble I know," Roosevelt went on to write, "but it is my duty to keep the Navy in a position where no chances, even the most remote, are taken."

Assistant Secretary of the Navy Franklin D. Roosevelt at a shooting range in 1917. (Four years later, Roosevelt was stricken with polio, paralyzing him from the waist down.)

Roosevelt started "borrowing trouble" the moment that Secretary Daniels left Washington on government business; while the secretary was away, Roosevelt leaked a memo to the *New York Times* revealing how undermanned the Navy was and that Congress needed to fund eighteen thousand more sailors with all due speed.

Roosevelt knew that Secretary Daniels would read about the memo, which the *Times* published in its entirety on October 22, 1914, and sure enough, Daniels was soon back in Washington and excoriating him. Roosevelt had to release a statement that he was not pushing for a buildup of forces and that he wouldn't even "consider it in [his] province to make any recommendations on the matter one way or another." But privately, Roosevelt had no regrets. "The country needs the truth about the Army and the Navy instead of a lot of soft mush about everlasting peace," he wrote to Eleanor.

In December 1914, Roosevelt joined a delegation of Navy brass to visit Great Britain and meet with Winston Churchill, the first lord of the Admiralty (the equivalent of the secretary of the Navy in the United States).

Roosevelt understood that the American people were firmly against the war, but he was determined to educate himself as much as possible on naval affairs, and the British had the most powerful fleet in the world. After a rather long, frigid journey across the Atlantic, the trip turned out to be a bust. Outraged that the United States was remaining neutral, Churchill refused to talk with Roosevelt and his delegates, and they returned home without even a handshake.

Forming a naval reserve was another of Roosevelt's personal undertakings. His goal was to build a training ground similar to the one his cousin Theodore and General Leonard Wood had established at Plattsburgh. Secretary Daniels tentatively consented to the plan but dragged his feet. The next time Daniels took an extended leave, Roosevelt, unchastened, formally stated to the press that the Navy was creating a reserve force of fifty thousand men. "Today I sprang the announcement," Roosevelt wrote to Eleanor on September 2, 1916. "It is of the utmost importance and I have failed for a year to get [Daniels] to take any action, though he never objected to it. Now I have gone ahead and pulled the trigger myself." Roosevelt braced himself for another trip to the woodshed, telling Eleanor, "I suppose the bullet may bounce back on me, but it is not revolutionary nor alarmist and is just common sense." This time Daniels apparently agreed, and Roosevelt was spared another tongue-lashing.

When the United States finally declared war, Theodore Roosevelt told his cousin to resign and "get into uniform at once." Franklin wanted to join Pershing's nascent army, but the decision was not his to make. Secretary Daniels, with the president's ardent support, refused to let Franklin enlist, he emphasized, because he was needed right where he was. His ideas and ingenuity had made him irreplaceable, and the Navy was better prepared to expand because of his foresight. Franklin was flattered and stayed in his position.

Among his first priorities was to prepare for the safe passage of the *Baltic* from New York to Liverpool. The ship had been shot at twice on its way to America, but both torpedoes missed. On board for its return trip to England would be General John Pershing and approximately a hundred handpicked officers who would comprise his General Staff. The ship would be at sea for ten days, and a single German submarine could essentially decapitate the U.S. military's high command with one well-aimed strike. The ship's location and purpose needed to remain under wraps.

It was among the worst-kept secrets in New York.

7.

Over There

ALL SORTS OF WISE bromides about bad beginnings making good endings were brought out by the weather yesterday morning as our party assembled at Governors Island in the pouring rain," General James Harbord wrote in his diary on May 29, 1917. Harbord was Pershing's chief of staff, and he diligently chronicled his experience with Pershing throughout the war, starting with their voyage from New York to England. One of his first observations upon arriving at their point of embarkation was the knuckleheaded decision of the Army supply departments to stencil A.E.F.—GENERAL PERSHING'S HEADQUARTERS in massive lettering on all of the crates accompanying the general and his staff on the *Baltic*, and to leave them on the pier "for the whole world to read" for days.

Harbord also noted how a large group of ladies had conspicuously gathered at the dock to see Pershing off. Their good intentions notwithstanding, it only brought unwanted attention, and Pershing turned them away. "The way the General's iron jaw clamped down on the proposition of the ladies to accompany us to Gravesend," Harbord wrote, "confirms my faith in the wisdom of the President in selecting him for France. The ladies disappeared." (Pershing did not notice, until it was too late, an artillery battery that was sent there to fire off a ceremonial salute, which, Pershing seethed, "made the announcement of our departure complete.")

There was one young lady Pershing was happy to see at the pier, and that was Anne Patton, sister of Pershing's trusted aide George Patton, who would also be sailing on the *Baltic*. Anne wasn't there for only her brother, however. Overwhelmed with loneliness and the pressures of his new assignment, Pershing had yearned for female companionship, and he had found it in the arms of twenty-nine-year-old Anne Patton. (Pershing was almost twice her age.) There was even talk of a marriage after the war.

Harbord, ever discreet, made no mention of Patton's sister, and wrote instead of how the crew passed the time once they set to sea. Lifeboat drills were conducted. Entertainers performed, some reciting Shakespeare and others leading the passengers in "Keep the Home Fires Burning," "My Country 'Tis of Thee," and "God Save the Queen." At night they stood on deck and watched as giant icebergs silently passed by. During the day, classes on French were offered as well as briefings on the military situation. "Colonel Puckle, of the British Army Service Corps," Harbord wrote, gave a lecture that concluded with some remarks, in general, about the average English officer "with whom we might have to deal." Harbord recorded Puckle's exact words:

> He is never demonstrative. He does not show his feelings. He does not wear his heart on his sleeve. He will shake hands with you when presented, possibly on parting, but probably never again. You enter his office, he may ask you to take a seat, and he may not, but he will nevertheless be glad to see you. You must not misunderstand his attitude for hostility, for it is not. To those of you who knew the British officer of other days I may say that you will find many new strange types that you will not recognize. The Old Army has passed away. It has gone forever.

Puckle's comment evoked a poignant realization. "I fancy we shall be saying [the same] a year from now, of our Army," Harbord wrote. "Many of that old Army of ours, of which we have grumbled and complained so much, and with which we have found so much fault, but which we have all the time loved so well, will lay their bones in the soil of France."

On June 8, the *Baltic* finally made land, and after a grand welcoming ceremony, Pershing and his most senior staff members were off on a series of formal lunches and dinners with other generals, heads of state, and members of the royal family. Harbord, usually by Pershing's side, took in every gossipy detail. "The King is a small man," Harbord noted about England's King George V.

> He has a good manly voice and either speaks readily or had well learned something some one had prepared for him. He has a nervous habit while speaking of shaking his left knee, his legs being very thin. He wore the service uniform of a British field marshal. His nose is rather red, though it is said that he had not been much of a drinker, I am obliged to say that physically he does not at all look the king.

King George took Pershing on a tour of Buckingham Palace and was keen to point out a statue of Queen Victoria that had almost been destroyed by German warplanes. "The god-damned Kaiser even tried to blow up his own grandmother!" the king exclaimed.

After ten days in England, Pershing and his staff crossed the Channel for the Boulogne wharf, where a regiment of French troops, journalists, local villagers, and musicians went wild with joy as they greeted their American visitors. Pershing and his officers snapped to attention when the band burst out with a rousing rendition of "The Star-Spangled Banner." And then they played it again. And one more time. "Even the General," Harbord recalled, "who stands like a statue, growled over the number of times they played it." The band wasn't done, however; now it was time for "La Marseillaise," which they also played several times.

There was yet more to come. "We stood up to the gangway while a dozen fuzzy little Frenchmen came up," Harbord wrote. "Each saluted the General and made a little speech, then sidestepped and was replaced by another until each little man had said his speech." The last one "was a big man with a sweeping moustache and the two stars on his sleeve which mark the French brigadier. His right hand was gone below the elbow; his chin and forehead were scarred. My theory for the lost arm was that he had lost it by standing with it up to his cap while a French band [endlessly] played 'The Star-Spangled Banner' followed by 'The Marseillaise.'"

Harbord's lighthearted tone turned somber when he was told what, in fact, had really happened to the man's arm. During the battle for Champagne, the officer was in command of a charging brigade when a German grenade landed right by his men—*mes enfants* ("my children"), he referred to them. He lunged for the grenade as it rolled on the ground and, just before it was out of his fingers, it exploded, blowing off his hand and much of his arm. At the same time, a German machine gunner put a bullet through his chin, breaking it, and grazing his forehead with another bullet.

Pershing, Harbord, and other generals embarked on a whirlwind tour of Paris over the next couple of days before meeting with Henri-Philippe Pétain, France's most senior officer, at his headquarters on June 16. Harbord and Pershing both recorded their first impressions of the sixty-one-year-old general. "Pétain is an erect soldierly looking man, bald, but originally with blond hair, wears a heavy moustache, walks briskly, and I should estimate him to be about fifty-seven, the age of our Chief [Pershing]," Harbord wrote.

Pershing described Pétain physically as well ("above medium height and weight, he wore a full moustache, lightly gray, and was then about sixty") but also took note of his personality: "He has a kindly expression, is most agreeable, but not especially talkative." What they did talk about, of course, was the war. "Our conversation after luncheon was almost entirely on military affairs," Pershing wrote, "including America's probable part in the war, which, as matters stood, gave little promise of becoming effective until the following spring," almost a year away.

Pétain had to leave for another engagement, but before he walked out of the room he looked at Pershing, expressed his gratitude that the United States had finally joined the Allies, and said, very seriously, "I hope it is not too late."

Pétain had been placed in command of all French troops only a month earlier, after the Army had come close to suffering a total breakdown in morale. Pétain's predecessor, Robert Nivelle, had proposed a massive offensive in April that would strike the Germans with such force above the Chemin des Dames plateau and along the Aisne River, ninety miles northeast of Paris, that it would provide the critical breakthrough the Allies needed. An artilleryman by training, Nivelle believed that after an overwhelming barrage, French infantry could sweep through with minimal resistance and reclaim the land.

Whether through overconfidence or sheer ignorance, Nivelle's plan was ill conceived from the start; the Germans were able to ride out most of the artillery by hunkering down behind protective ridges and inside an underground maze of tunnels and caves created over time by local stonecutters who had used the Chemin des Dames as a quarry for years. When French troops came storming over the lines on April 16 and 17 expecting only dead Germans in their path, they were confronted instead with rows of machine gunners and killed off by the thousands. The French did gain some ground—about six hundred yards, at a cost of ninety-six thousand dead. Officially, it was the Second Battle of the Aisne, but within France it became known as the Nivelle Offensive, forever tying the defeat to the name of the man most responsible for its execution.

Out of 112 French divisions, there were mutinies in 68. Soldiers dropped their rifles and simply refused to fight, regardless of the consequences. (An estimated fifty to seventy were executed, but out of ninety thousand court-martialed for desertion and insubordination.) Nivelle was replaced with Pétain, who immediately instituted several measures, large and small, to restore order. He provided the men with better food and more cigarettes, allowed them longer home leaves, and, most important, promised that their lives would no longer be needlessly squandered on large, sweeping attacks that achieved nothing. For these changes and the military acumen he later demonstrated, his countrymen would soon begin referring to Pétain as "the savior of France."

The first major contingent of U.S. soldiers, totaling fourteen thousand, disembarked in France on June 26, 1917. While the French who had lined the streets to greet them screamed with glee and showered the men with flowers, Pershing was thoroughly disappointed. To him, they looked shoddy and disorganized. Uniforms didn't fit. The men barely marched in order. Worst of all, Pershing knew that they were ill prepared for the harsh realities that lay ahead. Harbord also conceded that, despite their sparkling, energetic presence, the Americans were not exactly riding in like the cavalry. They had one meager division to offer, and it had never seen combat and wasn't even fully trained.

Two weeks later, on July 4, one of the division's regiments, the 16th, was selected to parade through the streets of Paris, ending at the burial site of the Marquis de Lafayette.

"What we have in blood and treasure are yours," a U.S. colonel proclaimed at the end of the ceremony. "In the presence of your illustrious dead we pledge our hearts and our honor in carrying this war to a successful conclusion. Lafayette, we are here!" Members of the crowd cried out in joy.

Whatever united front they showed in public, tensions between the generals were building behind closed doors. Pétain and Haig told Pershing that they wanted U.S. regiments to be broken up and dropped into British and French units the moment they set foot in Europe. Pershing adamantly opposed the idea. The Americans, he insisted, were going to serve under their own flag and in their own divisions.

Pétain and Haig argued that the war might be lost by then. It was a gut-wrenching decision, and one that was by no means obvious on either side, but Pershing held firm. Frustrated by Pershing's recalcitrance, his European allies even went over his head and communicated their demands to Secretary of War Newton Baker. They didn't know that, two days before Pershing left the United States, Baker had given him a top secret memo consisting of six directives that addressed the matter of Pershing's authority and independence. Point number five, the longest of the six, was the most consequential. Baker wrote:

> In military operations against the Imperial German Government, you are directed to cooperate with the forces of the other countries employed against that enemy, but in so doing the underlying idea must be kept in view that *the forces of the United States are a separate and distinct component of the combined forces* [emphasis added], the identity of which must be preserved. This fundamental rule is subject to such minor exceptions in particular circumstances as your judgment may approve. The decision as to when your command, or any of its parts, is ready for action is confided to you, and you will exercise full discretion in determining the manner of cooperation.

Harbord took some solace in noting that at least the French and British commanders' indignation wasn't entirely against the United States. "Our Allies seem to hate one another," Harbord wrote. "It is said that Sir John French wished to surrender Ypres in the autumn of 1914, which would have given the Germans Calais and the coast, and that [General Ferdinand Foch], our host at the Fourth of July dinner at Armenonville, grabbed Sir John by the shoulders and shook him up, and said 'By God you shall not surrender Ypres.' And he didn't."

Back at American headquarters in Washington, D.C., chaos reigned. "The new Brigadier General, Peyton March, who is to command our 1st Battery Brigade, gave us at dinner tonight a very graphic account of the way things are going in the War Department," Harbord wrote. "He says the Mail and Record room of the A.G.O. [Acquisitions and Grants Office] is piled six feet deep with papers not yet recorded, and that knowing there was a cable there from General Pershing asking for him, it took six days to get it from the A.G.O. to the Chief of Staff."

Harbord reflected on whether the United States really had the stomach for a drawn-out conflict. "Our American people are not, in my judgment, very keen for the war," Harbord wrote in his journal that June, when enthusiasm for the war was at its zenith. "They do not realize its perils. Losses in battle that also cost German lives they would understand, but if a troopship or two is torpedoed and a thousand or two American boys are drowned like rats, I wonder if the President could hold them in line."

When Woodrow Wilson's cabinet told the president in March 1917 that the nation was now clamoring for war, Wilson snapped that he didn't care about popular opinion. By June 1917 he had a very different view.

8.

Heaven, Hell, or Hoboken

P UBLIC OPINION POLLS WERE a relatively new phenomenon in
1917, and they were far from scientific. President Wilson and his
staff had some idea of the national mood through letters sent to the
White House, newspaper editorials, and old-fashioned word of mouth,
but they were uncertain as to how the general public would react to
policies that might require extraordinary sacrifices. It was one thing to
support a war in the abstract, quite another to be forced from one's
home and sent overseas to fight and possibly die in a foreign country.
Before America entered the war, one of the most popular songs in the
country was "I Didn't Raise My Boy to Be a Soldier" along with Irving
Berlin's "Stay Down Here Where You Belong," in which the devil
exhorts his son not to venture up to the war-torn earth, a true hell.

On April 13, 1917, President Wilson created the Committee on
Public Information (CPI), the most far-reaching and powerful propaganda campaign in American history to that point. Wilson put George
Creel, a former police commissioner and newspaperman who had
backed the president's reelection campaign, in charge of the agency.
Creel denied that his purpose was to spread propaganda. He claimed he
wished to advance positive messages that would support the war effort
and bolster the nation's morale. The CPI published its own daily newspaper, produced three feature films (*Pershing's Crusaders*, released in

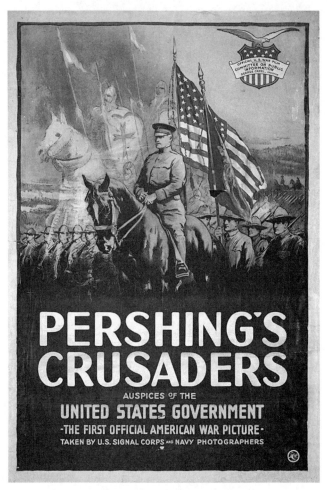

*Official poster for the first movie produced by the
Committee on Public Information.*

May 1918, was the first), and designed more than fourteen hundred
buttons, cartoons, and posters. But whatever else the CPI did, it, along
with several self-described patriotic organizations such as the American
Defense Society and the National Security League, enflamed anti-
German hysteria throughout the country.

Libraries banned and burned German books. Schools stopped teaching the German language. Words that even hinted of anything

Germanic were renamed. Sauerkraut and hamburgers became "liberty cabbage" and "liberty sandwiches." Dachshunds were referred to as "liberty dogs." Even German measles were preposterously renamed "liberty measles." Germania, Iowa, changed its name to Lakota; New Germany, Minnesota, became Motordale; Germantown and Berlin, both in Nebraska, changed to Garland and Otoe, respectively; and Ohio's New Berlin became North Canton. And countless men and women with German last names also altered them to look and sound more American.

Orchestras stopped playing works by Richard Wagner and other German composers, and the conductor of the Boston Symphony Orchestra, Karl Muck, was arrested because he had apparently refused to play "The Star-Spangled Banner" during a concert in Rhode Island. Muck was born in Switzerland, not Germany, as some reports stated, and he wasn't responsible for the playlist; Henry Lee Higginson, the BSO's founder and main financier, chose what songs were to be performed. (Higginson wasn't opposed to the national anthem. He merely felt it didn't fit in with the concert's classical-music theme.) Higginson tried to defend Muck, but the fifty-seven-year-old conductor was sent to an internment camp at Fort Oglethorpe, Georgia, for people accused of being traitors or spies.

Vigilante mobs also targeted individuals based on hearsay or the slimmest of evidence. Robert Prager was a German-born coal miner who had moved to Collinsville, Illinois, where he was quickly suspected of being un-American based on his accent and an abrasive, antisocial personality. (Prager actually considered himself extremely patriotic and had tried to enlist in the U.S. Navy but was rejected for being blind in one eye.) Local police locked him up one evening, for his own protection, after a group of coal miners went to his house and confronted him. When word got out that "a German spy" was in the local jailhouse, a crowd forced their way inside, and then half carried and half dragged Prager a mile outside Collinsville to an area known as Mauer Heights. Three hundred townspeople watched as members of the mob strung a noose around Prager's neck, threw the rope over a thick tree branch ten feet off the ground, and hoisted Prager up into the air until he was strangled to death. Eleven men were arrested for the murder, but the trial was a farce and they were all acquitted after the jury deliberated for less than an hour. "The city does not miss him," the editor of the *Collinsville Herald* said of Prager. "The lesson of his death has had a wholesome effect on the Germanists of Collinsville and the rest of the nation." Even major papers far from Collinsville endorsed what the mob had done. "In spite of excesses such as lynching," the *Washington Post* commented, "it is a healthful and wholesome awakening in the interior of the country."

President Wilson didn't condone the killing of Robert Prager, but he didn't speak out against it, either. Wilson's top priority was building an army. Initially he had hoped that enough young men would volunteer to serve without the government having to institute a draft, but after six weeks, only seventy thousand people had signed up, and at least a million were needed.

At the urging of Secretary of War Newton Baker, Wilson put forward the Selective Service Act of 1917, requiring all males ages twenty-one to thirty to register for the military. A key component of the bill was that, unlike in the Civil War, a draftee could not purchase his way out of service. Riots had broken out in New York City during the summer of 1863, when unemployed and low-income workers learned that the rich could pay a "commutation fee" of about $300 and avoid becoming a soldier.

Wilson signed the Selective Service Act into law on May 18, 1917. Although the vote had passed by overwhelming majorities in Congress, it was not without its critics. "I protest with all my heart and mind and soul against having the slur of being a conscript placed upon any men of Missouri," said Speaker of the House Champ Clark, from the Show Me state. "In the estimation of Missourians there is precious little difference between a conscript and a convict." Another House member stated that the draft would be counterproductive, creating a "sulky, unwilling, indifferent army." And indeed some tried to run off to

Canada, and the Canadian government eventually closed its border to any draft-age American. Others thought that a quick marriage would make them ineligible. It did not; the law exempted only men who were married before April 6, 1917, the day Congress declared war, and even then the selectee had to prove that his wife and family were dependent on him. Overall, hundreds of thousands of young men refused to register.

"It was a great day when we went to War with the Imperial German Government," Maury Maverick recalled sarcastically after heading off to train to be a machine gunner with the 157th (1st Colorado) Infantry Division.

> The statements of the President and Congress said that we were going to war with the German Government—*Imperial Government*—and not the people of Germany. It was very consoling, indeed, to know that we were merely fighting Imperialism, and that when we killed a German we were only taking a pot-shot at the Government. Also, when we died we could feel that we had not been killed by the German people, but by the Imperial German Government. In that way, we could *requiescat in pace*—that is, lie easy in our graves.

Maverick's name was literally synonymous with obstinate, independent-minded thinking. The twenty-two-year-old recruit from San Antonio, Texas, was the grandson of the rancher Sam Maverick, who stubbornly refused to brand his cows, and the word "maverick" became associated with anyone who went his or her own way regardless of rules or popular opinion.

Apparently some of his ancestor's blood coursed through Maury Maverick's veins, as he frequently questioned authority and had an irreverent streak.

"Tons of propaganda rolled in from Washington," Maverick noted after he enlisted. "I had not then heard of George Creel, but it was

George's stuff, and it dripped with nobility of phrase, and fine patriotic sentiments. We were ordered to digest it, and then make flaming speeches to our troops."

Maverick was referring to George Creel's Four-Minute Men, seventy-five thousand in all, who came from various backgrounds and lines of work—business, education, law, ministry—and gave short, patriotic pep talks, mostly at movie houses throughout the United States, where the speakers had a captive audience. (Creel kept their speeches to four minutes because he figured that was about the attention span of his listeners, and it was also the time it took a projectionist to change a film reel.)

Maverick's commanding officer, Colonel Rice Means, ordered Maverick to become a Four-Minute Man himself and fire up the regiment's troops. For Maverick, there were just two small problems. First,

Maury Maverick.

most of his soldiers were Mexican Americans who couldn't speak English. And second, Maverick's heart just wasn't in it. "I did not pretend to know the cause of the war myself," he said. "In fact, I very well knew that we had no business in the war, and I had no personal interest in it."

Maverick called in another lieutenant, Boley Brush, and instructed him to give the speech. Brush seemed even less enthused than Maverick, and asked him what he was supposed to say. Maverick told him to emphasize that "we are fighting to make the world safe for democracy, as Colonel Means said."

"That ain't so," Brush retorted.

"What?" exclaimed Maverick, feigning outrage. "Do you mean to tell me that we are not fighting for democracy and freedom? For liberty?"

Not realizing that Maverick was playing with him, Brush answered sincerely. "J. P. Morgan caused this war," he said, referring to the financial tycoon who had loaned the British and French millions of dollars to support their economies in the early years of the war. "It's enough that I join the army to fight for my country without me lying to a bunch of Mexicans from New Mexico and my own friends from Colorado. I ain't going to make any speech; I am for my country, all right, but I ain't going to lie—we are a bunch of collectors, that's what we are." And with that, Brush walked away, leaving Maverick to give the speech himself.

Instead of expressing his true beliefs, Maverick decided to ham it up and make the most rousing "speech on patriotism as no American ever heard before." And which no member of his Spanish-speaking men would understand anyway.

"I told them about Nathan Hale regretting that he could die only once for his country. . . . I told them of the men who suffered in Valley Forge," he said. Maverick was ultimately quite satisfied with his performance, and stated, "I was proceeding at a great rate and was on the verge of weeping at my own oratory."

Realizing that Colonel Means might quiz the men on what they had been told, Maverick repeated—by his estimation—*twenty times* that America had gone to war "to make the world safe for democracy."

It didn't stick.

When Maverick asked Pedro Salazar, one of the men who he thought knew at least some English, why they were going to war, Maverick prayed that he would provide an enthusiastic answer that would "inspire all of [his] men to go forth in battle, and plant the Stars and Stripes on the Kaiser's front yard."

Instead, Salazar very timidly replied that the "draft board, he send me here."

Whatever skepticism Maverick and other men might have felt, overall the Selective Service Act was a resounding success; by June 5— less than three weeks after it was enacted—more than nine million men had signed up. And some of the inductees who could have legitimately obtained a deferment became gung ho to fight. One of them was a debt-ridden farmer from Missouri who was struggling to run an oil business, Morgan & Co., in Kansas City, after having been unable to strike it rich mining for zinc and lead.

"I seem to have a grand and admirable ability for calling tails when heads come up," Harry S. Truman lamented to his fiancée, Elizabeth "Bess" Wallace in late May 1917. No matter how hard he tried, he just couldn't catch a break. "[I worked], really did, like thunder for ten years to get that old farm in line for some big production. Have it in shape and have had a crop failure every year. Thought I'd change my luck, got a mine, and see what I did get."

Although discouraged professionally, Truman went on to emphasize in the same letter that his relationship to Wallace was what kept his spirits aloft. "I'm the luckiest guy in the world to have you to love," he wrote, "and to know that when I've arrived at a sensible solution of these direful financial difficulties I've gotten into, that I'll have the finest, best-looking, and all the other adjectives in the superlative girl in the world to make the happiest home in the world with." And Truman had quite a home in mind (two, actually). He'd told Wallace only months earlier that he'd fantasized about living a life of luxury, with a house in the city and one in the country, several automobiles, his own airplane, and even a yacht, with her by his side "to boss the whole layout."

Truman did not immediately enlist after April 6, for both business and personal reasons. At the age of thirty-three, he was two years past the military's desired age range, and there was the not-so-minor factor that he was essentially blind without his glasses, with 20/50 vision in his right eye and 20/400 in his left. Also, the oil company was conceivably beneficial to the war effort, since the military relied on a steady supply of petroleum products. Ultimately, though, Truman couldn't turn a profit, and he returned to the family farm. (Truman's luck was even worse than he had thought; one of the fields that Morgan & Co. had explored and abandoned later proved to be worth millions of dollars; Truman's company simply hadn't drilled down deep enough.)

Truman had been fascinated by the military since he was a small boy. He devoured books about warfare and had applied to West Point when he was eighteen but was rejected because of his eyesight. Just after his twenty-first birthday, in May 1905, when, in his own words, he "could do as I pleased," he joined Missouri's National Guard and trained in a light artillery unit.

Truman finally decided to forgo his dreams of wealth and grandeur and reenlisted in the Missouri National Guard. On the evening of July 14, 1917, he attended a regimental banquet in Kansas City, where the seriousness of his decision hit him for the first time. Two of their senior officers, Colonels Karl Klemm and Arthur Elliott, sternly reminded the men what they had truly committed themselves to by signing up. "According to [Klemm and Elliott]," Truman wrote to Wallace later that night, "we have placed ourselves on a position of placing the American Government above everything, even our lives. . . . If we are ordered to Berlin, go we must—or be buried on the way."

On September 25, Truman shipped out to Fort Sill in Oklahoma. The send-off was so rushed that he didn't even have a chance to see or call Wallace, but he mailed her a few hastily written postcards from the train. Wallace had suggested that they get married before he left, but Truman was opposed to the idea, for her sake. He didn't want her to be tied to either a "cripple" or a "sentiment," should he be wounded or killed. He assured her that he would remain as faithful as a husband to her while away, even if she wanted to date other men, although he conceded that he would be "jealous as the mischief" if she did.

At Fort Sill, Truman's work ethic and organizational abilities quickly earned him a stellar reputation among enlisted men and officers alike. Truman excelled, it turned out, at running the canteen. His profits were so impressive (he made $3,000 in one week alone) that his superiors grew suspicious and ordered a thorough review of his sales. The auditing committee reported back that Truman's numbers were real: he had the most lucrative and cleanest canteen on base.

Truman did admit to Wallace that he was so desperate to hear from her that when the post office boy brought him one of her letters or packages, Truman let the kid take all the candy, apples, and soda pop he wanted. He begged Wallace to write to him more frequently.

Truman's real focus, however, was on learning artillery warfare. Throughout the fall and winter, he began drilling with 75mm guns. "We are working almost night and day to perfect our regiment," Truman reported to Wallace. "They are weeding out incompetent officers and men [so] I may get sent home yet." Truman also wrote that if he was booted out for ineptitude, at least he could return home "with a clear conscience." Then he immediately added: "I'd rather be shot though."

Eight days later, a British colonel who had served on the Western Front gave a speech at Fort Sill that profoundly affected Truman. "He made us all want to brace up and go to it with renewed energy," Truman told Wallace in his most impassioned defense of why he felt obligated to serve.

> He made us feel like we were fighting for you and mother earth and I am of the same belief I wouldn't be left out of the

greatest history-making epoch the world has ever seen for all there is to live for because there'd be nothing to live for under German control. When we come home a victorious army we can hold our heads up in the greatest old country on earth and make up for lost time by really living. Don't you think that would be better than to miss out entirely?

Catching himself aware that this might come across as bluster, Truman suggested that this letter should just be set on fire in "the kitchen stove." He ended it, as always, by expressing his deep love for Wallace and his desire to get back to her as quickly as possible.

Truman and his men were transferred to Camp Merritt, New Jersey, and rumors of their imminent departure to France came almost daily. Although the men weren't given the chance to return home to say good-bye to their loved ones, they did receive a short leave to New York City. It was Truman's first visit to Manhattan, and he was decidedly not a fan. "We went to the Winter Garden Sunday night and saw the rottenest vaudeville show I ever saw or ever hope to see," Truman wrote to Wallace. "It couldn't even play at the Globe and get by in Kansas City. New York is a very much overrated burg. It merely keeps its rep by its press agents' continually harping on the wonder of it. There isn't a town west of the Mississippi of any size that can't show you a better time."

Truman also went into Manhattan not to sightsee but to acquire several backup pairs of eyeglasses for his deployment. He was furious to realize that, based on a very reasonable price an optician there gave him, his eye doctor back home had been bilking him all along. Truman complained to Wallace:

> I accidently ran into an honest optician who happened to belong to my goat tribe (ie Scottish Rite) and he sent me to the best or one of the best oculists in the city. He gave me a complete and thorough examination a prescription I can use

Harry S. Truman.

in Paris or Vienna and lots of good conversation all for the whole sum of $5.00 and then he asked me if I thought I could stand that. How is that for the crookedest town in the universe? Then the optician who also gave me lots of good advice only charged me $17.50 less 10% for two complete pairs of regulation aluminum frames and glasses, throwing in an extra lens that he happened to chip on the edge in the grinding. I can't understand it. Watts stung me for $22.00 for two pairs and Dr. Leonard charged me $10.00 the last time I bought any and they were supposed to be friends of mine, too. This place is on Madison Ave. just off 42nd St. and I

know he pays more rent for a week than Watts does for a
month. Evidently these men are patriotic even if one of them
is named Haustettee.

Because he had a drastically uneven prescription, Truman needed
special lenses that could be worn without frames, with just a nose clip.
Although less stable, the pince-nez glasses were essential because they
could be used with a gas mask. Truman ended up packing a total of six
pairs.

Truman sent off one last letter to Wallace before sailing to Europe
from Hoboken, New Jersey, where the main port of embarkation was
located—and the port that troops hoped to return to if they survived
the war. "[I was] kept here until nearly two o'clock reading orders and
instructions as to how we must act, what we must say and not say when
we arrive in General Pershing's jurisdiction," he wrote. "About all we
can write is 'I am well if you are well it is well,' and if we were to put
that down S.V.B.E.V. they'd destroy the letter and probably hang us for
spies." (Truman missed an E, but he was abbreviating the Latin phrase
Si Vales, Bene Est. Ego Valeo.) He ended with a cheerful boast: "I am
hoping to cable you from Berlin soon."

9.

Under the Gun

Twelve of our men were taken prisoners and three were
killed and two wounded. Some one told us that the
Germans came two hundred strong in the night and got
them. . . . The German prisoner, captured by the Americans, was nearly stripped of his clothes for souvenirs, and
when they were amputating his arm, he bravely asked
if they wanted that, too!

—*American ambulance driver Amy Owen Bradley,*
describing in a letter home the first combat action
of the war between AEF and German troops

O N SEPTEMBER 6, 1917, Pershing settled into his new headquarters in Chaumont, a bucolic town that gave, in Pershing's
words, "relief from the depression of Paris," 170 miles to its west, where
almost every woman wore black mourning and disabled soldiers hobbled
around begging for food. Chaumont was located along a major railway
connected to southern ports such as Saint-Nazaire, vital nodes for incoming American troops and supplies. The French were concentrated
more in central France, to protect Paris, and the British were in the
north, by the English Channel. Chaumont was also closer to the German
lines. Pershing believed there were intelligence and communication ad-
vantages to being as near to the enemy as possible, within reason.

From the moment he arrived, Pershing was inundated with meetings and ceremonial duties. The local commanding general hosted a welcoming luncheon that included city officials and their families. Pershing was especially taken by the general's blond-haired daughter, "a beautiful child of six," he wrote, who no doubt reminded him of his own lost golden little girls. Pershing tried chatting with her in French, but she didn't respond. After several more attempts, he finally asked, "*Comprenez-vous?*" With unabashed frankness, she told him, "*Non.*" Pershing's language skills apparently hadn't improved much since his West Point days.

On September 10, Secretary of War Newton Baker wired Pershing a confidential cable:

> I am especially concerned that our troops should not be engaged in actual fighting in France until they are there in such numbers and have made such thorough preparation that their first appearance will be encouraging both to their own morale and to the spirit of our people here. I think it goes without saying that the Germans will make a very special effort to strike swiftly and strongly against any part of the line which we undertake to defend, in order to be able to report to their people encouragingly about our participation and also with the object of discouraging our soldiers and our people as much as possible. I have no doubt that this has all been present to your mind.

Pershing hardly thought of anything else. Every decision he made, every problem he had to overcome, related to training and supplying his troops. And he was keenly aware of public relations as well. American journalists in the States and those writing dispatches from Europe were almost unanimous in their desire to promote the heroism and sacrifices of AEF soldiers and Marines.

Three days before Baker's cable, German warplanes bombed a field hospital, blowing to pieces a twenty-seven-year-old doctor from Kansas City, Kansas, named William T. Fitzsimons. Although not a combatant, Fitzsimons was the first AEF fatality of the war. By coincidence, former president Theodore Roosevelt was a contributing editor to the main newspaper in Kansas City (*The Star*), and Roosevelt used his death to honor the doctor's humanity and demonize Germany. Roosevelt wrote:

> There is sometimes a symbolic significance to the first death in a war. It is so in this case. To the mother he leaves, the personal grief must in some degree be relieved by the pride in the fine and gallant life which has been crowned by the great sacrifice. We, his fellow countrymen, share this pride and sympathize with this sorrow. . . .
>
> As part of her deliberate policy of frightfulness, [Germany] has carried on a systematic campaign of murder against hospitals and hospital ships. The first American to die in our army was killed in one of these typical raids. We should feel stern indignation against Germany for the brutality of which this was merely one among innumerable instances. . . .
>
> We are in the eighth month since Germany went to war against us; and we are still only at the receiving end of the game. We have not in France a single man on the fighting line. The first American killed was a doctor. No German soldier is yet in jeopardy from anything we have done.

Roosevelt's impatience was felt by many, none more so than the man responsible for putting Americans onto that fighting line. This was Pershing's predicament; he, his officers, his troops, the French, the British, and all the other allies were pushing for action. But the men weren't ready.

Part of the problem concerned supplies. Pershing was especially irritated by the confusion in the States when it came to sending over provisions. Ships weren't being filled to capacity. Items were broken due to careless packing. And many supplies seem to have been selected by an "antiquated desk soldier long since retired," Pershing wrote. In one testy cable, he instructed the War Department to *stop* sending over floor wax, lawn mowers, bathtubs, window shades, and spittoons, which were absolutely unnecessary, and expedite the shipment of winter clothing, weapons, and similar matériel. (One of those spittoons did, for the record, end up in Pershing's office.)

There was also a problem on the receiving end. Pershing had complained to the War Department that U.S. troops were pressed into service unloading cargo at the ports in southern France when these men needed to be preparing for combat. The French had lent them "a few prisoners and some women," Pershing noted, but that was hardly satisfactory, and the docks were at risk of becoming "hopelessly congested" without the stevedores he had requested.

As confident as Pershing was in the fighting spirit of the AEF troops, they were untested. How they performed under fire for the first time would, as Secretary Baker reminded him, influence the faith the other Allied commanders had in him, and in whether the Americans could turn the tide of the war.

Ideally, each division would undergo at least three stages of training before engaging in any large-scale action. The first consisted of military basics, from digging foxholes to shooting a gun. Everyone, not only infantrymen, Pershing insisted, had to be proficient in using their rifles, including their bayonets.

Troops then moved on to learning their specialty skills. Artillerymen learned how to target mortars. Signal corps soldiers were shown how to lay telephone wires and establish other forms of communications between units and their commanders. Even a weapon as seemingly simple as a grenade required extensive instruction. Americans, raised on playing baseball, assumed it should be thrown overhand, like a pitch. But the Brits recommended an underhand method, based on how a cricket player would toss a ball. The trick was to give it a bit of an arc, so it would more likely drop into the narrow slit of a trench. The grenades were notoriously temperamental, and it was unnerving just to hold one; they were timed to explode after five seconds, but some detonated within three. If it was thrown too quickly, however, the enemy might have a chance to fling it back.

Having already been paraded before cheering citizens and military officials after they had arrived in Paris in early July 1917, 1st Division—the only division the United States had in France—was frequently put on display during its training period throughout September and October in Gondrecourt, thirty-seven miles north of Chaumont. French officers were getting anxious. The Americans were training too slowly, they felt, and weren't focusing on trench warfare. They continued to plead that the soldiers be scattered into French regiments to replace their casualties, and Pershing still refused. The Americans would fight together, and they would be taught what Pershing referred to as "open warfare," a more offensive approach to battle, rather than hunkering down in trenches and endlessly firing shells at the enemy while trying to avoid incoming artillery.

Pershing frequently visited 1st Division in Gondrecourt to see how it was progressing, and he was as anxious about its readiness as anyone. He had never been close with its commanding general, William Sibert, though they had attended West Point together. Sibert was a skilled engineer who had helped build the Panama Canal, but he had never led men in combat. He had been assigned to 1st Division before the war only because he happened to be one of the highest ranking generals in the Army. It was an appointment due more to seniority than to merit.

When Pershing visited Gondrecourt on October 3, the men demonstrated for him a new tactical maneuver that Major Theodore Roosevelt Jr., the former president's thirty-year-old son, had devised to overtake entrenched forces. Pershing asked Sibert what he thought of the exercise, and Sibert gave a vague, fumbling reply. Pershing exploded. He tore into Sibert for his uninspiring leadership and blamed him for the division's overall lack of preparation and professionalism. Deeply humiliated in front of his troops, Sibert was shocked into silence. But his chief of staff, Captain George Marshall, was so enraged by Pershing's censure and the demeaning way it was conducted that he grabbed the AEF commander's shoulder as he was walking away and blurted out, "General Pershing, there's something to be said here, and I think I should say it because I've been here longest."

Before anyone could stop him, Marshall unleashed a torrent of grievances. He railed at Pershing for how poorly the men were clothed and equipped, some without even shoes, and their insufferable living conditions, spread out as they were in unventilated barns and haylofts. He concluded by saying that all of these problems were more the fault of upper command than of General Sibert.

Pershing glared at Marshall and said only, "Well, you must appreciate the troubles we have."

"Yes, General, but we have them every day and many a day," Marshall replied, his voice still rising in anger, "and we have to solve every one of them by night."

After Marshall finished his tirade, the rest of the men stood there frozen, astonished by the confrontation they had witnessed and convinced that Marshall had just ended his military career.

But Pershing said nothing. He walked briskly back to his waiting automobile, marked "U.S. No. 1," and returned to his headquarters.

Pershing made no mention of the clash with Marshall in his private diary, but the next day, October 4, he sent another secret cable to Secretary of War Baker:

> I am making every effort to inculcate a strong, aggressive fighting spirit among our forces, to overcome a more or less perfunctory attitude engendered by years of peace. I hope you will permit me to speak very frankly and quite confidentially, but I fear that we have some general officers who have neither the experience, the energy, nor the aggressive spirit to prepare their units or handle them under battle conditions as they exist to-day.

Number one on Pershing's enclosed list of generals to be relieved of command was General Sibert.

Pershing paid another visit to Gondrecourt three days later, on

George Marshall.

October 7, and sought out the brash young captain named Marshall. His intention was not to demote or even reprimand him, even if Marshall's verbal broadside bordered on insubordination. Pershing was impressed with Marshall's candor and grasp of details, and Pershing could certainly empathize with the pressures Marshall was under, although Pershing's were exponentially more complex and demanding. Pershing recognized that at the very least he could count on Marshall for unvarnished reports of how the 1st Division was functioning and what assistance it needed. The 1st Division had been nicknamed Pershing's Pets because it had been formed out of the Punitive Expedition in Mexico, and he admittedly had a special fondness for its soldiers. He also knew they were about to be the first Americans sent to the front.

ALONG WITH ALL of the professional demands on Pershing's time, the general's personal life was proving to be complicated as well. In the middle of October, Pershing received a letter from Anne Patton, written from California:

> It is just at the hour of dark when all the world seems to bow
> its head in prayer. If you were only here we would go out
> onto the porch and watch daylight fade, but because you are
> so far away I do not go alone. It would make me sad. The
> hurt of our parting would be too severe.
>
> It was a Sunday evening when we kissed good-bye. So
> many weeks have gone since then. All kinds of things have
> happened. For you many wonderful things, experiences that
> have marked epochs in world's history. But in it all our love
> has lain warm in our hearts. Just think if you had gone away
> before you asked me if I loved you. Unspoken love is such a
> feeble thing, a prey to so many doubts and fears. I thank God
> that He let us have those unforgettable weeks, that we could
> see each other and kiss away each other's tears before we
> parted.

Anne soon realized, both from the tone of his response and the scarcity of letters, that Pershing was drifting from her. "Darling John," she wrote several weeks later, "you seem very far away tonight, and detached from me. It is such ages since I heard from you. I feel as if you were a part almost of another existence. I do not like to feel this way."

Anne was unaware that Pershing was already falling for someone else, a Romanian-born twenty-three-year-old living in Paris named Micheline Resco. Pershing had been introduced to her in June, three months before he moved out to Chaumont. A talented artist, she had met the general at a cocktail party and asked him if she could paint his portrait. He immediately agreed, and the two began to spend many private hours together.

His first letter to her was written on August 29. Resco had

apparently been sick, and he jotted off a quick note in French to let her know that he was thinking of her. (His misspelling of the word *mademoiselle* is in the original letter.)

> Madamoiselle, As I do not have the pleasure to see you
> today, I hope you are not suffering too much, which I would
> truly regret. Please accept, Madamoiselle, my respectful
> esteem and all my wishes for your speedy recovery.
>
> *JJ Pershing.*

Pershing had to be discreet about seeing Resco. At first he told his chauffeur and other staff members that he was visiting her to sit for his portrait. Eventually he started telling them that she was teaching him French, which was, no doubt, at least partially true.

Though he continued to use the more formal *vous*, rather than *tu*, when he addressed her, Pershing was falling deeply in love with Resco. "My dear Micheline," he wrote on September 5, before departing for Chaumont,

> Truly, today I am very very sad when I think that I cannot see
> you for many days. In fact it makes me feel ill. You are my
> dearest, isn't it so? And your courage and devotion to high ideas
> of propriety have given me only the greatest respect for you.
>
> Now I am all alone and truly nothing could make me more
> happy than to see you again. But I must wait with patience for
> the day when that happens. I care for you very much,
>
> *Your friend, J*

Pershing added a postscript: "This letter is for you only and in total confidence."

Pershing was mindful of another relationship in his personal life— being an attentive and caring father to his eight-year-old son, Warren. He frequently wrote to Warren in Nebraska, where the boy was being raised by Pershing's sister, May.

My dear Warren,

I have just had a very pretty horseback ride along the Marne.
It is a beautiful river and has a canal along its entire course.
The banks of the canal are level and grassy and, usually, lined
with trees. This morning I rode along the banks for about
two miles and came to a point where the canal runs across
the river and into a tunnel through a mountain. The bridge
that carries the canal is very deep of course and is made of
iron. I thought you would be interested to know about this.

I have a very good horse, a bay. He has a splendid trot, a
nice canter, and gallops well when you want him to. The only
thing that was lacking this morning in making my ride a
complete joy was that you were not here to go with me. I often
wish you were with me when I see beautiful things as I travel
about the country. I would also like to have you with me
always under all circumstances. I especially miss you at night.

I am just dictating this short note while I am eating
breakfast, so good-bye. Write me very often.

With much love, Papa.

Warren also spent time with Senator and Mrs. Warren, who lived
in Wyoming, and in late October he sent the following to his father:

Dear Papa,

I was at Cheyenne a week ago and had a fine visit with
Grandpa we drove out over the ranches a great deal I did not
get behind in school I went to Billie's birthday party to-day
and saw you in the pic-tures at the Orpheum they were fine. I
think of you so much and would like to see you with all my
love Warren.

Pershing's letters to Warren were for the most part tender and lov-
ing, but the notoriously tough general didn't hesitate to gently scold his
old son if he felt it was necessary.

Warren's handwritten letter to his father.

My dear Warren,

Your dear letter of October 27th came with Aunt Bess' and I
am more than pleased that you had such a satisfactory and
delightful visit with your grand-pa, and that you had a chance
to see the ranches and ride the ponies again.

I wish that I could see you in reality instead of looking at
you when out in the audience as I appear in the moving
pictures. You know I have not seen many of these moving
pictures myself and have often wondered just how good
they were.

Very confidentially, I am going to whisper this to
you: please be a little more careful in writing your letters

and be sure that you spell them out so they can be
plainly read.

    With many kisses and much love, I am

    Affectionately yours,

Papa

BY MID-OCTOBER 1917, the 1st Division had been moved to Sommerviller, fifty miles east of Gondrecourt, to be put in actual trenches
for the first time. Sommerviller had specifically been selected because
it *wasn't* very active. The French and German troops there had essentially come to an understanding that it was in nobody's interest to run
around trying to kill one another. Every so often their artillerymen
would fire a shell, to keep their superiors happy, but they mostly hit
empty fields or some faraway spot in no-man's-land. The Americans
were deployed to this quiet sector to ease them into combat by giving
them at least a general idea of trench life.

    For some it was too quiet. "The first thrill of service in the trenches
soon passed with a realization of the mud and other discomforts and the
dearth of excitement," George Marshall later grumbled about the experience. But every few days, there was enough activity to enable the
1st Division to rack up a series of "firsts."

    A few minutes after 6:00 a.m. on October 23, Sergeant Alex Arch of
Battery C, positioned just to the east of Sommerviller, fired the first
American artillery shot of the war at the German guns less than two
miles behind their trenches. (A war reporter who had talked his way
into the 1st Division's company of four artillery batteries retrieved the
shell casing and held on to it for Sergeant Arch.)

    Four days later, the AEF captured its first prisoner, a twenty-year-old
German named Leonard Hoffman. Hoffman had wandered off too far
from his own line and was spotted and shot. American soldiers took
him to a field hospital, but he couldn't be saved and was dead by the
next morning. The medics who had tried to keep him alive later came

to the macabre realization that they hadn't recorded the event for history. Hoffman's body was placed back on the operating table and posed to make it look as if he were being treated, and the doctors all stood around him with their surgical masks on as a photographer snapped a picture for posterity.

On October 28, Lieutenant D. H. Harden earned the distinction of being the first AEF officer wounded, after a shell fragment struck his knee. Major Theodore Roosevelt Jr., every bit his father's son, rushed over to Harden and, although envious that he hadn't been the first to be injured, congratulated Harden on his "achievement."

While replacing the 1st Battalion of the 16th Infantry after their ten-day stint, the incoming 2nd Battalion was told that the area was essentially peaceful. "I shot six Germans sneaking up on me one night," a private named Quincy Mills recalled, "and when daylight came they were all the same [tree] stump."

During the predawn hours of November 3, all that changed. A heavy rain was falling and, with dark clouds shutting out the moonlight, the night was pitch black. A platoon of nearly fifty men, all from 1st Division's Company F, were in the most forward section of trenches, approximately five hundred yards from enemy lines.

At precisely 3:00 a.m., the Germans commenced an artillery barrage that lasted for forty-five minutes. Company F's platoon was boxed in by shell fire, preventing them from retreating or moving forward. The trapped platoon watched in horror as out of the swirling smoke came hundreds of charging Germans. Many of them had crawled up to the wire during the shelling and were virtually on top of the Americans. The AEF machine gunners opened up on the advancing troops, but they were coming at them from every direction and soon the Americans were outflanked on all sides.

The sudden onslaught of German soldiers caused confusion; some Americans assumed the hulking figures running by them were other AEF troops and let their guard down. Corporal James Gresham came face-to-face with a soldier who asked him in perfect English, "Who are you?"

Gresham replied, "I'm an American, too, don't shoot!" The German instantly fired a bullet into Gresham's head.

Private Merle Hay was also killed by a man he assumed was an American. And Private Thomas Enright was found the next morning bayoneted so forcefully through the neck that he was nearly decapitated.

Along with killing Gresham, Hay, and Enright, the Germans wounded several AEF soldiers and took eleven more as prisoners. The raid lasted for only fifteen minutes, but nearly half of the men in Company F's platoon were casualties of the German assault. The French soldiers there had never before been hit with such a massive barrage—several thousand shells fired in less than an hour.

American journalists weren't entirely certain how to cover the story. HUNS KILL 3 PERSHING MEN, a *Chicago Herald* headline blared in an eight-column banner. But in the accompanying story, the editors made it clear that in the larger scheme of things the incident was of "no particular military significance." The German press, predictably, gloated about the "American defeat."

Later in the morning after the raid, General Bordeaux and Captain Marshall walked through the trampled, shell-pocked area and into a nearby dressing station to speak with survivors and determine exactly what had happened. From the tone and content of Bordeaux's queries, Marshall was beginning to sense that the general was questioning whether the American soldiers had put up much of a resistance.

Marshall, never one to hold his tongue if he believed his men were being insulted, said in a sharp tone, "General Pershing is going to be very much interested in that reaction of a French commander to American troops." Marshall went on to remind Bordeaux that Bordeaux was the one who wouldn't allow the Americans to conduct night patrols, which is what caused them to be taken by surprise. Having had his say, Marshall informed Bordeaux that he would not be returning to headquarters with him and, turning his back on the general, bid him farewell.

Well aware of how tenuous and important relations between French and American commanders were, General Bordeaux went out of his way to make amends. He organized an elaborate military funeral to honor the three young AEF combatants killed in Sommerviller, and personally presided over the ceremony, giving an impassioned eulogy. "In the name of the Eighteenth Division, in the name of the French Army, and in the name of France, I bid farewell to Corporal Gresham, Private Enright, and Private Hay, of the Sixteenth Infantry, American Army," he proclaimed.

> These graves, the first to be dug in our national soil, at but a short distance from the enemy, are as a mark of the mighty hand of our allies, firmly clinging to the common task, confirming the will of the people and Army of the United States to fight with us to a finish. . . .
>
> Thus the death of this humble corporal and of these two private soldiers appears to us with extraordinary grandeur. We will therefore ask that the mortal remains of these young men be left here—be left to us forever. We will inscribe on their tombs: "Here lie the first soldiers of the United States Republic to fall on the soil of France for justice and liberty." The passerby will stop and uncover his head. The travelers of France, of the allied countries, of America, the men of heart who will come to visit our battlefield of Lorraine, will go out of their way to come here—to bring to these graves the tribute of their respect and of their gratefulness.
>
> Corporal Gresham, Private Enright, Private Hay: In the name of France, I thank you. God receive your souls. Farewell!

A twenty-one-gun salute shattered the reverential silence, and then the sad, soulful notes of "Taps" played out across the countryside.

Captain George Marshall, the sole senior AEF officer who attended the service, was deeply impressed with General Bordeaux's eloquence and the effort he and his men had put into paying tribute to Gresham, Enright, and Hay.

Pershing had been attending a series of high-level meetings in Paris at the time of the funeral, which had been quickly arranged, but word got back to him through Marshall about the ceremony. Pershing later wrote how touched he was by Bordeaux's "beautiful oration" and the "large number of French troops [who] also came informally to pay their final tribute. This joint homage to our dead, there under the fire of the guns, seemed to symbolize the common sacrifices our two peoples were to make in the same great cause."

Both the French and the Americans had a vested interest in sustaining a strong alliance. But whether it was in the gilded palaces where the commanding generals met and dined or in the flooded trenches in which AEF and French troops shivered side by side, tensions were beginning to surface. Regarding those "high-level" meetings that Pershing had to participate in during early November, at the end of the day he was frustrated by the lack of unity among the Allies. "The undercurrent at the moment, as nearly as could be learned, showed a continued lack of accord among the different nations," Pershing wrote. "Each nation has its own aspirations and each sought to gain some advantage over the others."

General James Harbord, Pershing's chief of staff, noted in his diary that after having spent months in France he'd come to the conclusion that the French were "the most delightful, exasperating, unreliable, trustworthy, sensitive, unsanitary, cleanly, dirty, artistic, clever and stupid people the writer has ever known." Harbord then wondered "if we do not feel as much like fighting them as we do the Germans before the war is over." Behind closed doors, French generals were grousing about their American counterparts, too.

Despite the lofty sentiments of *fraternité* and common cause that were spoken at the funeral for Gresham, Enright, and Hay, the strain between the French and American soldiers at Sommerviller manifested itself only days later. Major Theodore Roosevelt and his younger brother Archibald, also an officer in the 1st Division ("Archie" was a captain), wanted to organize a retaliatory raid. General Bordeaux and

General Sibert signed off on it, and George Marshall assisted with the planning. The Roosevelt brothers trained with French troops to assault a building in the sector they believed German patrols frequently passed through in the evening.

Archie led the small detachment of mostly French soldiers, and when they arrived at the building, they found it was empty. Archie wanted to stay, and tempers flared when the French insisted on retreating. There was also an acrimonious dispute about which direction they should go. The jolly, one-for-all-and-all-for-one band of warriors that had taken off into the night hours earlier returned disgruntled and snapping at one another.

"This was the first American raid in the World War," Marshall later noted, "and what Theodore [Roosevelt] said to me at this time about the French will not bear repeating." The grand partnership was only just beginning.

10.

Show of Force

When they got up in the morning their shoes were frozen
stiff and they had to burn paper and straw in them before
they could get them on. Men hiked with frozen feet, with
shoes so broken that their feet were in the snow; many
could be seen in wooden sabots or with their feet wrapped
in burlap. Hands got so cold and frost-bitten that the rifles
almost dropped from their fingers. . . . [But] they got on
through spirit. The tasks were impossible for mere flesh and
blood, but what flesh and blood cannot do, spirits can make
them do.

—From a January 1, 1918, diary entry by Father
Francis Patrick Duffy, chaplain for New York's
165th Infantry Regiment

ON NOVEMBER 10, 1917, exactly a week after the tragedy at
Sommerviller, a troopship named the *Tunisian* pulled into Liverpool, England, carrying members of the 1st Battalion, 165th U.S. Infantry Regiment, part of Douglas MacArthur's 42nd "Rainbow" Division. Colonel MacArthur wasn't the commander, only its chief of staff, but he had conceived of the division when President Wilson and Secretary of War Baker were debating in April 1917 how to incorporate the National Guard into the regular Army. Guard units were state

Douglas MacArthur.

militias that could be federalized during wartime or national disasters, and MacArthur proposed forming a division of guard units from different states, that would, in his words, "stretch across the country like a rainbow." He believed it should be one of the first divisions sent overseas so that, from the beginning, Americans representing every region of the country would have a stake in the fight, and their loved ones would feel a sense of national pride in their mission. In the end, twenty-six states were represented.

Heading up the 165th's 1st Battalion was Major Bill Donovan, a Wall Street lawyer with a military background and expertise in international affairs. In 1912, Donovan led a cavalry troop in the New York National Guard. In March 1916, he was brought to Europe by the State Department as part of a relief commission established to assess the extent of the refugee crisis precipitated by the war, alleviate food shortages, and bring medical attention to those in need. The man most responsible for feeding displaced Europeans was Herbert Hoover, head of the American Relief Administration. At its height, the ARA was providing nourishment to more than ten million starving people a day. Donovan sailed for England on March 14, 1916, and hit the ground running, shuttling back and forth between the warring countries to coordinate the shipment and distribution of everything from crates of powdered milk to mass quantities of clothing for impoverished refugees.

Donovan cut his trip short after General Pershing launched the Punitive Expedition in the spring of 1916. Donovan's National Guard regiment was called up, and Donovan returned to New York in July, had a brief reunion with his wife and son, and then jumped onto the first train to Texas. Donovan took over Troop I in McAllen, a town directly south of San Antonio and ten miles north of Mexico. Most of the units, including Donovan's, were there to patrol the border, and many of the soldiers grew bored and listless, playing dice, napping, and writing long letters home. Except Donovan's men. Donovan filled their hours with target practice, 25-mile hikes, and 250-mile horse rides. There was nothing he demanded of them that he wouldn't do himself. Despite the exhausting drills, their morale soared.

When war was declared in April 1917, Donovan heard that his boyhood hero Theodore Roosevelt was trying to organize a regiment to fight in France. Donovan immediately volunteered. After President Wilson rejected Roosevelt's appeal and MacArthur designated the 165th Regiment as part of the 42nd Division, Donovan joined the 42nd.

Father Francis Duffy, a Canadian-born priest who had settled in New York and built the Our Savior Church in the Bronx, volunteered to become the 165th's chaplain. Ninety-five percent of the men were Irish Catholics, and Duffy often joked that their regiment added some much-needed "green" to MacArthur's rainbow.

Duffy was impressed with Donovan from the start. At thirty-four,

William Donovan (left) and Father Francis Patrick Duffy.

Joyce Kilmer.

Donovan was almost twice the age of some recruits, and he was, as Duffy noted in his journal, "very attractive in face and manner, an athlete who always keeps himself in perfect condition. I like him for his agreeable disposition, his fine character, his alert and eager intelligence."

The 1st Battalion's voyage overseas and slog to its forward position presaged what so many other American troops would experience over the next six months, starting with the wretched passage through the Atlantic's frigid, sub-infested waters. Oliver Ames, Donovan's aide, wrote to his mother and father:

> If you ever want to appreciate your family and friends, just try a 3,000-mile trip across the ocean in a rotten little tub, a huge life preserver with you every minute, and a feeling every minute that you may have to swim for it, and the water looking oh, so cold, to say nothing of the glorious future of participating in an Allied drive in the spring which may bring you glory and martyrdom; I wonder how I'll like to be a martyr; my chief occupation on the trip has been one long attempt to persuade myself I'll like it.

Next came the journey to whatever distant patch of land the men had been assigned to. For Donovan and his soldiers, that was the village of Naives-en-Blois, in northeastern France. After a miserable night in Southampton, England, where the troops sat or tried to sleep on wooden boards in an unheated "rest" camp as their teeth chattered, the battalion was ferried across the English Channel to Le Havre, France. From there, it was a five-mile hike to a railroad station where the men were packed into French freight trains that had "40 Hommes/8 Chevaux" (forty men or eight horses) written on the side, giving them an indication as to the luxuries they could expect once they were crammed inside. No effort had been made to clean the cars after the horses had been moved out, and the men had to lay their blankets, which were already torn and frayed, on top of the urine- and manure-saturated hay. There were no latrines, and the men did their best to hold out until they stopped in a small town, where they'd all rush from the train, relieve themselves, and scurry back on board. But often they had to resort to opening the massive Pullman side doors while the train was still moving, and lean out or squat down with their naked rear ends hanging over the tracks.

After arriving in Naives-en-Blois and shaking off the rank, nauseating hay from their blankets, most of the men were ordered to billet themselves in barns and stables, which meant more wet, reeking hay.

One of Donovan's favorite soldiers, the New York poet Joyce Kilmer, recalled that it was in Naives-en-Blois that their troubles really began. Kilmer recalled:

> The hell of it was the foulup in clothing. Here we were in the Vosges Mountain area, with what was to be one of the worst winters in French history beginning, and half the men didn't have their overcoats. Can you imagine that? Hardly any of them had winter brogans [heavy boots]—many were walking around in those light shoes you'd wear in a dress parade during the summer. Why, the next thing you knew a lot of the boys had rags on their feet. And the blankets—we had lightweight summer ones.

Kilmer had already achieved some measure of fame before he volunteered for the 165th. In 1913 his poem "Trees" ("I think that I shall never see / a poem lovely as a tree . . .") was published, and although widely ridiculed by literary critics as overly simplistic and sentimental fluff, it was well received by the general public. His 1914 book *Trees and Other Poems* became one of the top-selling works of poetry in America, and he lectured and gave readings throughout the country. Kilmer, age thirty, was married and had five children. Donovan described him as having a "gentleness" about him, but Kilmer turned down a cushy officer's position as a statistician so he could serve as an enlisted man with the infantry. (The decision would eventually cost him his life; Kilmer was killed in action on July 30, 1918, by a bullet to the head.)

Donovan himself was temporarily sent to field officers' school to learn from French combat veterans about coordinating artillery barrages with infantry attacks, firing rifle grenades and mortars, and charging trenches with fixed bayonets. One simulated exercise was done in front of General Pershing. Donovan wrote to his wife, Ruth, that in person the general looked shorter than his stated six feet, had a muscular chest, but was "not so well set up in the legs." (Pershing was actually bowlegged.) Donovan admired Pershing's "snappy" attire and remarked that his "face is softer than [it seems] in his pictures, and he has not the grim expression seen in them. He looks like a real he-man."

Donovan was outwardly the more personable of the two men, but he and Pershing were similar in their physical bearing and mental outlook. Both men had a demeanor that inspired fear and admiration, and they were both despised and revered for their leadership style, drilling and pushing their men to the breaking point. And they had no patience for slackers. When Donovan returned from officers' school, he took his men on grueling marches through rain and snow. Joyce Kilmer summed up one such day of drudgery in his diary: "December 10, hiked 10 kilometers—many of the men without shoes—weather freezing. One meal, some kind of stew."

But also like Pershing, Donovan was never harder on his men than he was on himself. When Donovan led his troops on a more realistic combat exercise, in which they dashed over and across natural and man-made obstacles—rocks, trees, ravines, coils of barbed wire—with full packs on their backs, he turned around and saw his men hunched over, wheezing, unable to move on.

"What's the matter with you guys?" he yelled. "I've got the same fifty pounds on my back as you men, and I'm ten years older."

On December 29, 1917, Donovan and his battalion were transferred from Naives-en-Blois to Longeau, where they received advanced training in trench warfare. Upon reaching the town, Donovan was informed that he had performed so well at the field officers' school that he had earned a promotion. This also meant, however, that he would be separated from his men and sent to another officers' school. Donovan of all people knew that orders had to be obeyed, but he had established a tight bond with his troops and wanted to lead them into combat.

Donovan rushed to the division's headquarters to meet with Douglas MacArthur to make his case. Colonel MacArthur empathized with Donovan but explained that not even the 42nd Division's commanding general, Charles Menoher, could reverse the order. Only Pershing could do that. MacArthur thought for a moment and said, impulsively, "Let's go, Bill. Don't let them get you away from the line. Fighting men are the real soldiers."

Off they drove in MacArthur's staff car to Chaumont, more than forty miles away. Pershing was there and agreed to see them without an appointment. MacArthur laid out the argument on Donovan's behalf, and Pershing was in total agreement. He rescinded the order; Donovan could stay with his troops, thereby forfeiting a safer assignment and a promotion. Donovan couldn't have been happier.

For the next two months the 1st Battalion's training intensified, and the men were outfitted with better gear. Some items, however, pricked the battalion's sense of Irish pride. On January 23, 1918, Father Duffy noticed a commotion alongside a road and went over to see what the problem was. "Val Dowling, the supply Sergeant, picked up a uniform out of a pile and held it up," Duffy wrote in his journal. "Look at the damn thing!"

Realizing he had just sworn in front of a priest, Dowling apologized and then explained himself:

"Excuse me, Father, but you'll say as bad when you look at it. They want us to wear this."

"He held it out as if it had contagion in it, and I saw it was a British tunic, brass buttons and all," Duffy recorded in his journal. "I disappointed my audience—I didn't swear out loud. 'Got nice shiny buttons,' I said. 'What's the matter with it?' 'Didn't I know it was a *British* [emphasis added] uniform?' Dowling asked."

British boots were an exception. At least with the footwear, Duffy reasoned, his men had "the satisfaction of stamping on them."

Two and a half weeks later, it was Duffy who was put off by English influences. "I had a little clash of my own with some of these enthusiastic youngsters," Duffy wrote in his journal on February 10.

> In the British school of the bayonet they teach that the men ought to be made to curse while doing these exercises. I see neither grace nor sense in it. If a man swears in the heat of a battle I don't even say that God will forgive it; I don't believe He would notice it. But this organized blasphemy is an offense. And it is a farce—a bit of Cockney Drill Sergeant blugginess to conceal their lack of better qualities. If they used more brains in their fighting and less blood and guts they would be further on than they are.

At the end of February 1918, the 165th Regiment was marched to the French trenches near Lunéville, in what was believed to be another "quiet" sector. On March 1, Donovan's 1st Battalion made history by storming across no-man's-land and driving German soldiers from their position, marking the first permanent gain made by AEF soldiers in France, albeit a small one. Out of the fifty Americans who went forward, four were killed.

The Germans launched wave after wave of attacks over the next several days, but they were all repelled. Donovan seemed to be everywhere at once. "Actually he was the calmest man under fire I ever saw," one sergeant recalled. "Oh, you'd think he was standing at the corner of Broadway and Forty-second Street, not in the middle of a barrage."

When the 1st Battalion was rotated out of the trenches and replaced by the 2nd Battalion, Donovan stayed on to assist the commander, Major William Stacom. On the evening of March 7, Donovan and Stacom were standing inside the command post when an out-of-breath young soldier came running in to report that a German shell had exploded on top of a massive dugout in a forested area known as the Rouge Bouquet, causing the sides to cave in and burying twenty-five French and American soldiers under tons of dirt and rock. Donovan turned to Stacom, who looked paralyzed by the news. Donovan asked for permission to verify the story for himself and offer whatever help was needed.

"No," Stacom said. "Majors are not expendable."

Donovan pressed him more firmly, and Stacom relented. As Donovan rushed to the site, he tried to buck up scared young soldiers under shell fire and prepare them for further possible German attacks. Donovan noticed seventeen-year-old Eddie Kelly on guard and could tell that he was frightened out of his mind. Donovan ran over, put his arm around Kelly, and asked him if he was "going to let those damned Dutchmen get his goat?" Emboldened, Kelly grabbed his rifle a little more firmly and emphatically told Donovan that no one would get through.

Donovan was also gathering men to dig out the buried soldiers, assuming any were still alive. Suddenly one of the worst sounds a soldier could hear blared through their position; it was from the Klaxon alarms, indicating that gas had been detected. Members of the 165th's 1st Battalion were the first Americans to be gassed in the war. Men frantically grappled with their masks, which were uncomfortable, fogged up, hindered vision, and were extremely hard to breathe through, causing light-headedness and a feeling of being suffocated alive. Some men tore the masks off after only a matter of seconds, and the other soldiers watched in dismay as the poison took hold and left its victims quivering on the ground.

Donovan heard the alarm and made certain that all of the men were protected. Minutes passed, and Donovan lifted his own mask to see if the air was clear. Once he felt the situation was safe, he told the other men to take off their masks as well.

When Donovan arrived at the collapsed dugout, he was shocked to see the dead body of Eddie Kelly, the boy he had tried to bolster up on his way from the command post. Once the German barrage had begun, another officer ordered Kelly to find shelter, and as he ran toward the entrance of the dugout, the closest cover he could find, a shell fragment struck him in the head.

Seven men had already been freed by the time Donovan pulled out a small entrenching tool and began digging. The dirt kept slipping down over the walls and even threatened to bury the rescuers, but Donovan and the other men only worked more furiously. The muffled cries of one young soldier, barely alive, could be heard through the rubble. "Come on, come on, fellows!" he begged, and then he started calling out for his mother as his voice faded to silence.

Nothing could be done. The dirt and stones were packed too tightly over the men, and the diggers were at risk of getting swallowed up in it all as well.

"I wish I could give you the picture," Donovan wrote to his wife, Ruth, after it was over. "The winding stairway shattered, covering held by a few broken posts, one candle lighting our work, two young officers on the stairway tense and white and tired, and while willing to face all the personal dangers rapidly losing their nerve at the cries of the poor devils and the absolute futility and hopelessness of it all."

The French awarded Donovan the Croix de Guerre for his actions. He agreed to accept it on the condition that the sergeants and lieutenants working alongside him received the medal as well, which they did.

Within the battalion there was a discussion as to whether they should bring in the engineers to exhume the bodies from the dugout for a proper burial. Joyce Kilmer made an eloquent plea to leave them where they were, entombed together in a kind of natural vault and memorial. The other men agreed, and Father Duffy went down to bless the mass grave. Kilmer also wrote a poem about the deceased that Duffy later read at a larger service.

> *In a wood they call the Rouge Bouquet,*
> *There is a new-made grave to-day,*
> *Built by never a spade nor pick*
> *Yet covered with earth ten metres thick.*
> *There lie many fighting men,*
> *Dead in their youthful prime,*
> *Never to laugh nor love again*
> *Nor taste the Summertime.*
> *For Death came flying through the air*
> *And stopped his flight at the dugout stair,*
> *Touched his prey and left them there,*
> *Clay to clay.*
> *He hid their bodies stealthily*
> *In the soil of the land they fought to free*
> *And fled away. . . .*

TEN MILES SOUTH of the 1st Battalion, Colonel Douglas MacArthur was with three other 42nd Division battalions. Just like his protégé, Donovan, MacArthur was proving his mettle under fire. On February 20, 1918, only days before Donovan's 1st Battalion was moving into their sector near Lunéville, MacArthur was on the other side of the town with French troops under the command of General Georges de Bazelaire. Bazelaire's men were preparing for a night raid on the German lines, and MacArthur insisted on tagging along. Bazelaire discouraged the idea, explaining that it was too dangerous, which only encouraged MacArthur's persistence. "I cannot fight them if I cannot see them," MacArthur argued. Bazelaire finally acquiesced.

When MacArthur arrived at the jumping-off point, the French soldiers couldn't believe what they were seeing. MacArthur was dressed from toe to tip as if he were attending a British foxhunting followed by an outdoor cocktail party. His polished cavalry boots shone like mirrors (which wasn't exactly ideal for stealthy nighttime maneuvers), his riding breeches were perfectly pressed, and he was wearing a turtleneck sweater, with a four-foot-long scarf, knitted by his mother, fluttering around his neck like a small flag when he walked. He clasped a cigarette holder between his teeth, and his only "weapon" was a riding crop. Finding steel helmets too uncomfortable and lacking in style, he wore an ascot cap.

After daubing their faces with black mud, MacArthur and the French *poilus* crouched down and braced themselves before going over the top. The signal came—an exploding grenade—and the men lurched forward, cutting through barbed wire and crawling in and out of shell holes. They came up almost to the edge of one trench when a German guard heard them and started shooting. Although MacArthur was right next to the French soldiers, he later wrote about the brief skirmish as if he were an observer impervious to enemy weapons. MacArthur recalled:

> The alarm spread through the trench, across the front. Flares soared and machine guns rattled. Enemy artillery lay down a barrage in front of the lines, trapping the party. But the raid went on. They leaped into the trenches, and the fight was savage and merciless. Finally, a grenade, tossed into a dugout where the surviving Germans had fled, ended it. When we returned with our prisoners those veteran Frenchmen crowded around me, shaking my hand, slapping me on the back, and offering me cognac and absinthe. . . . General de Bazelaire pinned a Croix de Guerre on my tunic and kissed me on both cheeks.

High on a ridge over the trenches was General Menoher, watching the assault from a safe distance. He had no idea that his chief of staff, a full colonel, was right in the thick of it. Far from being upset, Menoher awarded MacArthur a Silver Star and told a *New York Times* reporter that he "was one of the ablest officers in the United States Army and one of the more popular."

Combat, for MacArthur, was addictive. As his distant cousin Winston Churchill famously remarked, "Nothing in life is so exhilarating as to be shot at without result." On the evening of March 8, the 42nd Division was plotting three major raids. Figuring there was no point in even trying to dissuade MacArthur, General Menoher let him join a battalion from the 168th Infantry tasked with overtaking German troops at Salient du Feys.

Zero hour was 5:05 a.m. The French were going to launch a withering barrage against the German lines, and the 168th's battalion would charge in afterward. MacArthur described the intense few minutes before racing into the storm.

> Our officers and sergeants stood poised and ready, whistles in their teeth, counting off the minutes past five. Two minutes. Three. And now five. Our roaring guns suddenly lowered sights, and laced a blanket of exploding shells just in front of our line.
>
> "All ready, Casey?" I yelled into the ear of "F" Company's battalion commander, Captain Charles J. Casey. "Okay, Colonel," he said, and the whistles blew. "Up you go," I heard his ringing voice. . . . "Don't rush or you'll get your own barrage on your neck."
>
> I went over the top as fast as I could and scrambled forward. The last was like a fiery furnace. For a dozen terrible seconds I felt they were not following me. But then, without turning around, I knew how wrong I was to have doubted for even an instant. In a moment they were around me, ahead of me, a roaring avalanche of glittering steel and cursing men. We carried the enemy position.

MacArthur was being modest. Colonels did not normally participate in frontline combat operations against entrenched enemy positions. But aside from his own thirst for action, MacArthur knew that
many of the Company F soldiers had never been under fire before, and
he wanted to set an example to spur them on. Menoher wrote in an
official commendation report that MacArthur "accompanied the assault wave of the American companies engaged with the sole view of
lending his presence where it was reassuring to the troops who were
then unaccustomed to this manner of endeavor." Menoher also bestowed on MacArthur the Distinguished Service Cross, the second-
highest military award, after the Medal of Honor.

MacArthur's flouting of military regulations nearly cost him his life
the next day. He rarely carried a gas mask with him, and on March 11,
the Germans began hurling thousands of shells loaded with mustard gas
along the American lines. MacArthur was caught up in the fumes and
had to be hospitalized. Initially it was feared that he would be blind for
the rest of his life, but after eight days of rest, the doctors removed the
bandages from his eyes and his vision had returned.

Donovan's battalion was hit even harder with mustard gas ten days
later. Father Duffy recorded in his journal how heroically the men
acted. "Harry McCoun was struck by a shell which carried away his
left hand," Duffy wrote. "He held up the stump and shouted, 'Well,
boys, there goes my left wing.'"

But an artery in McCoun's left arm had also been severed, and
although two other soldiers rushed him to a first-aid station, "where
Doctor Patten tore off his mask to operate on him, McCoun died the
next morning," Duffy related. Dr. Patten himself went blind from gas
exposure after removing his mask to try to save Harry McCoun.

THE AMERICANS DIDN'T KNOW that the barrage was the prelude to a
much larger German attack being coordinated along the Western Front
and spearheaded by General Erich Ludendorff, the German Army's

second in command, after Paul von Hindenburg. It was Ludendorff who had convinced Kaiser Wilhelm II to resume unrestricted submarine warfare, even if it drew the United States into the conflict. Ludendorff had argued that the Americans would never be able to bring enough trained soldiers to Europe to blunt a well-timed German offensive in the spring. The timing was perfect; not only was the weather warming up, but Russia, with the largest army in the world, was now out of the war: after suffering nine million casualties, the Russians overthrew their imperial government in March 1917, and by October 1917 Vladimir Lenin's Bolsheviks were in charge. On March 3, 1918, the Bolsheviks signed a treaty with Germany ending all hostilities. Ludendorff himself had attended to oversee the negotiations. A million German troops were suddenly freed up from the Eastern Front to fight in the west.

Pershing was also unaware of the German juggernaut to come, and at the same time Ludendorff was amassing his troops, Pershing found escape from the everyday pressures of war by writing letters to family members, particularly Warren, about whom he was constantly worried. "Don't you wish you had a stenographer to whom you could dictate your letters, so you would not have to write them?" Pershing began a March 19, 1918, missive to his son.

> I guess you do wish so. At least I would think so from the
> way the bad pen and the bad pencil seem to work for you. . . .
> I remember when I was a little boy I used to be just the same
> way. It is not so easy to write, but then you know how little
> boys must learn to do things well, even if it is a little hard to
> learn. And it is always better to learn when you are a little
> boy because it comes easier then when you grow up. There
> are lots of things I wish I had learned better when I was a
> little boy, as I might not have to work now.
>
> You know little boys' school days pass very quickly. They
> do not seem to pass very quickly, but the first thing you
> know they are gone, then you are a man and you cannot go

to school any more because you have to work, and may be you have a lot of other things to think about and do not get much time to study and learn to write. I think if you wrote letters oftener it would soon come quite easy for you. Try it and see.

The pictures of [you in] the little Field Marshal [uniform from Madame Joffre] came to-day. They have been a long time on the road. I do not know what happened to them, but I suppose they have been piled under a lot of other mail somewhere and probably got lost for awhile. Anyway, I think they are very good. . . . I picked out two for Madame Joffre which I shall send her probably tomorrow. Auntie May wrote me about your putting on the uniform and wearing it to school. I think that was a very nice thing to do, because all the little boys and girls now know what a real Marshal of France looks like, and they did not know it before. You cannot tell as much by looking at pictures as you can from seeing a real Marshal in a real uniform. I expect they will remember that a long time. . . .

You know a boy who has a nice uniform like that, a nice sword and cap and everything ought to be very careful about riding his wheel and not take too many chances about running into street cars, and when he sees a street car coming (and he ought to be on the lookout for them all the time) he should stop until the street car passes by. How do you suppose I knew about your running so close to a street car? I won't tell you now. I will have to tell you some other time. May be you can guess, but you must be very careful, because I would like to think of you as being careful.

You know it takes a long time for letters to reach me, and I think for that reason we must write to each other more frequently than we do. I will write you as often as I have time, and you promise to write me as often as you have time.

Of course I know little boys have to have a lot of time to play,
and I want my little boy to have lots of time to play. . . . Play
is very necessary and I am glad you like to play, as I want you
to be out of doors and grow big and strong.

I hope you got well over the measles, and am glad you
had them. You won't have to have them again, may be.

Good night, many kisses,

Papa

Pershing also dashed off that same day a handwritten letter, in
French, to Micheline Resco. "Cherie: Do you recall the very happy
days we spent during last summer?" he asked, referring to when they
first met and she painted his portrait.

Days that I could never, never forget. You, with much
composure, saying, "[It's a pleasure], when one loves the
model!" and me, saying, "and when one loves the artist!" Do
you remember such things?

Yours, J.

IN THE MEANTIME, the German Army proceeded apace, and at 4:40
a.m. on March 21, seventy-one German divisions prepared themselves
to push forward as more than 6,600 guns unleashed the largest bombardment of the entire war.

Once the Allied commanders realized the enormity of the campaign, panic ensued. Day after day, tens of thousands of German rounds
were obliterating everything in front of them, followed by masses of
rested, well-trained German soldiers.

After four days of nonstop shelling and infantry assaults, the French
and British pressured Pershing again to feed his troops into their ranks.
On the morning of March 25, General Maurice de Barescut, France's
chief of operations, was nervously pacing around the headquarters he

shared with General Henri-Philippe Pétain in the small town of Compiègne, when he encountered Colonel Paul Clark, their liaison officer to Pershing. "Go quickly to the telephone and tell your chief the situation," Barescut ordered Clark. "Urge him to give us without delay all the help he possibly can."

Clark called Chaumont and got ahold of one of Pershing's main aides, Colonel Carl Boyd, and passed on the message. Pershing was standing right there and replied that he would drive over to see Barescut and Pétain in person.

Clark hung up the phone and told him what Pershing had said.

"Mon dieu!" Barescut cried. "Why does he wait to come? Why doesn't he telephone what he will do?"

Barescut stepped into Pétain's office and explained what happened. He came out even more agitated than when he had gone in.

"Please go at once to the telephone and tell General Pershing not to come," Barescut instructed Clark. "General Pétain will likely be away and even were he here the imperative demands of the moment require his whole time and thought. He could not see anybody. Tell General Pershing very strongly not to come."

Clark called Boyd again, relayed Barescut's message as strongly as possible, waited a moment, and then recognized Pershing's voice in the background: "Tell Clark I will come to see General Pétain this afternoon."

Upon hearing this, Barescut was clearly enraged but said nothing.

Under the best of conditions, it took several hours to drive from Chaumont to Compiègne. Afternoon came and went, and Clark was asked numerous times to check in with Chaumont. The answer was always the same, "General Pershing is on his way."

Pétain delayed his dinner by an hour, but there was still no sign of Pershing.

Clark decided to wait outside in the cold simply to spare himself from the derisive looks of the French generals who were furious at Pershing for what they perceived to be his inexcusable rudeness.

By 10:30 p.m., they were apoplectic. An aide came outside and blew up in Clark's face: "Doesn't he think we want to sleep at all!? Does he not know that since March 20 we have been without sleep!? He says he's coming! You tell him not to come! He replies that he is coming! But he *doesn't* come! *Mon dieu!*"

Fifteen minutes later, Pershing's khaki-colored limousine came driving up to the door. Pershing stepped out, appearing calm and poised.

"The roads are choked with troops and trains of automobiles and refugees to such an extent that much of the time I could not make headway," he told Clark. "I am sorry to have caused any inconvenience."

Clark warned him: "They waited on dinner for you and have been very impatient for you to come."

Pershing walked inside and found Pétain looking visibly distraught. The hour was already late, and Pétain was also preoccupied with the logistics of having to move his headquarters farther away from the advancing Germans. He quickly got to the point with Pershing, showing him on a map where he wanted American troops to be spread out. Pétain gave a detailed response as to why, under the present circumstances, this was the best option. Pershing was unmoved. The two men went back and forth but ultimately left the matter unresolved.

On March 27, they met with Supreme Allied Commander General Ferdinand Foch and Georges Clemenceau, France's prime minister. During a side conversation with Foch, Pershing stated: "I have come to tell you that the American people would consider it a great honor for our troops to be engaged in the present battle. I ask you for this in their name and my own."

Foch was so stirred with emotion that he pulled Pershing into the room where Pétain and Clemenceau were having their own meeting and asked Pershing to repeat what he had just said.

He did so, and the two men beamed, thinking they had finally broken the impasse. As they would later find out, however, Pershing still had no intention of scattering his troops throughout French and British units. Pershing had only four divisions in France—the 1st, 2nd, 26th, and 42nd—and he later reiterated that he wanted them united, as a corps. He was more than willing to have them help counter the German offensive, but on his own terms. It was because of just these types of misunderstandings that, a frustrated Clemenceau stated, the Allied commanders "often parted with smiles that on both sides concealed gnashings of teeth."

Unexpectedly, the Allies were spared from a complete rout; the German firestorm had burned itself out. The artillery barrage was so destructive that supply wagons and trains couldn't keep up with their own men, giving French and British troops an opportunity to regroup and strike back. The Allies still needed American soldiers, but the threat was diminished. For the time being.

11.

Divisions

A s Pershing was sparring with his British and French counterparts over amalgamating American troops into Allied units, senior officers back in the United States were starting to challenge Pershing's decisions and authority, particularly after General Peyton March became the Army's chief of staff. Other generals were embittered by Pershing's power and felt slighted or unappreciated by him, causing the AEF commander even more headaches.

Peyton March's military career had closely paralleled Pershing's. March was a plebe, or freshman, at West Point when Pershing was a firstie, or senior. March not only fought in the Spanish-American War, he demonstrated such promise as a young officer that the real estate titan John Jacob Astor IV gave him practically a blank check to recruit troops for and command an entire artillery unit, which was known as the Astor Battery. March served in the Philippines, first as an aide to General Arthur MacArthur—Douglas's father—and then, like Pershing, as a provisional governor. Pershing and March also worked together in the War Department in Washington, D.C., when the first General Staff was established in 1903. In 1905, during the Russo-Japanese War, Pershing and March traveled to Russia together as observers. And in the Punitive Expedition, March led a field artillery regiment on the Mexican border.

Sent to France in June 1917 with the first wave of U.S. officers, March was initially assigned to the 1st Division's 1st Field Artillery Brigade. The two men weren't personally close, but Pershing respected March. Secretary of War Newton Baker was looking to appoint a new chief of staff for the Army, and Pershing let him know that, while he would prefer his friend General John Biddle (who had many of the same credentials as March but would be more loyal to Pershing), he supported March as well. "I have an idea that March would make a good executive," Pershing told Baker. "I have always had a high opinion of March and had often thought of him as timber for Chief of Staff."

Baker chose John Biddle first, partly on Pershing's advice, but the job proved too overwhelming, and Baker quickly replaced him with March. Before returning to Washington, March met with Pershing at Chaumont for a comprehensive briefing about the AEF's strengths and shortcomings as well as Pershing's own aims and priorities. March also inspected the supply headquarters, which still seemed hopelessly disorganized, and spoke with soldiers in the trenches to get a better grasp on the grunt's-eye view of the war. Pershing and March had a cordial parting, but Pershing knew of March's reputation for being domineering and hardheaded. When March left Chaumont, one of Pershing's aides turned to him and remarked, "That man is going to cause you trouble."

Pershing nodded. "I know," he said.

Their first major clash came just weeks later. Needing to fill high-ranking positions in the AEF, Pershing had cabled to Washington his list of generals he wanted confirmed by the Senate. But when Pershing saw March's revisions, which had cut his list by more than half without even conferring with Secretary Baker, he was incensed. His recommendations had always been followed, and he sent another message to March insisting that Baker be shown the first list and sign off on it.

"The American Expeditionary Forces is only a part of the American army," March fired back, scolding Pershing as if he were an ignorant child, "and whatever promotions to the grades of Major General and Brigadier General are necessary will be made . . . from the entire army. You were directed to submit recommendations as were other general officers. . . . There will be no changes in the nominations already sent to the Senate."

March was technically correct. As the chief of staff, he represented the entire Army, not just the AEF, and there were only two individuals he had to defer to, President Wilson and Secretary Baker, regardless of whether past chiefs of staff had essentially rubber-stamped whatever Pershing had requested, which they all had. Pershing, in this case, wasn't looking for a fight, so he wrote March a conciliatory response, clarifying—gently—that he was only trying to prevent untested and unqualified officers from being sent to France. With that, he let the matter rest.

Upon learning of the squabble, even Secretary Baker felt that March's tone was inappropriate. At the bottom of March's condescending reply to Pershing, Baker scribbled to himself: "An excellent illustration of the way not to send a message."

Baker had described March as an "arrogant, harsh, [and] dictatorial" tyrant who rode "rough-shod over everyone." But Baker and Pershing conceded that March got results. He cut the turnaround time for troopships nearly in half, and to the ire of the men sailing in those ships, March packed them together so tightly that every bunk was assigned to three people, forcing them to sleep in shifts. Within a month, March more than doubled the number of troops arriving in France.

Despite the seemingly infinite number of details Pershing and March had to worry about, one of their biggest spats concerned the leather strap that officers wore over their shoulder. Created in 1870 by a British colonel named Sam Browne, the strap served as a kind of suspender. Browne came up with the idea after his entire left arm had been cut off during a battle in India; the strap was easier to manage with one hand. He also thought it added extra support to pants that were often weighed down with ammunition and a sword. The Sam

Browne belt acquired a more symbolic role over the years, first in the
British Army and then with the Americans, as part of an officer's uniform, but now March wanted it done away with.

Pershing won that argument and the strap stayed, although in 1918
it was renamed a Liberty belt. (And in just about every photograph of
Pershing and March together, March isn't wearing one.)

Whatever disagreements that Pershing and March had were mostly
professional. But few generals felt—or demonstrated—more insolence
toward Pershing than Leonard Wood, the man who believed he should
have been picked to lead the American Expeditionary Forces. Wood
was more senior than Pershing, and he was a Medal of Honor recipi-
ent, which Pershing was not. But Wilson and Baker personally disliked
him and questioned whether he was healthy enough for such an enormous job: starting in 1910, Wood had been treated for a series of brain
tumors.

During the fall and winter of 1917, Secretary Baker sent more than
thirty divisional commanders to Europe so they could better understand the situation in person, instead of through media accounts or War
Department memoranda. Pershing met with all of the commanders,
and then he quietly composed a list of ten who should not be allowed
to return. Pershing handed the highly confidential report to an old
friend of his, General J. Franklin Bell, to pass on to Secretary Baker.
Since the envelope containing the message was sealed, Bell was unaware that he was one of the ten that Pershing deemed unqualified.
Insensitive as it might have seemed, Pershing was sending an implicit
message to Baker that, when it came to wartime commanders, he
wasn't playing favorites.

Among the generals who traveled to France and England was Leonard Wood. Wood was highly opinionated and couldn't contain himself.
In meeting after meeting with British and French officials, he denigrated
the AEF, the War Department, President Wilson (whom he referred to as
a "rabbit"), and especially Pershing.

Wood's trip to Europe was extended for almost a month due to a

General Peyton March standing next to General John Pershing, wearing a "Liberty" belt.

ghastly accident. Wood had paid a visit to the Sixth Army School of Automatic Arms in a small French village called Fère-en-Tardenois, and the school's commandant wanted to show Wood a trench mortar demonstration. Wood and a small group of observers stood about ten feet behind a French artillery officer who began firing mortars at various distances. During the fourth shot, the mortar exploded inside the barrel, sending shrapnel in every direction. One piece struck the school's assistant commandant in the heart, killing him, and a larger shard blew off the head of the commandant, who was standing right next to Wood. Blood and brain matter sprayed across his face.

Miraculously, only a splinter of metal hit Wood himself, slicing a nerve in his right arm. Members of his staff quickly put a tourniquet around the wound and tried to get him into a car and off to the hospital. To Wood's credit, he insisted that the other injured men—several soldiers were seriously hurt (about ten in all were killed)—be helped first. Doctors were eventually able to chloroform Wood, mostly to start operating on him but also to get him to stop talking and giving orders. Wood spent three weeks in Paris resting, and, in a gesture of goodwill, Pershing invited him out to Chaumont, where Wood could finish his convalescence in a more comfortable environment.

But not even a day passed before Wood was back to his old ways; during his first dinner, Wood leveled one criticism after another at the AEF commander and his staff about how the war was being conducted. Pershing knew there was no point in arguing and endured Wood's disparaging comments while barely saying a word, just silently eating and seething.

Wood had hoped to pass through Paris and London again on his way back to the States, but Pershing arranged it so that he was sent right to America and, ultimately, to Camp Funston in Fort Riley, Kansas, where he commanded the 89th Division. (General Fred Funston was so beloved that an Army training camp was named in his honor almost immediately after he died in February 1917.) Wood had asked to see Pershing one last time before his departure, but Pershing brushed him off, saying that he was feeling unwell.

While the 89th Division was slated to fight in France, Pershing dreaded the idea of Wood remaining as its commander. Pershing, fortunately, had an ally in both President Wilson and Secretary Baker, both of whom had heard from numerous sources of Wood's indiscreet comments while he was in Europe. Pershing and Baker took solace in the fact that Wood, with his history of poor health, wouldn't pass the mandatory Army physical that allowed divisional commanders to serve overseas. All of the "blame" would therefore fall on the medical board, who would inevitably fail him.

They did not. The doctors gave Wood a thorough examination and declared him able to serve.

When word of this reached Chaumont, Pershing was incredulous. "How in the hell any board could bring itself around to believe that General Wood is fit for active service is more than I can understand!" he fumed. "He is a cripple and that is all there is to it, and there is no use in sending cripples over here to do men's work."

Secretary Baker was also stunned when the Army doctors gave Wood a clean bill of health. With the backing of General Pershing and Chief of Staff Peyton March, Baker devised a plan that would still keep Wood in America. For any division, the process of packing up gear and traveling to New York or New Jersey from where they'd sail was an ordeal that usually took several weeks. Customarily, the divisional commander stayed behind for most of the process to ensure that no soldier was left behind and all administrative matters had been settled. As soon as the 89th Division was in motion, Baker sent Wood a telegram that stated: "You are assigned to command Western Department. You will remain at Camp Funston until departure of last unit of the 89th Division, when you will proceed to San Francisco, California, and assume command of Western Department."

Although not a demotion, since department commanders wielded significant power, the order was essentially an exile; California was about as far removed from Washington, D.C.—not to mention Europe—as one could go in the continental United States.

As Baker's telegram came over the wire into Wood's Camp Funston office, Wood was already in New York. He had suspected that Baker might try something to thwart his desire to serve in France, so he had already raced to the East Coast, believing that it would be harder for Baker to turn him away if he was with his men, ready to sail. Once a copy of Baker's telegram was forwarded to him in New York, confirming his worst fears, Wood was livid and promptly left Manhattan for Washington, D.C., to confront Baker, Chief of Staff Peyton March, and, if necessary, President Wilson.

Wood's first meeting was with the chief of staff, and he demanded to know who was responsible for the decision to leave him behind. General March, characteristically, did not mince words: "General Pershing has asked specifically that you not be sent to France, and the War Department is going to back him."

Wood felt sucker-punched; he had assumed it was a political move by President Wilson, a Democrat, and not another soldier—and particularly not the man who had been given the assignment that Wood believed was rightfully his. Yes, Pershing had led troops in the Punitive Expedition, but that mission was, in Wood's words, a "grotesque fizzle" that should have disqualified Pershing, not elevated him.

Wood then met with Baker, who confirmed that Pershing requested that Wood not lead the 89th—or any division—in Europe.

"General Pershing most positively does not want you in France," Baker said, "and, frankly, General Wood, I must state that if I were commanding general in France, I should not want you, as I fear you would not be subordinate."

Trying to maintain his composure, Wood said, "Then I am to understand that the reputation of any officer in the United States Army is placed in General Pershing's hands to make or break as he sees fit?"

"We will not send any officer to France nor keep any officer there against General Pershing's will. We must have a homogeneous working force," Baker replied.

Humiliated, Wood lashed out, denigrating Pershing's reputation by dredging up long-dismissed rumors that he had fathered Filipino children when he was in the Philippines more than a decade earlier. Baker told Wood that such an argument was "irrelevant and unworthy of consideration."

Wood then demanded to see President Wilson, who, as a courtesy, agreed to meet. Wood began by feigning appreciation and friendship, but when it became clear that Wilson was in agreement with Secretary Baker about Pershing's decision, Wood went off on spurious tangents about Pershing's character and, as he had done with Baker, accused

Pershing of having illegitimate children in the Philippines. Having put up with enough of Wood's initially fawning and then churlish behavior, Wilson ended the meeting by saying he would think the matter over, which he had no intention of doing. The issue was resolved.

The whole affair with Wood was an exasperating distraction to Pershing, at the worst possible time. The massive German offensive that had flamed out in late March reignited on April 9. General Erich Ludendorff's Sixth Army and Fourth Army began hammering exhausted British troops in northern Belgium at the Lys River, intending to cut them off from their supply lines near the Channel. On April 11, with the prospects of his soldiers looking bleak, Field Marshal Douglas Haig issued an order to all his men emphasizing what was at stake:

> Three weeks ago to-day the enemy began his terrific attacks against us on a 50-mile front. His objects are to separate us from the French, to take the Channel ports and destroy the British Army.
>
> In spite of throwing already 106 divisions into the battle and enduring the most reckless sacrifice of human life, he has yet made little progress towards his goals.
>
> We owe this to the determined fighting and self-sacrifice of our troops. Words fail me to express the admiration which I feel for the splendid resistance offered by all ranks of our Army under the most trying circumstances.
>
> Many amongst us are now tired. To those I would say that victory will belong to the side that holds out the longest. The French Army is moving rapidly and in great force to our support.
>
> There is no other course open to us but to fight it out! Every position must be held to the last man; there must be no retirement. With our backs to the wall, and believing in the justice of our cause, each one of us must fight on to the end. The safety of our homes and freedom of mankind alike depend upon the conduct of each one of us at this critical moment.

Haig was not exaggerating. If the Germans drove a wedge through the British and French armies and blocked their supply route, England would almost certainly be forced to capitulate. But with tremendous support from Canadian and Australian soldiers, along with French reinforcements, the Allies—at a cost of 120,000 casualties—once again thwarted the Germans, and Ludendorff halted the offensive.

Throughout April, Pershing was also focused on training the 1st Division, now 26,500 soldiers strong, to retake the town of Cantigny, in northern France, at the end of May, giving them five weeks to prepare for the battle. Pershing had replaced William Sibert, the general he memorably dressed down in public, with the more aggressively minded Robert Lee Bullard.

Pershing gave his first major address to AEF troops when he spoke to the division's approximately one thousand officers on April 16. Although hardly insecure, Pershing disliked public speaking and did it rarely. (Even when he landed in France almost a year earlier, he asked one of his aides, Colonel Charles Stanton, to make the triumphant declaration "Lafayette, we are here!") Now, however, perhaps with Haig's moving "With our backs to the wall . . ." appeal in mind, Pershing better understood the importance of a commander's words to lead and inspire. "I did not come here to make a speech, I am not given to speech-making, so only a word more," Pershing stated, halfway through his April 16 speech.

> I have every confidence in the 1st Division. You are about to enter this great battle of the greatest war in history, and in that battle you will represent the mightiest nation engaged. That thought itself must be to you a very appealing thought and one that should call forth the best and noblest that is in you. Centuries of military tradition and of military and civil history are now looking toward this first contingent of the American Army as it enters this great battle. . . .
>
> Our people today are hanging expectant upon your deeds. Our future part in this conflict depends upon your action. You

are going forward and your conduct will be an example for succeeding units of our army. I hope the standard you set will be high—I know it will be high. You are taking with you the sincerest good wishes and the highest hopes of the president and all of our people at home. I assure you in their behalf and in my own of our strong belief in your success and of your confidence in your courage and in your loyalty, with a feeling of certainty in our hearts that you are going to make a record of which your country will be proud.

That same month Pershing found the solution to a problem he had been struggling with for some time. The Allies were still constantly pressuring him for large numbers of U.S. troops to be put under their command, and in April he finally relented, giving the French Army four regiments of soldiers who were ready to fight. And not in fleeting, hit-and-run raids in "quiet" sectors, but in major offensives. Why these particular Americans were chosen, however, was not entirely in line with the high ideals of which Pershing had spoken so stirringly.

12.

Black Jack and the Hellfighters

INITIALLY, it was Nigger Jack.

Over time General John Pershing's nickname became the less derogatory Black Jack, which even Pershing embraced since it was slang for a lead-filled billy club and was, therefore, synonymous with toughness. But Pershing had been called the more offensive epithet first, soon after he returned to West Point in 1897, at the age of thirty-seven, to teach tactical warfare. Pershing was merciless in doling out harsh punishments for the smallest infractions, and the cadets loathed him. Bigotry was so pervasive that a white person associated in any meaningful way with blacks was often assailed with the same vicious insults, and because Pershing had served with the 10th Cavalry Regiment, an all-black unit, the cadets started referring to him as Nigger Jack behind his back.

Pershing's own thoughts about African Americans were complicated and inconsistent. "My attitude toward the Negro was that of one brought up among them," Pershing wrote, reflecting on his years as a young man teaching black children in a public school in Missouri. "I had always felt kindly and sympathetic toward them and knew that fairness and due consideration of their welfare would make the same appeal to them as to any other body of men."

Pershing had praised the 10th Cavalry soldiers he had fought alongside with for their bravery under fire, and in 1899 he specifically appealed to the War Department to serve with them again in the Spanish-American War. During World War I, however, some of Pershing's actions and writings reflected the prejudices of the era.

And racial discord in the United States was surging, exacerbated by the rebirth of the white supremacist organization the Ku Klux Klan and tectonic shifts in regional demographics. Formed in the aftermath of the Civil War, the original KKK lasted barely a decade and dissolved in the early 1870s. But it was revived forty years later, primarily due to director D. W. Griffith's artistically groundbreaking but overtly racist film *The Birth of a Nation*. Griffith lionized Klan members as the valiant defenders of white women from predatory African American men, and he depicted black legislators, appointed to positions of power during Reconstruction, as alcoholic ne'er-do-wells spitefully using their new-found influence to enact laws against whites.

Released in February 1915, the movie was a huge commercial success. On Thanksgiving night of that same year, a former Methodist preacher named William Joseph Simmons, inspired by *The Birth of a Nation*, hiked to the top of Stone Mountain, near Atlanta, and with fifteen other men conducted an elaborate ceremony to inaugurate the new Klan, culminating with the burning of a large wooden cross. (The original Klan didn't burn crosses; Simmons got the idea from Griffith's film.) Starting with that small band of sixteen individuals, the Klan grew exponentially to four million members within a matter of years.

Race relations were also deteriorating because President Woodrow Wilson himself fanned the flames of intolerance. Despite having promised African Americans "absolute fair dealing" during his first presidential campaign, upon being elected, Wilson's administration went about reversing years of progress. He had black workers throughout the government fired without cause and segregated agencies that had been integrated by Wilson's predecessors, Republicans and Democrats alike. Wilson insisted he was unbiased, but he had a record of making racially demeaning and specious comments.

George Bowles, the same public relations mastermind who helped publicize Pershing's Crusaders, *also promoted* The Birth of a Nation.

On the matter of slavery, Wilson held the opinion that "domestic slaves, at any rate, and almost all who were much under the master's eye, were happy and well cared for." Regarding the post–Civil War period, Wilson argued that the Republican Party, the party of Abraham Lincoln, was unpopular during Reconstruction for elevating blacks into legislative roles "because the dominance of an ignorant and inferior race was justly dreaded." And of the original KKK, Wilson contended: "The white men were roused by a mere instinct of self-preservation—until at last there had sprung into existence a great Ku Klux Klan, a veritable empire of the South, to protect the Southern country."

The new KKK was finding a receptive audience among whites

nationwide, particularly during the war years, with the majority of their members coming from northern and midwestern cities. As millions of white men left their jobs to serve overseas, thousands of African Americans in the South, many of them the children of slaves and still living in abject poverty, migrated north in search of better employment. Whites resented the mass influx of blacks into their communities, and tension escalated into violence.

Lynchings were also on the rise. In 1915 they averaged one a week. By 1917 that number had increased by almost 50 percent. For some vigilantes, lynching wasn't brutal enough. On May 22, 1917, the Memphis newspaper *The Commercial Appeal* ran a headline announcing MOB CAPTURES SLAYER OF THE RAPPEL GIRL: ELL PERSONS TO BE LYNCHED NEAR SCENE OF MURDER; MAY RESORT TO BURNING. Persons was an African American man accused of murdering a white girl named Antoinette Rappel, and before he was even tried, a citizens group in Memphis decided to kill him themselves. The main "evidence" against Persons was based on a new theory that the last image a victim saw was imprinted on his or her eyes, so, after the county sheriff had Rappel's body exhumed, the authorities looked into her dead pupils and swore they saw Persons's face. Five thousand spectators showed up at the execution site, and instead of lynching Persons, several men chained him to the ground, poured gasoline over his entire body, and set him on fire. Persons's charred corpse was then dismembered and his head cut off. The newspaper praised the crowd the next day for being "orderly" and exhibiting "no drunkenness, no shooting and no yelling."

In East St. Louis, later that summer, thousands of whites descended on the city's relatively new African American community. "For an hour and a half last evening I saw the massacre of helpless Negroes at Broadway and Fourth streets," a *St. Louis Post-Dispatch* reporter wrote on July 3, 1917, in a story that was picked up over the wires by other newspapers.

> I saw man after man with hands raised, pleading for his life,
> surrounded by groups of men—men who had never seen him

before and knew nothing about him except that he was black—and saw them administer the historic sentence of intolerance, death by stoning. I saw one of these men almost dead from a savage shower of stones, hanged with a clothesline, and when it broke, hanged with a rope which held. Within a few paces of the pole from which he was suspended, four other Negroes lay dead or dying. . . . I saw Negro women begging for mercy and pleading that they had harmed no one, set upon by white women of the baser sort, who laughed and answered in coarse sallies of men as they beat [the Negroes'] faces and breasts with fists, stones and sticks.

In all, an estimated one hundred black men, women, and children as young as two years old were shot, stoned, hanged, beaten, or burned to death.

Seven weeks after East St. Louis, a simple misunderstanding between a black woman and a white policeman in Houston, Texas, triggered a series of events that caused the city to explode into a full-scale race riot, with the U.S. Army's all-black 3rd Battalion, 24th Infantry Regiment right in the middle of it.

Transferred from Columbus, New Mexico, where they had been patrolling the Mexican border after serving in the Punitive Expedition with Pershing, the soldiers of the 3rd Battalion were guarding a new Army base under construction, Camp Logan, two miles outside Houston. From the moment they arrived, the troops endured constant insults and threats of violence by white workers at Camp Logan and residents of Houston.

Jim Crow laws had essentially been nonexistent in Columbus, and the troops had grown accustomed to walking through the town without being harassed. In Houston, segregation was strictly enforced, and the 3rd Battalion soldiers grew angrier by the day at how they were bullied and disrespected.

On August 23, a police officer named Lee Sparks barged into the home of Sara Travers while in pursuit of a man seen gambling on a street corner. Sparks and another officer, Rufus Daniels, thought the suspect had tried to escape by dashing across Travers's yard. Travers, the mother of five children, had been quietly ironing when Sparks burst in and asked if she had seen anyone run through. When she said no, he accused her of being a "God damn liar" and then ranted that ever since "these God damn sons of bitches of nigger soldiers come here you are trying to take the town." Sparks searched the house, and when he found nothing, Travers inquired if there was anything else he wanted.

"Don't you ask an officer what he wants in your house," Sparks yelled at Travers. "I'm from Fort Ben and we don't allow niggers to talk back to us. We generally whip them down there." And then he slapped her, causing Travers to shriek in pain.

Officer Rufus Daniels heard the scream and rushed inside. When Sparks told Daniels what Travers had said, Daniels called her one of those "biggety nigger women," and the two men dragged Travers outside to arrest her.

Private Alonzo Edwards, from the 3rd Battalion, saw two white men pummeling a helpless black woman and hurried over. Sparks promptly bashed him on the head with the butt of his gun, asking, "What you got to do with this?" and then arrested Edwards on the spot.

Another member of the 3rd, Corporal Charles Baltimore, was walking past when he saw Edwards being hauled off. Baltimore was a military police officer and actually responsible for calming volatile situations. Without provocation, Sparks beat and arrested Baltimore as well. One neighbor claimed that Sparks even shot at Baltimore, but, if so, the bullets missed.

A rumor got back to Camp Logan that Baltimore had been killed and the police were on a rampage, randomly beating up African Americans. Enraged, more than 150 soldiers with the 3rd Battalion raided the supply tents for ammunition and rifles. Sergeant Vida Henry led the soldiers into Houston, where they encountered armed civilians and cops. A firefight broke out and fifteen white men, including five members of Houston's law enforcement, were killed. (Rufus Daniels was among the dead, but Lee Sparks was unharmed.) After accidentally shooting a military officer they mistook from a distance as a Houston policeman, the men scattered in different directions before heading back to Camp Logan. Vida Henry knew what his fate would be, calmly shook hands with some of the men before they disbursed, and informed them he was going off to commit suicide. His dead body was found the next day.

A battalion of white infantrymen and two companies of white artillerymen were rushed to Houston, and the city was temporarily placed under martial law. One hundred fifty-six members of the 3rd Battalion were disarmed, rounded up, and sent back to New Mexico to await trial, officially, for "mutiny." None of the men turned on another, and in the flurry of the violence, no witnesses could reliably claim that they could identify who, among the 156, fired the fatal shots. But there had to be some form of retribution for the deaths of 17 white men, and the military sentenced 29 members of the 3rd Battalion to be executed, with almost 50 more given life sentences in prison.

An internal War Department review came to the conclusion that the "ultimate cause of the riot" was "racial," and the men of the 3rd Battalion had been pushed to the breaking point. "[They] resolved to assert what they believed to be their rights as American citizens and United States soldiers," the lead investigator stated. "They failed, and in some cases refused to obey local laws and regulations affecting their race, [and] they resented the use of the word 'nigger.' . . . It is my belief that the tension had reached that point where any unusual occurrence would have brought on trouble."

Secretary of War Newton Baker accepted the report's finding that Houston's Jim Crow laws were the real cause of the unrest, and he worked to commute ten of the twenty-nine death sentences to life without parole. The military would eventually hang nineteen members of the 3rd Battalion, including Corporal Charles Baltimore, who had tried to defuse the situation with Officer Lee Sparks but was beaten for his efforts.

Within this toxic environment of riots, lynchings, and KKK rallies across the country, Secretary Baker struggled with the need to assemble an army of able-bodied men, white and black, without inciting racial unrest throughout the military. Baker knew that blacks wanted to serve and, ideally, fight on the front lines, where they could demonstrate their courage in battle. Many African American leaders saw the benefit of this as well and envisioned a time when black troops would return to America, having risked their lives for their country, and would finally be treated equally.

"The writer has all along held that the Negro, in order to keep his case clean, must perform all the duties of citizenship while he constantly renews his claim to all corresponding rights," James Weldon Johnson wrote in an editorial for the *Age*, a magazine published by and primarily for African Americans. Johnson was an acclaimed poet, lawyer, educator, songwriter (he wrote what became known as the first Negro national anthem, "Lift Ev'ry Voice and Sing"), and leader of the National Association for the Advancement of Colored People. And he was a major proponent of seeing black men in uniform and fighting for the country.

> Such a course of action does not mean that he should be led by any silly sentimentality in taking up the duty that faces him in the present hour. It does not mean he should forget his just cause for complaint. It means that guided by hard, common sense and remembering all that this country justly owes him, the Negro will take up and perform the duty that now falls to him; thereby strengthening his protest for his right and flinging a challenge to the white people of this country to rise to his plane of magnanimity and do their duty by him.

Secretary Baker was torn. Desegregating the Army was out of the question. Neither the public nor President Wilson, for that matter, would stand for it. The U.S. Marine Corps refused to accept blacks under any circumstances, and in the Navy, blacks could serve only as mess hands, preparing food. But Baker knew African American soldiers had already distinguished themselves in the Revolution, the Civil War, and every major conflict since. Baker was under tremendous pressure from African American leaders to deploy black soldiers into combat positions, but what happened at Houston, no matter how culpable the local whites were for goading the 3rd Battalion soldiers, cast a shadow over all black troops. Considering the sheer number of soldiers involved, white and black, it was impossible to separate them entirely or to keep black troops from training near white communities. Logistics simply wouldn't allow it.

The next potential clash started brewing one week after the Houston killings. On August 31, 1917, the mayor of Spartanburg, South Carolina, J. F. Floyd, was dumbfounded to learn that the War Department was sending the 369th Infantry Regiment to Camp Wadsworth, right outside Spartanburg. The Rattlers, as they were known—their flag showcased a rattlesnake—were, except for a handful of white officers and Puerto Rican volunteers, all African American soldiers from New York.

"With their northern ideas about race equality, they will probably expect to be treated like white men," Spartanburg's mayor told the *New York Times*. "I can say right here that they will not be treated as anything except negroes." Floyd, alluding to Houston, stated that sending the 369th to Spartanburg in the aftermath of such mayhem was like "waving a red flag in the face of a bull, something that can't be done without trouble."

The head of Spartanburg's chamber of commerce fully agreed, telling the *New York Times*:

> We asked for the camp for Spartanburg, but at that time we understood that no colored troops were to be sent down. It is a great mistake to send Northern negroes down here, for they do not understand out attitude. We wouldn't mind it if the

Government sent us a regiment of Southern negroes; we understand them and they understand us. But with those Northern fellows it's different.

I can tell you for certain that if any of those colored soldiers go in any of our soda stores and the like and ask to be served they'll be knocked down. Somebody will throw a bottle. We don't allow negroes to use the same glass that a white man may later have to drink out of.

On October 10 and 11, soldiers with the 369th poured into Camp Wadsworth to train with the forty thousand white members of the 27th Division. Only hours after they arrived, eight soldiers—four black and four white—walked arm in arm, in a display of solidarity, into Spartanburg for a night on the town. While passing a gang of young white men loitering about, someone shouted obscenities at the soldiers. Within moments fists were flying, and the row continued until military police swarmed in minutes later. Not one black soldier, however, had thrown a punch; all of the fighting had been done between the white soldiers and the locals.

The next morning the 369th's commanding officer, Colonel William Hayward, a white man, assembled his two thousand soldiers in an open field to candidly address the racial situation. Hayward was liked and respected by the men. He had almost single-handedly built the National Guard regiment over the past two years, and he was an accomplished officer in his own right. His military training started at the University of Nebraska-Lincoln, where John Pershing was one of his instructors (Pershing taught military tactics at UNL between 1891 and 1893), and he went on to serve with Pershing in the Spanish-American War.

Hayward mentioned both Houston and Spartanburg's less than hospitable welcome to explain to his regiment why he had called them together. While not excusing it, Hayward stated that Spartanburg's attitude was based on ignorance and misunderstanding. But no matter what happened, Hayward said, the regiment had to show restraint.

How they reacted to verbal taunts or even physical abuse could jeopardize not only the 369th, but the reputations of all African American soldiers in the Army. He beseeched them to show forbearance. He ended the talk by asking every man to raise his right hand and promise "to refrain from violence of any kind under every condition." Another white officer, Major Arthur Little, watched as "a sea of hands shot up over that sea of heads—and the meeting was dismissed."

Hayward had faith in his men and knew that he had an advantage no other regiment did: the best marching band in the entire AEF, led by an African American officer in the regiment, 1st Lieutenant James Reese Europe. Hayward intended to use the band to win over the people of Spartanburg.

Before the war, Jim Europe had established himself as one of the most brilliant jazz and ragtime composers in the United States. In 1910, he founded the Clef Club, a concert hall and gathering spot in Harlem for black musicians to riff and rehearse together. Europe's Clef Club Orchestra was the first African American orchestra to perform at Carnegie Hall, to rave reviews. Europe put his entire music career at risk by enlisting in the 369th, at the age of thirty-six, not only to lead the regiment's band but to fight as a machine gunner.

When Europe told Noble Sissle, the lead baritone in the Clef Club, what he had done, Sissle was thunderstruck. "Gracious, Jim, what's the idea? What time have you to devote to anybody's army?" Sissle was already feeling overwhelmed with work, and to lose Europe would only burden him with more obligations.

Europe told Sissle not to worry. He had volunteered his name, too.

"Oh no, you don't get me in anybody's army!" Sissle exclaimed, infuriated by Europe's presumptuousness.

"I have been in New York for sixteen years," Europe said to Sissle, "and there has never been such an organization of Negro men that will bring together all classes of men for a common good. And our race will never amount to anything politically or economically, in New York or anywhere else, unless there are strong organizations of men who stand for something in the community. . . . New York cannot afford to love this great chance for such a strong, powerful institution, for the development of the Negro manhood of Harlem."

Sissle relented and officially signed up as well.

Colonel Hayward scheduled the band to play a free open-air concert for the citizens of Spartanburg in the town's main square. Major Arthur Little vividly remembered the first performance. As the musicians were assembling their instruments, Little and other white officers, all wearing long coats with their collars raised to hide their ranks and insignia, paced among the crowd, listening for any murmurs of trouble. Little was anxious. "The talk which some of us overheard through that crowd during the early stages of the concert," Little recalled, "was by no means reassuring. At first it seemed, almost, as if an error of judgment had been made in forcing the colored regiment into prominence at so early an hour after our arrival." But once they actually started playing, everything changed. Little went on to say:

> There must be something in the time-honored line about music and its charms; for, gradually, the crowd grew larger, but the noises of the crowd grew less and less, until finally, in that great public square of converging city streets, silence reigned. Lieutenant Europe conducted, as was his custom, with but a few seconds between numbers, and the program appeared to be short. When the final piece had been played and the forty or fifty bandsmen had filed out of the stand in perfect order with the "Hep-Hep-Hep" of the sergeants as the only sound from their ranks, the flower of Spartanburg's citizenry looked at each other foolishly, and could be heard to say:—"Is that all?" while another would say:—"When do they play again?"

Little and Hayward were pulled aside by a committee of white businessmen, who apologized for their mayor's rude welcome and then assured the officers that it did not represent the true spirit of the citizenship of Spartanburg. Little was proud to note that the men praised the 369th for making such "a good start," "invited all of the officers of the regiment to consider themselves honorary members of the Country Club," and requested of Colonel Hayward "to let the band play for dancing at the club the following week."

Sadly, the band's influence extended only so far.

Soon after the concert, one of the regiment's few African American captains, Napoleon Bonaparte Marshall, was ordered off a trolley car after having paid his fare simply for being, in the words of the trolley driver, a "dirty nigger." Marshall was a highly successful, Harvard-educated lawyer who knew his rights, but he took Colonel Hayward's words about restraint to heart, swallowed his pride, and stepped back onto the street.

Henry Johnson, a five-foot-four private in the 369th, was thrown into the gutter by two local white men angling for a fight. Jeered as a coward, Johnson said he had promised his colonel he wouldn't strike back, and he walked away without retaliating.

Two white soldiers from another regiment saw how Private Johnson was mistreated, stormed over to the town bullies, and, after declaring that they hadn't made any promises to *their* colonel not to fight, bashed them to the ground for insulting a U.S. soldier.

Confrontations were on the rise, precipitated by white agitators who were only emboldened by the 369th soldiers' "turn the other cheek" mentality, and Hayward wondered how long his men could hold out. Hayward knew Secretary of War Newton Baker personally, and he decided to take a train up to Washington at his own expense to plead with Baker to send the 369th to the front lines of France. Where they'd be safer.

On Sunday, October 21, 1917, the day after Hayward left, the 369th teetered on the precipice of having its own "Houston." It all began when Lieutenants James Reese Europe and Noble Sissle, having just given another ovation-worthy performance, went into town to get a bite to eat. After finding a food stand that served blacks, Europe asked a local citizen who was also black where he could purchase some New York newspapers. The man pointed to a hotel and said they sold papers in the lobby. Europe was assured that, even though it was a "white" hotel, "colored folks" were allowed inside.

"Go on, Siss," Europe said, "and get every paper that has the word 'New York' on it. I never knew how sweet New York was 'til I landed here."

Sissle was apprehensive.

Once again, the black citizen assured him it was perfectly safe.

Sissle ventured in, bought the papers without incident, and headed out the door.

But before he made it outside, he felt a hand knock the hat off his head, and a sinister voice behind him hollered, for all to hear, "Hey, nigger, don't you know enough to take your hat off?" It was the hotel owner.

Sissle initially feared he had indeed broached military etiquette—until he looked around and saw that every white officer in the lobby had his hat on. When Sissle bent over to pick up his hat, the proprietor kicked him hard, knocking Sissle over. Sissle scrambled outside with the hotel owner cursing and striking him all the way to the curb.

Once again it was the white soldiers, incensed by what they had seen, who were poised to fight. "Let's kill the so and so," one of the white soldiers called out, referring to the hotel owner, "and pull his dirty old hotel down around his ears." The crowd was a powder keg, primed for a single spark to set the whole situation aflame.

"*Atten . . . shun!*" a powerful voice boomed over white and black soldiers alike. Everybody froze. "Get your hats and coats and leave this place, quietly," the voice commanded.

It was Jim Europe. He then came face-to-face with the hotel's owner, Europe's towering frame looming over the slightly built man. His blood pressure still up, the hotel owner pointed at Sissle and told Europe that the "nigger did not take off his hat, and no nigger can come into my place without taking off his hat too." Pushing his luck, the owner looked up at Europe and demanded that he, too, remove his cap.

Sissle, watching all this from a distance, cringed. Europe was one of the proudest men in the regiment, and there was no way he would remove his hat for a man who had just dishonored a soldier of the 369th, especially since the policy didn't apply to whites. But Europe had other considerations in mind. His next move could mean the difference between a massive riot, possibly larger than Houston, or having to humiliate himself in front of his men, an act that would itself have far-reaching repercussions.

"I'll take off my hat," Europe said, seeming to have acquiesced. "But," he added, there was a condition: "I just want to find out one thing. Why did you strike Lieutenant Sissle for? Did he commit any offense?"

"No! I told you he did not take his hat off, and I knocked it off. Now you get out of here." With quiet dignity, Europe turned his back, and walked into the street.

Little cabled Hayward in Washington and described what had occurred, further emphasizing why they needed to get away from Spartanburg as soon as possible. Hayward met with Secretary Baker, and they agreed that the current situation was untenable.

Two days later, the regiment returned to Camp Whitman outside New York to prepare for their journey overseas. But even on their home turf they had to watch their backs. Placed in barracks right next to theirs at Camp Whitman was an Alabama regiment, the 167th, whose soldiers expressed revulsion at the idea of being in such close proximity to black troops.

Also at the camp was New York's "Fighting Irish" 165th Regiment. When word got out that the Alabama 167th was planning a nighttime raid against the 369th, who were unarmed, a white captain in the regiment named Hamilton Fish Jr. went over to the 165th and discreetly appealed to them for ammunition. (Muscular and six-foot-four, Fish was an imposing presence. While playing football for Harvard in 1909, he struck a West Point cadet—Eugene Byrne—with such force during a game that it killed him. Byrne's death was one of several that caused football players to start using helmets instead of leather caps.) The Fighting Irish were sympathetic to their brother New Yorkers and decided to provide Fish with the ammo.

That evening, Fish located several Alabama officers and informed them that his troops were now armed and would fight back if attacked. "It would be a massacre," he said to them, "on both sides." Fish then added that "bloodshed between our troops was entirely unnecessary. Black or white, we were all Americans who had been called to fight a common enemy overseas; the war was in the trenches in France, not between the barracks at Camp Whitman." The officers assured Fish that they would do everything they could to prevent any violence, and the night passed uneventfully.

Finally, in mid-November, the two thousand soldiers of the 369th Infantry Regiment readied themselves to board the troopship *Pocahontas* for Europe. Built by the Germans seventeen years earlier and originally named the *Princess Irene*, the ship was seized by the United States while docked in Hoboken, New Jersey, when the war started. German sailors had damaged as much of the machinery as they could, and nature had taken its toll on the vessel as well. Boilers, bulkheads, sidings, and common areas were run-down due to rust and corrosion, and the whole ship, inside and out, was filthy. Hosed down, repainted, and patched up as best as possible, the *Pocahontas* was graded seaworthy after one precarious round-trip to France and back. For the men of the 369th, it would have to do.

And they weren't the only ones restless to get moving; the commander of the port of embarkation, General David Shanks, had thousands of turkeys packed on board, and Shanks wanted them delivered to frontline troops in time for Thanksgiving, less than two weeks away.

Upon setting sail, Colonel William Hayward was standing next to Major Arthur Little on the bow. "Well, you old pirate and buccaneer,"

Hayward said to Little, thinking of all they had endured, "we're on our way! Isn't it wonderful?"

Then, a hundred miles from shore, the engine's aging piston rods snapped apart, and the ship had to limp back to port.

Days passed and General Shanks was having a minor fit. "Goodness gracious, Colonel," he cabled to Hayward, "are you ever going to get those coons and turkeys to France?"

Thanksgiving came and went, and the troops were now scheduled to sail on December 12. After steaming out of its dock in Hoboken, the *Pocahontas* slipped into the Lower Bay off Sandy Hook, New Jersey. Much to Colonel Hayward's displeasure, no destroyers would accompany them to defend against German submarines. The destroyers had been redirected to protect grain shipments to England, a mission the Navy determined to be more critical.

On the night of December 14, while crowded next to other ships that would form their convoy, the *Pocahontas* was slammed into by a British tanker, crushing several lifeboats and punching a six-foot gash in her starboard side. The opening was well above seawater, and Colonel Hayward decided that the damage could be repaired at sea. The alternative was to be left out of the convoy, delaying their departure another several weeks. As the ship rocked back and forth in the choppy waves and with freezing December winds whipping around them, Hayward's men worked bare-handed to bolt new steel plates over the hole, and they sailed on to France.

Soon after they arrived, disappointment quickly set in; the men of the 369th were informed that they were to be used as stevedores at and around the ports and would not receive further training for combat. For three months, the men toiled loading and unloading cargo, repairing train tracks leading into the shipping yards, and performing other backbreaking work.

In April, the 369th received word that General Pershing had decided that the regiment should, in fact, be put into combat—but with the French Army. For Pershing it was a way to appease France's incessant demands for

U.S. troops to replace their losses; the 369th was, in a word, expendable. They would be entirely under French control, and they would have to use French weapons they were unfamiliar with, including the Lebel rifle, which fired only three shots at a time. The Springfield rifles they had trained with used cartridges that carried seven bullets.

Although Colonel William Hayward wanted his men to fight and knew they wanted to fight, too, he assumed it would be as part of the American Expeditionary Forces. "Our great American general simply put the black orphan in a basket, set it on the doorstep, pulled the bell, and went away," Hayward wrote to a friend back in the States about Pershing's decision.

The baby also came with a note attached. As France was integrating African American troops into its army, AEF headquarters issued a memorandum to French commanders titled "Secret Information Concerning Black Troops." General Pershing was not its author—his French liaison officer, Colonel Louis Linard, wrote the memo—but Pershing almost certainly approved its release.

"It is important for French officers who have been called upon to exercise command over black American troops, or to live in close contact with them, to have an exact idea of the position occupied by Negroes in the United States," the memo began. Although "secret" was in the title, the document was meant to be broadly distributed:

> The information set forth in the following communication ought to be given to these officers and it is to their interest to have these matters known and widely disseminated. It will devolve likewise on the French Military Authorities, through the medium of the Civil Authorities, to give information on this subject to the French population residing in the cantonments occupied by American colored troops.

In the next paragraph, Linard wrote, "The American attitude upon the Negro question may seem a matter for discussion to many French minds. But we French are not in our province if we undertake to discuss what some call 'prejudice.' American opinion is unanimous on the 'color question,' and does not admit of any discussion."

That statement was blatantly false; millions of white Americans were sympathetic to the plight of blacks in the United States, and the country had been having a rather intense "discussion" about the issue of race and prejudice since its founding.

Linard continued:

> The increasing number of Negroes in the United States (about 15,000,000) would create for the white race in the Republic a menace of degeneracy were it not that an impassable gulf has been made between them.
>
> As this danger does not exist for the French race, the French public has become accustomed to treating the Negro with familiarity and indulgence.
>
> This indulgence and this familiarity are matters of grievous concern to the Americans. They consider them an affront to their national policy. They are afraid that contact with the French will inspire in black Americans aspirations which to them (the whites) appear intolerable. It is of the utmost importance that every effort be made to avoid profoundly estranging American opinion.

Conceding that blacks were citizens of the United States, Linard wrote that "the black man is regarded by the white American as an inferior being with whom relations of business or service only are possible. The black is constantly being censured for his want of intelligence and discretion, his lack of civic and professional conscience, and for his tendency toward undue familiarity."

Once again, Linard was lumping all Americans together as being of one mind, and his reasons for why blacks were "constantly being censured" gave only the racist's perspective. At no point did he mention the centuries of injustices whites had committed against blacks.

Linard even went a step further. "The vices of the Negro are a constant menace to the American who has to repress them sternly," he wrote. He offered this evidence: "For instance, the black American troops in France have, by themselves, given rise to as many complaints for attempted rape as all the rest of the army. And yet the [black American] soldiers sent us have been the choicest with respect to physique and morals, for the number disqualified at the time of mobilization was enormous."

Linard concluded:

1. We must prevent the rise of any pronounced degree of intimacy between French officers and black officers. We may be courteous and amiable with these last, but we cannot deal with them on the same place as with white American officers without deeply wounding the latter. We must not eat with them, must not shake hands or seek to talk or meet with them outside of the requirements of military service.

2. We must not commend too highly the black American troops, particularly in the presence of Americans. It is alright to recognize their good qualities and their services, but only in moderate terms, strictly in keeping with the truth.

3. Make a point of keeping the native cantonment population from "spoiling" the Negroes. Americans become greatly incensed at any public expression of intimacy between white women and black men. They have recently uttered violent protests against a picture in the "Vie Parisienne" entitled "The Child of the Desert" which shows a [white] woman in a "cabinet particulier" with a Negro. Familiarity on the part of white women with black men is furthermore a source of profound regret to our experienced colonials who see in it an overweening menace to the prestige of the white race.

Military authority cannot intervene directly in this question but it can through the civil authorities exercise some influence on the population.

LINARD

Officers within the French Ministry were so appalled by the memo that they ordered copies of it to be gathered up and burned.

What was particularly astonishing about its release was that it came *after* black troops had already demonstrated extraordinary heroism in combat and brought some much-needed good news to the American effort.

On the evening of May 14, 1918, Private Henry Johnson and Private Needham Roberts of the 369th Infantry Regiment were serving with the French 16th Division just west of Verdun in a listening post two hundred yards in the middle of no-man's-land. Henry Johnson was the five-foot-four soldier who had been punched and kicked by whites in Spartanburg, South Carolina, but refused to strike back in order to prevent a larger riot. With only a thin circle of barbed wire protecting it, the post could easily be obliterated by a single shell or overpowered by little more than a small squad of enemy troops. Already vulnerable, Johnson and Roberts were equipped with only their French Lebel rifles and some hand grenades. Johnson had also brought along his own bolo knife.

At around 2:00 a.m., Johnson's ears perked up, and he whispered to Roberts, asking if he had heard anything. Roberts listened intently for a moment and then dismissed the noise as most likely rats gnawing on a piece of wood or bone. Unconvinced, Johnson crept out of the hole to move closer to where the sound was emanating from, and he came upon the sight of German troops stealthily snipping their way through the barbed wire.

Roberts had been focusing on what appeared to be a log, well off into the distance, that he hadn't recalled seeing before. Suddenly the "log" jumped up and raced forward, followed by about two dozen more Germans shooting and lobbing grenades as they advanced. A grenade exploded close to Roberts, sending him wheeling backward as shards of metal ripped through his legs and arms.

Johnson leaped up and fired off three shots, striking a German in the chest. Out of ammunition, he held on to his rifle and swung it like a club, smashing the face of a German who had a Luger aimed right at Roberts's head.

Johnson had also been hit by shrapnel and staggered for a moment. Looking over at Roberts, he realized that three Germans were trying to drag him off as a prisoner. Johnson used his rifle again to knock out one of the Germans, but the rifle cracked in half, rendering it useless.

Johnson pulled out his bolo knife and began slashing about wildly, driving the blade deep into one man's head. But Johnson didn't see another soldier rise up behind him and pump three bullets into his legs and arm. When the German lunged toward Johnson to finish him off, Johnson whirled around and, with his arm outstretched, gutted the German with a single stroke across his stomach.

Seeing French reinforcements coming in and horrified by the small tornado of violence Johnson had just inflicted on their comrades, the remaining Germans scurried back to their own lines. Johnson was able to get his hands on several grenades and tossed them at the retreating Germans. He then passed out and was taken, along with Roberts, to a dressing station.

Major Arthur Little, after being woken up and notified about the skirmish, threw a raincoat over his pajamas to get to the station as quickly as possible. Seeing how badly Johnson and Roberts had been shot up and injured by shrapnel, Little was almost certain the men would die. He was surprised to find them not only conscious but coherent and more than willing to talk about what had happened. Little was able to get the essentials of the incident before both men were placed inside an ambulance to take them to a larger French hospital.

Hours later, the first rays of sunlight revealed the true scope of what Roberts and Johnson had done. After Major Little cautiously went up to the listening post with an aide, he began tracing the path the Germans took to escape. It wasn't hard to follow.

"We trailed the course of the enemy retreat . . . to the bank of the river, where they crossed," Little recalled. "We trailed the course with the greatest of ease, by pools of blood, blood-soaked handkerchiefs and first aid bandages, and blood-smeared logs, where the routed party had rested." Like a forensic detective, Little could deduce exactly what had happened in the final moments of the confrontation.

As the Germans [were retreating], Johnson pelted them with grenades. We found evidence that at least one man had been terribly torn by the iron of these explosions. At the narrowest point in the [barbed wire] opening, where they could do no better than go in a single file, we found a terrible mass of flesh and blood, and the cloth of a coat, and the pulped material of a first aid packet—blown open. Upon the ground, in this opening, was the shell hole blown by the grenade. The hole was the size and shape of a five gallon punch bowl; and it was almost filled with thick, sticky blood.

Three American war correspondents—Irvin Cobb of the *New York World*, Martin Green of the *Evening World*, and Lincoln Eyre of the *New York Herald*—soon arrived on the scene. Their visit was not entirely by chance, as they had heard about this all-black regiment from New York and had been searching nearly all over France for them. But their timing, on this particular day, could not have been more fortuitous.

Cobb was the first to ask Little if "any interesting experience[s]" had occurred that might be of interest to his readers.

"Why yes, we did have a little fight this morning, that was good while it lasted," Little responded. A couple of the men had "a real pitched battle" and "did very well, too." Little had just finished writing up the account and asked the reporters if they cared to read it.

All three answered, enthusiastically, in the affirmative.

They also wanted to see where the battle took place, and, although warned that they could encounter German snipers along the way, they were all eager to go.

"The sun beat down mercilessly upon the shadeless plain," Little recalled. "I did want those writers, however, to see that grenade-blown punch bowl filled with blood."

After showing them the sector and sharing his written report with the journalists, Little also took them directly to the hospital where Roberts and Johnson were recuperating. Having heard of his physical exploits, the reporters were stunned to see the pint-sized Johnson in person.

Front-page articles with blaring headlines heralded Johnson and Roberts in newspapers throughout America.

Irvin Cobb had publicly stated that, before the war, he deemed African Americans to be inferior to whites. But men like Roberts and Johnson were causing him to change his beliefs. "As a result of what our black soldiers are going to do in this war," he wrote in his profile of Roberts and Johnson, "a word that has been uttered billions of times in our country, sometimes in derision, sometimes in hate, sometimes in all kindliness—but which I am sure never fell on black ears but it left behind a sting for the heart—is going to have a new meaning for all of us, South and North too, and that hereafter n-i-g-g-e-r will merely be another way of spelling the word American."

As THE 369TH continued to see action and other members showed the same courage and ferocity as Roberts and Johnson, the regiment started being referred to as the Harlem Hellfighters.

German intelligence hoped to counter these reports with propaganda flyers dropped from the air that encouraged black troops from the United States to question why they would defend a country that discriminated against them. "Hello, boys, what are you doing over here? Fighting the Germans? Why?" the leaflet began.

> Have they ever done you any harm? Of course some white folks and the lying English-American papers told you that the Germans ought to be wiped out for the sake of humanity and Democracy. What is Democracy? Personal freedom; all citizens enjoying the same rights socially and before the law. Do you enjoy the same rights as the white people do in America, the land of freedom and Democracy, or are you not rather treated there as second class citizens?

Can you get into a restaurant where white people dine? Can you get a seat in a theatre where white people sit? Can you get a seat or a berth in a railroad car, or can you even ride in the South in the same street car with the white people?

And how about the law? Is lynching and the most horrible crimes connected therewith, a lawful proceeding in a Democratic country? Now all this is entirely different in Germany, where they do like colored people; where they treat them as gentlemen and as white men, and quite a number of colored people have fine positions in business in Berlin and other German cities. Why, then, fight the Germans only for the benefit of the Wall Street robbers, and to protect the millions that they have loaned to the English, French, and Italians?

You have been made the tool of the egotistic and rapacious rich in America, and there is nothing in the whole game for you but broken bones, horrible wounds, spoiled health, or death. No satisfaction whatever will you get out of this unjust war. You have never seen Germany, so you are fools if you allow people to make you hate us. Come over and see for yourself. Let those do the fighting who make the profit out of this war. Don't allow them to use you as cannon fodder.

To carry a gun in this service is not an honor but a shame. Throw it away and come over to the German lines. You will find friends who will help you.

Enticing as the offer might have been (and, undeniably, the leaflet raised questions that black troops had been asking themselves and one another), the vast majority of African American soldiers believed that if they continued to fight with honor in the war, as they were doing, it would benefit the larger cause for equality back in the States.

At the War Department in Washington, there was concern that German propaganda might ultimately persuade African American

Privates Needham Roberts (right) and Henry Johnson.

soldiers to desert. A memo marked "confidential" was sent to General Peyton March on the morale and condition of these soldiers:

> Reference to your cablegram 1523, the stories probably invented by German agents that have been widely circulated among colored people in the United States to the effect that colored soldiers in France are always placed in most dangerous positions and sacraficed [*sic*] to save white soldiers; that when wounded they are left on ground to die without medical attention etc. are absolutely false. . . .
>
> A tour of inspection just completed among American negro troops by officers of the Training Section, these headquarters, shows a comparatively high degree of training and efficiency among these troops. . . . Colored troops in trenches have been particularly fortunate, as one regiment had been there a month

before any losses were suffered. This almost unheard of on western front.

Exploit of colored infantrymen [re: Roberts and Johnson] some weeks ago repelling much larger German patrol killing and wounding several Germans and winning Croix de Guerre by their gallantry has roused fine spirit of emulation throughout colored troops all of whom are looking forward to more active service. Only regret expressed by colored troops is that they are not given more dangerous work to do. They are especially amused at the stories being circulated that the American colored troops are placed in the most dangerous positions and all are desirous of having more active service than has been permitted them thus far. I cannot commend too highly the spirit shown among the colored combat troops who exhibit fine capacity for quick training and eagerness for the most dangerous work.

This memo was not written by Colonel Louis Linard or any other AEF staffer. It was authored and signed by the chief himself: PERSHING.

13.

The Eyewitness

Just how does it feel to be shot on the field of battle? Just
what is the exact sensation when a bullet burns its way
through your flesh or crashes through your bones? I always
wanted to know.

As a police reporter I "covered" scores of shooting cases,
but I could never learn from the victims what the precise
feeling was as the piece of lead struck. For long years I had
cherished an ordinate curiosity to know that sensation.

—*War correspondent Floyd Gibbons*

FOUR MONTHS AFTER *Chicago Daily Tribune* reporter Floyd
Gibbons's front-page article about the German U-boat's sinking
of the *Laconia* made him famous, he found his way to England in time
to greet General Pershing when he arrived in June 1917, and managed
to convince Pershing to let him accompany him across the English
Channel to France. Gibbons relished being first but also in uncovering
the small details that brought stories to life, such as a brief exchange
that Pershing had hours before he appeared in front of thousands of
wildly excited French citizens. Gibbons wrote:

It was a beautiful sunlit day. It was not long before the coast
line of France began to push itself up through the distant

Channel mists and make itself visible on the horizon. I stood in the bow of the ship looking toward the coast line and silent with thoughts concerning the momentousness of the approaching historical event.

It happened that I looked back amidships and saw a solitary figure standing on the bridge of the vessel. It was General Pershing. He seemed rapt in deep thought. He wore his cap straight on his head, the visor shading his eyes. He stood tall and erect, his hands behind him. . . .

As we drew close to the shore, I noticed an enormous concrete breakwater extending out from the harbour entrance. It was surmounted by a wooden railing and on the very end of it, straddling the rail, was a small French boy. . . . As we came within hailing distance, he gave us the first greeting that came from the shores of France to these first arriving American soldiers.

"*Vive L'Amerique!*" he shouted, cupping his hands to his mouth and sending his voice across the water to us. Pershing on the bridge heard the salutation. He smiled, touched his hand to his hat and waved to the lad on the railing.

Five months later, in October 1917, Gibbons was with the 1st Division at Sommerviller, when Sergeant Alex Arch became the first AEF soldier in the war to fire an artillery round at the Germans. Gibbons not only chronicled the event, he was the journalist who retrieved the shell casing and saved it for Arch.

By May 1918, the 1st Division was still the only fully trained American division in France. Were it to soundly defeat the Germans in a major battle, the victory would reverberate throughout the Allied lines—and Germany's.

Cantigny was the target. Seventy-five miles north of Paris and occupied by the 82nd German Reserve Division, the small village represented the westernmost tip of the German salient. It rested at the top of a hill, an ideal observation point for the surrounding area of Picardy. H hour for the main artillery barrage was scheduled for 4:45 a.m. on May

28, and Colonel Hanson Ely's 28th Infantry Regiment would lead the ground charge, accompanied by fourteen French tanks.

Organizing the logistics was Lieutenant Colonel George Marshall. He and the division's commander, General Robert Lee Bullard, had picked out an area twelve miles to the rear with terrain similar to Cantigny where Ely's regiment could rehearse their advance, which depended on carefully following a rolling barrage provided mostly by French artillery. Since training with actual cannons would have been too dangerous and also given away their position, men holding leafy tree limbs ran in front of the 28th's soldiers, arching the branches high in the air and then swooping them down into the ground with a crash, as if they were the exploding rounds. Ely's troops had to learn that if they moved forward too quickly, they'd be hit by their own shells, but too slowly and the Germans would have time to regroup. Bullard also had the men practice with flamethrowers, a weapon they had never used before. Bullard wanted them prepared for all contingencies.

So when the Germans launched a surprise offensive on May 27, the day before the scheduled assault, it threw their plans into chaos. Twenty German divisions attacked the French lines at Chemin des Dames Ridge, dramatically affecting the Cantigny operation because the heavy French artillery guns so integral to the assault were now needed to reinforce French troops trying to save Paris. General Ferdinand Foch agreed to let the guns stay long enough to provide the initial barrage on May 28, but they would be withdrawn immediately afterward. Except for a small number of light guns, the Americans would have no artillery support for the duration of the battle.

On a smaller scale, George Marshall was coping with his own personal calamity. He had carelessly mounted his horse without checking the saddle, and the saddle slipped to the side as Marshall started riding off. Marshall's right foot was caught in the stirrup, and as he fell to the ground, he snapped his ankle. Protesting that he didn't have the time, Marshall refused to go to a hospital for an X-ray to see if the bone had been broken. A local doctor taped up his foot, and it had to be propped up to reduce the swelling and allow it to heal. Unable to sleep due to the throbbing pain, Marshall worked up to eighteen hours a day for an entire week with almost no rest.

And then more bad news. Two days had passed since a lieutenant named Oliver Kendall had left on a mission to place heavy entrenchment and engineering tools in key depots close to the front lines. The 1st Division's officers were more concerned with the detailed maps that Kendall had been carrying than with the life of the young man himself. If Kendall had been caught with the papers, the Germans could pinpoint exactly where the Americans would be on D-day. No one knew if Kendall had evaded capture or, if not, if he was able to tear up the maps beforehand or otherwise dispose of them.

In light of these developments—the loss of all French heavy artillery after the first barrage; the fact that the man planning the drive, George Marshall, was in tremendous pain and drifting in and out of consciousness from fatigue; and the significant probability that the Germans had gotten hold of 1st Division's battle plans—there was, understandably, some discussion of perhaps canceling the operation. Pershing was at General Bullard's command headquarters to oversee everything in person, and he rejected postponing the attack. Any delay would be perceived as weakness. Defeat, of course, would have worse repercussions, but Pershing was willing to take that gamble.

Germany's 82nd Reserve Division had known for days that American troops were in the Picardy sector and had found shelter in neighboring towns, most of which had long ago been bombed into oblivion, and they sporadically sent over harassing fire, including 210mm rounds.

"A 3-inch shell," George Marshall wrote of the varying rounds, "will temporarily scare or deter a man; a 6-inch shell will shock him; but an 8-inch shell, such as these 210-mm ones, rips up the nervous system of everyone within a hundred yards of the explosion."

Floyd Gibbons marveled at how the men could steal even a moment's rest amid all the shelling. "It is strange how sleep can come at the front in surroundings not unlike the interior of a boiler factory, but it does," he observed. For some, the extended periods of quiet were even more unsettling. "Stranger still was the fact that at midnight when the shelling almost ceased, for small intervals almost every sleeper there present was aroused by the sudden silence."

"I don't sleep any more," Robert McCormick confided to Tiffany Blake, a friend and coworker from Chicago. "I hear every shot. The first buzz of the telephone wakes me." A graduate of Yale University and Northwestern University School of Law, McCormick was the editor and publisher of the *Chicago Daily Tribune*, Floyd Gibbons's employer, and a member of Chicago's city council. McCormick was also an expert horseman, and he had joined the 1st Cavalry Regiment of the Illinois National Guard in June 1916. Within a month he was in Mexico patrolling the border. McCormick earned the gratitude of officers and enlisted men alike for dipping into his extensive personal funds to provide them with extra supplies.

Fluent in French, McCormick was sent to Paris in July 1917 to work in Pershing's intelligence office as a liaison officer between the French and the American armies. Ostensibly his role was to gather and exchange information so that the two countries were on the same page when it came to war plans and military organization. But McCormick suspected that the French were withholding critical details from the United States, and he secretly began going through his counterparts' files to uncover what they were hiding. To divert their attention, McCormick would have an American colleague instigate a heated argument with a French officer down the hall, drawing staff members out to see what was going on, and then McCormick would sneak into their offices and skim through their files.

Even with such subterfuge to enliven his days, McCormick grew tired of office work and appealed to General Pershing and U.S. Army Chief of Staff Peyton March for a combat assignment. A few years shy of his fortieth birthday and untrained in the use of weaponry, McCormick was nevertheless sent to artillery school, where he excelled. By February 1918, Major McCormick was with the 1st Division's 5th Field Artillery Regiment. General Bullard was pleased to have him on his team, well remembering that McCormick used his own money to buy ammunition for the troops when the two men served on the Punitive Expedition back in 1916. Bullard also allowed McCormick his eccentricities; he wore a monocle over one eye and always carried a cane, which McCormick claimed he needed after a serious football injury. (He had in fact hurt himself playing polo, but McCormick thought football sounded manlier.)

After months of training and preparation, he was taken out of the battle just as it was starting. Several days before the H-hour assault on Cantigny, McCormick came down with the flu. Soon he could barely breathe or walk. He made one final inspection of his men the morning of the attack before he was transferred to a hospital in Paris.

Floyd Gibbons was with a group of artillerymen as they launched their early-morning barrage, and he watched as the 28th Infantry Regiment marched up to take their positions near the front. As Gibbons crouched alongside the gun crew, he noted their amusement when the infantry soldiers almost jumped out of their skin after a well-camouflaged howitzer nearby suddenly shattered the air with a deafening blast. Gibbons wrote:

> Upon such occasions the gun crews would laugh heartily and indulge in good natured raillery with the infantrymen [nicknamed doughboys].
>
> "Whoa, Johnny doughboy, don't you get frightened. We were just shipping a load of sauerkraut to the Kaiser," said one ear-hardened Marine gunner. . . .
>
> "Gwan, you leatherneck," returns an infantryman. "You smell like a livery stable. Better trade that pitchfork for a bayonet and come on up where there's some fighting."
>
> "Don't worry about the fighting, little doughboy," came another voice from the dark gun pit. . . . "If you don't get killed the first eight days, the orders is to shoot you for loafing. You're marching over what's called 'the road you don't come back on.'"

Rivalries aside, the artillery provided a well-executed rolling barrage that enabled the 28th Infantry Regiment to storm into Cantigny and gain control of much of the village in less than an hour. On May 29, American newspapers were calling the operation a total triumph. U.S. TROOPS CAPTURE TOWN proclaimed the *Chicago Daily Tribune*. The first line of the paper's lead article stated that the "American attack was a success in ten minutes."

It was neither that fast nor, at the time, a confirmed victory. While the Americans had indeed overtaken most of Cantigny by sunrise, they still had the challenge of holding on to it. And with the French artillery and tanks pulling out to face the German divisions barreling down on Paris, the AEF troops were now much more vulnerable.

Much of the fighting was house to house and man to man. German soldiers hiding in cellars fared the worst. With nowhere to escape, they could only watch as grenades came clattering down the cellar stairs and exploded. Others were cremated alive by flamethrowers.

Communication wires had been severed in the fighting, and General Robert Bullard and Lieutenant Colonel George Marshall at division headquarters relied on runners and carrier pigeons for much of their information. On May 30, two days after the *Tribune* and other papers had declared the battle over, a bird came into headquarters with a dire message that the Americans were on the verge of being overrun. Marshall's heart sank. "For the 1st Division to lose its first objective was unthinkable and would have had a most depressing effect on the morale of our entire Army as well as on those of our Allies," he recalled.

When Marshall looked more closely at the tiny, tissue-paper message, he noticed something odd. Although undated, the sender wrote the exact hour it was released—6:00 p.m. Marshall looked at his watch. It was 5:55 p.m. Unless the pigeon had magically flown back in time, something was amiss. Marshall was eventually able to determine that the note had been written twenty-four hours before and, much to his relief, the crisis had already been resolved. Apparently, the bird who brought the message had developed an affection for another carrier pigeon in Cantigny and lingered there for almost a day before leaving its newfound mate. By May 31, after seven failed counterattacks, the Germans finally gave up. Cantigny was entirely within American hands.

Out of four thousand American combatants in the battle, almost one in three was a casualty. "The price paid was a heavy one but it demonstrated conclusively the fighting qualities and fortitude of the American soldier," George Marshall later wrote. "The enemy's rush on Chateau-Thierry and the dramatic entrance of our troops at that point, at the psychological moment, naturally attracted the undivided attention of the public in America."

Less than a week after Cantigny was definitively won, Floyd Gibbons was back in Paris hunting down his next story. In early June he heard rumblings that the 2nd and 3rd divisions were about to clash with German troops in and around a forest fifty miles east of Paris called Belleau Wood. Within the 2nd Division was General James Harbord's Marine Brigade. Harbord had been Pershing's chief of staff, an enormously powerful position, but he had been pressing for a combat assignment.

This would be the Marines' first major action in the war, and Gibbons wanted to be in the thick of it. With their gruff, bombastic, and fearless manner, the Marines could be counted on for "good copy."

On the morning of June 6, Gibbons jumped into a car with a driver from the U.S. Press Bureau and Lieutenant Oscar Hartzell, who was a former journalist for the *New York Times*, and the three men drove to the Marine headquarters at La Voie-du-Châtel, just west of Belleau Wood. Gibbons handed the staff driver an urgent dispatch that said, "I am up at the front and entering Belleau Wood with the U.S. Marines" and told him to rush it back to the press office in Paris, with the explanation that Gibbons would fill the rest in later.

Inside the 5th Marines regimental headquarters, Gibbons and Hartzell found Colonel W. C. Neville and informed him of their plan to proceed to the front. "Go as far as you like, but I want to tell you it's damn hot up there," Neville warned.

That's exactly what they wanted to hear. Gibbons and Hartzell hiked to Lucy-le-Bocage, a town on the edge of Belleau Wood that was under heavy fire. Bullets and shrapnel clipped off leaves and branches as the two men made their way through a nearby forest, stepping over shell craters and blasted-out tree stumps. Little pieces of paper were fluttering through the smoke-filled air, and Gibbons grabbed a few to inspect them more closely. They were, he realized, torn-up personal letters the Marines had received from parents and sweethearts back home. "The tired, dog-weary Marines had been forced to remove [them] from their packs and destroy [them]," Gibbons wrote, "to ease the straps that cut into the aching grooves in their shoulders" as they pressed forward as swiftly as possible.

Several minutes before 5:00 p.m., Gibbons and Hartzell came across an American machine-gun nest, and a lieutenant asked them what they were doing in an active combat zone. Gibbons replied that he was a journalist pursuing the "big story" and Belleau Wood was it.

"If I were you I'd be about forty miles south of this place," the young Marine said, "but if you want to see the fun, stick around. We advance in five minutes."

Exactly five minutes later, the Marines sprinted forward in packs, each one providing cover for the next as they moved across the open field. As Gibbons and Hartzell followed, they encountered Major Benjamin Berry, battalion commander of the 5th Marines. Berry was astonished to see the two men there, armed with only writing pads and pencils, and he told them to turn back.

"But Major," Gibbons pleaded, "I want to get up there and cover this as an eyewitness for my paper."

"Well, then you'll come at your own risk," Berry said.

They crept down a sloped hillside that led to a sunken road. The bodies of French soldiers and U.S. Marines were strewn everywhere, freshly killed.

To Berry's south was Major Burton Sibley, with the 6th Marines.

Overseeing both battalions was General Albertus Catlin, watching through binoculars from a distant hill. Berry's men, Catlin could tell, had the tougher charge; the field in front of them was much longer and more open, but there was no other way to go.

Berry, Gibbons, and Hartzell came to an opening that led into the V-shaped field with forests on both sides. German machine gunners were hiding behind the trees, but Berry motioned for the men to follow him forward.

"Then the woods about us began to rattle fiercely," Gibbons wrote of the harrowing moment.

> Major Berry had advanced well beyond the center of the field when I saw him turn toward me and heard him shout:
>
> "Get down everybody."
>
> We all fell on our faces. And then it began to come in hot and fast. Perfectly withering volleys of lead swept the tops of the oats just over us. . . .
>
> I was busily engaged flattening myself on the ground and looked forward. Then I heard a shout in front of me. It came from Major Berry. . . . The Major was making an effort to get to his feet. With his right hand he was savagely grasping his left wrist.
>
> "My hand's gone," he shouted. One of the streams of lead from the left had found him. A ball had entered his left arm at the elbow, had travelled down the side of the bone, tearing away muscles and nerves of the forearm and lodging itself in the palm of his hand. His pain was excruciating. . . .
>
> "You are twenty yards from the trees," I shouted to the Major. "I am crawling over to you now. Wait until I get there and I'll help you. Then we'll get up and make a dash for it."

Pulling himself forward with his elbows and pushing with his toes, Gibbons slowly started making his way toward Berry.

"And then it happened," Gibbons recalled.

A bullet hit the upper part of his left arm. Gibbons felt like he had been touched on the skin with "the lighted end of a cigarette." That was all.

Gibbons looked at his arm and didn't see any blood flowing. He also didn't feel any stiffness or weakness, so he kept using it to inch forward.

Seconds later, another bullet pierced his left shoulder blade, and again, to Gibbons's surprise, the affect was minimal. The wound stung, but the pain was bearable, and he could still move his arm.

Gibbons called out to Major Berry to assure him he was on his way.

In order to protect his head as much as possible, Gibbons was pressing his left cheek into the ground and had the rim of his helmet covering the right side of his brow. It wasn't enough.

"Then there came a crash. It sounded to me like someone had dropped a glass bottle into a porcelain bathtub," Gibbons recalled, "and everything in the world turned white. That was the sensation. I did not recognise it because I have often been led to believe and often heard it said that when one receives a blow on the head everything turns black."

The third bullet had ricocheted off a large stone in front of Gibbons's face, pierced his left eye socket, fractured the top of his skull, and punched a three-inch hole through his helmet.

Unable to see anything, Gibbons seriously wondered if he might be dead, and he pinched himself with his right arm and determined that he was still alive. He didn't know that his left eyeball was hanging out of its socket, but the bullet had missed his brain by less than an inch, and he maintained consciousness. Gibbons adjusted the rim of his helmet to look out of his right eye, and he watched Major Berry stand up, despite the oncoming fire, and stumble back into the woods. Berry called in an artillery strike on the machine-gun nest, and it was successfully wiped out. There were still German snipers in the area, however, and Gibbons dared not move.

Hartzell, uninjured, had dropped down not far from Gibbons, and in a low voice he called over to ask him if he was seriously wounded.

"I don't think so," Gibbons replied. "I think I'm all right."

"Where are you hit?" he asked.

"In the head," Gibbons said.

Hartzell cursed at Gibbons and told him he was going over to help him.

"You damn fool," Gibbons snapped, "don't move in my direction. I think they think I'm dead."

Hartzell stayed put, but the two men kept up their quiet conversation, and they agreed to give each other the contact information for their wives, in the event one of them didn't make it through the night.

After an agonizing three hours waiting for the sun to set, the two men crawled back into the woods at nightfall and began to retrace their steps to find any kind of assistance. A mile down the path they encountered a medical corpsman, who removed the handkerchief that Gibbons had drooped over his dangling eye and bandaged it with gauze.

The corpsman directed the men to an aid station another mile away, and as they were limping along the side of the road, a Ford ambulance came sputtering up behind them. Gibbons squeezed into the passenger seat, and Hartzell sat on the running board. Four men filled the back of the ambulance. One of them had been shot through the lungs, and the other three had broken legs, their bones splintered by machine-gun rounds. Every time the car's wheels hit a rock or pitched into a shell crater, the men yelped in pain. The driver was going as slowly as possible so that the jolts wouldn't hurt as much, but the man with the chest wound tasted blood coming up into his throat and mouth and, barely able to speak, begged the driver to speed up.

"If I go fast," the driver said, "you guys are going to suffer the agonies of hell, and if I go slow this guy with the hemorrhage will croak before we get there." The closest medical facility was ten miles away.

Without pause, the men with the broken legs all told the driver to go faster, and they made it there in time to save the man's life. Gibbons also received his first real care since he had been shot. (The corpsman in the woods didn't even have water to clean Gibbons's wounds or flush out the congealed blood in his left eye socket.) The makeshift treatment center had been set up in a church, and the wounded were everywhere, lying on the dirt floor or propped upright against the hard, wooden pews. Gibbons apparently made quite an impression when he staggered through the entrance. "My God," he heard another patient gasp, "look at what they're bringing in."

Word got back to the U.S. Press Bureau in Paris that Gibbons had been shot multiple times, including in the head, and did not survive. As a tribute to Gibbons, the censors agreed to release the story about the Marines at Belleau Wood and gave him credit for the exclusive, even though it was generally against protocol to mention specific units (the entire number of Marines in the AEF was equal in size to a single Army division), and the battle was far from over.

Gibbons was actually still clinging to life on the morning of June 7, when he was crammed into an ammunition truck with about twenty other casualties and rushed to a hospital farther in the rear. An over-worked medical officer took one look at Gibbons, made a quick diagnosis that he wouldn't live through the day, and had him wheeled to an out-of-the-way corner of the building where the mortally wounded were left to die. Lieutenant Hartzell was able to locate Gibbons, rescue him from the "dead pile," and get him into an ambulance headed for the U.S. military base hospital at Neuilly in Paris.

There, Gibbons was greeted with a friendly face. "I know you," a young sergeant named Stephen Hayes said when Gibbons came in. "I'm from Chicago also. I used to go to Hyde Park High School. We're going to fix you up right away."

Gibbons confessed to feeling a sense of "utter helpless childishness" as he was prepped for surgery. No one had informed him of the true extent of his injuries since he'd been shot, and his mind was a whirlwind of questions. "Was the operation to be a serious one or a minor one?" he wondered. "Would they have to remove my eye? Would they have to operate on my skull? How about the arm? Would there be an amputation? How about the other eye? Would I ever see again?"

Gibbons was busy making mental notes about the procedure, and he was particularly intrigued by the anesthesiologist, who, while dispensing the ether, was paying little attention to Gibbons but chatting nonstop with a colleague.

"Are you feeling my pulse?" Gibbons asked, trying to get his attention.

"Now, never you mind about your pulse," he replied peevishly.

"You will pardon me for manifesting a mild interest in what you are doing to me," Gibbons remarked, "but you see I know that something is going to be done to my right eye and inasmuch as that is the only eye I've got on that side, I can't help being concerned."

"Now, you just forget it and take deep breaths," the man said, and then promptly returned to his other conversation: "Charlie, did you see that case over in Ward 62? That was a wonderful case. The bullet hit the man in the head and they took the lead out of his stomach. . . . Talk about bullet eaters—believe me, those Marines sure are."

A few more minutes passed when Gibbons heard the anesthesiologist casually say, "All right, he's under now; where's the next one?"

"The hell I am!" Gibbons exclaimed with, in his words, "visions of knives and saws and gimlets and brain chisels [going] through my mind."

More ether was administered, and Gibbons eventually drifted off. When he woke up, he was relieved to find he still had one good eye and that the doctors hadn't amputated his arm.

BY JUNE 8, the fight for Belleau Wood was still raging, and Gibbons was going crazy not being there to cover it in person. But with the help of a Marine major named Frank E. Evans, who relayed information from the battlefield to him in his hospital bed, Gibbons was able to weave together what he had experienced with Evans's reports and spotlight with obvious awe the actions of the Marines. After referencing brave warriors from a distant age, Gibbons claimed to have witnessed a "new ideal" of

Floyd Gibbons.

heroism in Belleau Wood. "A small platoon line of Marines lay on their faces and bellies under the trees at the edge of a wheat field," Gibbons began the story that would transform Belleau Wood into legend.

> Two hundred yards across that flat field the enemy was located in the trees. I peered into the trees but could see nothing, yet I knew that every leaf in the foliage screened scores of German machine guns that swept the field with lead. The bullets nipped the tops of the young wheat and ripped the bark from the trunks of the trees three feet from the ground on which the Marines lay. The minute for the Marine advance was approaching. An old gunnery sergeant commanded the platoon

in the absence of the lieutenant, who had been shot and was out of the fight. This old sergeant was a Marine veteran. His cheeks were bronzed with the wind and sun of the seven seas. The service bar across his left breast showed that he had fought in the Philippines, in Santa Domingo, at the walls of Pekin, and in the streets of Vera Cruz. . . .

As the minute for the advance arrived, he arose from the trees first and jumped out onto the exposed edge of that field that ran with lead, across which he and his men were to charge. Then he turned to give the charge order to the men of his platoon—his mates—the men he loved. He said:

"COME ON, YOU SONS-O'-BITCHES! DO YOU WANT TO LIVE FOREVER?"

Dan Daly, the forty-four-year-old Marine who exhorted his young comrades to advance, survived the battle, which lasted until June 26. One thousand other Marines did not. (Daly would later claim that he never used profanity and actually yelled: "For Christ's sake, men—come on! Do you want to live forever?" But Gibbons's version is quoted more frequently.)

For Gibbons, some of the greatest testimony regarding the Marines' grit and determination at Belleau Wood came from the Germans themselves. "The individual soldiers are very good," Gibbons quoted from an intercepted intelligence report:

They are healthy, vigorous, and physically well-developed men, of ages ranging from eighteen to twenty-eight, who at present lack only necessary training to make them redoubtable opponents. The troops are fresh and full of straightforward confidence. A remark of one of the prisoners is indicative of their spirit: "We kill or get killed." . . .

Only a few of the troops are of pure American origin; the majority is of German, Dutch and Italian parentage, but these semi-Americans, almost all of whom were born in America and never have been in Europe before, fully feel themselves to be true born sons of their country.

Gibbons observed this same sense of national unity in the hospital where he was recovering. "There were fourteen wounded American soldiers in my ward," Gibbons wrote.

> There was an Irishman, a Swede, an Italian, a Jew, a Pole, one man of German parentage, and one man of Russian extraction. All of them had been wounded at the front and all of them now had something nearer and dearer to them than any traditions that might have been handed down to them from a mother country—they had fought and bled and suffered for a new country, *their* new country.
>
> Here in this ward was the new melting pot of America. Not the melting pot of our great American cities where nationalistic quarters still exist, but a greater fusion process from which these men had emerged with unquestionable Americanism. They are the real and new Americans—born in the hell of battle.

There was one other group of Americans that Gibbons lauded in his articles, and they were the women who had come to Europe to serve however they could. Some had been in France and England since 1914, sweating through gas attacks and air raids and driving ambulances under shell fire. Others worked for the Red Cross, the Salvation Army, and the Y.M.C.A. to bring comfort to wounded and homesick soldiers. Not one of them had been drafted. They were all volunteers. And by June 1918, they were more than sixteen thousand strong.

14.

An Army of Angels

After the war there is going to be a difference between
those who were in France and those not. I realize perfectly
that those at home work just as hard if not harder, and that
they have all the dirty uninteresting things to do, but after
the war there is going to be a fellow feeling and esprit de
corps amongst those who have been to the front which
every man will be glad to be a part of. You have no
conception how different things are here from what you
really think. . . . It is all very interesting and I am sorry you
are not here to get a taste of it.

—American nurse Nora Saltonstall, writing to her friend
Clara Danielson on July 5, 1918

THE MAJORITY OF THE WOMEN, approximately ten thousand
in all, were U.S. Army nurses. And the sentiments they expressed
in their letters and journals were nearly indistinguishable from those
written by American soldiers and Marines—especially their early sense
of exuberance about heading over and their desire to get as close to the
front as possible.

"If my spectacular arrival here last night is to be a criterion of what
lies before me," Alta May Andrews wrote on December 1, 1917, from
Camp Custer in Michigan to her mother in Illinois,

I believe that I shall experience a great deal of excitement.
Such an interesting beginning to this—my Great Adventure!

Mother dear, I am afraid that I won't be able to convey to
you even a remote idea of how happy I am to be going.

You can't possibly know how much I have lived for this
occasion. To think that my childhood ambition is about to be
realized. To know that such an unusual wish was at last
materialized is nothing short of remarkable.

How I always longed to emulate father's heroine, Mrs.
Briggs. How often I have listened to those fascinating stories
of that dear old Civil War Nurse. . . .

But, who would ever dream that in this period of
civilization there could possibly develop a war of such
magnitude that it would include even me? But, if it has to be
that this world must be embroiled in a tremendous "War to
end Wars," I am glad that I, too, may play a part in it.

After five months of training, Andrews finally received the news
she had been waiting to hear. "My darling Mother," Andrews exclaimed, "tonight finds me among a group of ten nurses who are considered just about the most fortunate creatures on earth! . . . We are to
be sent overseas!!!!"

Although enthusiastic, Andrews was not ignorant of the dangers
ahead. Germans were bombing hospitals and dressing stations, and
nurses were treating patients with highly infectious diseases and dying
by the hundreds as a result.

Before embarking, Andrews was issued a Certificate of Identity
card that included her fingerprint, a photograph of her face, and several
basic personal details, including her age ("27"), height ("5 ft. 5 1/2 in"),
and weight ("162 lbs"). There was also a line called "Remarks," under
which Andrews noted one small physical defect: "Tips of middle finger, left hand, amputated." The certificate served as her official I.D.,
and it would also be used to identify her body in the event that she was

killed, possibly even en route to Europe. Ten days before Andrews departed from Hoboken, New Jersey, a German submarine sank six U.S. ships in sight of New York City and laid mines that caused further casualties.

"Because of the fact that several boats had been torpedoed off the Jersey Coast last Sunday," Andrews wrote in her second diary entry, "it was essential that zigzagging begin the moment we left the harbor. The twelve weirdly camouflaged transports, each with its cargo of troops and nurses, immediately took up their designated positions." (The strange camouflage that Andrews mentions refers to a technique called "dazzling." Instead of painting a ship to blend in with its environment, which—unlike on land—is impossible to do on water, ships were painted in bold, oddly patterned colors that, in theory, would make it harder for submarines to estimate their heading, speed, and distance.)

After two weeks at sea, Andrews arrived in England and promptly informed her family that she was safe and that her letters from here on might be a bit "namby-pamby" due to government restrictions on what could and could not be shared. "I shall try to avoid bringing into operation the cruel scissors of the censors [who would, truly, cut out pieces of letters], however, by eliminating all news of supposed military importance."

Censorship was intended not only to prevent the enemy from discovering troop movements and locations (letters captured on Allied trains or ships or pulled from the corpses of soldiers on the battlefield could yield valuable information), but also to ensure that messages were cheerful and optimistic. Andrews's own morale could not have been higher.

"Mother dear, I love it all!" she continued in her first letter home from Europe. "These past six months have literally been packed with sensational thrills—thrills exciting, supreme, each one surpassing the preceding ones. First, the call to service, then the coveted assignment overseas. Later, that breathtaking sensation of walking up a gang-plank into whatever Fate holds in store for you."

In Andrews's private diary, the entries were as upbeat as her letters, but she did allow for the occasional complaint. Upon settling into her new quarters in France, and seeing the lumpy mattress on steel slats that she'd be sleeping on, Andrews griped: "I really believe that I now understand why the Guillotine was invented! It must have been to make a fitting finish to the man who invented this bed to which I have been assigned."

Andrews wrote to her sister that the other nurses were expressing a much greater disappointment, that their location in Neuilly was "too far behind the lines," and they were impatient to put their training into action.

They would not have much longer to wait.

As the fighting at Belleau Wood and surrounding areas intensified, the wounded started streaming into Neuilly, and Nurse Andrews was overwhelmed by what she saw.

"How utterly disgusted I have been with myself today!" she admitted in her diary on July 11, 1918.

> After having reached my coveted objective, I came precariously near to spoiling it all. While I was engaged in the simple task of bed-making this morning, the appearance of the dressing cart caused the wounds of all of the sixty-eight patients in the ward to be exposed simultaneously. An ugly looking stump of a leg here, an amputated arm there, a long, jagged wound in a chest, a face horribly mutilated with gaping holes in abdomens and backs! But, most frequent of all, the ugly stumps, stumps, stumps! . . .
>
> This ghastly exposure taking me so completely by surprise, I became deathly sick. I grew cold and my head pounded. I tried to look away from one sickening sight only to behold others.

One French soldier, unknowingly, helped Andrews steel herself and regain her composure. "Gritting my teeth," she wrote,

Alta May Andrews and the ship she sailed to France on,
with "dazzling" camouflage.

I compelled myself to watch the dressing of a poilu whose leg
had been almost entirely stripped of flesh by mutilating shrapnel. He was sitting up calmly taking in the entire situation
without a flicker—without a murmur. To him I owe a debt of
gratitude! Then and there, my troubles were over and I knew
that I would never again allow myself to be affected.

Three days later, Neuilly, along with all of Paris, came perilously
close to being overrun. General Erich Ludendorff and the German
high command had specifically chosen July 15 as the date of a final,
all-out blitz code-named *Friedensturm*, or "peace offensive." Ludendorff
was so confident of victory that he believed the Allies would be suing
for peace within a matter of days.

On July 14, Bastille Day, the Germans were hoping that many
French troops would be too drunk or hungover after a night of carousing to fight. What they didn't know was that Allied commanders had
already learned of their plans after interrogating German soldiers captured during a raid near Reims on July 11. The prisoners even divulged
the exact time—12:10 a.m. on the fifteenth—that the Germans would
begin their artillery barrage, followed by a sweeping infantry attack.

At 11:00 p.m. on the fourteenth, the Allies launched their own barrage, catching the Germans entirely off guard. The French had also
moved many of their troops into secondary trenches, so when the Germans started shelling the front lines, very few soldiers were there. Once
the German infantry passed by the first line of trenches, they found
themselves up against French forces virtually untouched by the initial
bombing and primed to fight.

General Pershing also ordered several divisions to reinforce the
French. In a repeat of August 1914, the Germans came close to breach-
ing the French lines near a bulge in the Marne River, near Paris, but
this time it was the American 3rd Division that held them back.

By July 16, the German offensive was stalling, and General Foch saw
an opening to strike back. One of his main objectives was to cut the

highway between Soissons and Château-Thierry, the Germans' primary communications and supply route in the Marne region. General Charles Summerall's 1st Division and General James Harbord's 2nd Division, having just won the battle for Belleau Wood two weeks earlier, would lead the assault. Combined, the two divisions became III Corps, led by General Robert Bullard. Bullard's stellar performance at Cantigny with the 1st Division had earned him the promotion to corps commander.

H hour would be 4:35 a.m. on the morning of July 18. The seventy thousand American troops, along with the French Foreign Legion, had to move into position near the Forest of Retz, outside Villers-Cotterêts, without alerting the Germans, including their aerial reconnaissance, that such a massive operation was in motion. They were helped by the fact that the moon was shrouded by dark rain clouds on the evening of July 17.

"All night long those furtive forces moved through the forest," an American reporter embedded with III Corps wrote of the preparation.

> There was some suspense. We knew that if the Germans had the slightest advance knowledge about that mobilisation of Foch's reserves that night, they would have responded with a downpour of gas shells, which spreading their poisonous fumes under the wet roof of the forest, might have spelt slaughter for 70,000 men.
>
> But the enemy never knew. They never even suspected. And at the tick of 4:35 a.m., the heavens seemed to crash asunder, as tons and tons of hot metal sailed over the forest, bound for the German line. . . .
>
> All through that glorious day of the 18th, our lines swept forward victoriously. The First Division fought it out on the left, the Foreign Legion in the centre and the Second Division with the Marines pushed forward to the right. Village after village fell into our hands. We captured batteries of guns and thousands of prisoners.

On through the night the Allied assault continued. Our
men fought without water or food. . . . By morning of the
19th, we had penetrated the enemy's lines that we had crossed
the road running southward from Soissons to Chateau-Thierry,
thereby disrupting the enemy's communications between his
newly established base and the peak of his salient. Thus exposed to an enveloping movement that might have surrounded
large numbers, there was nothing left for the Germans to do
but to withdraw.

"The Germans began backing off the Marne," the reporter concluded. "From that day on, their movement to date has continued
backward. It began July 18th. Two American Divisions played glorious
parts in the crisis. It was their day. It was America's day. It was the turn
of the tide."

The reporter who accompanied the American troops throughout
the battle had only just recently been released from the hospital after
nearly being killed five weeks earlier, with three still-healing bullet
holes in his body attesting to his brush with death. But he was unwilling to let anything prevent him from missing the historic Second Battle
of the Marne. He was Floyd Gibbons.

FOR ALL OF Gibbons's glory-filled language and almost sanitized
depictions of warfare, victory came at an enormous cost, and thousands
of American and Allied troops were killed or permanently disfigured.

"The night of the 16th we began to witness the result of the desperate fighting which had stopped, for awhile at least, the determined
German drive toward Paris," Nurse Alta May Andrews wrote in her
diary on July 18.

Our hospital alone received over five hundred American
wounded. . . . Some were brought in with both legs amputated, others with the loss of an arm or a leg. Others with both

arms shattered or torn by shrapnel. Some had gaping wounds in their backs, abdomens, chests or faces. It was horrible! After literally dumping the patients into the assigned beds, the stretcher bearers hurried back to the receiving ward or operating rooms for others. . . . Our Chief Nurse was right! We have no further cause to complain of being denied the opportunity to nurse wounded soldiers right here!

Despite the onslaught of incoming patients, individual soldiers made a deep impression on Andrews. She recognized that each of them was somebody's child. On July 19, she went into detail about "a fine American lad of eighteen" named Rogers. Andrews wrote in her diary:

Upon my appearing for duty at seven [p.m.], the day nurses reported his condition as critical, advising me to watch him closely. Interspersing other duties about the ward with frequent trips to his bedside, I was always questioned by the semiconscious lad about his mother. Each time I went to him, he would gasp, "Hasn't-my-mother-got-here-yet? They've-sent-for-her-you-know."

Upon my answer that she would be here any minute, he would always seem greatly relieved.

Shortly after midnight, I found his pulse almost imperceptible. Parting the blue gingham shield I raised the lantern and saw that Death was but a matter of a few moments. Without opening his eyes, but sensing my hand on his, he smiled and softly whispered, "Oh! mother-is-it-you? I-knew-you'd-come. You did-get-here-didn't-you-mother? Talk-to-me!"

Oh! It was terrible! This dear boy "Going West!" How I wondered where his mother was and what she would do if she knew that this was happening to her boy.

I summed all of my courage and patting his hand so wet with beads of cold perspiration, answered, "Yes! Son, mother is here! And mother knows that everything will be all right soon."

He tried to answer but his words were inaudible. I stood there hurting all over inside, and in another minute or two he was gone. . . .

To think of these young lads alone, dying far from home and loved ones! It's the most tragic thing in the world.

Along with their physical injuries, Andrews recorded how profoundly the men had been affected mentally by combat. "Last night the quiet of the ward was disturbed by a penetrating shriek, followed by sickening groans," Andrews wrote to her mother and sister. "I rushed to the bedside of a dreamer who had 'seen' two Germans standing at the foot of his bed about to bayonet him. The poor boys! I'm afraid that they will suffer from this nervous shock to their systems for many months to come—perhaps for years. Surely they can never be the same."

Andrews worked the night shift, caring for up to seventy men at a time by herself. She marveled at the resilience of her patients. With the exception of those who might involuntarily scream out during a nightmare or were delirious from anesthesia and momentarily groaned in agony before they slipped into unconsciousness, the men bore their pain as quietly as possible. "The dear boys, brave, patient sufferers—reconciled to lie there uncomplainingly—grateful to you for whatever attentions you can give them, and expecting no more," Andrews wrote in another letter to her family. "The wonderful consideration they have for their 'buddies' is truly remarkable. They suffer in silence in deference to those around them who may have found peace and surcease from misery in blessed sleep."

Although Andrews focused on her "boys" in the letters she wrote home, occasionally she touched on war-related events, being careful not to reveal anything that went against military censorship. In her diary she could divulge whatever she wanted, and the entries, for the most part, are more candid and emotional than her correspondence. On July 23, 1918, Andrews noted with sadness in her diary that an

American airman had been shot down near Château-Thierry. Pilots were still depicted in the press as modern-day knights, but by 1918 the novelty and allure of flying had worn off to some degree, and Germany's spring and early summer ground offensives had monopolized the media's attention.

The loss of the young American aviator, however, whose death was reported on around the world, renewed an interest in the sacrifices these men were making and the perils they faced. Reporters might have moved on, but these dangers were worse than ever.

15.
_____

Their Crowded Hour

Death by burning was the death we dreaded more than any
other. Our planes were constructed of wooden frameworks
covered with fabric. The fabric was treated with "dope," a
highly combustible fluid that drew up the cloth and
stretched it tight. We Americans had no parachutes. Some
German pilots and all their balloon observers were
equipped with [them]. . . .

A major in the Paris headquarters of the Air Service told me
that the service did not believe in parachutes. "If all you
pilots had parachutes," he told me coolly, "then you'd be
inclined to use them at the slightest pretext, and then the
Air Service would lose planes that might otherwise have
been brought down safely."

—*World War I flying ace Eddie Rickenbacker*

O N FEBRUARY 18, 1918, the Lafayette Escadrille, the squadron
of U.S. airmen formed in April 1916, was officially dissolved into
the new American Air Service under General Pershing's command.

By that time, many of the escadrille's most beloved pilots were dead.
Three months after Victor Chapman was killed, in late June 1916, his

close friend Kiffin Rockwell was shot down. On September 23, Rockwell and Raoul Lufbery were flying two brand-new Nieuports over German lines when Lufbery had to return to base because his machine gun was malfunctioning, leaving Rockwell alone. Rockwell flew on, spotted a German Albatross observation plane a mile below him, and dove right at it. The Albatross was a two-seater, and the gunner in the rear quickly swiveled around and unloaded a stream of lead into Rockwell's plane, tearing off one of the wings and sending Rockwell plummeting to earth. French soldiers near the crash site found that he had been hit with an exploding bullet in the chest and was dead before impact.

Rockwell had spoken and written often about dying. Whether it was to comfort his parents or himself, or both, he claimed he was totally at peace with whatever might happen. "I don't want you to worry about me," he told his mother in a letter. "If I die, I want you to know that I have died as every man ought to die fighting for what is right. I do not feel that I am fighting for France alone, but for the cause of all humanity, the greatest of all causes."

To his friend Paul Pavelka, Rockwell was a bit more cavalier. On the night before he was shot down, almost as if he had experienced a premonition, Rockwell instructed Pavelka what to do in the event that he was killed. "Take whatever money you happen to find on me," Rockwell said, "and drink to the destruction of the damn Boche."

Pavelka himself died soon thereafter. If anyone had a reason to feel indestructible, it was Pavelka. Having been honorably discharged from the U.S. Navy in 1915, he enlisted in the Foreign Legion and was bayoneted while fighting in Champagne. He recuperated and then joined the escadrille in June 1916. On August 13, he was flying over Verdun when the nose of his plane burst into flames. With thick smoke spewing into his eyes, Pavelka was able to land in a wet marsh and scramble out of the plane just before the engine exploded. A year later he was in a car heading back to base when the driver lost control of the vehicle on a bridge and went over the side, plunging into a rocky ravine below.

Thrown through the windshield, Pavelka badly cut up his face, broke his jaw, and fractured both of his legs. Two weeks later, with bandages around his knees and his mouth wired shut, Pavelka got back in a plane and was flying missions again. And then, later that fall, Pavelka learned that an old comrade, a British cavalryman from the Foreign Legion, was visiting a nearby regiment to bring them some new horses. On a whim, Pavelka, an experienced ranch hand from his youth in Montana, mounted one of the mares. The animal reared up and fell to its side, crushing Pavelka to death. On November 11, 1917, the man who had been stabbed by a bayonet, walked away from a fiery crash landing, and barely survived an automobile accident was done in by an untamed horse.

By December 1917, more than a thousand Americans had been sent to Issoudun, the AEF's largest aviation training camp, located in central France. "I am now plugging along from day to day, doing my work, and enjoying my flying," twenty-year-old Quentin Roosevelt wrote to his fiancée, Flora Whitney, from Issoudun, on December 8. Quentin was the youngest son of former president Theodore Roosevelt, and his letters exuded the same enthusiasm that the Lafayette Escadrille pilots had expressed years before. "These little fast machines are delightful," he wrote, referring to the Nieuport 18s they used.

> You feel so at home in them, for there is just room in the cockpit for you and your controls, and not an inch more. And they're so quick to act. It's not like piloting a lumbering Curtis[s], for you could do two loops in a Nieuport during the time it takes a Curtis[s] to do one. It's frightfully cold, now, tho'. Even in my teddy-bear,—that's what they call these aviator suits,—I freeze pretty generally, if I try any ceiling work. If it's freezing down below it is some cold up about fifteen thousand feet. Aviation has considerably altered my views on religion. I don't see how the angels stand it.

Roosevelt had been drawn to airplanes since he was eleven years old. In the summer of 1909, he was with his family vacationing in France when he watched his first air show. "We were at Rheims and saw all the aeroplanes flying, and saw Curtis[s] who won the Gordon Bennett cup for the swiftest flight," Roosevelt wrote to a school friend, referring to aviation pioneer Glenn Curtiss. "You don't know how pretty it was to see all the aeroplanes sailing at a time." (Ironically, when Roosevelt later learned to fly, his least favorite planes were those built by Curtiss, whose name he also regularly misspelled. Roosevelt had suffered a serious back injury in college, and he found the Curtiss planes extremely uncomfortable.)

Roosevelt had started his flight training at the age of nineteen in Mineola, New York, where there was an aviation school less than half an hour from his family's home in Oyster Bay. Graduated as a lieutenant, he was assigned to Issoudun. Roosevelt was an experienced mechanic—he grew up tinkering with broken-down motorcycle and car engines—and along with his flight duties, he was put in charge of maintaining and repairing more than fifty trucks. He was also given supply duties and, because he was fluent in French, frequently asked to serve as an interpreter for senior American officers when they had to converse with French officials.

Roosevelt earned the admiration of the enlisted men and junior officers for an incident involving a clash with an obstinate captain who wouldn't give the men desperately needed winter boots. "When, as flying cadets under the command of Lieut. Quentin Roosevelt," a fellow lieutenant named Linton Cox recalled to a newspaper back in the States, "we were receiving training at Issoudun in the art of standing guard in three feet of mud and were serving as saw and hatchet carpenters, building shelters for the 1,200 cadets who were waiting in vain for machines in which to fly, affairs suddenly reached a crisis when it was discovered that the quartermaster refused to issue rubber boots to us, because the regular army regulations contained no official mention or recognition of flying cadets."

Quentin Roosevelt.

Cox went on to relate how appeal after appeal was rejected, and the men were starting to get sick, standing for hours in freezing mud up to their knees. Roosevelt decided to approach the captain, who, in Cox's words, "was a stickler for army red tape, and did not have the courage to exercise common sense," and requested that the soldiers be given the proper boots. When Roosevelt was refused as well, he demanded an explanation. Infuriated by the young lieutenant's impertinence, the captain ordered him out of his office. Roosevelt wouldn't budge.

"Who do you think you are—what is your name?" the captain demanded.

"I'll tell you my name after you have honored this requisition, but not before," Roosevelt said. He wasn't afraid of identifying himself; he simply didn't want there to be even the appearance of expecting favoritism because of his famous last name.

The confrontation escalated, and, according to Cox, "Quentin, being unable longer to control his indignation, stepped up and said, 'If you'll take off your Sam Browne belt and insignia of rank I'll take off mine, and we'll see if you can put me out of the office. I'm going to have those boots for my men if I have to be court-martialed for a breach of military discipline.'"

Two other officers who overheard the yelling intervened before any fists were thrown, and Roosevelt stormed out of the office and went directly to the major of the battalion. He explained the situation, and the major agreed with Roosevelt and assured him that the boots would be provided.

"Roosevelt had hardly left the major's office when the quartermaster captain came in and stated that there was a certain aviation lieutenant in camp whom he wanted court-martialed," Cox recounted.

"Who is the lieutenant?" asked the major.

"I don't know who he is," replied the captain, "but I can find out."

"I know who he is," said the major. "His name is Quentin Roosevelt, and there is no finer gentleman nor more efficient officer in this camp, and from what I know, if anyone deserves a court-martial you are the man. From now on you issue rubber boots to every cadet who applies for them, armed regulations be damned."

The boots were immediately issued, and the cadets were loud in their praise of Lieutenant Roosevelt.

Apologizing to his family and fiancée that his letters were "unutterably dull and uninteresting," Roosevelt explained that he remained mired in bureaucratic and official duties. (He had also suffered from recurring pneumonia and a case of the measles, information he withheld from his family until he had fully recovered.) Disorganization and delays plagued the entire Air Service; in a January 15, 1918, letter to his mother, Roosevelt railed against the "little tin-god civilians and army fossils that sit in Washington [and] seem to do nothing but lie" about how well things were supposedly progressing in France. "I saw one official statement about the hundred squadrons we are forming to be on the front by June," he wrote. "That doesn't seem funny to us over here,—it seems criminal, for they will expect us to produce the result that one hundred squadrons would have." Currently, there were all of two squadrons at Issoudun. Congress had appropriated funding to build five thousand American warplanes, but by early 1918, U.S. manufacturers were unable to construct anything comparable to what either the Allies or the Germans had developed. Without even checking with the War Department, General Pershing ordered several thousand planes from the French, at a cost of hundreds of thousands of dollars.

"There's one good thing about going to the front," Roosevelt continued in his letter to his mother. "I shall be so busy worrying about the safety of my own neck that I shan't have time to worry about the way the war is going." He also felt an obligation, as a Roosevelt, to be in the fight. "I owe it to the family—to father, and especially to Arch and Ted who are out there already and facing the dangers of it." Less than a month later, Roosevelt was offered a plum assignment in Paris to fly planes from their factories in the capital out to their designated airfields throughout France. Although not dangerous, the job was, in fact, critical, and it offered the thrill of flying different types of aircraft, with the added benefit of living in posh quarters. Roosevelt turned it down.

Another two months passed, and Roosevelt was still stuck at Issoudun. There was, however, some good news to report. "Things are beginning to hum here at school," he wrote to his mother on April 15, 1918. "For one thing, we hear that they are not going to send any more pilots over here from the states for the present, which is about the first sensible decision that they have made as regards the Air Service. As it is they must have two thousand pilots over here, and Heavens knows it will be ages before we have enough machines for even half that number."

Among those who had been coming over to Issoudun were the remaining members of the Lafayette Escadrille. The most admired was

Major Raoul Lufbery, one of the squadron's original pilots. With seventeen verified kills, "Luf" was the escadrille's top ace. (A pilot needed to have shot down at least five planes to be considered an ace.) Solemn and quiet, Luf was somewhat of a loner. He even preferred to go out on missions by himself. But he did so, mostly, in order to come to the rescue of younger, less experienced pilots when they found themselves outnumbered. The only time he showed a more whimsical side was when he roughhoused with the escadrille's mascot, a lion named Whiskey, adopted as a cub from a Paris zoo. The airmen fed him only grains so that he wouldn't grow accustomed to eating meat, and even in adulthood he acted more like an affectionate puppy dog than a lion.

"Everything I learned, I learned from Lufbery," Eddie Rickenbacker recalled of the man who became his mentor in the 94th Aero Squadron. Rickenbacker had been a celebrity in his own right racing "speed demon" cars before the war, and he sailed to France on General Pershing's ship, the *Baltic*, having signed up to serve as a military chauffeur. In France, Rickenbacker mainly drove Colonel Billy Mitchell, one of Pershing's main advisers and eventually the chief of the American Air Service.

While in Paris, Rickenbacker bumped into an old acquaintance from the States who was also working for the Air Service and, well aware of Rickenbacker's expertise with machines, asked him on the spot if he wanted to be the chief engineer at Issoudun. Rickenbacker agreed, but only with Colonel Mitchell's blessing. Mitchell had grown fond of Rickenbacker and hated to lose him, but he recognized it was an opportunity that Rickenbacker shouldn't pass up. Mitchell even pulled some strings to get Rickenbacker into a basic-training program for pilots near the city of Tours before heading to Issoudun.

Rickenbacker spent seventeen days at Tours. He loved the adrenaline rush of flying, which reminded him of his race-car days. After being transferred to Issoudun, he would sneak out on his own, without an instructor, to teach himself more advanced maneuvers. He nearly killed himself—and a few others—in the process. While flying over

Raoul Lufbery with Whiskey.

Eddie Rickenbacker.

the fields at Issoudun one day he noticed the other pilots playing football and decided to show off a bit by executing a spin directly above them. He momentarily lost control of his plane and came within fifty feet of crashing into the ground before finally pulling up, causing players and spectators alike to dash for cover. One of Issoudun's commanding officers was so furious that he grounded Rickenbacker for thirty days.

Lufbery, however, saw potential in Rickenbacker, and on March 6, 1918, he asked Rick, as he called him, and another pilot, named Douglas Campbell, to participate in the 94th's first patrol over German lines. Issoudun was so behind in adequately equipping its pilots that their planes were still unarmed. But Rickenbacker and Campbell jumped at the chance to fly with Lufbery and learn from the master, and the three set out at 8:15 in the morning. Lufbery took them over the front lines between Reims and Verdun. Rickenbacker was shocked by what he saw below. "Armies had been fighting over that once-beautiful farmland for more than three years," Rickenbacker remembered of the moment, "and what was left was wasteland. Not a house, not a barn, not a tree was left standing."

Suddenly Rickenbacker's attention was diverted by large puffs of black smoke; German shells were exploding all around him. "After my first moment of terror had passed, I realized that, in spite of all the turbulence and noise, neither my plane nor I had suffered a scratch," Rickenbacker later recalled. "A feeling of elation surged through me. I had been fired at, and I had kept my wits about me. The flight home was one of my most exquisite flying experiences. I had passed my first test."

When the three men landed, the other pilots and mechanics were already gathered around, waiting to hear about their experience. "We had the air completely to ourselves," Rickenbacker reported, flush with confidence. "Neither friend nor enemy had dared to join us in the sky."

Lufbery chuckled and asked, "Sure there weren't any other planes around, Rick?"

"Not a one!" he replied.

Lufbery shook his head and said: "Listen. One formation of five Spads crossed under us before we passed the lines. Another flight of five Spads went by in about fifteen minutes, five hundred yards away. Damn good thing they weren't Boches. And there were four German Albatrosses ahead of us when we turned back and another two-seater closer to us than that. You must learn to look around."

Lufbery then walked over to Rickenbacker's plane. "He poked his finger through a hole in the tail and another through the wing," Rickenbacker said. "Then he pointed to where another piece of shrapnel had gone through both wings not a foot from the cockpit. Just a few inches and I would have been a hero all right—a dead hero."

Having spent years flying in freezing conditions and sleeping in damp, drafty quarters, Lufbery had developed a severe case of rheumatism. His assignment was only to teach and advise the new pilots; he was under no obligation to serve in combat. But over the next few months, especially once the 94th finally received planes with machine guns, he continued to fly his solo patrols.

On May 19, Lufbery was in the barracks when he saw a German Albatross dare to fly directly over Issoudun. He rushed to the hangar and jumped into a plane, knowing he could catch up with it.

Rickenbacker and the other pilots watched from below as Lufbery shot several rounds at the Albatross, but the bullets appeared to simply bounce off the heavily armored plane. The German gunner returned fire, and Lufbery's engine burst into flames. Lufbery was clearly trying to maneuver his plane to extinguish the fire, but it only flickered deeper into the cockpit and set his flight suit ablaze.

Lufbery scrambled out of the cockpit, held on to the side of the plane, and then let go, thousands of feet above the ground. From that high up, a pilot could see the curve of the horizon. The wide expanse of multicolored earth took on a greater and greater clarity with every passing second. There was a stream that Lufbery seemed to be aiming for in a desperate attempt to break his fall. But instead, the wind carried him over toward a farmhouse, and his body slammed into a wooden fence at 120 miles per hour. By the time the members of his squadron raced over to the site, the French farmers who lived there had already removed Lufbery's body from the spikes and covered it with flowers.

NOT EVEN THE death of someone as legendary as Lufbery dampened the zeal of the younger pilots to head into harm's way. "I am now a member of the 95th Aero Squadron, 1st Pursuit Group," Quentin Roosevelt proudly announced to his mother a month after Lufbery was killed. "I'm on the front—cheers, oh cheers—and I'm very happy."

On July 11, he sent her a more detailed letter describing his experiences. "I got my first real excitement on the front for I think I got a Boche," Quentin wrote.

> I was out on high patrol with the rest of my squadron when we got broken up, due to a mistake in formation. I dropped into a turn of a vrille [i.e., a dive]—these planes have so little surface that at five thousand you can't do much with them. When I got straightened out I couldn't spot my crowd any where, so, as I had only been up an hour, I decided to fool around a little before going home, as I was just over the lines. I turned and circled for five minutes or so, and then suddenly,—the way planes do come into focus in the air, I saw three planes in formation. At first I thought they were Boche, but as they paid no attention to me, I finally decided to chase them, thinking they were part of my crowd, so I started after them full speed. . . .
>
> They had been going absolutely straight and I was nearly in formation when the leader did a turn, and I saw to my horror that they had white tails with black crosses on them. Still I was so near by them that I thought I might pull up a little and take a crack at them. I had altitude on them, and what was more they hadn't seen me, so I pulled up, put my sights on the end

man, and let go. I saw my tracers going all around him, but for some reason he never even turned, until all of a sudden his tail came up and he went down in a vrille. I wanted to follow him but the other two had started around after me, so I had to cut and run. However, I could half watch him looking back, and he was still spinning when he hit the clouds three thousand meters below. . . .

At the moment every one is very much pleased in our Squadron for we are getting new planes. We have been using Nieuports, which have the disadvantage of not being particularly reliable and being inclined to catch fire.

Three days later, Quentin was surrounded by German fighters and, unable to shake them, was shot twice in the head. His plane spun out of control and crashed behind enemy lines.

News of Quentin's death was reported worldwide. Even the Germans admired that the son of a president would forgo a life of privilege for the dangers of war, and they gave him a full military burial with honors.

A pilot's view of the landscape below.

General Pershing knew Quentin personally, and when his death was confirmed, it was Pershing's turn to send a letter of sympathy to his old friend Theodore Roosevelt: "I have delayed writing you in the hope that we might still learn that, through some good fortune, your son Quentin had managed to land safely inside the German lines," Pershing began.

> Now the telegram from the International Red Cross at Berne, stating that the German Red Cross confirms the newspaper reports of his death, has taken even this hope away. Quentin died as he had lived and served, nobly and unselfishly; in the full strength and vigor of his youth, fighting the enemy in clean combat. You may well be proud of your gift to the nation in his supreme sacrifice.
>
> I realize that time alone can heal the wound, yet I know that at such a time the stumbling words of understanding from one's friends help, and I want to express to you and to Quentin's mother my deepest sympathy. Perhaps I can come as near to realizing what such a loss means as anyone.
>
> Enclosed is a copy of his official record in the Air Service. The brevity and curtness of the official words paint clearly the picture of his service, which was an honor to us all.
>
> *Believe me, Sincerely yours, JPP*

"I am immensely touched by your letter," Roosevelt replied. He well remembered the trauma that Pershing himself had endured before the war. "My dear fellow," Roosevelt continued, "you have suffered far more bitter sorrow than has befallen me. You bore it with splendid courage and I should be ashamed of myself if I did not try in a lesser way to emulate that courage."

Due to Roosevelt's status as a former president, he received countless letters and telegrams from other heads of state, as well as total strangers, offering their sympathy for the family's loss. Roosevelt

The remains of Quentin Roosevelt and his airplane.

usually responded with a short message of appreciation, but there were two letters of condolence, one to him and one to Mrs. Roosevelt, from a woman named Mrs. H. L. Freeland, that particularly touched them, and on August 14, 1918, exactly a month after Quentin was killed, Theodore sent back a lengthy, handwritten reply.

> Last evening, as we were sitting together in the North Room, Mrs. Roosevelt handed me your two letters, saying that they were such dear letters that I must see them. As yet it is hard for her to answer even the letters she cares for most; but yours have so singular a quality that I do not mind writing you of the intimate things which one can not speak of to strangers.
>
> Quentin was her baby, the last child left in the home nest; on the night before he sailed, a year ago, she did as she always had done and went upstairs to tuck him into bed—the huge, laughing, gentle-hearted boy. He was always thoughtful and considerate of those with whom he came in contact. . . .

It is hard to open the letters coming from those you love who are dead; but Quentin's last letters, written during his three weeks at the front, when of his squadron on an average a man was killed every day, are written with real joy in the "great adventure." He was engaged to a very beautiful girl, of very fine and high character; it is heartbreaking for her, as well as for his mother; but they have both said that they would rather have him never come back than never have gone. He had his crowded hour, he died at the crest of life, in the glory of the dawn. . . .

Is your husband in the army? Give him my warm regards; and your mother and father and sister. I wish to see any of you or all of you out here at my house, if you ever come to New York. Will you promise to let me know?

Faithfully yours, Theodore Roosevelt

After Quentin's death, the once boisterous former president was more subdued, and his physical health declined rapidly. In his final days, Roosevelt often went down to the family's stables to be near the horses that Quentin as a child had so loved to ride. Lost in sorrow, Roosevelt would stand there alone, quietly repeating the pet name he'd given his son when he was a boy, "Oh Quenty-quee, oh Quenty-quee . . ."

The Roosevelts decided to leave Quentin buried in Europe, but they did retrieve the mangled axle from his plane, which they displayed prominently at their home in Oyster Bay.

16.

Captain Harry

I shall be happy if I can only get to order my battery to fire one volley at the Hun [even] if I get court martialed the next day. You know that would be something really worthwhile. An infantry man can only shoot one bullet at a time with his little pop gun but I can give one command to my Irish battery and put 848 bullets on the way at once. . . .

If I hadn't been a battery commander they would in all probability have sent me home as an instructor. I hope they don't do it until I have earned a gold service stripe and have seen the front much as I would like to be home. I'd be forever apologizing for not having gotten to the front.

—Harry Truman writing to his fiancée, Bess Wallace, August 4, 1918

WHEN HARRY TRUMAN EMBARKED for Europe in March 1918 and promised his fiancée, Bess Wallace, that he would soon be cabling her "from Berlin," it was as much a playful boast as Truman's way of encouraging her not to worry about him. Once in France, Truman still had several months of training to get through, and there was the possibility that he would prove to be an inadequate officer and sent home without firing a single shot at the enemy.

Assigned to the AEF's artillery school near Chaumont, Truman was thrust into what he called "the most strenuous week I ever spent in my life." His days, Truman explained to Wallace, began at 7:00 a.m. and lasted until 9:30 p.m., when he and the other officers had to spend at least ninety minutes studying before collapsing from exhaustion. There was some physical drilling involved, but mostly it was constant class-room instruction on a college level—and Truman had only graduated from high school—about everything from trigonometry and loga-rithms to astronomy and engineering. The intensity of it all was so overwhelming that Truman thought he might literally go crazy or, as he put it, become "nuttier than an Arkansas squirrel." Truman also told Wallace, after taking one of his first exams, that the test was so befud-dling it would have made "the president of Yale University bald . . . [from] scratching his head" trying to figure out the answers.

As an example of the type of complex questions that Truman had to solve, he recorded one in his notebook:

> Battery in position at an altitude of 121 meters. Registration point has Y az of 918 map range from 4210 altitude 111 meters. Target A is a Telegraph Central Y az 786. 1002 Map Rn5600 Altitude 110. At 14 o'clock you are ordered to fire on Target A and you decide to use a Trans out of fire from registration Pt. Use HE shell I fuse +++ Pvrd Temp +10
>
> Soundage at 14 o'clock
> Wind 31-5 Pressure sea level 761
> 200 32-4 Temp +17
> 500 32-5
> You decide to fire enough rounds on registration point to get lot Ks or Dvo. Adjusted data on registration is Y az 900 & elevation (including site 8 57'). What is your Ko or Dvo and what is initial elevation for Target A.

After two months in France, Truman learned that he had been pro-moted before he'd left the States. He proudly exclaimed to Wallace that he was finally "a real Captain in Uncle Sam's Armee." Having excelled in both his classroom and on the field, Truman was eventually sent to Camp Coëtquidan in western France, where he would undergo his final training before being sent to the front—assuming that he continued to perform well and could command a battery of 194 men and four 75mm guns.

Truman could hardly have been assigned a more difficult group of individuals: Battery D of the 2nd Battalion, 129th Field Artillery, 35th Division, the majority of whom were Irish Catholics from Kansas City, Missouri. They were a rough, rambunctious lot, infamous for their drinking. They had been nicknamed the Dizzy D ("dizzy" being slang for drunkenness), and four other commanders had tried and failed to keep them in line. Colonel Karl Klemm, whom Truman had known from Missouri, had resolved to break up the entire battery and spread the men around if they failed to behave themselves under Truman.

The Dizzy D had actually liked its last captain, John Thacher, but he was deemed too lenient with the men and was placed in another battalion. "Thacher had been well loved by all the men in the battery," bugler Albert Ridge said at the time of the replacement, "[and when] it was learned that Captain Truman had been assigned to Battery D, there was a good deal of talk about mutiny, about causing trouble."

Truman was an odd choice to lead the group. He didn't have a reputation for being tough, he wasn't Irish or Catholic, and, with his pince-nez glasses, he looked more like an accountant than a man ready to lead soldiers into battle.

"[Thacher] was an emotional-type guy, but Truman wasn't," Private Vere Leigh recalled of Truman's first encounter with the men. "He was kind of a rather short fellow, compact, serious face, wearing glasses; and we'd had all kinds of officers, and this was just another one, you know. And he announced to the battery that he was going to be in charge, and when he gave orders he wanted them carried out. He made it pretty plain."

Private Albert Ridge, the bugler, remembered what happened after Truman gave his brief introductory speech:

He looked the battery over, up and down the entire line, about three times, and the men were all waiting for the castigation that they really knew they were entitled to from a new commander because of their previous conduct. But Harry Truman, he just continued to look at them, and his only command to the battery was—"Dismissed!"

Well, of course the dismissed battery went toward their barracks. But I think that that command to the Irish group was a sort of benediction. He had not castigated them. He had dismissed them as much as to say—like the Good Lord said to Mary Magdalene—"Go and sin no more." From that time on I knew that Harry Truman had captured the heart of those Irishmen.

They didn't let Truman off quite that easy. The moment he turned his back they all gave him the Bronx cheer, which Truman chose to ignore.

One of Truman's first acts was to gather his noncommissioned officers together and explain what he expected of them. "I am sure you men know the rules and regulations," he said. "*I* will issue the orders and *you* are responsible for them being carried out. I didn't come over here to get along with you. You've got to get along with me. And if there are any of you who can't, speak up right now and I'll bust you right back [a rank] now."

The men were impressed with his directness, but they were even more appreciative that he entrusted them to do their jobs without interference, so long as they did them well. Gradually, Truman developed a reputation for being strict but fair. He also made a point of taking an interest in each man, learning about him personally and focusing on his strengths. Eventually they started referring to him affectionately as either Captain Harry or Captain O'Truman, indicating that they saw him as one of their own.

Truman also drilled the men extensively, and their sense of pride swelled as they were whipped into shape and began outperforming other batteries, thanks to Truman's own proficiency in using the 75mm guns. French-made, the 75s were a particular favorite of the Americans. They were significantly smaller than the German 210mms, but the 75s were much easier to maneuver, they fired accurately and rapidly (they had a range of five miles and could shoot a round every two to three seconds), and they also had a pneumatic recoil system that prevented the entire gun from rolling backward after every shot, enabling the gunners to better keep it on target or quickly adjust it if necessary. Although the gun was two decades old, no other country could replicate it, and the French kept the specifics about its design and composition classified.

Battery D and other units of the 35th Division finally received their orders in mid-August to move to the front, albeit to *un secteur tranquil*, just as the first infantry regiments had started off in quiet sectors before experiencing sustained combat. Truman and his men had been assigned to Mount Herrenberg, just outside the town of Kruth, in Alsace. Crammed into the "40 Men/8 Horses" cattle cars, Battery D made the three-day journey across France. Upon their arrival, Truman and his soldiers looked out across no-man's-land and saw a huge banner spread out in front of one of the German trenches that said "Welcome 35th Division."

After having scouted out a perfect location on Mount Herrenberg and set up his guns, Truman was ordered to shift them to an area about a mile closer to the German lines. Normally such an arduous task would take twenty-four hours. Truman and his men were given six. Adding to their misery, a rainstorm broke out, causing the mountain trails to become even more slippery and treacherous for the horses and men pulling the 75s and caissons. Everything had to be done as quietly as possible in the darkness so that the Germans wouldn't see or hear them moving into their new position. Burlap bags were placed over the mouths of the horses to muffle their snorting, cloths were wrapped around the metal-rimmed wheels of the guns, and extra grease was slathered on the carriage axles to reduce squeaking.

H hour was 8:00 p.m. on August 29, 1918. The battery received its ammunition only hours before—five hundred rounds of "No. 5" and "No. 4" shells, the former containing collongite and the latter hydrogen cyanide. Captain Harry Truman's first artillery assault of the war would be with poisonous gas. (The "No. 4" rounds were essentially deemed obsolete by the French due to enhancements the Germans had made to their gas masks, so the French unloaded their surplus on the Americans. But the "No. 5"'s were still considered highly effective.)

Truman's first night in combat was almost his last. Between 8:00 and 8:36 p.m. precisely, D Battery discharged almost all of its rounds. Truman was on his horse observing the barrage when the Germans returned fire, and an incoming shell blew up a mere fifteen feet away from him. Even though he wasn't hit, the explosion sent Truman's horse rearing back into a crater, where it fell directly on top of him. With the full weight of the thousand-pound animal pressing down on him, Truman couldn't breathe. He was within seconds of suffocating to death when one of his lieutenants, Vic Housholder, saw what was happening and rushed over to wrench Truman free.

Horses and some of Truman's men scattered in all directions when the German bombs fell, and Truman unleashed a torrent of profanities unlike anything his men had heard from him before. One by one, they sheepishly came back, and later that night the battery returned to a base position for food and a chance to sleep. They had been up for almost four days straight.

Truman wrote to his fiancée, after his first taste of combat.

Dear Bess,

I am the most pleased person in the world this morning. I got two letters from you and have accomplished my greatest wish. Have fired five hundred rounds at the Germans at my command, been shelled, didn't run away thank the Lord, and never lost a man. . . .

My greatest satisfaction is that my legs didn't succeed in carrying me away, although they were very anxious to do it. . . .

I am in a most beautiful country and it seems like a shame
that we must spread shells over it, but as the French say
Boches are hogs and should be killed. Please don't worry
about me because no German shell is made that can hit me.
One exploded in fifteen feet of me and I didn't get a scratch,
so you can see I have them beaten there. . . .

Yours always
Harry

Truman's coolness under fire only enhanced his reputation within
Battery D, but he confessed to his fiancée that he wasn't as fearless as he
seemed. "The men think I am not much afraid of shells but they don't
know," Truman wrote in his next letter to Wallace. "I was too scared
to run and that is pretty scared."

After their August 29 baptism of fire, Battery D was ordered farther
north. They began with a short train ride but then had to march the rest
of the way, sometimes eighteen to twenty miles a night. They—along
with five hundred thousand other American troops—were being sent
to a region around the German-occupied town of Saint-Mihiel.

General Pershing had had his eye on Saint-Mihiel since the moment he'd set foot in France in June 1917. Variously described as a
"thorn" or "fang" jutting into the French border, the triangle-shaped
stronghold was twenty-five miles across and sixteen miles deep. German soldiers had been there for so long that they had quartered themselves in French homes and refurnished the interiors to accommodate
their own tastes. They were also raising children, now old enough to
walk and talk, that they had fathered with local Frenchwomen.

By June 1918, Pershing had one million men under his command,
with three hundred thousand new troops coming in a month, and on
August 10 the American First Army was officially activated. Pershing
named himself as its commander, while still retaining his position as
the head of the entire AEF.

First Army's initial operation would be to retake Saint-Mihiel.

Marshal Ferdinand Foch had given his approval, and the attack was set for mid-September. On August 29, General Pershing moved his headquarters from Chaumont to Ligny, a town twenty-two miles southwest of Saint-Mihiel. From there he could better oversee what would be the largest military campaign in U.S. history.

Less than twenty-four hours later, First Army was already at risk of being broken apart. And the threat was coming from Pershing's own side.

17.

The Birthday Present

I never saw General Pershing looking or feeling better. He
is sleeping well. He is tremendously active. He will soon
strike with this field army. I know he will succeed. He is
not letting anything get on his mind to absorb it from the
all-important question of how to get a military victory.

—*General Charles Dawes, writing in his journal,*
August 25, 1918

O N A UGUST 30, 1918, Marshal Ferdinand Foch traveled to
Pershing's headquarters in Ligny to discuss a massive new Allied
offensive intended to smash through the entire Hindenburg Line, from
the British Channel down to the Meuse-Argonne region of France.

The two generals sat down at a table, and Foch unrolled the maps
and charts that detailed a battle plan to be launched in late September.
British and Belgian soldiers would intensify their ongoing assaults in
northern France and Belgium as French and American troops launched
an attack directly to their south. This would entail splitting up the
American First Army and placing its divisions under French and British
control to be used as reinforcements. In light of this, Foch told Pershing
that the Saint-Mihiel campaign would have to be severely limited or
scrapped entirely.

Pershing was incredulous. "Marshal Foch," Pershing said, trying to
keep his anger in check, "almost on the eve of an offensive, you ask me

to reduce the operation so that you can take away several of my divisions and assign some to the French Army?" Not only would Foch's proposal fragment the American First Army that Pershing had worked tirelessly to form, it would drastically diminish the number of troops under Pershing, relegating the general to a minor role in the larger offensive.

Foch asked Pershing what he recommended instead. Pershing reiterated that the American-led attack on Saint-Mihiel would go ahead as planned, and First Army would then join the Allied effort in the Meuse-Argonne, where the French would need the most assistance.

Foch replied that this was unrealistic; the Americans couldn't possibly defeat the Germans at Saint-Mihiel and still have the strength to attack an even larger number of battle-hardened German troops sixty miles away.

Pershing maintained that they could, so long as his divisions weren't taken from him.

Foch was losing patience. "Do you wish to take part in the battle?" he asked, essentially threatening the American general with being left out of the operation entirely. It was an empty bluff—the Allies couldn't prevail without the AEF—but the insult hit its mark.

"Most assuredly," Pershing shot back, "but as an American Army and in no other way."

Pershing then reminded Foch, "You have no authority as Allied commander in chief to call upon me to yield up my command of the American Army and have it scattered among the Allied forces where it will not be an American Army at all."

Foch said he "insisted" on the new plans as he had explained them.

"Marshal Foch, you may insist all you please," Pershing said, rising from the table, "but I decline absolutely to agree to your plan." For a split second, Pershing considered slugging Foch in the face but restrained himself.

Having come to an impasse, and well aware that Pershing had reached a boiling point, Foch rolled up his maps and left.

The following day, Pershing sent Foch a memo outlining how the American First Army could capture the Saint-Mihiel salient and then quickly regroup to fight in the Meuse-Argonne. Pershing then paid a visit to General Pétain, whom he had always found to be more understanding and more personable than Foch. Pétain agreed with Pershing that the First Army should not be fragmented.

Foch and Pershing met again on September 2 in Foch's headquarters. After enduring another of Pershing's clenched-jaw rebukes about not dividing up First Army, Foch relented.

The men agreed that Pershing's troops would assault Saint-Mihiel by September 11 or 12 and then descend on the Meuse-Argonne with an even larger force by September 26. Foch was anxious to hit the Germans as soon as possible because their morale was low after having been beaten back at the Marne, but a more important factor was the weather; the longer the Allies waited, the colder and rainier it would become, hampering their efforts to transport troops, set up artillery, and attack entrenched positions.

Surprise was critical. The Americans knew that the Germans had spies throughout the villages where Pershing and other Allied commanders were living. French civilians who had been either coerced or bribed by the Germans passed on information they had overheard or surreptitiously acquired. In light of this, American intelligence executed a brilliant counterintelligence operation.

In early September, Pershing sent General Omar Bundy to Belfort, 150 miles south of Saint-Mihiel where, Bundy was told, he would be leading First Army's VI Corps. In truth, the corps existed mostly on paper. Joining Bundy in Belfort was a seasoned intelligence officer named Colonel Arthur Conger, who knew exactly why they were there—to trick the Germans into thinking that the Americans were amassing their forces around Belfort. Fake radio messages were transmitted to AEF headquarters about the buildup. At night, Conger had a small number of tanks crisscross the area as many times as possible to convince German aerial reconnaissance crews, flying over Belfort during the day, that large numbers of American tanks were moving into the area. Conger's most cunning ruse involved a single piece of mimeograph paper. In his hotel room, he wrote up a phony report about the impending assault, crumpled up the carbon copy, and tossed it into the wastebasket. Conger walked down to the bar, enjoyed a leisurely drink, and returned to his room, whereupon he found that the trash can had been emptied, as he had hoped, by a local informant or hotel staff member working for the Germans. Soon after, German divisions were being transferred from the north to Belfort.

Back at Pershing's headquarters, staff members were in a frenzy planning the actual assault. Major General Hunter Liggett's I Corps, which included the 82nd, 90th, and 5th divisions, and Major General Joseph Dickman's IV Corps, comprised of the 89th, 1st, and 42nd ("Rainbow") divisions, would advance from the south of Saint-Mihiel, as General George Cameron's V Corps would come in from the northwest, with the 26th "Yankee" Division leading the charge. (Third Corps was being prepared for the Meuse-Argonne Offensive, and the bulk of II Corps had been assigned to the British, who felt they deserved these particular American troops because English officers had trained them.) The French II Colonial Corps, with 110,000 soldiers, would strike the tip of the salient. More than 670,000 troops would participate in all.

Along with the soldiers in the II Colonial Corps, the French provided the AEF with 260 light tanks, led by George Patton, and 800 airplanes, placed under the command of Billy Mitchell.

At precisely 1:00 a.m. on September 12, more than three thousand artillery guns roared to life, commencing a four-hour barrage on the German lines.

"As dawn broke I led my assault line forward," General Douglas MacArthur wrote of the infantry charge. "I had fought the German long enough to know his technique of defense. He concentrated to protect his center, but left his flanks weak. The field of action, the Bois de la Sonnard, lent itself to maneuver, and we were able with little loss to pierce both flanks, envelop his center, and send his whole line into hurried retreat." Fighting with the 42nd Division's 84th Infantry

Brigade, MacArthur noted that they had conquered their first objective, the village of Essey, by nightfall.

Lieutenant Colonel William Donovan and Father Francis Duffy, also with the 42nd, were at Essey as well. "French civilians were still living in this village, having spent the period of bombardment in a big dugout—the first civilians that we had the pleasure of liberating," Father Duffy wrote in his journal. "They laughed and wept and kissed everybody in sight and drew on their slender stock of provisions to feed the hungry men. The soldiers began wandering everywhere looking for souvenirs."

Duffy also noted how easily many of the enemy troops surrendered:

> The prisoners were mainly Austrians and Austrian Slavs. They had not been very keen about the war at any time and were made less so on finding that they had been left behind after the bulk of the army had withdrawn. Many of them had been in the United States, and the first question that one of them asked was, "Can I go back now to Sharon, PA?" One of them was found seated in a dugout with a bottle of Schnapps and a glass. He immediately offered a drink to his captor saying "I don't drink it myself, but I thought it would be a good thing to offer an American who would find me."

Soldiers in other divisions were experiencing a similar lack of opposition. Lieutenant Maury Maverick, serving with the 1st Division's 28th Infantry Regiment, was on horseback pulling carts of ammunition when in the chaos of battle he got separated from his battalion. Maverick left the ammo to seek out his men, and while galloping through the woods he rode straight into more than two dozen Germans, all of them armed.

Certain he was about to be shot full of holes, Maverick nearly fell off his horse in panic. To his amazement, though, the Germans all dropped their rifles, lifted up their hands, and screamed, "*Kamerad!*

Kamerad!" One officer approached Maverick and implored him, in broken English, to take them prisoner.

Pointing to the Allied lines, Maverick instructed the Germans to march in that direction and give themselves up. The Germans explained that they were afraid of being killed by less sympathetic Americans, and they wanted Maverick to personally lead them back. Two of the younger Germans started to cry. Feeling sorry for them, Maverick agreed to escort them as close to the rear lines as possible. Maverick later wondered if he should have made a bigger deal of having captured (as it turned out) twenty-six German soldiers. "I could have gotten a crowd together, made a record of it—and have gotten a batch of medals," Maverick recalled of the incident. "Since my uncle [James Luther Slayden] was in Congress, there would have been no limit."

The 26th Division, on the northwestern flank, made it into the town of Vigneulles by 2:00 a.m. on the morning of September 13, and hours later the 26th and 1st divisions came together as planned, essentially bringing the battle to an end.

Pershing was ecstatic. "The First Army attacked yesterday and the reduction of St. Mihiel salient is complete," Pershing wrote in his diary on September 13. "Our troops behaved splendidly. . . . This is my birthday and a very happy one."

Pershing later elaborated on the battle's significance:

> The reduction of the St. Mihiel salient completed the first task of the American Army. Its elimination freed the Paris–Nancy rail communications and the roads that paralleled the Meuse north from St. Mihiel. These at once became available for our use in the greater [Meuse-Argonne] offensive to be undertaken immediately. We had restored to France 200 square miles of territory and had placed our army in a favorable situation for further operations. No form of propaganda could overcome the depressing effect on the enemy's morale or the fact that a new adversary had been able to put a formidable army in the

field against him which, in its first offensive, could win such an
important engagement.

Among those who found themselves somewhat underwhelmed by
it all was George Patton. Patton had several close calls but survived, and
he detailed his experiences, including a brief encounter with Douglas
MacArthur, in a letter to his father (the misspellings, including that of
MacArthur's name, are a result of Patton's dyslexia):

> Dear Papa
> We have all been in one fine fight and it was not half so
> exciting as I had hoped, not as exciting as affairs in Mexico,
> because there was so much company. When the shelling first
> started I had some doubts about the advisability of sticking
> my head over the parapet, but it is just like taking a cold bath,
> once you get in, it is all right. And I soon got out and sat on
> the parapet. At seven o clock I moved forward and passed
> some dead and wounded. I saw one fellow in a shell hole
> holding his rifle and sitting down. I thought he was hiding
> and went to cuss him out, he had a bullet over his right eye
> and was dead.
>
> As my telephone wire ran out at this point I left the
> adjutant there and went forward with a lieutenant and four
> runners to find the tanks, the whole country was alive with
> them crawling over trenches and into the woods. It was fine
> but I could not see my right battalion so went to look for it,
> in doing so we passed through several towns under shell fire
> but none did more than throw dust on us. I admit that I
> wanted to duck and probably did at first but soon saw the
> futility of dodging fate, besides I was the only officer around
> who had left on his shoulder straps and I had to live up to
> them. It was much easier than you would think and the
> feeling, foolish probably, of being admired by the men lying
> down is a great stimulus.

I walked right along the firing line of one brigade they were all in shell holes except the general (Douglas Mcarthur) who was standing on a little hill, I joined him and the creeping barrage came along towards us, but it was very thin and not dangerous. I think each one wanted to leave but each hated to say so, so we let it come over us. The infantry were held up at a town so I happened to find some tanks and sent them through it. I walked behind and some boshe surrendered to me. At the next town all but one tank was out of sight and as the infantry would not go in I got on top of the tank to hear the driver and we went in, that was most exciting as there were plenty of boshe we took thirty.

On leaving the town I was still sitting sidewise on top of the tank with my legs hanging down on the left side when all at once I noticed all the paint start to chip off the other side and at the same time I noticed machine guns, I dismounted in haste and got in a shell hole, which was none too large every time I started to get out the boshe shot at me. I was on the point of getting scared as I was about a hundred yards ahead of the infantry and all alone in the field. If I went back the infantry would think I was running and there was no reason to go forward alone. All the time the infernal tank was going on alone as the men had not noticed my hurried departure. At last the bright thought occurred to me that I could move across the front in an oblique direction and not appear to run yet at the same time get back. This I did listening for the machine guns with all my ears, and laying down in a great hurry when I heard them, in this manner I hoped to beat the bullets to me. . . .

Then I walked along the battle front to see how the left battalion had gotten on. It was a very long way and I had had no sleep for four nights and no food all the day as I lost my sack chasing a boshe. I got some crackers off a dead one (he had not blood on them as in Polks story) they were very good but I would have given a lot for a drink of the brandy I had had in my sack. The Major of the left battalion was crying because he had no more gas. He was very tired and had a bullet through his nose, I comforted him and started home alone to get some gas. It was most interesting over the battle field like the books but much less dramatic. The dead were about mostly hit in the head. There were a lot of our men stripping off buttons and other things but they always covered the face of the dead in a nice way.

I saw one very amusing thing which I would have liked to have photographed right in the middle of a large field where there had never been a trench was a shell hole from a 9.7 gun the hole was at least 8 feet deep and 15 across on the edge of it was a dead rat, not a large healthy rat but a small field rat not over twice the size of a mouse. No wonder the war costs so much. . . .

This is a very egotistical letter but interesting as it shows that vanity is stronger than fear and that in war as now waged there is little of the element of fear, it is too well organized and too stupendous. I am very well much love to all.

Your devoted son

Secretary of War Newton Baker, in France at the time to see first-hand how the Americans were performing, was thrilled by the victory, as was President Wilson, who sent Pershing a telegram that read: "Accept my warmest congratulations on the brilliant achievements of the Army under your command. The boys have done what we expected of them and done it in a way we most admire. We are deeply proud of them and of their Chief. Please convey to all concerned my grateful and affectionate thanks."

Even the two men who had doubted Pershing the most cabled him gracious messages. "All ranks of the British Armies in France welcome with unbounded admiration and pleasure the victory which has attended the initial offensive of the great American Army under your personal command," General Douglas Haig wrote. "I beg you to accept and to convey to all ranks my best congratulations and those of all ranks of the British under my command."

Marshal Ferdinand Foch was equally as fulsome. "The American First Army under your command, on this first has won a magnificent victory by a maneuver as skillfully prepared as it was valiantly executed. I extend you as well to the officers and to the troops under your command my warmest congratulations."

On the morning of September 15, Prime Minister Georges Clemenceau traveled from Paris to meet with Pershing at his headquarters in Ligny and asked to see Thiaucourt, a town recaptured by the Americans near Saint-Mihiel. Much to Clemenceau's displeasure, Pershing told him it was too dangerous—unexploded shells and mines lay everywhere, and there still might be German snipers lurking about in range of the town as well—so Pershing sent a disgruntled Clemenceau off with two aides to safer areas. Pershing then had a lunch meeting with the president of France, Raymond Poincaré, and his wife in the village of Sampigny, where the couple had lived before the war. (These frequent day trips were a nuisance to Pershing, but he recognized the political importance of fostering friendly relations with French heads of state and American dignitaries, although some of his AEF staff members were less understanding. "Franklin Roosevelt and party," Lieutenant Pierpont Stackpole, aide to I Corps commander Hunter Liggett, wrote in his diary with a hint of disdain, "called at chateau [headquarters] and we sent them off on a joy tour under direction of Major Hunter Scott. Like everybody else they wanted to get shot at with a guarantee against a hit and smell dead men and horses.")

"After lunch we visited the site of their residence [in Sampigny] only to find that it had been completely demolished by German artillery," Pershing wrote of his excursion with the Poincarés. "It had been a beautiful though modest house and its location especially well chosen to give one a fine view of the Meuse valley. It was a sad occasion for them as they looked over the ruins, but they accepted it in the usual courageous French way by saying simply, 'C'est la guerre.'"

While strolling through the remains of Sampigny, they encountered two AEF soldiers quartered in what was left of the village. "When I told them who the visitors were," Pershing recalled, "they seemed to regard my remarks as an introduction." Instead of giving the French president and his wife a quick, deferential nod or salute and then walking away, the two Americans marched right up to the Poincarés, gave them each a hearty handshake, and then tagged along as they continued with the tour. Pershing was more amused than embarrassed by the soldiers' behavior and later noted that it was "just another illustration" of the democratic spirit instilled in the average Yank from the United States.

Although Saint-Mihiel had, without question, boosted the spirits of American and Allied troops alike, behind the scenes, however lavish their praise for Pershing, generals like Haig and Foch knew that the victory was not entirely what it seemed.

Several days before the attack began, Germany's most senior general, Erich Ludendorff, had instructed his local commanders to begin vacating large areas of the salient and leave behind mostly second- and third-rate soldiers. Ludendorff had drawn up the evacuation plans before he had any knowledge of the impending assault; Saint-Mihiel simply no longer had the same strategic value of other strongholds, where top-tier defenders were needed. The Americans had charged so rapidly through the salient not only because of their undeniable grit and courage, but because many of the German frontline positions had already been abandoned or were in the process of being reduced.

On September 15, the same day Pershing was meeting with Prime Minister Clemenceau and President and Mrs. Poincaré, he sent a secret cable to the War Department expressing his concern about how ready some AEF troops were for battle, after a recent crop had arrived in France with almost no training.

Pershing vented:

> These men have received little instruction [in] gas defense, bayonet exercise and combat, interior guard, march discipline,

school of soldier, [or] care and use of rifle. Some had never handled a rifle. Nevertheless these men had been in service about two months. Essential replacements should receive instruction in fundamentals before departure [from the] United States. . . . Current shortage in replacements requires men to be sent to first line divisions within five or six days after arrival in France. . . . Do not understand why this condition should prevail with anything like proper supervision over training in camps at home.

On September 21, Pershing moved AEF headquarters to Souilly in preparation for the Meuse-Argonne Offensive. On his way there, he visited Verdun and walked through the town to, in his words, "make a casual inspection of the citadel," the building Pétain had used as his command center during the nine-month Battle of Verdun in 1916 that cost 160,000 French lives. Pershing noticed the defiant vow that Pétain had etched on one of the walls, "On ne passe pas" ("No one will pass"), a pledge that Pétain and his troops honored. Pershing found himself so moved by these words that he stood there in total silence for several minutes. In five days, he would send into combat a force larger than Pétain's. Pershing had braced himself for a battle that could easily last as long as Verdun; he had requested that a total of one hundred divisions be sent to France by July 1919. While Chief of Staff Peyton March didn't argue with the time frame—he, too, expected that the war could continue well into the following summer—he rejected Pershing's request and said that the most the War Department could ultimately muster was eighty divisions. Pershing currently had forty.

Despite the fact that Pershing did not have his ideal number of divisions, Saint-Mihiel had given him the confidence that he would be able to handle any challenges he encountered in the weeks and months to come.

He would not.

18.

All In

In 1914, when the great German armies first marched to conquest, they had come through the Argonne, seized it, and had never been dislodged. The terrain was so difficult, so easily defended, that the French had never attempted to attack. It was so powerfully fortified over four years that doubts existed in Allied high circles that any troops in the world could drive out the Germans. The Germans, themselves, boasted they would drown an American attack in its own blood.

The Germans . . . had a machine gun nest behind every rock, a cannon behind every natural embrasure. Here was the key sector of the famous Hindenburg Line. . . . Breach it and there would be laid bare Sedan and Mezieres, the two huge German rail centers, through which all the German armies as far away as the North Sea at Ostend were supplied. Take Sedan and every German army to the west would be outflanked. . . . It would mean the capture of troops running into the hundreds of thousands. It would mean the end of the war.

—*General Douglas MacArthur*

During their meeting of September 2, General Pershing had assured Marshal Foch that the American First Army could fight the Germans at Saint-Mihiel and, before the battle was over, begin transferring entire divisions sixty miles north to the Meuse-Argonne region by September 26 to assault the Hindenburg Line. The Hindenburg Line, in fact, was not one long trench or fortification but a series of defensive positions (or, in German, *Stellungen*) named after witches from the German composer Richard Wagner's operas.

Pershing's plan for the first wave of attacks was ambitious. They involved General Hunter Liggett's I Corps, General Robert Lee Bullard's III Corps, and General George Cameron's V Corps. II Corps was still with the British in the north, and IV Corps, led by General Joseph Dickman, would be brought into battle weeks later.

The primary goal was for V Corps to capture Montfaucon ("Falcon Mountain") and the woods around it, which were all part of the Giselher Stellung, and then head four miles north to pierce the Kriemhilde Stellung, near the towns of Romagne and Cunel. General Pétain had warned Pershing that overtaking Montfaucon alone would require at least three months. Pershing wanted the Kriemhilde Stellung destroyed in less than twenty-four hours.

Third Corps would cover V Corps's right flank, where the Germans dominated the heights of the Meuse River, and I Corps would protect V Corps on the left side from the Germans entrenched in the Argonne Forest. To the west of I Corps would be France's Fourth Army, with three divisions. The ultimate target of *all* the French and American troops was the Sedan-Mézières railroad, thirty miles north of Romagne and Cunel, and twenty-five miles past the Freya Stellung, the last of the three Hindenburg Line fortifications between the First Army's jumping-off point and Sedan-Mézières. The rail line represented the jugular of the German military, the artery that sustained the rest of the army's body; sever it, and the wound would likely prove fatal.

While Pershing would, in the end, be held accountable for the outcome of the American role in the Meuse-Argonne Offensive, much of the preparation—and pressure—to execute it efficiently fell on the shoulders of Colonel George Marshall, who had been promoted to Pershing's staff because of his stellar work planning the battle for Cantigny. Marshall learned of his assignment less than three days before the assault at Saint-Mihiel, and while Pershing had conceived the master plan, Marshall had to work out the specific logistics of transferring more than 1.4 million soldiers and Marines into the Meuse-Argonne region and positioning them in accordance with Pershing's outline. (Approximately eight hundred thousand were needed for the first wave alone.) General Hugh Drum, First Army's chief of staff, told Marshall that the job had to be accomplished as quickly as possible. Marshall recalled:

> I immediately returned to my office to consult the map, [and] about ten minutes' consideration made it apparent that to reach the new front . . . would require many of these troops to get under way on the evening of the first day of the St. Mihiel battle, notwithstanding the fact that the advance in that fight was expected to continue for at least two days. This appalling proposition rather disturbed my equilibrium and I went out on the canal to have a walk while thinking it over. . . .
>
> I remember thinking during this walk that I could not recall an incident in history where the fighting of one battle had been preceded by the plans for a later battle to be fought by the same army on a different front, and involving the issuing of orders for the movement of troops already destined to participate in the first battle, directing their transfer to the new field of action. There seemed no precedence for such a course, and, therefore, no established method for carrying it out.

Marshall described the hours that followed as the "most trying mental ordeal" he had experienced in the war. He was fully aware that decisions he made in haste could cost the lives of countless men. But he was under a deadline, and "war," he reasoned, was a "ruthless taskmaster, demanding success regardless of confusion, shortness of time, and paucity of tools." Suddenly, Marshall had somewhat of an epiphany, called in a stenographer, and began dictating what he referred to as "the preliminary order for the Meuse-Argonne concentration." Conceding that it was "far from satisfactory," he had it delivered to General Drum's office by another aide. (Marshall was too afraid to do it himself, fearing Drum would summarily reject it after a quick scan.) The next morning, when Drum called Marshall into his office, Marshall expected to be censured. Instead, Drum praised the plan and said that Pershing himself had called it "a fine piece of work."

There were only three barely passable roads in and out of the Meuse-Argonne region to transfer more than one million men, and the undertaking had to be done under the cover of night. German commanders suspected some sort of major attack was in the works, but they expected it to come from Saint-Mihiel, where the Americans already had hundreds of thousands of troops. The idea of moving almost the entire First Army sixty miles north and into one of the Germans' most well-defended areas seemed nonsensical. As the other divisions filed out, Pershing kept the 26th "Yankee" Division near Saint-Mihiel and instructed them to continually "make their presence known" to convince the Germans that an assault there was imminent.

Along with organizing the men, Marshall had to coordinate the movement of all necessary supplies and matériel. According to Pershing's own calculations, the offensive required 3,980 guns of various calibers; 40,000 tons of ammunition, which needed to be replenished at a rate of 3,000 tons a day; 93,000 animals (mostly horses and mules); 164 miles of new light-rail lines; 34 evacuation hospitals; and enough trucks to transport 20,000 men at a time.

By the morning of September 25, everything was in place.

AT 11:30 P.M., the French Fourth Army unleashed a barrage of artillery from their position on the western edge of the Argonne Forest to make the Germans believe that an assault was coming from there. Three hours later, the Americans began their own barrage, the largest in human history.

Flying high above the Meuse-Argonne region was Captain Eddie Rickenbacker, now commander of the 94th Aero Squadron. He was mesmerized by the scene below. "Through the darkness the whole western horizon was illumined with one mass of jagged flashes," Rickenbacker observed from his plane. "The picture made me think of a giant switchboard which emitted thousands of electric flashes as invisible hands manipulated the plugs."

In the First Army's western sector, Captain Harry Truman and his D Battery alone fired off more than three thousand rounds, their four 75mm guns shooting so rapidly that, over the course of the bombardment, four hundred gallons of water were needed to cool down the red-glowing barrels. At 5:30 a.m., infantry regiments from the 35th Division advanced through a heavy mist toward Vauquois, a hilltop town defended by approximately fourteen hundred Germans. Most of the Americans had no battle experience, and their officers had been given a dire assessment the day before of what to expect. A confidential report from Pershing's headquarters warned:

> VAUQUOIS may be taken as the perfect example of German fortification, combining an elaborate trench system with the use of mines. The garrison is in deep dugouts affording protection from our largest shells. These are very comfortably equipped, having electricity, water supply and kitchens close at hand. . . .
>
> The fortress of VAUQUOIS, dominating the plain for 100 miles, is one of the points on the front where the Germans have installed themselves with great thoroughness. . . .
>
> From captured documents dated December, 1917, it appears that VAUQUOIS must be held at any cost.
>
> If the tactical situation eventually necessitates a retirement, the Commandant of VAUQUOIS is ordered to blow up all mined galleries.

The French had attempted to conquer Vauquois four times in 1914 and 1915, at a cost of tens of thousands of men, without success. They ultimately gave up trying, and referred to it as Le Mont des Morts, "the Hill of the Dead."

Shrouded in fog, the troops from the 35th Division were barely visible as they crept up on Vauquois the morning of September 26. Instead of encountering the fourteen hundred German soldiers that AEF intelligence had estimated, they found seventy-five. The German commander, a twenty-year-old lieutenant named Friedrich von Huellesheim, requested permission from his headquarters to abandon the town before blowing it up, which could have potentially killed an entire regiment of the 35th. But Huellesheim's superiors cabled back that he and his men were to stay and fight to the death. Less than forty-five minutes later, they surrendered instead.

Two miles north of Vauquois, the 35th stormed into the small but historic village of Varennes, where King Louis XVI and Marie Antoinette had been caught 127 years earlier while fleeing from antimonarchist revolutionaries and placed under arrest, before being taken back to Paris to be guillotined. With assistance from the 28th Division on its left flank, the 35th captured Varennes in three hours.

Cheppy, less than a mile to the east, was proving to be a tougher battle. At both Varennes and Cheppy, heavy Schneider and light Renault tanks from Lieutenant Colonel George Patton's 1st Tank Brigade were there to support the 35th. But the dense fog intermingled with artillery smoke, and with visibility less than ten feet, confusion reigned. Patton wrote to his wife, Beatrice:

> I started forward at 6:30 [a.m.] to see what was doing but
> could see little. Machine guns were going in every direction
> in front behind and on both sides. But no one could tell who
> they belonged to. I had six men—runners—with me and a
> compass so I collected all the soldiers I found who were lost
> and brought them along. At times I had several hundred.

> About 9:30 we came to a town called Cheppy. I went
> passed [*sic*] the infantry as we were supposed to have taken the
> place. But all at once we got shot at from all sides.

Matters only worsened when the morning mist burned off and soldiers and tanks alike were exposed to the sunlight, causing even more chaos.

"When we got here it began to clear up and we were shot at to beat hell with shells and machine guns," Patton told Beatrice. Upon seeing infantrymen from the 35th bolting from Cheppy to find cover, Patton "called them all sorts of names" to shame them into some semblance of order.

More than a hundred soldiers crouched down with him behind the crest of a hill, waiting for Patton's tanks to wipe out the German machine-gun nests around Cheppy. But they were nowhere to be seen. Patton was short-tempered under the best of circumstances, and his anger was rising by the second. The Germans had sighted the Americans' position, and small puffs of dirt, kicked up by German machine-gun and rifle bullets, started edging closer and closer to Patton and the other soldiers.

Enraged by the inaction and determined to investigate what the problem was, Patton stood up, ran down the slope that directly faced the enemy gunners, and discovered that the tanks were either bottlenecked at narrow crossovers or stuck in deep trenches. The walls had to be broken down to create a crude ramp the tanks could surmount.

"I went back and made some Americans hiding in the trenches dig a passage," Patton wrote to his wife. Patton himself jumped into the ditch, grabbed the shovels and picks kept on the side of the tanks for just these emergencies, and began furiously digging and tearing into the trench walls.

"I think I killed one [American] man here," Patton mentioned almost as an aside in his letter to Beatrice. But it wasn't by accident. "He would not work," Patton explained, "so I hit him over the head with a shovel. It was exciting for they shot at us all the time and I got mad and walked on the parapet." Screaming orders at the men below who were working to dislodge the cumbersome metal monsters, Patton believed he was impervious to the bullets plinking off the sides of the tanks and whizzing to each side of him.

He was armed only with a small sidearm and a walking stick, which he used to knock on his tanks to get the crews' attention. He believed the stick had a distinctive tapping sound so the crews would know it was him. Patton himself never rode in the tanks. They moved more slowly than a man could walk, and the peripatetic colonel needed to be up and around to evaluate the overall battle situation.

Patton wrote:

> At last we got five tanks across and I started them forward and yelled and cussed and waved my stick and said come on. About 150 dough boys started but when we got to the crest of the hill the fire got fierce right along the ground. We all lay down. I saw that we must go forward or back and I could not go back so I yelled who comes with me. A lot of dough boys yelled but only six of us started. My striker [Private Joe Angelo], me and 4 dough boys. I hoped the rest would follow but they would not. Soon there were only three but we could see the machine guns right ahead so we yelled to keep up our courage and went on.

With his adrenaline surging, Patton barely felt the bullet that struck him in the left hip until, after walking another forty feet, his leg gave way, and he crumpled to the ground.

Moments before he was hit, Patton experienced a vision of sorts involving his grandfather and great-uncle, both Confederate officers killed in the Civil War. "I felt a great desire to run," Patton recalled. "I was trembling with fear when suddenly I thought of my progenitors and seemed to see them in a cloud over the German lines looking at me. I became calm at once and saying aloud, 'It is time for another

Patton to die' called for volunteers and went forward to what I honestly believed to be certain death."

When Patton collapsed, Private Angelo rushed over and dragged him into a shell hole, where Angelo bandaged Patton's leg. Although his body was going into shock, Patton had the presence of mind to keep hollering out orders. German machine gunners were raking the top of the hole, and Patton and Angelo were trapped for several hours.

Once the machine guns were finally eliminated, Patton was carried for two miles on a stretcher by five men, Angelo dutifully at his side. Patton was placed in an ambulance but instructed the driver to take him to the 35th's headquarters so he could debrief their senior officers on the situation around Cheppy. Patton was finally evacuated to a hospital, from which he sent a letter to Beatrice about the wound. "The bullet went into the front of my left leg and came out just at the crack of my bottom about two inches to the left of my rectum," he wrote with characteristic frankness. "It was fired at about 50 m[eters] so made a hole about the size of a [silver] dollar where it came out. It has hurt very little and I have slepped fine. I will be out in ten days."

Both Patton and Angelo were awarded the Distinguished Service Cross for their actions (Patton recommended himself for the Medal of Honor but was turned down), and Patton praised Angelo publicly for being "without a doubt the bravest man in the American Army."

Patton regretted that he was out of the war for good, but he was proud of his brigade, who helped the 35th take Cheppy by the afternoon of September 26. "The tank corps established its reputation for not giving ground," he wrote to his wife. "They only went forward."

General Hunter Liggett's two other divisions in I Corps, the 77th and the 28th, were not progressing as rapidly as was the 35th. They were slogging their way through the Argonne Forest, its dense mass of trees and underbrush ideal for concealing machine-gun nests and trenches.

Pershing's most important objective of the day, however, remained Montfaucon. General Joseph Kuhn's 79th Division, flanked by the 37th and 4th divisions, was responsible for attacking the mountain head-on.

Within Pershing's headquarters, some privately questioned the decision to choose the 79th and its commander, Joseph Kuhn, for such a daunting, and pivotal, campaign. An engineer by training, Kuhn had never fought in a war, and the 79th was among the most inexperienced divisions in the entire First Army.

Kuhn was not without his bona fides. He had graduated first in his class at West Point, served as a military attaché in Japan during the Russo-Japanese War, and held a high position in the office of the Army chief of staff. He began a unique assignment in 1915, when he was appointed to a commission of senior Army officers sent to Germany to study how its armed forces were mobilized, instructed, and implemented. German commanders were so convinced of their military superiority that they believed the U.S. officers would come to the realization that a war against Germany was unwinnable and would therefore stay out of the conflict. Instead, the experience gave the Americans valuable insights into German strategy, tactics, manpower, and weaponry, as well as their vulnerabilities (a high degree of arrogance, apparently, being one of them). Kuhn's detailed analysis of Germany's strengths and weaknesses was greatly admired by his colleagues, and in 1917 he was named the president of the Army War College.

Among Kuhn's detractors was III Corps commander Robert Lee Bullard, a classmate of his at West Point. They both graduated in 1885, a year before Pershing. Born William Robert Bullard in Alabama, Bullard so idolized the Confederacy that at the tender age of six he asked his father to change his first two names to Robert Lee, in honor of the legendary Southern general, and his father complied. After West Point, Bullard, unlike Kuhn, went on to acquire extensive combat experience, fighting in the same three conflicts—the Spanish-American War, the Filipino insurrection, and the Pancho Villa Punitive Expedition—in which Pershing and so many of the AEF's other future generals had been involved. Although Pershing had given Bullard command of his beloved 1st Division, which distinguished itself at the battle for Cantigny, Pershing had named Kuhn to lead a division (the 79th) before Bullard, and Bullard felt slighted.

Pershing, however, saw enormous potential in Kuhn. He had the military bearing and temperament that Pershing thought an effective commander ought to exude, he was disciplined, and he was respected by his troops. Harry Parkin, a major who served in the 79th, reflected on the qualities he believed were required of a stellar leader, and his summation was influenced by his interactions with Kuhn: "Be just, be fair, be reasonable with soldiers, and do not fear to take a kindly interest in them and their troubles, but never be familiar. First you must gain their respect; obedience and loyalty will follow. Harshness and brutality will never make good soldiers. They will fail you in time of need. An officer can be strict, he must be, but he need not be harsh or unjust."

On the day before the attack on Montfaucon, Kuhn's men went about the myriad preparations a soldier makes before diving into battle. Officers studied their maps in detail, memorizing every important piece of terrain in their designated sector. Supply sergeants distributed the hand grenades, ammunition cartridges, and rations their men would carry with them for at least the first two days. The emergency food provisions consisted mostly of "hardtack"—the same rock-solid, stale-tasting crackers Civil War soldiers had relied on fifty years earlier—and canned corn beef, which troops in their more generous moments referred to as "corn willy" but, because of its repulsive taste and lumpy texture, was more frequently compared to monkey or horse meat. Men also spent hours cleaning and oiling their firearms. Members of the machine-gun units, aware of how easily their M1917 Enfields could jam, made sure they were in good condition, while the regular infantrymen focused on tending to their standard-issue Browning rifles. (Coincidentally, twenty-three-year-old Lieutenant Val Browning, the son of the guns' eponymous inventor, served in the 79th.)

Men also prayed, gave confession to their divisional chaplains, and held impromptu religious services. They wrote letters home to parents and sweethearts, making certain that no expressions of love were left unsaid in the event they never saw the person again. And some went crazy at the mere thought of the fighting to come. At least two men in the 79th shot themselves in the foot to keep from being sent into action.

If anyone had reason to go mad from fear it was the wire cutters, who snaked their way into no-man's-land at night and, without being seen or heard, snipped through coils of barbed wire and then marked the cleared lanes with white tape so that the infantry would have an unobstructed path to follow.

"At dusk [on September 24] we were ready to start, and I led the men, showing them the North Star, and told them to cut due north," wrote a lieutenant named Jack Bentley about their dangerous task. Bentley, a twenty-two-year-old Quaker from Maryland, played for the Baltimore Orioles before the war and could have legitimately used his faith to claim conscientious objector status and stay home to continue playing professional baseball. Instead, he enlisted. Bentley continued:

> I divided them up into eight teams, and they went to it. This was a hard job and the boys were exhausted when twelve o'clock came. . . . Our hands were torn and bleeding, clothing torn and wet, many of the boys had slipped into shell-holes filled with cold water, and the whole party was about in. It took us two hours to get back to camp and at daylight I was up, and reported to Colonel S[weezey] that the work was complete. He told me we were to go back that night and tape off the front and on the following morning we were to go over the top at five-thirty, preceding the infantry.

Leading the main charge at 5:30 a.m. on September 26 were the 79th Division's 314th Infantry Regiment, with the 315th behind them, and the 313th Infantry Regiment on their left, followed by the 316th. The 313th and 316th had to traverse a deep ravine called the Redoute du Golfe before entering the Bois de Cuisy and then penetrating the larger Bois de Montfaucon. The 314th and 315th had to pass through a valley ominously named Oeuvre du Demon ("Work of the Demon") before joining the other regiments to cross an open field, go down a steep hill, and then hike up Montfaucon itself.

With the 79th's artillery providing a rolling barrage, all of the regiments sprinted ahead in the first few minutes with almost no opposition. But when their own artillery units mixed in shells that were intended to provide the infantry with a concealing smoke screen, many of the inexperienced troops thought it was German poison gas, stopped to put on their masks, and waited for the fumes to clear. Some turned tail and ran back to the rear lines. Once order was reestablished, the men pushed on, but precious time had been lost.

Colonel William Oury's 314th came under sustained fire while trudging through a knee-deep bog past the bombed-out hamlets of Haucourt and Malancourt; several platoons of German soldiers inside the ruined homes opened up on them. The Americans suffered relatively few losses and were able to mount a swift counterattack that either killed or captured all of the German troops in the villages.

Next came the Oeuvre du Demon. The doughboys marched into the seemingly quiet valley not realizing that on every side were camouflaged machine-gun nests. The Germans waited for the Americans to funnel into the center of the dale and then commenced an enfilading fire. Those who weren't killed outright dropped to the ground and frantically looked around for anyplace to escape to. But there was nowhere to go.

The 313th, led by Colonel Claude Sweezey, was entering its own ambush, the Redoute du Golfe, which had more than a hundred machine guns lined across a ridge, as well as German soldiers wielding *Flammenwerfer*. Row after row of Sweezey's men rushed into the redoubt only to be shot dead or immolated by the flamethrowers. Despite having seen their comrades killed in droves, soldiers from the 313th continued to leap into the fray. Even enemy officers marveled at the tenaciousness of the previously untested soldiers. "The young American troops attacked with admirable pluck, though for the most part in unsuitable formations," a German colonel named Victor Keller observed. "Swarms of riflemen standing upright were no rarity. The American losses were considerable: 400 American soldiers were found dead in front of a single battalion sector."

Sweezey recognized the futility of the situation, ordered a pause, and sent runners off with urgent appeals for tanks and additional troops. Across the line, the entire advance was grinding to a halt. In stark contrast to the 79th's plight, however, the two divisions on its flanks—General Charles Farnsworth's 37th and General John Hines's 4th—were on track to meet their objectives for the day. Kuhn was especially dependent on the 4th, to his east, because Hines's division was supposed to drive past Montfaucon and then cut west to hit the fortress from behind, thereby relieving pressure on the 79th's troops when they got to the front of the mountain. Kuhn was unaware that General Robert Lee Bullard, commander of III Corps (which included the 4th Division), had changed the plan for his own benefit and had no intention of assisting the 79th.

Back at AEF headquarters, Pershing was practically beside himself, not knowing whether Montfaucon had been captured. When he finally received word at around 3:00 p.m. that Montfaucon was still in German hands and the assault was progressing slowly, he sought out V Corps's commander, General George Cameron, and ordered him to light a fire under the 79th. Cameron sent off a blistering message to Kuhn. "The Seventy-ninth Division is holding up the advance of the whole American Army," he wrote. "The Commanding General insists that the attack be pushed more vigorously." Kuhn immediately contacted the brigade commander of the 313th, General William Nicholson, and told him in no uncertain terms, "You must get Montfaucon tonight."

Vigor was not what the soldiers of the 79th lacked. Many of their communication systems had broken down, and the senior officers were unable to determine the exact location of their troops. Regimental commanders were also hindered. The 313th, to the left of Montfaucon, and the 314th, less than a mile away to its right, couldn't relay messages to each other to launch a coordinated strike. The 79th's artillery units, uncertain where the infantry regiments were, ceased firing (some were too far back to provide support anyway), leaving the soldiers even more exposed. And German snipers had begun targeting the 79th's field officers, knowing that without their leadership, the enlisted men would be thrown into disarray.

Despite the confusion, within a matter of hours Colonel Sweezey's 313th started to receive the assistance it needed. French Renault tanks and soldiers from the 37th Division converged on the Redoute du Golfe and helped the 313th punch its way into the Bois de Cuisy and, by early evening, all the way through to the northeastern edge of the Bois de Montfaucon.

Still unable to connect with the 314th, Colonel Sweezey's regiment tried to conquer Montfaucon on its own. A man of few words, in part due to a pronounced stutter, Sweezey gave his troops a direct, one-word command: "Forward!" And, at approximately 6:30 p.m., forward they went, crossing a field that offered no defenses except for the shallow, vermin-infested shell craters that were spread out haphazardly across the open ground. With sundown fast approaching, the French Renaults supporting Sweezey's men rumbled back into the forest, their crews explaining that they couldn't operate the tanks in the dark.

Having made it to the base of Montfaucon just after sunset, Sweezey's men were confronted with the hard truth that they had incurred massive casualties since leaving the Bois de Montfaucon, and a nighttime raid on the towering fortress would be suicidal. Sweezey ordered the 313th back to the woods they had charged out of only hours earlier. Adding to their already low spirits, a cold rain began to fall.

At 1:15 a.m. that night, General Robert Noble, commander of the 79th's 158th Brigade, received a message from General Kuhn to organize his men without delay and join up with Hines's 4th Division to surmount Montfaucon on its eastern side. Noble had two serious problems. General Robert Lee Bullard had ordered the 4th to bypass Montfaucon, which it did, and he told Hines not to turn back. Bullard's motivations were entirely personal. By pressing III Corps forward, he could boast to Pershing and his staff that he had gone farther than any other commander that day. The fact that he faced significantly less obstacles or resistance didn't matter. Pins and arrows on the maps at headquarters were the main measure of success, and Bullard's were well beyond the rest. Bullard had little respect for Kuhn, but he despised General George Cameron. Upon hearing that V Corps's 79th needed 4th Division's support at Montfaucon, Bullard turned to one of his colonels and said, in so many words, that he would be damned if he'd help Cameron "win any battle laurels." Bullard anticipated that as the size of the AEF expanded, Pershing was likely to form the American Second Army, and Bullard was determined to lead it. The more he outshone the other corps commanders, the better his chances.

General Robert Noble's second problem was even more critical— and embarrassing. He couldn't find his brigade. Earlier in the evening he had been separated from his men during a gas attack, and because their communication lines had become disengaged, he had to roam around in the darkness to seek them out. After finally finding them hours later, Noble decided against mounting an advance. With various units of the 79th still scattered about, Noble was afraid they might accidentally fire on one another. When General Kuhn arrived at 7:00 a.m. to check on Noble's progress, he was stunned by Noble's excuses and relieved him instantly. Kuhn then replaced Noble with Colonel William Oury and ordered him to link up with General William Nicholson's 157th Brigade. Within thirty minutes, Oury and Nicholson's men were storming up Montfaucon.

At the top of the mountain were an observatory, a church, and a cemetery. The Germans used all three for cover, even firing at the Americans from inside the aboveground mausoleums. Both sides were unable to resupply their ammunition, and once their bullets ran out, men began gutting one another with trench knives and cracking skulls with their rifle butts. By 11:30 a.m., after four hours of brutal hand-to-hand combat, the Americans finally prevailed.

Later in the day, General Nicholson returned to the 79th's headquarters, where he encountered General Kuhn.

"Where the hell have you been?" Kuhn shouted at Nicholson, who retorted, "I've been taking Montfaucon."

A carrier pigeon had already brought the message to the divisional headquarters, but no one had conveyed it to General Kuhn.

"OUR ATTACK STARTED well Thursday morning [September 26] and good advances were made along the whole front," Pershing wrote in his diary on Monday, September 30. "General Pétain called, much pleased at our progress. M. Clemenceau, who also came, very enthusiastic and started to Montfaucon, but road congestion prevented his reaching there."

Pershing's upbeat diary entry belied the AEF's true situation. General Bullard's III Corps traversed eight miles in one day, but the terrain it covered was the least formidable that any corps in First Army had to face. The 77th and 28th divisions, in Liggett's I Corps, were still bogged down in the Argonne Forest, and the 35th was on the brink of being decimated. Emboldened by their relatively quick victories at Vauquois, Varennes, Cheppy, and other small villages that the Germans had barely bothered to defend, the 35th unraveled when it was confronted with overwhelming artillery and machine-gun fire at the town of Exermont.

Unbeknownst to Pershing, before he'd written in his diary about Prime Minister Clemenceau's desire to see the conquered stronghold of Montfaucon for himself, Clemenceau had already thrown a tantrum over Pershing's leadership skills and wanted him fired. Clemenceau became apoplectic when, on his way to Montfaucon on September 29, his limousine came to a stop behind a seemingly endless convoy of mostly American trucks, ambulances, and horse-drawn artillery wagons on a dirt road that led to Montfaucon. Clemenceau was still peeved he hadn't been able to visit Thiaucourt, near Saint-Mihiel, two weeks earlier, but while that was due merely to safety concerns, the bottleneck Clemenceau encountered on the 29th, he believed, revealed gross incompetence within the AEF, for which Pershing was responsible. What he really wanted to see was the observatory, where the telescope that the German Crown Prince Wilhelm had looked through during the

*Backed-up vehicles on one of the few remaining roads
in the Meuse-Argonne region.*

battle for Verdun was still positioned. (Practically every American and French soldier who walked through Montfaucon made it a mission to peek through the telescope himself.) After an excruciating eight hours stuck in gridlock, the furious prime minister finally gave up and ordered his driver to return to Paris.

Clemenceau was hardly the only one frustrated with Pershing. "Reports from Americans . . . state that their roads and communications are so blocked that the offensive has had to stop and cannot be recommenced for four or five days," Field Marshal Sir Douglas Haig, commander in chief of the British Expeditionary Force, wrote in his diary on October 1. "What very valuable days are being lost! All this is the result of inexperience and ignorance on the part of [the American staff]."

And Field Marshal Sir Henry Wilson, chief of the British Imperial General Staff, commented in his diary that the "state of chaos the fool [Pershing] has got his troops into down in the Argonne is indescribable." He added later that on a personal level, Pershing was a "vain, arrogant, weak ASS."

Not even Montfaucon, conquered in less than thirty-six hours, could be hailed as a complete success. Because the 79th Division, abandoned by the 4th, failed to secure the mountain on September 26, the Germans had time to bring up ten entire divisions to reinforce their lines.

With the exception of Robert Lee Bullard's III Corps, Pershing made sweeping changes within First Army. All three of George Cameron's V Corps divisions—the 37th, the 91st, and especially the 79th, which some AEF senior staff members blamed for hampering the overall offensive—were sent to the rear. Cameron was given only two new divisions to lead, the 3rd and the 32nd, and a fairly minor assignment to take the Bois de Chauvignon, south of Romagne.

In Hunter Liggett's I Corps, the badly mauled 35th Division was replaced with the 1st. Their objectives were much more critical: the Côte Dame Marie and the Côte de Châtillon, along the Romagne Heights, which were among the stronger positions on the entire Kriemhilde line. A mile to the east were the Cunel Heights, which Bullard and his 4th, 80th, and 33rd divisions were responsible for capturing. There were other major cities and obstacles to be taken as well— Grandpré, Borne de Cornouiller (informally renamed by the Americans as Corn Willy Hill), and Bucanzy—but once the heights of Romagne and Cunel were vanquished, the Allies could move directly onto their main targets, Sedan and Mézières.

The 1st Division commenced its attack from the town of Exermont at 5:25 a.m. on the morning of October 4. The Germans had controlled much of the area after routing the 35th Division several days earlier, and the decaying corpses of soldiers from the 35th were visible in every direction, a vivid warning of the dangers ahead.

"Our company numbered two hundred men," Lieutenant Maury Maverick recalled of their early-morning charge outside Exermont. "Within a few minutes, about half of them were dead or wounded."

Maverick became pinned down in an area surrounded by dense trees that was coming under heavy shell fire, and he realized the only way out was through a narrow path that was cleared of brush and wire—but was also cluttered with the corpses of recently killed American soldiers.

"I felt sure there was a German machine gun on the other side. I did not want to go through that lane. But the men began to waver a little and I figured it would not be right for me to lay down or stop, so I moved ahead."

Maverick and four other men dashed forward, shooting as they went, and they made it through unscathed. But before Maverick could catch his breath, a shell burst directly above him. He was knocked down by the concussive force of the explosion and struck in the shoulder by shrapnel. None of the other men survived.

"I looked at my four runners," Maverick wrote, "and I saw that the two in the middle had been cut down to a pile of horrid red guts and blood and meat, while the two men on the outside had been cut up somewhat less badly, but no less fatally."

Maverick lost a considerable amount of blood and was near death himself before finally being taken to a base hospital. He recalled:

> When I came to from the operation I was in a ward for the severe cases. I was vomiting something that smelled like ether. There were ten of us, three Germans, seven Americans. A German, quite close to me, had most of his face shot out. He would sip a little milk. But the blood would trickle down into his stomach and he would puke milk and blood. . . . It was very difficult for him to talk, but he spoke English.
>
> "If I do not die," he said, "I will take a long vacation and get well. The surgeons are now great. They make new faces." I saw a twinkle in his eye.
>
> "I will visit my brother in Milwaukee." He continued: "Will you tell him for me that I shall soon visit?" But within an hour, with horrible paroxysms, he died.

Lying in his hospital bed and mourning the loss of his four comrades, Maverick found himself thinking back to his youth in San Antonio. "[Their deaths] reminded me of nothing I had ever seen before," he reflected, "except Christmas hog butchering back on the Texas farm. The only difference was that the hog butchering was done methodically, and the liver and [lungs] and hearts were properly saved. In other words, the hog butchering was relatively humane."

Later that day, Pershing entered in his diary a much gloomier evaluation of First Army's progress. "Attack resumed at 5:25 this morning. Met durable resistance, advance very slow. Our men have had to fight for every 100 yards they have gained, and it looks as though we will have a hard, slow advance. There is no course except to fight it out, taking the best possible advantage of the ground which now lays to the advantage of the Germans."

Not even the mighty 1st Division could break through to the Kriemhilde line. In less than a week of fighting the 1st had suffered seventy-five hundred casualties, the most of any division in the Meuse-Argonne region. Pershing ordered that they be pulled out and replaced by the 42nd "Rainbow" Division, officially led by General Charles Menoher but whose most popular officer was General Douglas MacArthur, commander of the division's 84th Brigade.

Before the 42nd had moved into place, AEF headquarters was consumed by a potentially disastrous story that the media was following intently.

On October 3, six companies of approximately 550 soldiers from the 77th Division, part of Hunter Liggett's I Corps, were near the village of Binarville, in the far western edge of the Argonne Forest, when they were surrounded by German forces.

Within a matter of days, three hundred of the men were killed by machine-gun and shell fire or taken prisoner. Word had gotten out to the press about the Lost Battalion, as they were referred to, and journalists were updating their readers on a regular basis about this dwindling unit's fate and whether the soldiers would get out alive.

With all of their runners either dead or captured, their last form of communication was a basketful of carrier pigeons. The senior commander, Major Charles Whittlesey, a bookish, bespectacled lawyer who had no real military training, scribbled out a note for the first pigeon to carry: "Many wounded. We cannot evacuate." The bird flew straight up—and was promptly shot dead in midair by the Germans.

Whittlesey dashed off another message: "Men are suffering. Can support be sent?" The next bird went up and it, too, exploded in a cloud of blood and feathers after it was struck by a perfectly aimed bullet.

Along with the threat of dying of thirst (an enticing, crystal-clear stream was just feet away but in full view of snipers) or being killed by a German shell, Whittlesey's men were being bombarded by their own artillery units, who had misjudged where the battalion was trapped and started dropping bombs right on top of them.

Only one bird was left, a female pigeon they had erroneously given a male name, Cher Ami ("Dear Friend"), and their survival depended on whether this bird would make it to headquarters. Whittlesey's final message was more detailed and indicated the urgency of the situation: "We are along a road parallel to 276.4. Our own artillery is dropping a barrage directly on us. For heaven's sake stop it."

All eyes were on Cher Ami. She soared straight up, seeming to understand intuitively the importance of her mission. And then, inexplicably, she settled onto a nearby tree branch, where she calmly began to groom her plumage as if she hadn't a care in the world. Members of the battalion yelled and threw rocks at her, and one soldier started to climb the tree and shake the branch until Cher Ami finally flew off. She was shot at, and although struck in the eye and leg, managed to make it to divisional headquarters twenty-five miles away. The bombardment stopped.

General Liggett organized a massive rescue mission involving the 28th and 82nd divisions, and on October 8 the remaining members of the Lost Battalion were finally saved. The story of these scrappy underdogs who endured five days of German attacks with no food or water dominated the news and gave the AEF a boost back in the States.

A thirty-year-old corporal in Liggett's 82nd would go on to become one of the most famous and decorated doughboys of the war. The third-oldest of eleven children in a family living near Pall Mall, Tennessee, Alvin Cullum York grew up carousing with a wild bunch, "wilder than wild bees when they're swarming," York himself would say of the friends he used to gamble and drink and shoot guns with. York became smitten with a local girl named Gracie Williams, who attended a fundamentalist congregation, the Church of Christ in Christian Union (CCCU), and York initially went to the services in order to spend time with her. Gradually, the sermons started to have an effect on him, and on New Year's Eve 1915 York experienced a spiritual epiphany and became a devout member of the CCCU.

Legally required to register for the draft after Congress instituted the Selective Service Act, York enlisted but tried numerous times to be exempted from combat due to the CCCU's staunch pacifism. York believed violence was a sin, but the draft board claimed CCCU wasn't a legitimate religious sect and denied his appeals.

Mustered into the 82nd, York fought at Saint-Mihiel with the division's 328th Infantry Regiment and proved to be a crack rifleman due to his many years of hunting in rural Tennessee. On the morning of October 8, York and his platoon were on a wooded hill designated on their maps as number 223, close to the village of Chatel-Chéhéry. After leaving the protection of the trees, they entered a large clearing when they came under enemy machine-gun fire. York later recalled:

> The Germans met our charge across the valley with a regular sleet storm of bullets. I'm a-telling you that there valley was a death trap. It was a triangular-shaped valley with steep ridges covered with brush and swarming with machine guns on all sides. I guess our two waves got about halfway across and then jes couldn't get no further nohow. The Germans done got us, and they done got us smart. They jes stopped us in our tracks. Their machine guns were up there on the heights overlooking us and well hidden, and we couldn't tell for certain where the

terrible fire was coming from. It 'most seemed as though it was coming from everywhere.

When their lieutenant was shot up "like a rag doll" in front of the platoon, Sergeant Harry Parsons took command and sent corporals Bernard Early, Murray Savage, William Cutting, and York with thirteen privates to attack Humserberg Hill, where most of the machine-gun nests seemed to be located. American artillery support came in at just the right moment, and York was able to flank the Germans without being seen and opened fire on the crew, picking off every one of them. With the nest wiped out, Early and the other squad members were able to come up from behind and surprise another, much larger group of Germans—about seventy total—and took them all prisoner.

Early's men were guarding the POWs when a German voice barked out a command, and, suddenly, all of the prisoners dropped to the ground as enemy machine guns opened fire on the Americans, who were still standing. Nine were killed and three others seriously wounded, including Early. Corporal York was now in charge, and he was determined to silence the remaining German machine guns. York later said of the incident:

> And those machine guns were spitting fire and cutting down the undergrowth all around me something awful. And the Germans were yelling orders. You never heard such a racket in all of your life. I didn't have time to dodge behind a tree or dive into the brush. . . . As soon as the machine guns opened fire on me, I began to exchange shots with them. There were over thirty of them in continuous action, and all I could do was touch the Germans off just as fast as I could. I was sharp shooting. . . . All the time I kept yelling at them to come down. I didn't want to kill any more than I had to. But it was they or I. And I was giving them the best I had.

During the assault, six German soldiers in a trench near York charged him with fixed bayonets. York had already fired every round in his rifle, so he drew out his pistol and picked off and killed all six soldiers before they could reach him. Counterintuitively, York targeted the Germans farthest from him first. York had learned the technique hunting turkeys in Tennessee; if the ones in the front were shot at first, those in the back immediately sought out cover, but if York started with the ones in the rear, he was more likely in the end to get them all.

German lieutenant Paul Jürgen Vollmer, commander of the 1st Battalion, emptied his pistol trying to kill York while he was contending with the machine guns. Failing to even injure York, and seeing his mounting losses, he offered in English to surrender the unit to York. By the end of the engagement, York and his seven men marched 132 German prisoners back to the American lines.

Upon returning to his unit, York reported to his brigade commander, General Julian R. Lindsey, who remarked, "Well, York, I hear you have captured the whole damn German army."

"No, sir," York replied. "I got only a hundred thirty-two."

AFTER THE LOST BATTALION'S SAGA highlighted how precarious and unreliable communications could be, an ingenious and unprecedented experiment was developed in Saint-Ètienne, southeast of the Argonne. Under the direction of Colonel Alfred Bloor, a secret message was called in by telephone ordering two companies of AEF soldiers to go from one small village to another. Bloor had decided that phoning the order was the only possible means of transmitting the urgent information; runners were relatively slower, he didn't have any carrier pigeons, and signal flares wouldn't provide the necessary detail.

Bloor was certain the Germans were listening in and attempting to decipher his text, since Bloor had earlier sent false coordinates over the same line, and soon after the Germans bombed that very location. (Nothing of value was there and no one was injured in the shelling, but it proved to Bloor that the Germans were eavesdropping.)

Bloor was confident that the new message was undecipherable. It wasn't based on any mathematical scheme and the words weren't any variation of English. They were sentences created by Choctaw Indians who were serving in the 142nd Infantry Regiment, 36th Division. Bloor had earlier overheard several of the Native Americans speaking with one another in their own dialect. Upon confirming that the vocabulary hadn't been recorded on paper and was passed down orally from generation to generation, Bloor had the idea of using Choctaw words as the basis of a new code. There weren't any direct translations of military words or phrases, so the Choctaws came up with rather simple replacements that would sound meaningless to nonspeakers but were understandable to them. When describing the number of units involved in a battle, for example, they would say the number (in Choctaw) followed by the words for "grains of corn." When referring to artillery, they spoke of "big guns"; casualties were "scalps"; poison gas was "bad air"; and "little gun that shoots fast," translated into Choctaw, referred to machine guns.

Bloor's idea was used in battles throughout the Meuse-Argonne campaign, and captured German soldiers confirmed that they had indeed intercepted the messages and were absolutely baffled by them.

BACK AT AEF HEADQUARTERS, Pershing's emotions were fluctuating by the hour, depending on the most recent cable or staff report. On October 10, Liggett's I Corps had driven the Germans entirely out of the Argonne Forest, a remarkable achievement. Pershing had also heard inklings of secret talks between the German government and the Allies about an armistice, a possible indication that, like their British and French counterparts, the Germans were exhausted after more than four years of warfare.

But Pershing was also wary of any overtures for peace expressed by the German government, as it could merely be a false pretext to stall the Meuse-Argonne Offensive, which was far from over. Despite Liggett's success in the Argonne, First Army still was well behind

Pershing's original schedule, and the casualty counts were mounting by the thousands with every passing day.

Pershing occasionally visited military hospitals. In one ward he met a young soldier who apologized to the general for not saluting him. When Pershing looked down and saw that the man's right arm had been completely blown off, Pershing said, "It is I who should salute you." Pershing maintained his composure, but once he got into the privacy of his car, he burst into tears, deeply moved by the soldier's gallant spirit. Pershing had recently confided to Douglas MacArthur that a general should never, ever let his soldiers see him "flinch."

Pershing had another fleeting but intense breakdown in front of his trusted personal aide-de-camp, Colonel John Quekemeyer. While driving through one battle-ravaged town after another, Pershing was struck again by the enormity of suffering the war was inflicting on his troops, and he began quietly calling out to his dead wife: "Frankie . . . Frankie . . . My God, sometimes I don't know how I can go on."

On top of all the other problems and pressures Pershing had to contend with in early October, there was a silent enemy creeping through the trenches, killing more of his men than bombs and bullets combined: the Spanish flu, a particularly virulent strain of influenza for which there was no vaccine or cure. Victims suffered from fevers that spiked to 104 degrees or more, relentless nausea, severe muscle aches, and coughing fits so violent that a person could tear his or her own rib cartilage. A red, frothy phlegm constantly filled the lungs, and blood dripped out of the ears and nose. Those unable to fight the virus or its accompanying complications, like pneumonia and tuberculosis, usually died within ten days.

The virus was highly contagious and spread quickly in trenches and other close quarters. It was also killing the people caring for those already infected; of the more than two hundred U.S. Army nurses who died during the war, almost every one of them was a victim of the Spanish flu. (Back in the States, the pandemic ultimately claimed the lives of more than six hundred thousand men, women, and children,

nearly the same number of people lost in the four years of fighting during the Civil War.)

By October 10, Pershing realized he could no longer assume
day-to-day control of both First Army and the AEF. The time had
come to delegate, and he informed Hunter Liggett that he would be
promoting him to commander of First Army.

Also on October 10, Pershing wrote a letter to his son, Warren, that
belied the strain of the moment.

> My dear Kiddie:
>
> I have your letter of Sunday (no date) written on letter paper
> with the Stars and Stripes on one edge. It makes very pretty
> writing paper. The letter was No. 8 so I suppose you can tell
> the date but I cannot.
>
> I have often promised in my various letters that you
> should come to France while I am still here, and I am going
> to keep this promise and you may count upon it. I do not
> know just when it will be nor how I shall arrange it, but we
> can work that out a little bit later.
>
> I want you to come so that you yourself can see something
> of the army and see something of France. I want you to know
> while you are still a boy something of the fine patriotism that
> inspires the American soldiers who are fighting over here for
> the cause of liberty. They are fighting as you know against
> Germany and her Allies to prevent the rulers of Germany
> from seizing territory that does not belong to them and from
> extending their rule over the people of other governments
> who do not wish to be ruled by Germany. I might add that in
> order to do this the German army, under orders from the
> Ruler of Germany, has committed most serious crimes, and
> for that also we are fighting in order to punish them.
>
> I want you to see some of the battlefields of France with
> me, over which the American soldiers have fought in

carrying out the great purpose of our people. It will enable you to realize later in life just what sacrifice means and just what degree of sacrifice our army is called upon to make and which they have made and are making bravely and courageously.

I think that you should talk this over with your Auntie and I want you to regard it, of course, as confidential, and let me have any suggestion that you and she wish to make regarding it. In the meantime, work as hard as you ought to work giving yourself plenty of time for play and exercise in the open air, to the end that you may prepare yourself as well as the average boy prepares himself, or better, for whatever calling you may follow in life. And might I add, as I have already said to you, that it is my hope that you will always be what I believe you to be—a very manly, upright, honest, industrious, wholesome, wide-awake boy. I look forward to your companionship with a great deal of pleasure, and after the war is over we can have many good times together.

Give my love to your Aunties, and believe me, as always,

Yours affectionately,

Papa

Three days later, Pershing met with Marshal Ferdinand Foch at Foch's headquarters. Foch admonished him for First Army's failure to keep pace with French and British forces to the north. He also raised the issue again of Pershing relinquishing some of his command and letting the French and British incorporate the Americans into their divisions. Pershing saw Clemenceau's meddling in this and, as he had done numerous times before, dismissed the idea out of hand.

"On all other parts of the front, the advances are very marked," Foch stated. "The Americans are not progressing as rapidly."

Pershing argued that the reason the Allies were moving forward more swiftly was the Germans had moved their divisions from the north and into the Argonne region to confront the Americans. Pershing's men were the ones bearing the brunt of the counterattacks. "No army in our place would have advanced farther than the Americans," Pershing said.

"Every general is disposed to say the fighting on his front is the hardest," Foch retorted. "I myself only consider results."

"The Germans," Pershing shot back, "could hold up any troops Marshal Foch has at his command."

"I judge only by results," Foch repeated.

Changing the subject, Pershing informed Foch that he was creating the American Second Army, which would be led by General Robert Lee Bullard (as Bullard had hoped and expected). Foch was then handed the specifics of the plan but set it down without reading it. Any general who led two or more full armies became a "group commander," a position Pétain and Haig had already achieved. Pershing was insisting now to be considered on the same level.

"Ah, yes," Foch said almost casually, "I am inclined to grant your request. However, you are not to construe this as a plan for you to withdraw to Chaumont"—that is, farther from the front lines.

"As usual," Pershing said, "my headquarters train will remain in the woods at Souilly. I will visit Army, Corps, Division, and Brigade as often as possible."

"Very good," Foch replied, and the two men bade each other good-bye.

Pershing went off to Paris for additional meetings that evening. He had a note hand-delivered to Micheline Resco's apartment. "My dear," he wrote. "I am here for the night. I arrived at nine and am departing at six in the morning. I am very sad that I won't be able to see you, kiss you, or embrace you at length, but the battle progresses. . . . All for you. J."

"THIS IS THE first opportunity I have had to write you since the day I wrote from the woods before the big drive began," another contrite and love-struck soldier wrote to his sweetheart. Harry Truman was apologizing to his fiancée, Bess Wallace, that he had been out of touch for more than three weeks after the Saint-Mihiel initiative.

> I am very sorry to have been so long but things have happened to me so rapidly I couldn't write. There was no chance to mail them if I could have. The great drive has taken place and I had a part in it, a very small one but nevertheless a part. The experience has been one that I can never forget, one that I don't want to go through again unless the Lord wills but I'd never have missed for anything. The papers are in the street now saying that the Central Powers have asked for peace, and I was in the drive that did it! I shot out a German Battery, shot up his big observation post, and ruined another Battery when it was moving down the road.

Truman started writing again to Wallace on a regular basis. He echoed Pershing's view about not letting the Germans off too easily if they truly were seeking an end to the war. President Wilson had given his Fourteen Points speech several months earlier, which had enumerated not just possible terms for an armistice but also conditions that related to other diplomatic and territorial problems around the world. It concluded by calling for an organization—which became the League of Nations—that could resolve international matters without resorting to warfare.

The German government had paid little heed to the speech when Wilson delivered it on January 8, 1918, but now that the Germans realized how dominant the American forces were becoming, they considered the prospect that Wilson might be easier to negotiate with than the Allies.

"The news sure looks well today," Truman wrote in late October. "When Austria begs our grand President for the privilege of peace it really looks like something. I'm for peace but that gang should be given a bayonet peace and be made to pay for what they've done to France. . . . When the moon rises behind those tree trunks I spoke of awhile ago you can imagine that the ghosts of the half-million Frenchmen who were slaughtered here are holding a sorrowful parade over the ruins. It makes you hope that His Satanic Majesty has a particularly hot poker and warm corner for Bill Hohenzollern [Kaiser Wilhelm II] when his turn comes to be judged and found wanting."

Having had an opportunity to rest and regroup, the American First Army, under General Hunter Liggett's control, was pressing forward with renewed vigor. One by one, the major towns and villages they needed to capture were beginning to fall—albeit at enormous cost. MacArthur's 84th Brigade of the 42nd Division was gassed as it approached the Côte de Châtillon, and MacArthur, who still refused to carry a mask himself (he claimed it impeded his movements), inhaled the poisonous fumes and was nearly forcibly evacuated to a hospital by his own men, but he refused to leave. General Charles Summerall, head of V Corps, bypassed the 42nd Division's commander, General Menoher, and told MacArthur directly: "Get me Chatillon or a list of five thousand casualties."

"If this brigade does not capture Chatillon you can publish a casualty list of the entire brigade with the brigade's commander at the top," MacArthur replied.

For two days, MacArthur and his men kept battering Côte de Châtillon until finally, on October 14, they were successful. That same day, Colonel Bill Donovan was also pushing his men tirelessly, calling to soldiers apparently too afraid to press on as shells were screaming past them: "Come on, fellows! It's better ahead than it is here." Moments later, he was hit in the leg and collapsed to the ground. He continued to issue orders as he lay wounded, until he was eventually carried back to a field hospital, more furious that he was out of the war than that he had been injured. Donovan saw Father Francis Duffy when he came into the treatment center, and Duffy recorded their brief exchange in his journal. "[Donovan] looked up from the stretcher and said to me smilingly, 'Father, you're a disappointed man. You expected to have the pleasure of burying me over here.' 'I certainly did, Bill, and you are a lucky dog to get off with nothing more than you've got.'"

More than twelve miles to the 42nd's west, the 78th Division was attacking Grandpré. After the Germans had been rooted out a week later, on October 23, a young infantryman in the 78th wrote to another soldier back in the States about his experiences against the "Jerries." Troops rarely shared graphic accounts of combat to loved ones, but they often did so with their comrades in the AEF, who could relate to what they had been through. "Dear Old Bunkie," the soldier began,

> Now don't go into epileptic fits or something like that when you read this letter, that is because I sent one to you as I know I haven't written you a letter for some time. Too busy with Uncle Sam's affairs just now and am working to beat hell.
>
> I guess you would like to know of a few of my experiences over here while the scrimmage was on so I'll give you a few little yarns.
>
> We were in the line up at Thiacourt (St. Michel Sector) at first and although we did no actual fighting as we were in reserve at first and then in support, we got a lot of strafing from Jerry in the nature of Artillery fire and Air raids.
>
> But in the Argonne Forest was where we got in it in earnest and even if I do say it myself, the good old Lightning (78th) Division will go down in history as second to none for the work they did there.
>
> It was here, old man, that I got my first Hun with the bayonet. That was on the day prior to taking Grandpré and we had just broke through the enemy first line defenses when this happened.
>
> We were pressing through a thicket when this big plug-ugly Hun suddenly loomed up in front of me and made a one-armed stab at me with his bayonet. You can make a hell of a long reach this way, but it's a rather awkward thrust as the bayonet makes the rifle heavy at the muzzle when you've got hold of your rifle at the small of the stock like this guy had. A homelier guy I never saw before in all my life and he'd

make two in size compared to Dad and you know what a big man my old Dad is.

Well you can imagine that this bud did not catch me unawares.

I was ready for him. I thought I was going to have a pretty stiff one-sided fight on my hands, with the odds in his favor, but he was a cinch. Before I even realized it myself I parried off his blow and had him through his throat. It was my first hand to hand fight.

It was all over in a second, that is it for Jerry. He never even made a shriek. He went down like a log.

It was hand to hand all the way through that section of the woods as it was considered a vulnerable point, but we finally cleared them out and opened up the way for an attack on Grandpré itself. . . .

While sneaking about the ruins of Grandpré "Mopping Up" we came across a Prussian Chap in a ruined building with a rifle. He was a sniper, alive and the reason he was still there was because he could not get out although the opening was big enough for him to crawl through. During the bombardment the roof of the building had fell through in such a way as to pin him there by the feet and although he was practically uninjured he could not get himself free. I'll explain better when I see you, as I can tell it better than I can write it. He begged us to help him and although we had been cautioned against treatury [sic] one of the fellows who was with me put down his rifle and started to crawl through to free him. The moment he got his head and shoulders through the hole which had been smashed by a shell, by the way, this Hun hauls off and lets him have a charge right square in the face.

Poor Dan never knew what happened. His face was unrecognizable. We didn't do a thing but riddle that hole, we were that furious, and we didn't stop shooting until our magazines were empty. . . .

Up near Bricksway we ran into another pretty stiff proposition. We had to fight through the woods that seemed to be full of machine gun nests. We had just cleared out one of them with hand grenades and while we were sneaking up a rather steep hill, thickly wooded, we saw these Huns suddenly appear and run about a dozen paces and disappear down into a clearly camouflaged dug-out.

The Yanks were pressing the Huns hard, they were some of the Famous Prussian Guard too, and after these three birds had gone down into their hole we sneaked right up. There were three of us together, all Buck Privates. I took a hand grenade out of my bag, pulled out the retaining pin and heaved it down into the dug-out. That's the only and safest way of getting a Hun out of a dug-out. There was a helluva an explosion in about six seconds. I threw two more down to join the first and keep it company. Well after the big noise had stopped down there we crept down to investigate.

There was only one room down there, a big concrete affair and only one entrance, the one we came down, and that room was a mess. There were fifteen dead Huns down there and the walls, floor and ceiling were splashed with red, so you can see what damage a hand grenade can do. . . .

I was also with a detachment of men who took a dozen prisoners out of a dug-out and the worst of the whole thing was that they were only mere kids.

Just think of it old man. Mere kids, that is the most of them and they all expected to be killed immediately. . . .

Well I guess this will be all for just now so with best regards and good wishes to you, Elmer, Mother Sutters, Pop, Mutt, and all the kyoodles, I close.

Your Old Friend and Comrade in Mischief
Dickwitch

P.S. Say you old slab of a lop-sided tin-eared Jackass, what's wrong with you anyhow. Got writer's cramp or what? Pick up a pen for the Love of Pete and write to your old buddie in France.

Few soldiers were more hell-bent on redeeming themselves than the men of General Joseph Kuhn's 79th Division, who had been placed in reserve after their brutal attempt to take Montfaucon on the first day of the overall offensive.

In late October they were put back into action and up against Corn Willy Hill, a stronghold not unlike Montfaucon, and several smaller hills surrounding it. This battle would prove equally as ferocious, and many of the same difficulties that plagued them a month earlier—lack of rations, poor coordination with their artillery, and general confusion in the literal and figurative fog of war—were still a factor.

Lieutenant Lloyd Palmer, with the 79th's 315th Infantry Battalion, chronicled their nearly ten days of combat. Famished almost from the start, Palmer and his men came upon the mostly rotting remains of a destroyed field kitchen from another division. Palmer wrote:

> They had evidently lit the fires in their kitchens and started boldly getting a meal within a few hundred yards of the front. I had to admire their courage, but their attempt to feed the men, almost on the front, met with disaster. The smoke from the kitchens must have attracted the Germans' attention for in the midst of their preparations the position was shelled violently. It was one of the worst messes that I ever saw. There were between twenty and thirty dead horses spread all over the scene. Mixed in with carcasses of the horses were the bodies of a number of gallant soldier cooks, and lying all about in various stages and conditions was the food which was intended for the hungry soldiers of the 29th division.
>
> Holding our noses and working among the debris we each found a few cans of tomatoes and meat which were safe to eat.

We also found a half a barrel of nice, sour pickles which appeared good, so we took along a tin hatful. It was not a pleasant place to salvage food, but it could not have tasted better served in grand style in a great hotel.

Finding freshwater was another challenge. Palmer wrote:

The little drop of water I had when I started had been passed to some friends and not a drop remained. Some of my men told me of a spring on the hillside not far away. Braving the bullets again I dodged along and finally found the "spring." It seemed nothing more than a puddle, but I drank deeply, filled my canteen, and went back to where I had left my company. In the gathering darkness I ran into Lieutenant Dodson wandering around aimlessly. I asked him what was the matter and he said something about two dead Americans nearby. He kept muttering something about all being killed and had a wild look in his eyes. He was as crazy as a loon.

Palmer began to feel his own nerves start to fray when his battalion came under intense artillery fire. He recalled:

I did my customary leap into a nearby shell hole and crouched waiting for the shelling to end. The shelling became more and more violent till the whole hillside was being raked. I also realized that fate had again dealt unkindly with us, as all the shells were coming from American guns. In the midst of this tornado of noise and thunder, a great shell roared overhead and burst on the crest of hill 378, blowing out a hole you could dump a three story house in. Three more of these shells burst and after each explosion the whole hill rocked and the area for half a mile was sprinkled with debris. . . . These four shells were from the great sixteen-inch naval gun, mounted on a

railroad carriage, and had been fired from Verdun, over twenty
miles away. . . .

After a particularly vicious burst, almost on the edge of the
shell hole I was occupying, I decided to move. Taking advantage of a partial lull in the firing, I jumped out of the hole and
started running. . . .

Dead Germans and Americans were lying everywhere on
the slope and mixed with the dead were a few surviving
wounded in pitiful shape. One chap cried out wildly to me for
help as I went by. His leg was off at the knee and he had already
lain there for two days. As I had nothing to eat or drink, I had
to pass him up. . . .

The fog and mist still hung heavy and if it had not been for
the mysterious rifle and machine gun fire out in the fog, I
might have thought myself absolutely alone. As I was again
very thirsty I thought I would look for the spring that I had
found the night before. After some search I found it but I
turned away after a glance at it. Two soldiers who evidently
had been getting water there had been hit directly with a large
shell. The head of one soldier had been completely blown
away, while the other was horribly mangled, and parts of both
were in the spring.

Despite all the hindrances that Palmer and his men encountered, they
continued to make extraordinary gains over the next several days, and
the 79th and other divisions finally penetrated the Kriemhilde Stellung
and forced the Germans into a full retreat. Hours before reaching their
final objective on the morning of November 11, Palmer described one
last, dreamlike image that caught his attention:

We were a ghostly crew that morning as we plodded along silently and stupidly in the enveloping fog. Of the two hundred
men all that could be seen, or heard, were two or three

shadowy figures ahead. As we neared our destination daylight
pierced the fog so we could see ten or fifteen feet on either side
of us. Suddenly I saw what appeared to be a pure white figure
with arms flung wide, lying on the ground nearby. It turned
out [to be] nothing more than a poor, dead American, but the
heavy frost of the night before had covered the worn, muddy
figure with a pure white cloak, beautiful to behold.

Palmer and his men "stumbled up" a hill and were met with what
he called "the worst hail of machine gun bullets that any had experienced," which killed a number of his comrades.

German artillery then opened up on them as well.

"It seemed that I just couldn't stand it to hear those shells come
whining down on me again," Palmer wrote. "The strain for the past
two weeks had been enough to break anybody and I was no exception.
All I could do was lie and wait for each shell to burst and it seemed that
every one that exploded in the vicinity screeched straight for me."

Palmer didn't know that the war was essentially over. Representatives from the German government had been meeting with General
Foch in a railroad car near Compiègne, and by 5:00 a.m. on November
11 they had agreed that the fighting would cease six hours later. The
Meuse-Argonne campaign, combined with the concurrent British
breakthrough in Macedonia, and the certain knowledge of the enormous American military might still coming on line, had been decisive.
German morale was shattered.

Runners had been sent out with the news, and by the order of General Pershing, attacks would not let up until 11:00 a.m. on the dot.
Pershing wanted to inflict as much damage on the Germans as he could
before the armistice ended all hostilities.

EARLY THAT SAME MORNING, just as he had flown above the Allied
troops and watched their artillery illuminating the sky in the first few

minutes of the Meuse-Argonne Offensive, Captain Eddie Rickenbacker took to the air an hour before the cease-fire to gain a unique, bird's-eye perspective on the final moments of the war. Rickenbacker wrote:

In the morning orders came down that all pilots should stay on the ground. About 10:00 [a.m.] I sauntered out to the hangar and casually told my mechanics to take the plane out on the line and warm it up to test the engines. Without announcing my plans to anyone, I climbed into the plane and took off. Under the low ceiling I hedgehopped towards the front. I arrived over Verdun at 10:45 and proceeded on toward Conflans, flying over no-man's-land. I was at less than five hundred feet. I could see both Germans and Americans crouching in their trenches, peering over with every intention of killing any man who revealed himself on the other side. From time to time ahead of me on the German side I saw a burst of flame, and I knew that they were firing at me. Back at the field later I found bullet holes in my ship.

I glanced at my watch. One minute to 11:00, thirty seconds, fifteen. And then it was 11:00 a.m., the eleventh hour of the eleventh day of the eleventh month. I was the only audience for the greatest show ever presented. On both sides of no-man's-land, the trenches erupted. Brown-uniformed men poured out of the American trenches, gray-green out of the German. From my observer's seat overhead, I watched them throw their helmets in the air, discard their guns, wave their hands. Then all up and down the front, the two groups of men began edging toward each other across no-man's-land. Seconds before they had been willing to shoot each other; now they came forward. Hesitantly at first, then more quickly, each group approached the other.

Suddenly gray uniforms mixed with brown. I could see them hugging each other, dancing, jumping. Americans were passing out cigarettes and chocolate. I flew up to the French sector. There it was even more incredible. After four years of slaughter and hatred, they were not only hugging each other but kissing each other on both cheeks as well.

Star shells, rockets and flares began to go up, and I turned my ship toward the field. The war was over.

The final battle had lasted forty-seven days and involved 1.2 million Americans. Of the 53,400 U.S. combat deaths in the entire war, half of them occurred in the Meuse-Argonne Offensive.

Of the momentous occasion, Pershing wrote in his diary:

> Left for Senlis, where I arrived at 11:45 and had a talk with the Marshal [Ferdinand Foch]. This was the very first time I had seen him since the confirmation of our victory. He was in high spirits and said a great many things about the splendid work of the American Army, my cordial cooperation and how he appreciated my straight-forward dealings. He said that he had always known my attitude on every question because I stated it frankly and clearly and then lived up to it. He became so enthusiastic and so did I, that both of us were unable to restrain the tears.

Not everyone on the American side, however, found himself in a celebratory mood. Using an old typewriter and some "liberated" German paper, a twenty-eight-year-old U.S. Army chaplain named Melville Montgomery wrote to his family in Kansas on November 13. "At the present sitting I am burning the last little piece of candle that I have," he began. (Montgomery consistently misspells "battalion" throughout the letter.)

> At about six o'clock on the morning of the 11 two batallions of the 129th went into the front trenches. There was to be a "hop over." Five thirty is usually the zero hour. There was a

delay in getting ready this time. At 9:10 the order was given. The men climbed over the trenches and started on a run out into the fog of no man's land. Soon Jerrie opened fire and the battle was on. At 9:15 the Adjutant of the Third batallion climbed over the top and shouted for the men to come back, but they were gone. . . .

One man was killed and several wounded. If the order had reached the line five minutes sooner they would have been saved. The order came to headquarters at 8:30 to stop all hostilities. Runners were sent to each batallion. The one to the third lost his way. Because of the delay they went over the top after peace was declared. . . .

Since then I have been seeing the gruesome results of war. I buried a man today who was killed in a swamp many days ago. He was a man hidden with a machine gun in the tall grass and killed at his post. No one knew he was there until some one happened to run across him today.

I have seen a German air plane crushed on the ground with the blood of the driver sprinkled over it. I have seen graves torn open with the remains of decaying men scattered about. I have seen wounded men and dying. I have seen men who have marched all night, wet, cold, and hungry go over the top with spirit. I have seen men suffering from gas. I was at the battle front just one night and until eleven o'clock the next morning. I have seen enough to do me. Others have been here for months, some for years. Truly war is hell.

Another chaplain, Father Francis Duffy with the 42nd "Rainbow" Division, found himself in equally somber spirits. He wrote in his journal:

I had always believed that the news of victory and peace would fill me with surging feelings of delight. But it was just the contrary. I knew that in New York and in every city at home and throughout the world men were jubilant at the prospects of peace. But I could think of nothing except the fine lads who had come out with us to this war and who are not alive to enjoy the triumph. All day I had a lonely and aching heart. . . .

My duties, like my feelings, still lay in the past. With men from all the companies I went round the battlefield to pay as far as I could my last duties to the dead, to record and in a rough way to beautify their lonely graves, for I knew that soon we would leave this place that their presence hallows, and never look upon it again.

Those who had witnessed the catastrophic loss of life on the front lines weren't alone in finding themselves overwhelmed by emotion and all that they had seen and experienced. "In a low, roughly finished ward on the fourth floor of our hospital, where the low gabled windows admit the light which brings into relief the rough red bricks of the unfinished walls, one finds the 'Jaw Ward,'" nurse Alta May Andrews wrote in one of the longest entries in her diary.

It is there that the true conception of the horrors of so-called "civilized warfare" are painfully evident. There, are congregated seventy of the most pathetic victims of the war. Strong, virile young men permanently disfigured. Deadly shrapnel has done its dastardly work in most of the "cases," while in others, bullets have exploded in their mouths. Some entire lower jaws are missing. Others have gaping ragged holes in their cheeks. Nearly all of them have lost their teeth and some have even sacrificed parts of their tongues and noses. Because of the intricate network of facial nerves in the head, these unfortunate lads are called upon to bear more than their share of suffering. It's all so horrible and cruel. . . .

One fellow, O'Rourke, a former pugilist, is lying in bed with a steel brace holding together the remnants of his face.

Both of his cheeks were entirely shot away—only a small section of his chin remains, while his broken and shattered jaws have been stripped of teeth, and the section of his nose remaining so loose that it can be moved in any direction.

What also deeply affected Andrews was how the men were coping with their condition. She wrote:

An atmosphere of heroic bravery and splendid courage is prevalent among them all, while their thoughts seem to be everywhere except upon themselves. Most of the patients are "up patients" and visit around the ward, playing games, helping one another and are continually "jollying" with their jovial banter.

All are fed nourishing liquid foods, such as raw eggs beaten with milk and cream, meat juices, and thin cereals. Most of them are fed through small tubes which are inserted through their nostrils or directly into their throats through the gaping wounds in the sides of their faces. They help in the feeding of one another, taking turns pouring the liquids into the funnels, often joking meanwhile about the enormous capacity someone may possess.

As the majority of cases are those whose entire lower jaws are missing, each one is provided with a rubber trough, fastened bib-like about his neck. Into those troughs there drains the uncontrollable saliva. Their speech is almost incoherent and it is difficult for us to understand them.

Oh! God! This surely must be the most pitiful part of war! Here they are, so happy and carefree now, so bravely enduring untold physical suffering while exhibiting an altruistic concern. But, how different it will be when they are separated and returned to civilian life. . . .

Of all my assignments, this one in the "Jaw Ward" has been the most horrible! Nurses are not kept here on duty long, but each one takes her turn. I fear that I shall always have those pitiful faces with those haunting, questioning eyes before me, but to offset the morbidity, there will be that other side of the picture—that fine, courageous spirit exemplified by these heroic martyrs.

Even with censorship lifted, Andrews refrained from going into much detail about the "Jaw Ward" in her letters home. But the subject of the ward came up when President Woodrow Wilson came to Paris in December 1918 to negotiate the Treaty of Versailles and to meet with and congratulate those who had helped win the war. ("It would have been difficult to have decided when the cheering was the loudest, whether it was when our President passed, or when that tall erect figure of General Pershing rode by," Andrews noted in a December 15 letter home about a massive parade in Paris the day before.) On December 22, Wilson and his wife visited Andrews's hospital. Andrews described the president in a letter to her family as "genial," greeting her with an outstretched hand and saying, "I wish to thank you personally for your services rendered here."

Awestruck, Andrews blurted out "a rather squeaky, 'Good morning, and thank you.'"

She was particularly impressed with how much time and attention Wilson gave to the soldiers, inquiring when and in which battle they were wounded and often tenderly placing a hand on their shoulders while expressing his gratitude for their service. "Some of the sickest patients," Andrews wrote, "were so overcome emotionally, that their lips trembled, and tears rolled down their cheeks."

Near the end of her letter, Andrews related to her mother and sister that Wilson was about to leave the hospital when he asked if he had missed anyone. An officer informed him that there was, indeed, another section they had not visited—the "Jaw Ward"—but that even hardened doctors and nurses found it to be a "terrible shock" to see. Wilson was adamant about going, and he and his wife were escorted there.

"The Wilsons, exhibiting splendid courage," Andrews wrote, "went through the entire ward, shaking the hand of every man—each so terribly disfigured. They talked to these poor boys, and endeavored to understand the incoherent replies which were given with such great difficulty."

Wilson had already met with hundreds of men who had lost limbs and suffered ghastly wounds, but nothing had shaken him like this. "Upon leaving this 'chamber of horrors,'" Andrews wrote, "the President was as white as death, and his hands trembled. He appeared to stagger! A look of suffering was on his face, and he seemed completely crushed."

Her perception of Wilson was instantly changed. "Although I am not entirely in accord with some of the policies of Mr. Wilson, being the daughter of a loyal Republican, still this amazing exhibit of courage and fortitude has gained for him a staunch admirer. I shall always adore him!"

Less adoring of Wilson were the heads of state he convened with in Paris to hammer out a permanent peace agreement. Along with Wilson, the three men who had the most influence in the talks were Vittorio Orlando, David Lloyd George, and Georges Clemenceau, the prime ministers of Italy, Great Britain, and France, respectively.

From the start, the other leaders felt that Wilson, whose country had suffered the least in the war, acted in a domineering manner. Wilson, in turn, believed that the Allies were foolishly pushing for terms that were far too onerous for Germany to bear. "Our greatest error would be to give [the Germans] powerful reasons for one day wishing to take revenge," Wilson said to Clemenceau. "Excessive demands would most certainly sow the seeds of war."

Clemenceau accused Wilson of being naïve. The Germans, he contended, would find some pretext for being treated unfairly and seek retribution regardless of the penalties imposed on them. The Allies, Clemenceau went on to argue, should therefore take advantage of Germany's weakened military situation and, among other conditions: create a buffer zone between Germany and France (an area later called the

Rhineland), demand massive financial reparations, and gut their armed forces. "Do not believe they will ever forgive us," Clemenceau told Wilson. "Nothing will destroy the rage of those who wanted to establish their domination over the world and who believed themselves so close to succeeding."

Exactly five years to the day that Gavrilo Princip assassinated Archduke Feranz Ferdinand, representatives from Germany and the Allied nations sat down inside the glittering Hall of Mirrors in the palace of Versailles and signed what became known as the Treaty of Versailles. The war that had claimed an estimated seventeen million lives, six million of whom were civilians, had officially come to an end.

ALONG WITH OVERSEEING THE return of U.S. troops and matériel to the States, General Pershing had one other extremely important task at hand after the armistice: creating the American Graves Registration Service and identifying the dead. The AGRS assumed the mournful duty of recovering the bodies of slain troops and, depending on the wishes of their families, burying them in American military cemeteries in Europe or returning them to the States.

Twenty-seven-year-old Lieutenant David Arthur Thompson was an executive assistant to the chief of the AGRS. His job became an intensely personal one when he sought out the body of his own brother, Joseph. Thompson related to his father how his brother's remains were retrieved and described the personal effects that were found with him.

> Dear Dad,
> I intended to write mother, but I can't tell her as much as I
> can you. When you read this, you can explain to her
> everything that you wish.
> I have just taken Joe from his grave in the woods to a lot
> in the national American Cemetery at Romagne, France. I
> had to supervise the work myself on account of the shortage

of officers; therefore, made a personal inspection of the body, which as you might know, I'd rather die than do, but which had to be done.

I'm going to be very plain in telling you, and know it might hurt, but I know you will wish to know. I am awful glad that it was I that could do it, and not any of you, as it would have drove any of you insane.

With three colored boys given me as a detail and a Dodge light truck, I made my way over the hills 40 miles. Sometimes the road was so bad we had to cross fields, and at one place had to build a small bridge over a place where the road was destroyed.

We left Romagne at 7:30 and got to the grave at the Harmont woods at noon. I had the colored fellows dig down the side of the grave until we struck the body, or could see the clothes. I saw his feet and legs first, and then the rest of his body, just as he fell.

He was dressed in new clothes, and had on his rain coat, and full pack, with the exception of the rifle and helmet. He was not in a box, as I expected, but merely a blanket thrown over the top of his body, and some loose boards over that.

We removed the blanket, boards, etc. And of course, the body was badly decomposed. The head was blown from the body by a high explosive shell, but what was left of the skull was lying there. The face was entirely blown away. I then unbuttoned the coats and found his other identification tag about his neck, which then and there identified him without going further.

I then placed him in a coffin we had brought with us and placed it in the car. We then got the body of Carl Coombs out, as we did Joe. Coomb's body was also badly decomposed, and he was a heavy boy to lift out.

The odor from both was terrible and I had to forget
for the moment who they were. I had rubber gloves,
but could hardly touch the bodies without cleaving the
flesh from the bone. Therefore, had to work carefully and slowly.

We then had both bodies in the car and drove back to
Romagne by going away around through the rear of the
German lines, and got back to the cemetery at Romagne
about 5:00 p.m.

There I turned both bodies over to the undertakers who
were present. I had the clothes removed and carefully
searched, with good results.

I found in his clothes: your last letter to him, a pocket
knife, fountain pen, his diary, testament, Book of Psalms,
another book with annotations of all mail received and
sent, some small pictures he had received from home,
about 10 Francs in money, two watches, one his own, the other
a German watch, a few German coins, and German post cards.

His diary is very interesting, and his Psalm book is
wonderful, and shows that he died with a clean soul. . . .

The poor kid prayed for peace and God gave it to him,
Dad. How thankful I am that God gave it instantly. He was
prepared to die, and did not suffer. I am happy over the
thoughts of it, but God only knows how I miss him. I loved
him so much.

Dad, these things are worth the world to you. I shall
preserve them carefully; although they are in pretty bad
shape, owing to the dampness of the ground and body. Also,
they are badly stained and smell bad. I have soaked them all
in gasoline, and in a day or so, they will be O.K.

I shall bring them to mother, everything. But I ask you all
for them to be kept in my family, when you leave us to join
poor Joe. I have gone through a living hell to get them, and
after you and mother, they are mine.

Joe now rests beside Carl Coombs in the Romagne Cemetery, with 35,000 others. It is a beautiful place and our national Monument in France. I pray that you will let his body lie there in peace. I know he would wish it.

He is now buried deep in a coffin; and on Memorial Day, his grave will be beautifully decorated. General Pershing will be there to pay his last respects to his men who fought under him and it will be a beautiful ceremony. . . .

They have started a movement in France to have some girl look after each grave, or group of graves. There is a young girl here that will look after them both, that is, Joe's and Carl Coombs'.

She is the only girl that has ever visited their graves. She went there only under great risk and hardships. Just because she wanted to be the one that could have charge of the graves after we are all gone. . . .

She has been reading Joe's diary, and Psalm book, and I tell you, it is enough to impress anyone. They have been very good friends to me here.

I know Ma will be pleased to have this stuff. To see his own writing will be more to her than his body. Please let it now Rest in Peace.

I feel now that I have accomplished everything possible. The grave location is: Section 9, Plot 3, Grave 155. Joe is buried in the Northeast corner.

Write soon, Dad, and love to all. Your Son, Art.

In World War I, all U.S. troops had been issued, for the first time, what became known as dog tags, and close to 99 percent of the 116,516 Americans who died in the conflict were identified. By comparison, approximately half of the soldiers lost in the Civil War were buried under gravestones with no name on them but simply the word "Unknown."

·   ·   ·

BEFORE RETURNING TO America, Pershing kept his promise to his son, Warren, and brought him to France, where they were reunited after being apart for almost two years. Outfitted in a miniature officer's uniform, Warren toured Europe with his celebrated father.

Pershing had thanked his troops for their service in an official bulletin ("General Orders No. 203") sent out on November 12, 1918, but the memo was mostly intended to emphasize the importance of maintaining a strict sense of discipline even though the war was over. In the months that followed the armistice, Pershing was deeply moved by the stories of sacrifice he heard almost everywhere he went about the Americans under his command, and he decided to pen a more heartfelt expression of gratitude, written in the form of a personal letter, that would be given to every member of the AEF.

"My fellow soldiers," it began.

> Now that your service with the American Expeditionary Forces is about to terminate, I can not let you go without a personal word. At the call to arms, the patriotic young manhood of America eagerly responded and became the formidable army whose decisive victories testify to its efficiency and its valor. With the support of the nation firmly united to defend the cause of liberty, our army has executed the will of the people with resolute purpose. Our democracy has been tested, and the forces of autocracy have been defeated. To the glory of the citizen-soldier, our troops have faithfully fulfilled their trust, and in a succession of brilliant offensives have overcome the menace to our civilization.
>
> As an individual, your part in the world war has been an important one in the sum total of our achievements. Whether keeping lonely vigil in the trenches, or gallantly storming the enemy's stronghold; whether enduring monotonous drudgery

at the rear, or sustaining the fighting line at the front, each
has bravely and efficiently played his part. By willing sacrifice
of personal rights; by cheerful endurance of hardship and
privation; by vigor, strength and indomitable will, made
effective by thorough organization and cordial co-operation,
you inspired the war-worn Allies with new life and turned
the tide of threatened defeat into overwhelming victory.

With a consecrated devotion to duty and a will to
conquer, you have loyally served your country. By your
exemplary conduct a standard has been established and
maintained never before attained by any army. With mind
and body as clean and strong as the decisive blows you
delivered against the foe, you are soon to return to the
pursuits of peace. In leaving the scenes of your victories, may
I ask that you carry home your high ideals and continue to
live as you have served—an honor to the principles for which
you have fought and to the fallen comrades you leave behind.

It is with pride in our success that I extend to you my
sincere thanks for your splendid service to the army and to
the nation.

Faithfully,

John J. Pershing

Commander in Chief

19.

Postscript

MORE THAN TWO MILLION Americans ultimately served overseas in what President Woodrow Wilson had called "the war to end all wars," and most of these men and women returned to the United States in 1919. For some it was an exhilarating experience that brought public adulation and was a source of great pride; for others it was a nightmare they refused to discuss.

Alvin York had been overlooked during the war but was profiled in a *Saturday Evening Post* story in April 1919 that catapulted him to fame. York had been awarded the Distinguished Service Cross for his actions of October 1918, when he helped wipe out numerous machine-gun nests near the village of Chatel-Chéhéry and rounded up 132 German prisoners. Once the wider public read the details of the dramatic story, York became one of the most honored and celebrated doughboys of the war. General Pershing himself endorsed York for the Medal of Honor, which York eventually received, and in 1941 the feature film *Sergeant York* was released, starring Gary Cooper as York. (Cooper received an Oscar for his performance.) York died peacefully at the age of seventy-six, leaving behind his beloved wife, Gracie, and eight children, most of whom were named after prominent Americans. The youngest girl was Betsy Ross York and the youngest boy Thomas Jefferson York.

Charles Whittlesey, the senior officer from the Lost Battalion, also received the Medal of Honor and was in constant demand, giving speeches and being asked to participate in Memorial Day and other patriotic parades. Both York and Whittlesey served as pallbearers during the first burial of the Unknown Soldier at Arlington National Cemetery on November 21, 1921. While York adjusted well emotionally to postwar life, Whittlesey remained haunted by the deaths of the three hundred men he saw killed when his battalion was trapped and under fire without food or water for five days deep within the Argonne Forest. Less than a week after attending the ceremony at Arlington National Cemetery, Whittlesey killed himself.

Even those who didn't endure combat were traumatized by the war. Dorothea and Gladys Cromwell, twin sisters who gave up a lavish, carefree lifestyle as high-society debutantes in Manhattan to serve as Red Cross nurses, arrived in France in February 1918 and worked at a hospital in Souilly until the end of the war. On January 21, 1919, they boarded SS *La Lorraine* to sail back to America. But during that journey something snapped, in both of them. Having seen and cared for so many young men maimed and disfigured for life, they couldn't bear the memories anymore and committed suicide together, jumping over the side of the ship into the freezing waters of the Atlantic.

Alta May Andrews, the U.S. Army nurse who briefly met President Wilson at the main Army hospital in Neuilly, left France on April 13, 1919. In a letter to her mother written on April 26, Andrews expressed that while she had been "privileged to play my little part in this Great War" she was thrilled that soon after returning home she would be discharged from the military. "I'm in splendid condition [physically]," she remarked, "discounting a case of 'nerves' which will probably amount to naught when once I get out of this 'man's army.'" Andrews was posted to a hospital in Fort Sheridan, Illinois, to finish out her service. She was not looking forward to the assignment. "I found my ward on the lower floor of a large, newly constructed wooden building," she wrote in her diary on May 5, 1919. "How I dreaded to enter! Gritting my teeth with a new determination to see this thing through,

I started down the huge ward through a centre aisle. There were six rows of beds in the ward which contained one hundred and twelve wounded from overseas." Suddenly, Andrews realized that she knew some of the patients, and they recognized her as well. "Even big handsome Sullivan from Peducah, a 'pet from my pet ward' is here, and oh! that dear boy, I had never dreamed that he would ever live to get even this close to his beloved Peducah! His smile was more wonderful than ever and it always did seem to have all others eclipsed." It was a joyful "old timers' reunion," Andrews wrote, and they all started to reminisce and even laugh together. The moment proved to be life-changing. "Upon leaving the ward," Andrews wrote in the last sentence of her diary entry, "I went directly to the office of Miss Wilson, the Chief Nurse. She was greatly astonished to hear my decision—'I guess I don't want my discharge after all! I am going to stay!'" And indeed, Alta May Andrews not only continued to nurse World War I soldiers, she reenlisted during World War II at the age of fifty-one.

Other veterans went on to distinguished careers in politics and business. Maury Maverick, the young lieutenant from Texas who fought with the 1st Division at both Saint-Mihiel and in the Meuse-Argonne Offensive, became a congressman in 1935 and then the mayor of San Antonio in 1939. For "gallantry in action and especially meritorious service," Maverick received the Silver Star and for his wounds, the Purple Heart.

On January 6, 1919, less than six months after his son Quentin was shot down and killed, former president Theodore Roosevelt passed away. But he lived long enough to see his four other children survive the war. Ethel had worked as a nurse in France. Kermit, who served in Mesopotamia with the English, earned the British Military Cross for his bravery. Both Archie and Ted Jr. were decorated for their courage under fire and for sustaining wounds in battle, but both men recuperated and went on to fight in World War II.

Eddie Rickenbacker, the "Ace of Aces" pilot and former race-car driver, launched the Rickenbacker Motor Company in 1920, which introduced four-wheel braking in U.S. automobiles. Rickenbacker became general manager of Eastern Air Lines in 1934 and, with other investors, bought it in 1938 and was the company's president for twenty years. Although he ultimately died of a stroke at the age of eighty-two, he was reported in the media to have been killed not once but twice before that. In late February 1941, Rickenbacker was flying in an Eastern Air Lines plane on business when it crashed near Atlanta, Georgia. Nine of the sixteen passengers were killed, and Rickenbacker sustained massive injuries. Several ribs pierced through his skin, his skull was fractured, his pelvis and left knee were broken, and his left eyeball had been dislodged. It took emergency crews almost twelve hours to find the wreckage, and Rickenbacker, soaked in blood and gasoline, had been pinned on top of another passenger, who was dead. When he was finally taken to the hospital, doctors focused on other survivors because they assumed Rickenbacker's condition was hopeless, while the others had a fighting chance. They eventually treated him and were even able to place his eyeball back into its socket.

Then, on October 21, 1942, Rickenbacker was flying in a B-17D bomber over the South Pacific to inspect islands in the area when a glitch in the plane sent them off course by hundreds of miles. Running out of gas, the plane ditched in the ocean. Rickenbacker and the other crew members were adrift on a life raft, sustaining themselves on only rainwater and the occasional fish they were able to catch. The Navy searched for two weeks and was about to give up when Mrs. Rickenbacker begged them to continue for one more week. After spending twenty-four days lost at sea, Rickenbacker and the other men were all finally rescued.

Rickenbacker had been highly decorated throughout and after World War I, including being awarded the Medal of Honor. But some heroes of the war never attained the recognition they deserved until long after they had passed away, if at all. Many of them had been overlooked simply because of the color of their skin. After Eugene Bullard, the U.S. soldier hit by shrapnel in the mouth and leg at Verdun, recuperated from his wounds, he decided he wanted to fly. And indeed, on May 5, 1917, after eight months of training, Bullard became the first African American combat pilot in history. But while the French conferred on him their highest military awards, his native country awarded him nothing. Bullard died on October 12, 1961, poor and in relative obscurity.

And only one member of the 369th Harlem Hellfighters, the regiment that spent more time under fire (191 days) than any other American unit in the war, was officially honored by the U.S. government— Henry Johnson, who received the Medal of Honor. But it was bestowed in 2015, decades after Johnson had passed away in 1929, broke, and also, at the time, essentially forgotten.

Numerous officers under General Pershing, including Douglas MacArthur, George S. Patton, George Marshall, William "Wild Bill" Donovan, and Harry Truman, were deeply influenced by their service in World War I and would go on to have a far-reaching impact on their country.

MacArthur's return to the United States in the spring of 1919 began on a sour note. MacArthur wrote to a former aide in the 42nd "Rainbow" Division on May 13, 1919:

> We reached New York on the 25 [of April], but where-oh-where was that welcome they told us of? Where was that howling mob to proclaim us monarchs of all we surveyed? Where were those bright eyes, slim ankles that had been kidding us in our dreams? Nothing—nothing like that. One little urchin asked us who we were and when we said—we are the famous 42nd—he asked if we had been to France. Amid a silence that hurt—with no one . . . to greet us—we marched off the deck, to be scattered to the four winds—a sad, gloomy end of the Rainbow.

After addressing some additional personal matters in the letter, MacArthur added a more philosophical note about the Treaty of Versailles, which was still being negotiated. "We are wondering here what is to happen with reference to the peace terms," MacArthur wrote. "They look drastic and seem to me more like a treaty of perpetual war than of perpetual peace."

When that peace was indeed broken two decades later, MacArthur would become one of the most powerful generals of World War II, named by President Franklin D. Roosevelt as commander of the U.S. forces in the Far East. Despite his extraordinary service in World War I and postwar promotions and appointments (MacArthur was superintendent of West Point from 1919 to 1922 and the Army's chief of staff from 1930 until 1935, among other influential positions), MacArthur nearly ended his military career after a volatile exchange in the White House with Roosevelt soon after he was elected in 1932. During a meeting with the president, MacArthur explained that the military's budget needed to be drastically increased. Roosevelt disagreed.

MacArthur castigated the president, saying that when the next war was lost "and an American boy, lying in the mud with an enemy bayonet through his belly and an enemy foot on his dying throat, spat out his last curse, I wanted the name not to be MacArthur, but Roosevelt."

Roosevelt exploded. "You must not talk that way to the president!" he bellowed.

MacArthur immediately apologized and offered his resignation on the spot. He was almost out the door when the president said to him calmly, "Don't be foolish, Douglas, you and the budget must get together on this." MacArthur was shaken by the confrontation and wrote in his memoirs that as he walked outside, he threw up on the White House steps.

MacArthur had also seen his popularity wane among AEF veterans when he opposed the Bonus March on Washington in the summer of 1932. More than seventeen thousand destitute AEF soldiers and their families converged on Washington to encourage Congress to authorize an advance payment on a bonus they had been promised, but which wasn't to be paid out until 1945. Financially devastated by the Great

Depression, the veterans needed their money right away. Many were literally starving. MacArthur, who was the Army chief of staff at the time, received orders from the president and secretary of war to break up the protest. MacArthur already thought that the demonstration stank of a Communist plot, and he was more than willing to use Army infantry, cavalry, and even tanks to displace the marchers. Washington police were the first to threaten the crowd, and two veterans were shot to death. On July 28, MacArthur mobilized his troops, with Major George Patton leading six battle tanks. Patton was confronted by one of the marchers, Joe Angelo, the same man who had pulled Patton to safety and treated his wounds when Patton was shot on the first day of the Meuse-Argonne Offensive. Patton had once called him "the bravest man in the army." When Angelo approached him, Patton said to several other officers: "I do not know this man. Take him away and under no circumstances permit him to return." The entire crowd eventually dispersed without any further loss of life, but for four more years the veterans pressured the government to assist them, and Congress finally approved the payments. President Roosevelt tried to veto the bill, but Congress overrode him.

When Roosevelt died, on April 12, 1945, Vice President Harry Truman became commander in chief. Unlike MacArthur, Patton, and Marshall, Truman wasn't close to or even known by General Pershing. Truman was just one of thousands of junior officers in the AEF. The two men did, however, come face-to-face in France, three months after the war was over. "We were inspected by Gen Pershing, the Prince of Wales and a whole troop of Generals, Colonels and Majors," Truman had written to Bess Wallace on February 18, 1919.

> Have been getting ready for the event since Friday. The General told me I had a nice looking bunch of men and that he wanted me to take them home as clean morally and physically as when they came over so that the home people could be as proud of them as he is. He gave us a little talk after we'd passed

in review and told us we'd covered ourselves with glory in the Meuse Argonne drive and that no carping politician could take that satisfaction away from us. Also he said America won the war and that there was no argument to that. That the 35th [Division] was an immense cog in the wheel and he was proud of us because we came from his part of the country.

Truman had admired Pershing's leadership during World War I, and after Truman was sworn in as president, one of his first official visits was to see General Pershing, then in poor health and residing at the Walter Reed Army Medical Center in Washington, D.C. Although they didn't meet for long, Truman wanted to pay his respects to his former "chief," and Pershing was grateful for the gesture.

Truman was extremely proud of his wartime experience and the fact that he didn't lose a single member of his Battery D soldiers in combat. As president, he remained in touch with many of his old comrades. In late May 1945, a letter was placed on Truman's desk that his staff knew he would want to read. It came from Vic Housholder, the man who had saved Truman's life when, during a German artillery attack, Truman's horse had fallen over and nearly suffocated him to death before Housholder wrenched him free.

"Dear President Harry," Housholder began, affectionately (but still respectfully), alluding to the way Truman's men used to refer to him as Captain Harry:

> I trust you received my wire of congratulations dated April 16th. [Did] not anticipate a reply and I don't want you to think that that is why I mention the matter now—I only mention it to let you know I sent one, because in all probability, you never saw it along with the thousands of other messages that were sent you.
>
> I have a very real reason for this letter, directed to you as it is and I do hope for some sort of response.

Housholder went on in detail to explain that his eldest son, Tom, was a P-51 Mustang pilot in Europe who, seven months earlier, had bailed out of his plane over Germany but hadn't been heard from since. Housholder was hoping that Truman could use his influence to help locate his son, dead or alive.

Housholder was uncertain if the president would in fact receive the letter, so he also wrote to the First Lady, Bess Truman, imploring her to make certain that the president saw his initial letter. Housholder mentioned that he had served alongside her husband twenty-seven years earlier, but he did not add that he had also essentially saved his life.

Having only been president for less than six weeks and under excruciating pressure to focus on winning the war, Truman nevertheless made finding Tom Housholder a priority and sent off messages to the proper officials within the War Department. After extensive back-and-forth exchanges between senior Army officers in Washington and Europe, it was finally determined that, sadly, Tom Housholder had not survived and his body had been buried and then disinterred before being laid to rest in an American cemetery southwest of Liege, Belgium.

Of all the AEF's high-ranking officers who went on to even more prominent roles in World War II, perhaps Truman's favorite was Army Chief of Staff George Marshall. The two men clicked personally, and while Marshall didn't have the public exposure of the more flamboyant generals such as George Patton or Douglas MacArthur, Truman knew that Marshall's logistical expertise, which he honed during World War I as the mastermind responsible for executing the battle plans for Cantigny, Saint-Mihiel, and the Meuse-Argonne offensives, is what secured the Allies' victory in World War II. Truman named Marshall to be the secretary of state in 1947, and Marshall put forth a massive proposal to spend billions of American dollars to rebuild Germany and other countries devastated by World War II. Much of postwar Europe was still in ruins and impoverished, and the Marshall Plan, as it came to be known, would help stabilize the Continent.

President Truman did not have the same rapport with MacArthur or Bill Donovan, now head of the Office of Strategic Services, the precursor to the CIA, as he had with Marshall. Truman found MacArthur's ego and need for attention unbearable, and when MacArthur publicly criticized President Truman's "limited conflict" while MacArthur was serving as the commander of all American and U.N. forces in the Korean War, Truman fired him. MacArthur came back to America like a conquering hero, welcomed home with parades and huge rallies almost everywhere he went. On April 19, 1951, he stood before Congress and gave his famous "Old Soldiers Never Die; They Just Fade Away" speech. Retired from the military, MacArthur joined the board of Remington Rand, a company known for its pistols, typewriters, and shavers.

Truman and Donovan wrangled over the future of the OSS, which Donovan had founded during Franklin D. Roosevelt's presidency. When World War II was over, Donovan wanted the OSS to continue its clandestine efforts. Truman was adamantly against the idea. "The OSS has been a credit to America," Truman said to Donovan during a May 14, 1945, meeting at the White House.

> You and all your men are to be congratulated on doing a remarkable job for our country, but the OSS belongs to a nation at war. It can have no place in an America at peace. I am completely opposed to international spying on the part of the United States. It is un-American. I cannot be certain in my mind that a formidable and clandestine organization such as the OSS designed to spy abroad will not in time spy upon the American people themselves. The OSS represents a threat to the liberties of the American people. An all-powerful intelligence apparatus in the hands of an unprincipled president can be a dangerous instrument.

Truman later changed his mind and endorsed establishing, in January 1946, a "central intelligence group" that would spy on foreign countries. But he never warmed to Donovan himself, and although Wild Bill was the clear choice to lead the new organization, Truman named Rear Admiral Sidney W. Souers, the former deputy chief of naval intelligence, to be the first director of the agency.

George Patton, one of General Pershing's favorites among his senior officers, had no relationship with President Truman, personally or professionally. Patton was in Europe, having led millions of troops during World War II, when Truman became president. Patton died in Heidelberg, Germany, on December 21, 1945, after a truck he was riding in collided with another vehicle. Patton broke his neck and was sent to a hospital, where he passed away twelve days later due to, according to official records, a pulmonary edema. (One of the most enduring conspiracy theories in American military history has it that Patton was murdered by Russian agents because of his strident anti-Soviet views. They first tried to kill him by staging the accident, and when that failed, they poisoned him in the hospital. The allegations are controversial, to say the least.)

IRONICALLY, one of the World War I–era veterans most influenced by Pershing—Dwight D. "Ike" Eisenhower—never saw combat or even set foot overseas during the war. But had it not been for Pershing, Eisenhower might have landed in prison at the age of thirty-two, permanently derailing his military career instead of going on to become the Supreme Allied Commander in Europe in World War II and then a two-term president of the United States.

Eisenhower was accepted into West Point in 1911 and, like Pershing, attended mostly for the free education. He didn't stand out academically or seem in any way destined for greatness. In fact, one of the classes he performed worst in was Military History. Eisenhower claimed he did poorly because the cadets, instead of being instructed to think analytically about strategy or tactics, were forced to memorize the names of generals who led certain battles. "I always did hate memory tests, although I have a pretty good memory," Eisenhower said. "But this wasn't the kind of thing that interested me."

What did appeal to Eisenhower was playing poker and smoking cigarettes, both of which violated West Point's strict code of conduct. Eisenhower racked up, in his own words, "a staggering catalogue of demerits." Life at West Point was exacting, and the myriad regulations could trip up even the most diligent cadet, but Eisenhower broke the academy's rules intentionally and practically gloated over his demerits, seeing them as badges of honor. "I didn't think of myself as either a scholar whose position would depend on the knowledge he had acquired in school, or as a military figure whose professional career might be seriously affected by his academic or disciplinary record," Eisenhower said, thinking back on his time at West Point. In a class of 164 cadets, Eisenhower ranked 125 "in conduct" when he graduated, in 1915.

His first assignment was to Fort Sam Houston, which was commanded by Major General "Fighting Fred" Funston. And it was there in San Antonio that Eisenhower met his future wife, eighteen-year-old Mamie Geneva Doud. They were introduced in October 1915, and four months later, on Valentine's Day 1916, Eisenhower proposed to Mamie, and she said yes.

When the United States declared war on Germany, Eisenhower was placed into the 57th Infantry Regiment, but only to coordinate logistics. He was desperate to see action overseas, but on September 20, he was sent to Fort Oglethorpe in Georgia to train new officers. On September 24, Mamie gave birth to their first child, a son, a towheaded tyke who very much resembled his father. The baby's given name was Doud Dwight Eisenhower, but his parents called him Little Ike or Ikky.

In December 1920, the Eisenhowers hired an amiable and hardworking young woman to help Mamie with the housekeeping, something Mamie's privileged upbringing hadn't prepared her for.

Several days later, something was wrong with Ikky.

First he developed a fever, and the Eisenhowers assumed he had simply come down with the flu. But his temperature kept rising, his throat became sore, and horrible red rashes started appearing on his body. He was rushed to the hospital, and a specialist carefully examined Ikky and diagnosed him as having scarlet fever. The doctor then told the Eisenhowers what they probably already knew: there was no cure. "Either they get well," the doctor stated, "or you lose them." The Eisenhowers later found out that their new maid was just getting over a bout of scarlet fever and, although her symptoms had gone away, wasn't entirely cured and passed the virus on to Ikky.

Compounding their anguish, the Eisenhowers had to immediately quarantine their son, which meant they couldn't hold or even be close to him. Ikky's hospital room had a porch attached to it, and the best his father could do was sit in a chair by the window and every so often wave at his little boy.

For ten days Ikky languished in his hospital bed until the fever turned into meningitis, and he died on January 2, 1921. "I have never known such a blow," Eisenhower later recalled. "This was the greatest disappointment and disaster in my life, the one I have never been able to forget completely." Mamie was also devastated, but she, too, saw how much the death affected her husband. "For a long time," she wrote, "it was as if a shining light had gone out of Ike's life. . . . The memory of those bleak days was a deep inner pain that never seemed to diminish much."

Ikky loved the color yellow, and on Ikky's birthday, September 24, Eisenhower had a bouquet of yellow roses delivered to Mamie every year for the rest of their lives.

While still trying to recover from the shattering personal loss he and Mamie had experienced in January 1921, Eisenhower was hit with a potentially catastrophic blow to his career. A fastidious adjutant general in the Army noticed that the financial forms Eisenhower had submitted improperly included a housing allowance that was higher than what Eisenhower should have received. "The Certificate which this

Dwight and Mamie Eisenhower on their wedding day.

Their first child, Doud Dwight "Ikky" Eisenhower.

officer filed with his pay vouchers for the months of May to August 1920 were on their face false and untrue," scolded the adjutant general. "And the result of this investigation leads me to the conclusion that Major Dwight D. Eisenhower, Inf[antry], be brought to trial." (To add insult to injury, the additional money was to cover the cost for an extra room in the Eisenhower's home for little Ikky.)

Eisenhower paid back the amount—$250.67—and swore that he was unaware of any wrongdoing. The fact that this whole misunderstanding centered on his dead two-year-old son generated no sense of pity or compassion whatsoever from the adjutant general, who thought Eisenhower should be court-martialed. He passed the matter up to the Army's inspector general, Eli Helmick, and Helmick was hardly more sympathetic. "Major Eisenhower," he said, "is a graduate of the [West Point] Military Academy, of six years' commissioned service. That he should have knowingly attempted to defraud the government, or, as he contends, that he was ignorant of the laws governing commutation for dependents, are alike inexplicable."

Eisenhower was fortunate to have a powerful ally on his side: Brigadier General Fox Conner, Pershing's chief of operations during the war, and one of the most revered officers in the U.S. military. Eisenhower was introduced to Conner by George Patton, and the two quickly became good friends. Conner helped Eisenhower get Pershing's assistance to resolve the "fraud" issue, and he also recommended Eisenhower to serve on the American Battle Monuments Commission, headed by Pershing. Eisenhower was given the task of writing *A Guide to the American Battle Fields in Europe*, which Pershing wanted to be the definitive book on the AEF's history and the American cemeteries and memorials throughout France and Belgium. The two men ended up traveling together throughout Europe (Eisenhower was allowed to bring Mamie along), visiting most of the places where Pershing's men had fought and that Eisenhower had carefully researched and written about. By the end of their tour, Eisenhower knew as much about the AEF as anyone, including Pershing himself, and the information would prove to be invaluable to Eisenhower when, in 1943, he became the Supreme Allied Commander in Europe.

THE YEARS AFTER World War I were good to General John J. Pershing. Pershing was hailed as a hero upon his return to the United States and given ticker-tape parades. On September 3, 1919, he was promoted to General of the Armies of the United States, essentially earning him a sixth star. No other American commander has ever received a higher ranking in his lifetime. (George Washington was named General of the Armies by an act of Congress in 1976, 177 years after his death, as part of the country's bicentennial celebration.)

Even before he returned to the States, Pershing was urged by Democrats and Republicans alike to run for president. History was in his favor; every previous major war had helped boost victorious leaders into the White House, from Washington after the Revolution to Pershing's hero, Ulysses S. Grant, in 1869. And Theodore Roosevelt's famous charge in Cuba in 1898 during the Spanish-American War had certainly elevated Roosevelt's political career. Pershing denied having any political aspirations and discouraged friends and family members from suggesting otherwise. When his younger brother James went against his wishes, Pershing was furious. "I am not a candidate for anything and don't expect to be," he wrote to James in late December 1918 from France, "but if I were, with you running around the country like a blatant ass making speeches whenever some bunch of advertisers desire to have you do so, it would not be long before we should all go to the scrap heap as a family of fools."

Pershing was more open to the idea than he let on, however. Although he found the *appearance* of seeking out public office distasteful, he later admitted that if a groundswell of Americans insisted that he be nominated by the Republican Party (and he considered himself a lifelong Republican), he would run. He especially wanted to blunt the ambitions of his old nemesis Leonard Wood, out on the trail actively stumping to be president. George Patton warned Pershing that if Wood actually became the commander in chief, Pershing could expect to be banished to some far-flung spot on the globe. "You will command the island of Guam," Patton stated, only half in jest.

Wood and Pershing, who barely campaigned (his heart really wasn't into it), were beat out at the Republican convention by Senator Warren Harding, the eventual winner of the national election. Pershing was a man not lacking in ego, and the idea of the United States rallying behind the old war hero to send him to the White House was not unappealing to him. But it also wasn't his life's goal. Wood's defeat also took the sting out of Pershing's own loss. "The victory is ours," Pershing said in a lighthearted cable to his close friend Charles Dawes. "I die content." The postwar assignment that Pershing did want was Army chief of staff, and on May 13, 1921, Secretary of War John Weeks appointed Pershing to the coveted position, replacing Peyton March. One of Pershing's first directives to his staff was to start wearing the Sam Browne belts that his predecessor so disdained.

Famous, handsome, and still a widower, Pershing was considered one of the nation's most sought-after and eligible bachelors. Although linked romantically to numerous women, Pershing downplayed the rumors in the press. "If I were married to all the ladies to whom the gossips have engaged me," Pershing told a *New York Times* reporter, "I would be a regular Brigham Young," referring to the Mormon founder and his more than fifty wives.

Anne Patton, George's sister, regarded herself as engaged to Pershing when he left for Europe in June 1917, and she assumed they would marry after the war. But over time she sensed from their correspondence that he had fallen out of love with her.

"You ask me when I am coming home," Pershing had written to Anne on December 27, 1918, from France. "As far as I can tell, it is no nearer now than it was when I started here in 1917 with the possibility of having to police up the rest of the world and with little prospect of getting home, although I should like to return home in the summer if things work out, but I have a great fear that things are not going to work out that way." There was no mention of his missing her. Or wanting to see her. Or looking forward to when they would be together again. He concluded his letter on a somewhat obligatory note, stating: "Please accept for yourself and your mother and Aunt Annie and your father my most affectionate Christmas greetings and very best wishes."

Anne decided that instead of waiting for Pershing to return, she would go to France to try to rekindle his feelings for her. The trip was a disaster. Upon her arrival, Pershing asked her rather curtly, "How long are you staying, and what are you going to do over here?" Once it became clear to Anne that she and Pershing had no future together, she turned right around, went back to California, and promptly instructed her family that, on the subject of her relationship with Pershing, "Let us *never never* speak of it again."

At war's end, Pershing was still in love with Micheline Resco, the young painter he had met soon after arriving in Paris in June 1917. Even when separated by thousands of miles, they continued their relationship. The normally staid and somber general expressed himself like an infatuated schoolboy in his letters to Micheline, still in France. "Ah, my dear, how I miss you each day and each night," he gushed in a letter dated February 13, 1920, six months after he returned to America. "I pray for you, for your presence, for your kisses, for the many ways you show your tenderness. When we get together again for the first time, I am sure that we are going to die. I am going to just eat you all up, as I am going to kill you with love, with a passion stronger than anything in the world. It is uncontrollable. It is mad!"

They were finally reunited a year later. Pershing was invited to Paris in 1921 to place a ceremonial Medal of Honor on France's Tomb of the Unknown Soldier, and while there he saw Resco as much as possible. She moved to Manhattan, temporarily, in 1922 to open an art gallery and studio, and she would spend her weekends with Pershing in Washington. Europeans were more tolerant than Americans of a sixty-two-year-old man having a lover who, at twenty-eight, looked young enough to be his granddaughter. Pershing and Resco were more discreet in the States. They avoided large social events and dining in public, preferring more intimate gatherings with close friends or quiet nights alone. (The only existing photographs of Resco are of very poor quality, and there are no known photographs of them together.)

When they were separated again, they exchanged effusively affectionate letters sent in sealed envelopes. But when Pershing was traveling, usually on official business, he often had to cable his messages to Resco, and these could be read by any number of people. So they devised a code. *Lucas* = *J'ai recu le cable* (I received the cable), *Teresa* = *Je suis tres triste* (I am very sad), *Radium* = *Je suis la plus heureuse du monde* (I am the happiest in the world), and, because Pershing's French was still far from perfect, Resco often used *Nicome*, which meant: *Je n'ai pas compris votre cable—les mots sont incomprehensible*, or, I did not understand your cable—the words are incomprehensible.

Pershing's sister May was especially disapproving of his relationship with Resco. Whether she regarded the age difference to be unseemly or felt a loyalty to her dead sister-in-law isn't known for sure, but whatever the reason, May could barely contain her contempt for Resco. Pershing never hid from Resco how emotionally scarred he remained by the loss of Frankie and his three young girls, and he believed himself very fortunate to have found someone who, instead of being threatened by the emotions Pershing still felt for his first wife, understood his suffering and offered him solace.

Pershing wrote to Resco on the evening of a fateful anniversary:

10 P.M. August 26

Cherie Darling,

This is a most depressing night—10 years ago it all
happened—and Warren and I were left alone—he a little boy
of 6, and I, well! what can one say? How well do I recall those
terrible days enroute from El Paso to San Francisco, and
after—Frances would have been 45, Helen 19, Anne 17,
Margaret 13. How proud I should have been of them all!

General and Mrs. Dawes were in Cheyenne the other day and
went out to decorate their graves. It touched me deeply to
have them do that. He is such a thoughtful friend to have.

Well! Cherie, I have you and you could not know what a
place you fill in my heart. I love you, little Cherie—goodnight—Yours.

Pershing could not have forgotten the fire and its horrible consequences even if he had tried to do so with his iron will. There were
endless reminders. Every holiday, every birthday, every former friend
or relative associated with Frankie and the girls brought back a surge
of memories. Throughout the 1920s and '30s, his grief was exacerbated
by appeals from people who had fallen on hard times and informed
Pershing that they had been the ones who had saved Warren's life and,
therefore, deserved money from the general. A woman claiming to be
their Filipino housekeeper, Flora Perez, told Pershing that she was afflicted with a spinal column fracture caused by grabbing Warren and
jumping from his bedroom window two stories to the ground to escape
the flames. Every written account of the incident, including by sworn
eyewitnesses, noted that a soldier named Fred Newsome climbed a lad-
der to the second floor and saved Warren. Perez had only been an
anxious onlooker.

"I have kept still for twenty-five years," another veteran wrote to
Pershing, insisting that he carried Warren down to safety, and was now
in need of work. He was counting on Pershing to use his connections
to find him a government job. Pershing's aides began to stop showing
him the letters because they only further depressed the general.

By the 1930s, Pershing's luster was beginning to dim, and his military advice was increasingly ignored. He had warned politicians about
making drastic reductions in the defense budget, but the national mood
was to cut the armed forces, just as it had been before World War I.
Like Woodrow Wilson, President Franklin D. Roosevelt campaigned
for reelection on a promise not to get the United States entangled in the

conflict raging, once again, throughout Europe. "I have said this be-fore, but I shall say it again and again and again," Roosevelt declared in October 1940. "Your boys are not going to be sent into any foreign wars." When the United States finally entered World War II, its mili-tary ranked seventeenth in the world. Italy and Portugal had larger armies.

Pershing had taken up residence at Walter Reed, and when Con-gress declared war against Japan on December 8, 1941, he cabled Presi-dent Roosevelt: "As one among those millions, I offer my services, in any way in which my experience and strength, to the last ounce, will be of help in the fight."

Roosevelt replied, "Dear General, You are magnificent. You always have been—and you always will be. Your services will be of great value." The message, while gracious, was perfunctory; at eighty-one years of age, Pershing was too old and his experience too outdated to serve in any official capacity as an adviser, which is what he had most wanted.

Pershing was, however, touched by the visits and messages he re-ceived from the men who'd once been his junior officers and were now the esteemed generals who'd be leading the Allies in Europe and the Pacific. General George Patton stopped by Walter Reed before em-barking, bringing along the two pistols that he had used during their first operation together, the hunt for Pancho Villa. After reminiscing, Patton knelt down, took Pershing's hand, kissed it, and asked for the general's blessing.

"Good-bye, Georgie," Pershing said, choking up. "God bless you and keep you, and give you victory."

Once Patton himself was ordering hundreds of thousands of men into battle overseas, he wrote to his mentor to emphasize how much Pershing's leadership had inspired him. "I can assure you that whatever ability I have shown or shall show as a soldier," Patton wrote, "is the result of a studious endeavor to copy the greatest American soldier, yourself."

In September 1939, George Marshall was promoted to chief of staff of the Army and became President Franklin D. Roosevelt's most senior military adviser throughout the war. Marshall wrote to Pershing:

> With distressingly heavy casualties, disorganized and only partially trained troops, supply problems of every character due to the devastated zone so rapidly crossed, inclement and cold weather, flu, stubborn resistance by the enemy of one of the strongest positions of the Western Front, pessimism on all sides and pleadings to halt the battle made by many of the influential members of the army, you persisted in your determination to force the fighting over all the difficulties and objections. . . . Nothing else in your leadership was comparable to this.

Most of Pershing's fellow Allied generals from World War I were long gone. Field Marshal Douglas Haig had died in January 1928, and Marshal Ferdinand Foch passed away just over a year later, in March 1929. Ten years earlier, Foch had been a strong advocate—along with Pershing—for being tougher on the Germans in the Treaty of Versailles. "This is not a peace," Foch insisted. "It is an armistice for twenty years." And World War II, indeed, exploded exactly twenty years later when Germany stormed into Poland in September 1939. (There remains considerable debate as to whether the Allies were, in fact, too harsh against the Germans. Adolf Hitler clearly manipulated Germany's festering sense of national humiliation in his rise to power. But his flagrant violations of the Treaty of Versailles—including but not limited to drastically rebuilding his armed forces, implementing mandatory military conscription, and then invading the Rhineland in March 1936—all went unchallenged and only emboldened the Nazis. Hitler himself later conceded that "if the French had marched into the Rhineland, we would have had to withdraw with our tail between our legs.")

Pershing was stunned to learn that his old colleague, General Henri-Philippe Pétain, whom he had considered a dear friend, was now reviled as a traitor by many in his homeland. After the Germans invaded Paris in June 1940, the onetime "savior of France" had agreed to head up what was essentially a puppet government in collaboration with the Nazis. When the war was over, Pétain was put on trial and condemned to death. He was spared only when President Charles de Gaulle, who had led the French Resistance, commuted Pétain's sentence to life in prison.

Warren Pershing grew up to be every bit his father's son; he was good-looking, well liked, and a natural leader. He attended the prestigious Phillips Exeter boarding school, where he was a mediocre but popular student, then went to Yale and was voted most likely to succeed. He joined the military before World War II started and was eventually deployed overseas.

While in France and Germany, the tables were turned, and it was Warren in war-torn Europe sending letters to the States. "We have just received word that we move again tomorrow," Warren wrote to his father ("Pere") and Aunt May on March 31, 1945.

> The gypsy life is to my liking, as it means the shortest way home. It also reminds me of last summer and fall when we were coming across France and Belgium, and just as fast, too. It begins to look as though this may be the last struggle the Germans will be able to put up, in this war at least. I hope we will have enough sense to sit on their heads for the next fifty years, either that or kill them all off, as there seems to be no peaceful solution to the German problem. They think they are born to rule, when in truth, they are only born to be dominated and we will be very foolish people if we ever forget it again.
>
> I like to think that you are with me as we traverse this area, in spirit anyway, as you certainly tried to convince people that we should have made this march in 1918. What a shame it is that we didn't. We might have been spared this war. I think you would have enjoyed going through this part of the country.

The other day as I rode down the Rhine I was reminded of our trip in the boat, as you will remember. A funny thing happened some months ago, it was back last August when we were still on the other side of Paris. The colonel asked me if I had ever been on the Rhine and I said I had. He then asked a lot of technical questions about the width and speed of the current. I could only guess, but told him it was around eleven hundred feet across and had a current of about seven or eight miles an hour.

Lately, we had a good chance to check out these measurements as we have built a number of bridges across it. They vary from just under a thousand to thirteen hundred, and the current has been measured at about seven miles an hour.

So, little did you think, or I either, that as we cruised down the Rhine and I asked all the questions that a boy of ten always asks, that the information would turn out to be of any practical use!

The war in Europe ended five weeks later, and General Dwight D. Eisenhower sent Pershing a message on V-E Day. "As the commander of this second American Expeditionary Force," Ike wrote on May 8, 1945, "I should like to acknowledge to you, the leader of the first, our obligation for the part you have played in the present victory." Ike was alluding to Pershing's earlier efforts to expand and reorganize the Army and its training system.

Micheline Resco had moved to Washington during the war and saw Pershing at Walter Reed on a regular basis, much to the consternation of Pershing's sister May. May tried to keep Resco from coming by, informing her that the general's car, which would normally drive Resco to and from the hospital, was being used elsewhere. Or May would simply tell her that the general was too tired to entertain visitors, when the opposite was true; even Pershing's doctors noticed how improved he seemed when Resco was there. The two played cards together, listened to the radio, and made small talk, and Resco also brought along books and newspapers to read to him.

After a twenty-nine-year-long "courtship," Pershing finally proposed to Resco, and they were secretly wed on September 2, 1946, at Walter Reed, with no one in attendance except the French-born priest—Father Jules Baisnée—who married them.

DURING WORLD WAR II, Warren made a comment in a letter about his two young sons, Jack and Richard, both of whom were born during the war. "Let's hope that maybe Jackie and Dickie can avoid what tripped up both their father and grandfather, and I might add even their great-grandfather [who had served in the Civil War]," Warren wrote to his father from Europe. "It looks to me as though the law of averages ought to begin to operate in their favor and maybe skip their generation."

Sadly, that turned out not to be the case; Warren's life was ultimately bookended by tragedy. Once they reached adulthood, both Dick and Jack joined the Army in peacetime, and they both went to Vietnam when hostilities broke out in Southeast Asia. On February 17, 1968, Dick Pershing was killed while trying to rescue a wounded member of his platoon. He was posthumously awarded the Silver Star for bravery.

Warren's only consolation was that his father was no longer alive to bury yet another member of their family. General John J. Pershing had passed away at the age of eighty-seven on July 15, 1948, due to congestive heart failure.

The old general had two final requests before he died. On December 20, 1929, he had written (in English) a letter to Micheline Resco that he handed to Warren and asked him to give to her when he passed away.

> My Dear Michette,
> What a beautiful love has been ours! How perfect the
> confidence and the communion! How happy have been the

days we have spent together! At the twilight of my life God sent you to be near me. In my hours of sadness you have been my strength. In my moments of triumph you have been there to share them with me. Ever since we first met you have been in my thoughts by day and my dreams by night. Your beauty, your greatness of soul, your brilliance of mind have been the inspiration of the sincerest admiration and the purest love. I fain would think your presence, unseen perhaps, has always filled my heart. As my dear companion in life you will be with me through eternity. I can not but believe, chérie, that together we shall pluck the flowers that grow in some fairer land. So, do not weep, be brave, say not goodbye, but say goodnight, and in some brighter clime bid me good morning, where you will hold me in your dear arms, and I shall be your own. In all the future the lingering fragrance of your kisses shall be fresh on my lips.

As always, much love . . .

Pershing's second request was a more public one. Instead of being buried under any sort of elaborate memorial or prominent headstone, as so many other generals had been honored, Pershing asked to be interred at Arlington National Cemetery next to the troops he had served with thirty years earlier in World War I. He rests there now, under the exact same simple white marker that adorns the graves of his men, his fellow soldiers.

General Pershing's grave at
Arlington National Cemetery.

Acknowledgments

Every writer is dependent on two critically important factors when working on a book: that the subject matter is one the author feels passionately about from start to finish and that a brilliant and nurturing editor will be there to help craft the manuscript and shepherd it to its completion. Fortunately, I was blessed, from day one, to have the steady and supportive guidance of one of the best editors in publishing, Scott Moyers. Scott immediately understood the passion behind this book when I first proposed it, and along with his extraordinary skills as an editor, he demonstrated a degree of patience and encouragement that went above and beyond the call of duty. I doubt I will ever be able to fully express how indebted I am to him for all of this.

I am, of course, eternally grateful to Ann Godoff, the founder, president, and editor in chief of Penguin, who also understood the spirit of this project from the beginning. And Ann has assembled an incredible team at Penguin. Along with Scott, I was very fortunate to work with his colleague Christopher Richards, who seems far too young to be as wise and talented as he is and who also put in double time to help get this book completed. I also want to thank editorial assistant Kiara Barrow, production editor Ryan Boyle, and copy editor Mark Birkey. Copy editors are truly the unsung heroes of publishing, who take on the painstaking chore of going over every letter and punctuation mark in a manuscript to ensure its accuracy. (Having said that, if there are any mistakes in this book, the fault is entirely my own.) Finally, regarding the Penguin team, I want to thank designer Darren Haggar for finding that stunning picture of John Pershing for the cover. I had never seen it before, and it couldn't be more perfect.

None of this would have come about in the first place if it weren't for my agent, Miriam Altshuler, who introduced me to Penguin. Miriam has remained, over more than twenty-five years, not only the most phenomenal agent an author could have, but a great friend, a trusted shoulder to lean on, and simply one of the most caring and admirable people I've ever known, professionally or personally. I am also extremely indebted to Reiko Davis, who began as Miriam's assistant and is now a sensational agent in her own right.

This book—like several others I've worked on previously—is part of a much larger effort I launched in 1998 to encourage Americans to seek out and preserve wartime correspondences as a way of honoring and remembering the military men and women who have served this nation. I am deeply grateful to all of the veterans, troops, and their loved ones who have shared with me more than one hundred thousand letters from every conflict in U.S. history.

The project began after our family's home in Washington, D.C., burned down years ago. Fortunately, no one was hurt in the blaze, but just about everything we had went up in smoke. Sometime later, a distant cousin of ours named James Carroll Jordan heard about the fire and checked in to see how we were doing. I told him that we were all fine physically but were rather dismayed at having lost all of our personal possessions, including irreplaceable photographs and letters. This apparently struck a chord, and James told me that he had just been going through his old World War II memorabilia and found a letter he'd written when he was a twenty-three-year-old P-51 pilot in Europe and had just walked through a recently liberated Nazi concentration camp. "Dear Betty Anne: I saw something today that makes me realize why we're over here fighting this war," he wrote on April 21, 1945. He then went on to describe in rather graphic detail what the Germans had done to their victims.

James sent me the original letter, and I'll never forget holding that thin onionskin paper in my hands and thinking how delicate and fragile it seemed—and what a stark contrast this was to the weight and significance of his words. When I told him that I would, of course, return the letter, he said, "Go ahead and keep it. I was probably going to toss it out anyway." The idea that he would even consider discarding something so valuable was stunning to me, and although I didn't know it at the time, it was the first war letter I would acquire.

The second letter came from outside our family, but it was equally as significant. While telling a friend of mine named Anne Tramer about our house fire and then receiving my cousin's remarkable letter, she told me that she had a somewhat similar experience: her grandfather Erwin Blonder also fought in World War II, and when he, too, was twenty-three years old, he wrote to his brother and father about his combat experiences in Europe. "I am writing this letter to you to get certain things off my mind," he began. "I am telling this to you because I want to spare Shirlee the horrible details of war and I don't want this letter shown to either her [or] Mother." (Shirlee was his fiancée.) As it turned out, Erwin was almost killed three weeks later but survived the battle and then the war. Erwin read his September 30, 1944, letter aloud to his entire family at his and Shirlee's fiftieth wedding anniversary. Anne had never heard that side of her grandfather before (like many veterans, he rarely spoke about what he endured or witnessed in wartime), and when Anne put me in touch with him, he became a kind of mentor, encouraging me to seek out additional letters and to especially focus on African American soldiers, war nurses, Navajo Code Talkers, and other service members who were often overlooked in the history books. Erwin was especially interested in Japanese American troops because he and his battalion were rescued at one point by the 442nd Regimental Combat Team, a group of Japanese American soldiers whose unit ultimately became among the most heavily decorated in our country's history.

Thanks to James Carroll Jordan and Erwin Blonder—the men to whom this book is dedicated—the Legacy Project, as I initially called it, was born. And the person most responsible for giving it its first bit of national exposure, in 1998, was Dear Abby, and I will be forever indebted to her for her generosity and friendship over the years.

In 2013, the Legacy Project's letters were donated to Chapman University in Orange, California, and now represent the foundation of an institute, the Center for American War Letters, that is archiving and cataloging the existing correspondences while also working to bring in more. I fell in love with the school when one of its theater professors, John Benitz (who has since become a dear friend), suggested workshopping a play there based on the letters and my travels around the United States and the world to find them. The students, the faculty, and the administration were all extremely supportive of the overall mission of the project and, most important, showed profound respect for the servicemen and -women who wrote the letters, and I eventually decided that Chapman would be the perfect home for this massive and growing collection. Along with John Benitz, I especially want to thank President Daniele Struppa (and his predecessor Jim Doti) for making me a part of the Chapman community, and I'm also very grateful to the professors and staff members I've gotten to know within the entire university: Julie Artman, Dean Charlene Baldwin, Sheryl Bourgeois, Rand Boyd, William Cumiford, Laurie Cusalli, Gregory Daddis, Doug Dechow, John Encarnacion, Brett Fisher, Patrick Fuery, Marilyn Harran, Jennifer Keene, Nina LeNoir, Lauren Menges, Essraa Nawar, Heidi Negrete, Jan Osborn, Kyndra Rotunda, Angela Ruiz, Robert Slayton, Char Williams, and Tom Zoellner.

For going out of their way to help with my research, there are numerous historians, archivists, and librarians throughout the United States whom I wish to thank, including: Cornelia Read, who helped me with all of the photographs; Nicole J. Milano, who runs the Archives of the

American Field Service and AFS Intercultural Programs Inc.; Lesley Martin at the Chicago History Museum Research Center; Regina Green at the Choctaw Nation of Oklahoma Capitol Museum; Richard Dean, the president of the Columbus (New Mexico) Historical Society, which owns and operates the town's main museum, and where I saw the picture of John Pershing standing next to Pancho Villa that reignited my interest in Pershing; Jocelyn K. Wilk at the Columbia University Rare Archives and Manuscript Library; Robin Hutchison and Jennifer Reibenspies at the Cushing Memorial Library and Archives, Texas A&M University; Deanna L. Kolling and Kathy Struss at the Dwight D. Eisenhower Presidential Library, Museum, and Boyhood Home; Denzil Heaney, probably the foremost living expert on Pershing and whose assistance has been especially valuable, at the General John J. Pershing Boyhood Home State Historic Site; Kurt Graham, Jim Armistead, David Clark, Sam Rushay, and Randy Sowell at the Harry S. Truman Library and Museum; Juliana Kulpers at the Harvard University Archives; David P. Miros, who helped me with the Pershing letters to Micheline Resco, at the Jesuit Archives: Central United States; Bruce Kirby, Jeffrey Flannery, and Michelle Krowl in the Manuscript Division of the Library of Congress; James Zobel at the MacArthur Memorial; Jeffrey S. Kozak at the George C. Marshall Foundation; Lynn Heidelbaugh, Susan Smith, and Patricia Raynor at the National Postal Museum; Eric Blevins at the North Carolina Museum of History; Amanda Bahr-Evola at the St. Louis Public Library; Sue Sarna at Sagamore Hill National Historic Site; Marine Corps historian Patrick Mooney; Marie Cutchiss and Genna Rollins at the Theodore Roosevelt Association; and Doran Cart, Jonathan Casey, Mike Vietti, and Stacie Peterson, who helped me find the Alta May Andrews letters and diaries, at the National World War I Museum and Memorial.

Along with my parents, who have, of course, been incredible throughout this whole endeavor, there are a host of other family members and friends to whom I am grateful: Allison Agnew, Ted Alexander, Sharon Allen, Chris Aprato, Meredith Ashley, Rye Barcott, Scott

Baron, Chris Beach, Kate Becker, Peter Benkendorf, Bob Bergman, Rob Berkley and Debbie Phillips, Margaret Bernal, Cliff and Anna Blaze, Todd Boss, Doug Bradshaw, Joy and Chad Breckenridge, Lawrence Bridges, Anne Tramer Brownlee (and the entire Tramer family), Christopher Buckley, Jon Burrows, Lisa Catapano, Chris and Liz Carroll, Lucinda and Sophia Carroll, Ross Cohen, Craig Colton, Frank Correa, Allan Cors, Dan Dalager, Dave Danzig, Richard Danzig, Connie and Tom Davidson Sr., Elissa and Tommy Davidson, Chris Davies and Stephanie Martz-Davies, Frank Davies, James Dourgarian, Chris Dunham, Tom Dunkel, Deanna Durrett, Chris Epting, Dave Gabel, Joan Gillcrist, Larry Goins, Erin Gruwell, Parker Gyokeres, Joyce Hallenbeck, Darell Hammond, Tom Hare, Linda Howell, Ed Hrivnak, Nick Irons, Ryan Kelly, Yumi Kobayashi, Chrissy Kolaya, Tina and Zoltan Krompecher, Gene and Joanna Kukuy, Greg and Maureen Lare, Tom Leitzell, Lisa Lesane, Jack Lewis, Kathy Lowy, John McCary, Liz McDermott, Pam McDonough, James and Meribeth McGinley, Ann Medlock, Doug Meehan, Jimmie Meinhardt, Brad Meltzer, Justin Merhoff, Mike Meyer, John Meyers, Nathan Mick, Allen Mikaelian, Brook Miller, De'on Miller, Rusell Miller, Marja Mills, Janet Min, Pat Moran, K. K. Otteson, Jon Peede, David Pelizzari, James Percoco, Pam Putney, Cheryl Richardson, Joe Rubinfine, Cathy Saypol, Jeff Shaara, Thad Sheeley, Dr. Robert Siegel, Denis Silva, Pete Sluszka, Lucy Roberts Smiles, Charles Smith, Kelsey Smith, Kerner Smith Jr., Kerner Smith III, Maggie Smith, Patty Smith, Megan Smolenyak, Steve Stevenson, Will Strong, Sean Sweeney, Adrian Talbott, Chris and Becca Tessin, Chuck Theusch, Bill Thomas, Kyriakos Tsakopoulos, Martin Vigderhouse, Todd Vorenkamp, Jamie Wager, Stephen Webber, Matthew Wheelock, Megan Willems, Rob Wilson, Thomas Young, and Lydia Zamora. And finally, a very, very special thanks to Ellen Wingard.

Notes on Sources

Since many of the following publications are used as sources in multiple places throughout this book, the full list of titles is provided in the bibliography for easy reference, and abbreviated references are also listed in the notes below. Smaller publications, such as magazines, newspapers, and political flyers, are usually cited in full in the text of this book, but where they are not, all of the relevant information is provided in their respective chapter summaries below.

Letters, diaries, and similar personal writings provided by the family members of World War I veterans, museums, archives, and other institutions are also listed individually within the chapter notes below.

All of the letters to and by John Pershing in this book as well as his journals, unless noted differently, are archived at the Library of Congress. With one exception (the letter on pages 352–53), Pershing's letters to Micheline Resco are at the Jesuit Archives: Central United States in St. Louis, Missouri. All letters by George Patton are also in the Library of Congress, and all letters by Harry S. Truman are archived at the Harry S. Truman Presidential Library and Museum, Independence, Missouri.

Finally, to keep the main narrative moving along at a pace that is as brisk and uninterrupted as possible, various comments and asides that address potentially conflicting information have been added, in parentheses, within the chapter notes below. These are intended to explore certain discrepancies in original materials and, ideally, attempt to set the record straight.

FOREWORD
John Pershing letters to "Aunt Eliza" and "Dear Anne" are part of the author's private collection; Tuchman, *The Guns of August*; Bernstein, *The Willy-Nicky Correspondence*; Goldhurst, *Pipe Clay and Drill*; Smith, *Until the Last Trumpet Sounds*; Greenwood (editor), *My Life Before the World War, 1860–1917*. (Greenwood's book is actually an edited version of a previously unpublished manuscript that Pershing wrote about his life before 1917. Pershing wrote about his war years in detail in his two-volume *My Experiences in the World War*, which was published in 1931 and won the Pulitzer Prize. Despite the award, critics panned the memoir for being dry and somewhat tedious, and Pershing himself confided to friends and family members that he loathed working on the manuscript but thought it would be valuable to history.)

1. AUGUST 26
Zuckerman, *The Rape of Belgium*; Toynbee, *The German Terror in Belgium*; Horne and Kramer, *German Atrocities 1914*. (Since the publication of Toynbee's description of German atrocities against Belgian citizens in 1917, historians have debated the veracity of these accounts, with some arguing that the stories were fabricated by the Allies for propaganda purposes and were neither as lurid nor as prevalent as reported. In recent years, however, uncovered documents in Germany's own archives have confirmed that many of the atrocities did indeed occur and were widespread throughout Belgium.) Smythe, *Pershing*; Vandiver, *Black Jack*, vols. 1 and 2. (Of all Pershing's biographers, Vandiver gives the most detailed description of the loss of Pershing's wife and three daughters at the Presidio.) Smith, *Until the Last Trumpet Sounds*; Goldhurst, *Pipe Clay and Drill*. Photograph of Louvain reprinted by permission of Trinity Mirror/Mirrorpix/Alamy. Photograph of John Pershing and his family courtesy of the Library of Congress.

2. THE FIRST TO GO
"American Volunteers Bled and Led Way to WWI 100 Years Ago," Reuters, February 18, 2015; Werstein, *Sound No Trumpet*; Seeger, *Letters and Diary of Alan Seeger*; Anonymous, *Letters from André Chéronnet-Champollion, 1914–1915*; Gleason, *Our Part in the Great War*; Hansen, *Gentlemen Volunteers*; Howe (editor), *The Harvard Volunteers in Europe*; Geller (editor), *The American Field Service Archives of World War I, 1914–1917*; Buswell, *Ambulance No. 10*; Bradley, *Back of the Front in France*; Dexter, *In the Soldier's Service*; Carisella and Ryan, *The Black Swallow of Death*; Greenly, *Eugene Bullard*. Photographs of A. Piatt Andrew and General Stephen Galatti at the AFS headquarters in Paris, taken by H. C. Ellis, courtesy of the Archives of the American Field Service and AFS Intercultural Programs; and photograph of Mrs. W. K. Vanderbilt in front of the cathedral at Reims is also courtesy of the Archives of the American Field Service and AFS Intercultural Programs. Photograph of Verdun skeletons courtesy of the San Diego Air & Space Museum (John McGrew Collection).

3. HUNTING PANCHO
Smythe, *Guerrilla Warrior*; Welsome, *The General and the Jaguar*; Cramer, *Newton Baker*; Hirshson, *General Patton*; D'Este, *Patton*; Smith, *Until the Last Trumpet Sounds*;

Goldhurst, *Pipe Clay and Drill*; Vandiver, *Black Jack*, vol. 2. (The official date of Pershing's birthday, September 13, 1860, which is on his grave marker at Arlington National Cemetery as well as on various statues in his honor, and which Pershing himself cited throughout his adulthood, is almost certainly inaccurate. It is now believed that Pershing was born nine months earlier, sometime—the exact day still isn't known—in January 1860. Recently discovered documents indicate this change, including a letter from his grandmother to a maternal aunt, written in February 1860, in which she states that "John and Ann [Pershing's parents] had a little boy last month and they are thinking of naming him John." And the February 1860 census from Pershing's birthplace near Laclede, Missouri, also lists a newborn boy named John in the Pershing household. Pershing is believed to have changed the date himself when he was about twenty-two years old for a very specific reason: he was applying to West Point for the free education, and if he had stated that he was born in February 1860, he would have been too old to be admitted. By moving his birthday to September, he was able to just slip in under West Point's age limit. Once he started celebrating his birthday in September, he apparently stuck with it for the remainder of his life. Pershing was known throughout his career for his honesty and forthrightness, and justifiably so, but in this particular case, the evidence suggests he wasn't entirely truthful.

4. Lafayette's Boys
Rockwell, *War Letters of Kiffin Yates Rockwell*; Weeks, *Greater Love Hath No Man*; Chapman, *Victor Chapman's Letters from France*; Roseberry, *Glenn Curtiss*; Mortimer, *The First Eagles*; Flood, *First to Fly*; Parsons, *Flight into Hell*; Hall and Niles, *One Man's War*; Gordon, *The Lafayette Flying Corps*. Photograph of Kiffin Rockwell reprinted by permission of the North Carolina Museum of History.

5. Countdown
Larson, *Dead Wake*; Auchincloss, *Woodrow Wilson*; Berg, *Wilson*; Cooper, *Woodrow Wilson*; Tuchman, *The Zimmermann Telegram*; Gibbons, *And They Thought We Wouldn't Fight*; Brands (editor), *The Selected Letters of Theodore Roosevelt*; Neu, *Colonel House*. Photograph of the Zimmermann telegram courtesy of the National Archives.

6. The Promotion
Pershing, *My Experiences in the World War*, vol. 1; Smith, *FDR*; Cramer, *Newton Baker*; Sears, *The Career of Leonard Wood*; McCallum, *Leonard Wood*; Smith, *Until the Last Trumpet Sounds*; Vandiver, *Black Jack*, vol. 2. Photograph of Franklin D. Roosevelt courtesy of the Franklin D. Roosevelt Presidential Library and Museum, Hyde Park, New York.

7. Over There
Harbord, *Leaves from a War Diary*; Pershing, *My Experiences in the World War*, vol. 2; Smith, *Until the Last Trumpet Sounds*; Goldhurst, *Pipe Clay and Drill*; Vandiver, *Black Jack*, vol. 2.

8. Heaven, Hell, or Hoboken
Auchincloss, *Woodrow Wilson*; Berg, *Wilson*; Cooper, *Woodrow Wilson*; Henderson, *Maury Maverick*; Maverick, *A Maverick American*; Ferrell (editor), *The Autobiography of*

Harry S. Truman; Giancreco, *The Soldier from Independence*. Photograph of Harry Truman courtesy of the Harry S. Truman Library and Museum, Independence, Missouri.

9. UNDER THE GUN

Bradley, *Back of the Front in France*; The Society of the First Division, *History of the First Division During the World War, 1917–1919*; Cray, *General of the Army*; Marshall, *Memoirs of My Services in the World War 1917–1918*; Harbord, *Leaves from a War Diary*; Pershing, *My Experiences in the World War*, vol. 2; Smith, *Until the Last Trumpet Sounds*; Goldhurst, *Pipe Clay and Drill*. George Marshall photograph courtesy of the George C. Marshall Foundation, Lexington, Virginia.

10. SHOW OF FORCE

Duffy, *Father Duffy's Story*; Dunlop, *Donovan*; Manchester, *American Caesar*; MacArthur, *Reminiscences*; The Society of the First Division, *History of the First Division During the World War, 1917–1919*; Pershing, *My Experiences in the World War*, vol. 2; Smith, *Until the Last Trumpet Sounds*; Goldhurst, *Pipe Clay and Drill*; Vandiver, *Black Jack*, vol. 2.

11. DIVISIONS

The Society of the First Division, *History of the First Division During the World War, 1917-1919*; Davenport, *First Over There*; Sears, *The Career of Leonard Wood*; McCallum, *Leonard Wood*; Pershing, *My Experiences in the World War*, vol. 2; Smith, *Until the Last Trumpet Sounds*; Goldhurst, *Pipe Clay and Drill—John J. Pershing*; and Vandiver, *Black Jack*, vol. 2.

12. BLACK JACK AND THE HELLFIGHTERS

Stokes, *D. W. Griffith's* The Birth of a Nation; Lehr, *The Birth of a Nation*; Barbeau and Henri, *The Unknown Soldiers*; Sammons and Morrow, *Harlem's Rattlers and the Great War*; Fish, *Memoir of an American Patriot*; Williams, *Torchbearers of Democracy*; Edgarton, *Hidden Heroism*; Little, *From Harlem to the Rhine*; Harris, *Harlem's Hell Fighters*. (Although Harris refers to the 369th as Hell Fighters, their nickname is often spelled as one word: Hellfighters.) Colonel Linard's memo about African American troops was published in its original French with an English translation in "The Crisis," XVIII, May 1919.

13. THE EYEWITNESS

Gibbons, *And They Thought We Wouldn't Fight*; Gibbons, *Floyd Gibbons*; Bullard, *Personalities and Reminiscences of the War*; Davenport, *First Over There*; Gustaitis, *Chicago Transformed*; Gies, *The Colonel of Chicago*; Smith, *The Colonel*; Cray, *General of the Army*; Marshall, *Memoirs of My Services in the World War 1917–1918*; Harbord, *Leaves from a War Diary*; Catlin, *With the Help of God and a Few Good Marines*; Martin (editor), *The Greatest U.S. Marine Corps Stories Ever Told*.

14. AN ARMY OF ANGELS

Keene, *World War I*; Graham (editor), *Out Here at the Front*; Wigle, *Pride of America, We're with You*; letters and diaries by Alta May Andrews courtesy of the National

World War I Museum and Memorial, Kansas City, Missouri; Gibbons, *And They Thought We Wouldn't Fight*; Gibbons, *Floyd Gibbons*. Photographs of Alta May Andrews and camouflaged ship reprinted by permission of the National World War I Museum and Memorial, Kansas City, Missouri.

15. THEIR CROWDED HOUR
Roosevelt (editor), *Quentin Roosevelt*; Brands (editor), *The Selected Letters of Theodore Roosevelt*; Groom, *The Aviators*; Gordon, *The Lafayette Flying Corps*; Carisella and Ryan, *The Black Swallow of Death*; Greenly, *Eugene Bullard*; Rickenbacker, *Fighting the Flying Circus*; Rickenbacker, *Rickenbacker*. Photograph of Quentin Roosevelt's corpse and crashed airplane reprinted by permission of Trinity Mirror/Mirrorpix/Alamy. Photograph of aerial view of landscape courtesy of the San Diego Air & Space Museum (John McGrew Collection).

16. CAPTAIN HARRY
Ferrell (editor), *The Autobiography of Harry S. Truman*; Giancreco, *The Soldier from Independence*; "'Twas in 1918, in France, in World War I—Columbus Man Saves Missouri Captain,"*Columbus Daily Advocate*, August 16, 1950; Hoyt, *Heroes of the Argonne*.

17. THE BIRTHDAY PRESENT
Dawes, *A Journal of the Great War*, vol. 1; Dunlop, *Donovan*; The Society of the First Division, *History of the First Division During the World War, 1917–1919*; Smith, *Until the Last Trumpet Sounds*; Pershing, *My Experiences in the World War*, vol. 2; Goldhurst, *Pipe Clay and Drill*; Vandiver, *Black Jack*, vol. 2; Duffy, *Father Duffy's Story*; MacArthur, *Reminiscences*; Manchester, *American Casear*; Parsons, *The American Engineers in France*; Cray, *General of the Army*; Marshall, *Memoirs of My Services in the World War 1917–1918*; Henderson, *Maury Maverick*; Ferrell (editor), *In the Company of Generals*; Maverick, *A Maverick American*; D'Este, *Patton*; Eisenhower, *Yanks*.

18. ALL IN
MacArthur, *Reminiscences*; Manchester, *American Ceasar*; Yockelson, *Forty-seven Days*; The Society of the First Division, *History of the First Division During the World War, 1917–1919*; Liggett, *A.E.F.*; Liggett, *Commanding an American Army*; Smith, *Until the Last Trumpet Sounds*; Pershing, *My Experiences in the World War*, vol. 2; Goldhurst, *Pipe Clay and Drill*; Vandiver, *Black Jack*, vol. 2; Cray, *General of the Army*; Marshall, *Memoirs of My Services in the World War 1917–1918*; Walker, *Betrayal at Little Gibraltar*; Hoyt, *Heroes of the Argonne*; Jack Bentley memoir courtesy of the Cushing Memorial Library and Archives, Texas A&M University; D'Este, *Patton*; Eisenhower, *Yanks*; Mastriano, *Alvin York*; Perry, *Sgt. York*; Britten, *American Indians in World War I*; Krouse, *North American Indians in the Great War*; Farwell, *Over There*; Rickenbacker, *Fighting the Flying Circus*; Rickenbacker, *Rickenbacker*; Knock, *To End All Wars*; "Dear Old Bunkie" letter reprinted by permission of and copyright by Susan Koelble; Lloyd Palmer account of the Meuse-Argonne Offensive reprinted by permission of John M. Palmer; Melville Montgomery letter reprinted by permission of and © by Elizabeth Dowey; Duffy, *Father Duffy's Story*; letters and diaries by Alta May Andrews courtesy of the National World War I Museum and Memorial, Kansas City, Missouri. David Arthur Thompson letter courtesy of Merrilee A. Foley; American Graves Registration

Service information is provided by the American Battle Monuments Commission; the "My Fellow Soldiers" letter is from the author's private collection; Smith, *Until the Last Trumpet Sounds*. Photograph of the traffic jam in the Verdun sector reprinted by permission of the Everett Collection Historical/Alamy.

19. POSTSCRIPT

Duiker, *Ho Chi Minh*; letters and diaries by Alta May Andrews courtesy of the National World War I Museum and Memorial, Kansas City, Missouri; Mastriano, *Alvin York*; Greenly, *Eugene Bullard*; MacArthur, *Reminiscences*; Manchester, *American Ceasar*; Sears, *The Career of Leonard Wood*; McCallum, *Leonard Wood*; Cray, *General of the Army*; O'Reilly and Dugard, *Killing Patton*; Patton, *Killing Patton?*; Wilcox, *Target Patton*; Dunlop, *Donovan*; American Battle Monuments Commission, *A Guide to the American Battle Fields in Europe*; D'Este, *Eisenhower*; Perret, *Eisenhower*; Miller, *Ike the Soldier*; Pershing, *My Experiences in the World War,* vol. 2; Smith, *Eisenhower in War and Peace*; Smith, *Until the Last Trumpet Sounds*; Goldhurst, *Pipe Clay and Drill*; Vandiver, *Black Jack,* vol. 2. Photographs of Dwight D. Eisenhower with his wife, Mamie, and of their son, Ikky, courtesy of the Dwight D. Eisenhower Presidential Library, Museum, and Boyhood Home, Abilene, Kansas. Letter by Pershing to Resco dated December 20, 1929, was acquired by the author through an antiques dealer in Paris and is part of the author's private collection. Photograph of Pershing's grave at Arlington National Cemetery taken by the author.

Bibliography

AMERICAN BATTLE MONUMENTS COMMISSION. *A Guide to the American Battle Fields in Europe.* Washington, D.C.: Government Printing Office, 1927.

ANDREW, ABRAM PIATT. *Friends of France: The Field Service of the American Ambulance Described by Its Members.* Boston and New York: Houghton Mifflin Company, 1916.

———. *Letters Written Home from France in the First Half of 1915.* Privately published by Helen M. Andrew, 1916.

ANONYMOUS. *Letters from André Chéronnet-Champollion, 1914–1915.* New York: Privately printed, 1915.

AUCHINCLOSS, LOUIS. *Woodrow Wilson: A Penguin Life.* New York: Viking Penguin, 2000.

BARBEAU, ARTHUR E., AND FLORETTE HENRI. *The Unknown Soldiers: African-American Troops in World War I.* Philadelphia: Temple University Press, 1974.

BERG, A. SCOTT. *Wilson.* New York: The Berkley Publishing Group, 2014.

BERNSTEIN, HERMAN. *The Willy-Nicky Correspondence: Being the Secret and Intimate Telegrams Exchanged Between the Kaiser and the Tsar.* New York: Alfred Knopf, 1918.

BLUMENSON, MARTIN, ED. *The Patton Papers: 1885–1940.* Boston: Houghton Mifflin Company, 1972.

BRADLEY, AMY OWEN. *Back of the Front in France: Letters from Amy Owen Bradley, Motor Driver of the American Fund for French Wounded.* Boston: W. A. Butterfield, 1918.

BRANDS, H. W., ED. *The Selected Letters of Theodore Roosevelt.* Lanham, MD: Rowman & Littlefield Publishers, Inc., 2001.

BRITTEN, THOMAS A. *American Indians in World War I: At War and at Home.* Albuquerque: University of New Mexico Press, 1997.

BULLARD, ROBERT LEE. *Personalities and Reminiscences of the War.* Garden City, NY: Doubleday, Page & Company, 1925.

BUSWELL, LESLIE. *Ambulance No. 10: Personal Letters from the Front.* Boston and New York: Houghton Mifflin Company, 1917.

CARISELLA, P. J., AND JAMES W. RYAN. *The Black Swallow of Death: The Incredible Story of Eugene Jacques Bullard, the World's First Black Combat Aviator.* Boston: Marlborough House, Inc., 1972.

CATLIN, ALBERTUS W. *With the Help of God and a Few Good Marines.* New York: Doubleday, Page & Company, 1919.

CHAPMAN, JOHN JAY. *Victor Chapman's Letters from France.* New York: Macmillan & Company, 1917.

COOPER, JOHN MILTON, JR. *Woodrow Wilson: A Biography.* New York: Vintage, 2009.

CRAMER, C. H. *Newton Baker: A Biography.* Cleveland: The World Publishing Company, 1961.

CRAY, ED. *General of the Army: George C. Marshall, Soldier and Statesman.* New York: Cooper Square Press, 1990.

DAVENPORT, MATTHEW J. *First Over There: The Attack on Cantigny, America's First Battle of World War I.* New York: Thomas Dunne Books/St. Martin's Press, 2015.

DAWES, CHARLES GATES. *A Journal of the Great War. Vols. 1 and 2.* Boston: Houghton Mifflin Company, 1921.

D'ESTE, CARLO. *Eisenhower: A Soldier's Life.* New York: Henry Holt and Company, 2002.

———. *Patton: A Genius for War.* New York: HarperCollins, 1995.

DEXTER, MARY. *In the Soldier's Service: War Experiences of Mary Dexter, England—Belgium—France, 1914–1918.* Cambridge, MA: The Riverside Press, 1918.

DUFFY, FRANCIS P. *Father Duffy's Story: A Tale of Humor and Heroism, of Life and Death with the Fighting Sixty-ninth.* New York: George H. Doran Company, 1919.

DUIKER, WILLIAM J. *Ho Chi Minh: A Life.* New York: Hyperion, 2000.

DUNLOP, RICHARD. *Donovan: America's Master Spy.* New York: Skyhorse Publishing, 2014.

EDGARTON, ROBERT B. *Hidden Heroism: Black Soldiers in America's Wars.* Boulder, CO: Westview Press, 2001.

EISENHOWER, JOHN S. D. *Yanks: The Epic Story of the American Army in World War I.* New York: The Free Press, 2001.

FARWELL, BYRON. *Over There: The United States in the Great War, 1917–1918.* New York: W. W. Norton & Company, 1999.

FERRELL, ROBERT H., ED. *The Autobiography of Harry S. Truman.* Columbia: University of Missouri Press, 1980.

———. *In the Company of Generals: The World War I Diary of Pierpont L. Stackpole.* Columbia: University of Missouri Press, 2009.

FISH, HAMILTON. *Memoir of an American Patriot.* Washington, D.C.: Regnery Gateway, 1991.

FLOOD, CHARLES BRACELEN. *First to Fly: The Story of the Lafayette Escadrille, the American Heroes Who Flew for France in World War I.* New York: Atlantic Monthly Press, 2015.

GELLER, L. D., ED. *The American Field Service Archives of World War I, 1914–1917.* Westport, CT: Greenwood Press, Inc., 1989.

GIANCRECO, D. M. *The Soldier from Independence: A Military Biography of Harry Truman.* Minneapolis: Zenith Press/MBI Publishing Company, 2009.

GIBBONS, EDWARD. *Floyd Gibbons: Your Headline Hunter.* New York: Exposition Press, 1953.

GIBBONS, FLOYD. *And They Thought We Wouldn't Fight.* New York: George H. Doran Company, 1918.

GIES, JOSEPH. *The Colonel of Chicago: A Biography of the Chicago Tribune's Legendary Publisher, Colonel Robert McCormick.* New York: E. P. Dutton, 1979.

GLEASON, ARTHUR. *Our Part in the Great War.* New York: Frederick A. Stokes Company, 1917.

GOLDHURST, RICHARD. *Pipe Clay and Drill: John J. Pershing—The Classic American Soldier.* New York: Thomas Y. Crowell Company, 1977.

GORDON, DENNIS. *The Lafayette Flying Corps: The American Volunteers in the French Air Service in World War One.* Atglen, PA: Schiffer Military History, 2000.

GRAHAM, JUDITH S., ED. *Out Here at the Front: The World War I Letters of Nora Saltonstall.* Boston: Northeastern University Press, 2004.

GREENLY, LARRY. *Eugene Bullard: World's First Black Fighter Pilot.* Montgomery, AL: NewSouth Books, 2013.

GREENWOOD, JOHN T., ED. *My Life Before the World War, 1860–1917: A Memoir.* Lexington: The University Press of Kentucky, 2013.

GROOM, WINSTON. *The Aviators: Eddie Rickenbacker, Jimmy Doolittle, Charles Lindbergh, and the Epic Age of Flight.* Washington, D.C.: National Geographic Society, 2013.

GUSTAITIS, JOSEPH. *Chicago Transformed: World War I and the Windy City.* Carbondale: Southern Illinois University Press, 2016.

GUTIÉRREZ, EDWARD A. *Doughboys on the Great War: How American Soldiers Viewed Their Military Experience.* Lawrence: University Press of Kansas, 2014.

HALL, BERT, AND JOHN J. Niles. *One Man's War: The Story of the Lafayette Escadrille.* New York: Henry Holt and Company, 1929.

HANSEN, ALREN J. *Gentlemen Volunteers: The Story of the American Ambulance Drivers in the First World War.* New York: Arcade Publishing, 1996.

HARBORD, JAMES G. *Leaves from a War Diary.* New York: Dodd, Mead & Company, 1925.

HARRIS, STEPHEN L. *Harlem's Hell Fighters: The African-American 369th Infantry in World War I.* Washington, D.C.: Potomac Books, 2003.

HENDERSON, RICHARD B. *Maury Maverick: A Political Biography.* Austin: University of Texas Press, 1970.

HIRSHSON, STANLEY P. *General Patton: A Soldier's Life.* New York: HarperCollins, 2002.

HORNE, JOHN, AND ALAN KRAMER. *German Atrocities 1914: A History in Denial.* New Haven, CT: Yale University Press, 2001.

HOWE, M. A. DeWOLFE, ED. *The Harvard Volunteers in Europe: Personal Records of Experience in Military, Ambulance, and Hospital Service.* Cambridge, MA: Harvard University Press, 1916.

HOYT, CHARLES B. *Heroes of the Argonne: An Authentic History of the Thirty-fifth Division*. Kansas City: Franklin Hudson Publishing Company, 1919.

KEENE, JENNIFER. *World War I: The American Soldier Experience*. Lincoln, NB: University of Nebraska Press, 2011.

KNOCK, THOMAS J. *To End All Wars: Woodrow Wilson and the Quest for a New World Order*. New York: Oxford University Press, 1992.

KROUSE, SUSAN APPLEGATE. *North American Indians in the Great War*. Lincoln: University of Nebraska Press, 2007.

LARSON, ERIK. *Dead Wake: The Last Crossing of the Lusitania*. New York: Crown Publishers, 2015.

LEHR, DICK. *The Birth of a Nation: How a Legendary Filmmaker and a Crusading Editor Reignited America's Civil War*. New York: PublicAffairs, 2014.

LIGGETT, HUNTER. *Commanding an American Army: Recollections of the World War*. Cambridge, MA: Riverside Press, 1925.

———. *A.E.F.: Ten Years Ago in France*. New York: Dodd, Mead & Company, 1928.

LITTLE, ARTHUR W. *From Harlem to the Rhine: The Story of New York's Colored Volunteers*. New York: Covici Friede Publishers, 1936.

MacARTHUR, DOUGLAS. *Reminiscences*. Annapolis, MD: Naval Institute Press, 1964.

MANCHESTER, WILLIAM. *American Caesar: Douglas MacArthur, 1880–1964*. New York: Dell Publishing, 1978.

MARCH, PEYTON. *The Nation at War*. Garden City, NY: Doubleday, Doran & Company, 1932.

MARSHALL, GEORGE C. *Memoirs of My Services in the World War 1917–1918*. Boston: Houghton Mifflin Company, 1976.

MARTIN, IAIN C., ED. *The Greatest U.S. Marine Corps Stories Ever Told: Unforgettable Stories of Courage, Honor, and Sacrifice*. Guilford, CT: Lyons Press, 2007.

MASTRIANO, DOUGLAS V. *Alvin York: A New Biography of the Hero of the Argonne*. Lexington: The University Press of Kentucky, 2014.

MAVERICK, MAURY. *A Maverick American*. New York: Covici Friede Publishers, 1937.

McCALLUM, JACK. *Leonard Wood: Rough Rider, Surgeon, Architect of American Imperialism*. New York: New York University Press, 2006.

MILLER, MERLE. *Ike the Soldier: As They Knew Him*. New York: G. P. Putnam's Sons, 1987.

MORTIMER, GAVIN. *The First Eagles: The Fearless American Aces Who Flew with the RAF in World War I*. Minneapolis: Quarto Publishing Group USA, 2014.

MULLEN, ROBERT W. *Blacks in America's Wars: The Shift in Attitudes from the Revolutionary War to Vietnam*. New York: Pathfinder, 1973.

NEU, CHARLES E. *Colonel House: A Biography of Woodrow Wilson's Silent Partner*. New York: Oxford University Press, 2015.

O'REILLY, BILL, AND MARTIN DUGARD. *Killing Patton: The Strange Death of World War II's Most Audacious General*. New York: Henry Holt and Company, 2014.

PARSONS, EDWIN C. *Flight into Hell: The Story of the Lafayette Escadrille*. London: John Long, 1938.

PARSONS, WILLIAM BARCLAY. *The American Engineers in France*. New York: D. Appleton and Company, 1920.

PATTON, MRS. [his wife], Patton's Soldiers, and a War Correspondent. *Killing Patton? His Life, His Death, Told by Those Who Loved Him*. Self-published, 2014.

PERRET, GEOFFREY. *Eisenhower*. New York: Random House, 1999.

PERRY, JOHN. *Sgt. York: His Life, Legend & Legacy*. Nashville: B&H Publishing Group, 1997.

PERSHING, JOHN J. *My Experiences in the World War. Vols. 1 and 2*. New York: Frederick A. Stokes, 1931.

RAMIREZ, JOSÉ A. *To the Line of Fire: Mexican Texans and World War I*. College Station: Texas A&M University Press, 2009.

RICKENBACKER, EDDIE V. *Fighting the Flying Circus*. Garden City, NY: Doubleday & Company, 1965.

———. *Rickenbacker: An Autobiography*. Englewood Cliffs, NJ: Prentice-Hall, 1967.

ROCKWELL, PAUL AYRES. *War Letters of Kiffin Yates Rockwell*. Garden City, NY: The Country Life Press/Doubleday, Page & Company, 1925.

ROOSEVELT, KERMIT, ED. *Quentin Roosevelt: A Sketch with Letters*. New York: Charles Scribner's Sons, 1921.

ROSEBERRY, C. R. *Glenn Curtiss: Pioneer of Flight*. New York: Doubleday & Company, 1972.

SAMMONS, JEFFREY T., AND JOHN H. MORROW JR. *Harlem's Rattlers and the Great War: The Undaunted 369th Regiment and the African American Quest for Equality*. Lawrence: University Press of Kansas, 2014.

SEARS, JOSEPH HAMBLEN. *The Career of Leonard Wood*. New York: D. Appleton and Company, 1920.

SEEGER, ALAN. *Letters and Diary of Alan Seeger*. New York: Charles Scribner's Sons, 1917.

SMITH, GENE. *Until the Last Trumpet Sounds: The Life of General of the Armies John J. Pershing*. New York: John Wiley & Sons, Inc., 1998.

SMITH, JEAN EDWARD. *Eisenhower in War and Peace*. New York: Random House, 2012.

———. *FDR*. New York: Random House, 2007.

SMITH, RICHARD NORTON. *The Colonel: The Life and Legend of Robert McCormick, 1880–1955*. Boston: Houghton Mifflin Company, 1997.

SMYTHE, DONALD. *Guerrilla Warrior: The Early Life of John J. Pershing*. New York: Charles Scribner's Sons, 1973.

———. *Pershing: General of the Armies*. Bloomington: Indiana University Press, 2007.

SOCIETY OF THE FIRST DIVISION, THE. *History of the First Division During the World War, 1917–1919*. Philadelphia: The John C. Winston Company, 1922.

STOKES, MELVYN. *D. W. Griffith's* The Birth of a Nation: *A History of "The Most Controversial Motion Picture of All Time."* New York: Oxford University Press, 2007.

TOYNBEE, ARNOLD J. *The German Terror in Belgium—An Historical Record*. New York: George H. Doran Company, 1917.

TRUMAN, HARRY S. *Memoirs by Harry S. Truman. Vols. 1 and 2*. Garden City, NY: Doubleday & Company, 1955, 1956.

TUCHMAN, BARBARA. *The Guns of August*. New York: Macmillan Publishing, 1962.

———. *The Zimmermann Telegram: America Enters the War, 1917–1918*. New York: Macmillan Publishing, 1958.

VANDIVER, FRANK E. *Black Jack: The Life and Times of John J. Pershing. Vols. 1 and 2*. College Station: Texas A&M University Press, 1977.

WALKER, WILLIAM. *Betrayal at Little Gibraltar: A German Fortress, a Treacherous American General, and the Battle to End World War I*. New York: Scribner, 2016.

WEEKS, ALICE S. *Greater Love Hath No Man*. Cambridge, MA: The Riverside Press, 1930.

WELSOME, EILEEN. *The General and the Jaguar: Pershing's Hunt for Pancho Villa*. Lincoln: University of Nebraska Press, 2006.

WERSTEIN, IRVING. *Sound No Trumpet: The Life and Death of Alan Seeger*. New York: Thomas Y. Crowell Company, 1967.

WIGLE, SHARI LYNN. *Pride of America, We're with You: The Letters of Grace Anderson, U.S. Army Nurse Corps, World War I*. Rockville, MD: Seaboard Press, 2007.

WILCOX, ROBERT K. *Target Patton: The Plot to Assassinate General George S. Patton*. Washington, D.C.: Regnery Publishing, 2008.

WILLIAMS, CHAD L. *Torchbearers of Democracy: African-American Soldiers in the World War I Era*. Chapel Hill: The University of North Carolina Press, 2010.

YOCKELSON, MITCHELL. *Forty-Seven Days: How Pershing's Warriors Came of Age to Defeat the German Army*. New York: NAL Caliber, 2016.

ZAMORA, EMILIO, ED. *The World War I Diary of José de la Luz Saenz*. College Station: Texas A&M University Press, 2014.

ZUCKERMAN, LARRY. *The Rape of Belgium: The Untold Story of World War I*. New York: New York University Press, 2004.

Index

Note: Page numbers in *italics* refer to illustrations.